VIOLENCE IN BETWEEN

The **Institute of Southeast Asian Studies (ISEAS)** was established as an autonomous organisation in 1968. It is a regional centre dedicated to the study of socio-political, security and economic trends and developments in Southeast Asia and its wider geostrategic and economic environment.

The Institute's research programs are the Regional Economic Studies (RES, including ASEAN and APEC), Regional Strategic and Political Studies (RSPS), and Regional Social and Cultural Studies (RSCS).

ISEAS Publications, an established academic press, has issued more than 1,000 books and journals. It is the largest scholarly publisher of research about Southeast Asia from within the region. ISEAS Publications works with many other academic and trade publishers and distributors to disseminate important research and analyses from and about Southeast Asia to the rest of the world.

The **Monash Asia Institute (MAI)** is a multi-disciplinary research unit at Monash University in Melbourne, Australia. Founded in 1988, the MAI brings together a wide range of Asia-related activities at the university to promote and support Monash's expertise and interest in the Asian region.

MAI Press is an imprint of Monash University Press, and specialises in books and working papers about Asia. The books represent a range of disciplines, such as politics, history, women's studies, business and the environment. MAI Press welcomes authors from many countries and diverse backgrounds. MAI Press books are distributed in Australasia, North America, Southeast Asia and Europe.

Violence in between

Conflict and security in archipelagic Southeast Asia

Damien Kingsbury
Editor

Monash Asia Institute
Clayton

Institute of Southeast Asian Studies
Singapore

First published in Australia in 2005
for distribution in Oceania and North America by
Monash University Press
Monash University, Victoria 3800, Australia
www.monash.edu.au/mai

First published in Singapore in 2005
for distribution in Southeast Asia and Europe by
ISEAS Publications
Institute of Southeast Asian Studies
30 Heng Mui Keng Terrace, Pasir Panjang, Singapore 119614
E-mail: publish@iseas.edu.sg   Website: bookshop.iseas.edu.sg

© Monash Asia Institute 2005

National Library of Australia cataloguing-in-publication data:

Violence in between : conflict and security in archipelagic Southeast Asia.

Bibliography.

ISBN 1-876924-37-3 (Monash University Press)

ISBN 981-230-351-0 (ISEAS Publications)

1. Terrorism - Asia, Southeastern. 2. Terrorists - Asia, Southeastern. I. Kingsbury, Damien. II. Monash University. Monash Asia Institute. (Series : Monash Papers on Southeast Asia ; no. 62).

303.6250959

Cover design by Minnie Doron, Maiim Design.
Printed by Brown Prior Anderson, Hawthorn, Victoria, Australia.

Contents

Preface vi

Contributors viii

Introduction 1
Damien Kingsbury

Chapter 1   Terrorism in archipelagic Southeast Asia 9
Clinton Fernandes and Damien Kingsbury

Chapter 2   New terrorism in Southeast Asia 53
Carlyle Thayer

Chapter 3   Islam, Islamism and politics in Indonesia 75
Greg Barton

Chapter 4   Maritime security in Southeast Asia 105
Craig Snyder

Chapter 5   Instability in archipelagic Southeast Asia 127
Damien Kingsbury

Chapter 6   Dynamics of Muslim separatism in the Philippines 155
Kit Collier

Chapter 7   The tyranny of invented traditions: Aceh 175
Stephen Sherlock

Chapter 8   Greed: the silent force of conflict in Aceh 203
Lesley McCulloch

Chapter 9   Security forces in Ambon: from the national to the local 231
Muhammad Najib Azca

Chapter 10 East Timor in transition: an Australian policy challenge 255
Clinton Fernandes

Chapter 11 East Timor border security 277
Damien Kingsbury

Bibliography 299

Preface

This book began life as a discussion between a group of colleagues connected to Deakin University who specialise in issues of security, defence, international relations and area studies. This group agreed that it would be useful to contribute to a collected volume exploring security issues in the Southeast Asia region. The intention was to bring various areas of expertise to bear on one interesting, if somewhat troubled part of the world.

Between the idea and completion, the region that was being looked at underwent a series of significant changes. This should have been and largely was expected, hence the view that such a book was necessary. But while all knew that the situation was difficult and unstable when this project began, none could foresee the events of 11 September 2001, which not only focused world attention on issues of terrorism but, through earlier events and some of the consequences of the US-led attack on Afghanistan, also gave impetus to an incipient politico-religious movement in archipelagic Southeast Asia.

Again, this should not have been surprising, as the connections between organisations such as Al Qaeda and regional terrorist and militia groups had already been well established, as were the many deeply philosophical, ideological and religious links that underpinned many of the groups active in the region. For some observers, it took a much more local event than the aircraft attack on the World Trade Center in New York to begin to uncover regional terrorist groups, along with the already known *jihad*-ist elements that had been causing grief and mayhem amongst various regional communities. That event was the bombing of a nightclub in the tourist resort of Kuta, Bali, in Indonesia, on 12 October 2002, which left 202 people dead, more than half of whom were foreign tourists. If nothing else, it shook some regional governments out of their complacency. Meanwhile, other regional conflicts also received greater attention as being seen, accurately or not, as linked to these more spectacular events. Combined with other regional conflicts, the whole regional picture started to look decidedly unstable and unpredictable.

This turmoil forced all to reconsider their views and positions. These essays, then, are the product of this rethinking. While the editing of this volume fell largely to one person, I would like to thank Clinton Fernandes for his helpful comments, insights and early reading of some drafts. I would also like to thank the contributors who agreed to put their hard-earned research towards this volume. Finally, I would like to thank my wife, Fiona Delahunt and children

Cailan and Alexandra, for putting up with my disappearances both to the region and to my office.

Damien Kingsbury, Melbourne, January 2005.

Contributors

Dr Greg Barton is a senior lecturer in politics at Deakin University.

Dr Kit Collier is a research fellow at the Research School of Pacific and Asian Studies at the Australian National University.

Dr Clinton Fernandes was awarded a PhD from Deakin University in 2005.

Dr Damien Kingsbury is Director of International and Community Development at Deakin University.

Dr Lesley McCulloch is a former Australia Research Fellow researching the Indonesian military.

Muhammad Najib Azca is a lecturer in sociology at the University of Gadjah Mada, Yogyakarta.

Dr Stephen Sherlock is a freelance consultant on Indonesia.

Dr Craig Snyder is a senior lecturer in international relations at Deakin University.

Professor Carlyle Thayer is Convener of the Centre for Defence and Strategic Studies, Canberra, on behalf of Deakin University, on secondment from the Australian Defence Force Academy, University of New South Wales.

Introduction

Damien Kingsbury

The attack on the World Trade Center in New York on 11 September 2001 sharply focused international attention on a new type of international terrorism and cast into sharp relief a shifting international security agenda. The consequent 'war on terrorism', notably in Afghanistan[1], dispersed Islamic militants from their bases, in many cases to Southeast Asia, and highlighted the existing presence of such militants in Southeast Asia, many of whom were 'alumni' of the Afghanistan *jihad* (holy struggle). The 'war on terrorism' also had the effect of polarising world opinion, not least among many Muslims. Most were driven away from militant violence, although expressing strong concern that attacks by US-led coalitions were directed more at Islam as such, rather than at terrorism. But a critical minority felt further driven towards a more militant position, providing a small but important stream of recruits. In Southeast Asia, a series of terrorist attacks, the uncovering of a large terrorist network and a string of continuing regional conflicts all added to an awareness that the region, long regarded as relatively benign[2], was among the world's most troubled areas.

Not only are the terrorist attacks and other conflicts deeply troubling in their own right, but this region sits astride one of the most heavily shipped and strategically important waterways in the world. Beyond this, the region is the source of significant oil and natural gas reserves, has one of the world's two last great rainforests, and is home to more than 300 million people. What is now happening in archipelagic Southeast Asia is of critical concern not just to its own region, but to the world.

Yet this most recent focus on terrorism, and in particular Islamic terrorism, neglects political violence in the post-independence period that in many cases continues into the present. Indeed, a long history of conflict and violence has characterised archipelagic Southeast Asia—the 'islands in between'[3]—since records were first kept. Early settlement of the region was characterised by conflict as new migrants displaced original inhabitants, and along with the establishment of states and proto-states came conflict between them over territory, population and suzerainty. States with imperial aspirations in Java and Sumatra attacked and often conquered their neighbours, regional powers rose and fell and from the 16th century, European powers began to impose their will on the region. This led to a new series of conflicts that were433 not resolved until 1949, although it could be argued that many of the conflicts are a continuation of unresolved legacies of colonialism and, perhaps, of earlier imperial aspirations.

The introduction of Islam to the region was of itself not a cause for conflict. Islam is believed to have come with traders and to have been a predominantly sufi-ist or mystical version of Sunni Islam that often fitted in well with pre-existing belief systems (in particular in Java). But Islam was a rallying point against colonial imposition, in West Sumatra and Aceh, Central Java, South Sulawesi and the southern Philippines. Even the traditional piracy of northern Borneo and the Sulu Archipelago was often understood in Islamic terms, at least when practiced against colonial shipping.

Indeed, piracy—ambiguously defined—had been a hallmark of the region since time immemorial. Early records of Singapore show it as a haven for pirates, its beaches strewn with the bleached bones of their victims, while the narrow Malacca Straights have historically been prey to pirates-cum-regional sea powers. It is no coincidence that five sites of regional power —Sri Vijaya, Malacca, Aceh, Penang and Singapore—were located along these strategic straights. Further afield, the sailors of southern Sulawesi have long had a reputation as able seamen. Colonisation of northern Borneo, in fact, was delayed and ultimately encouraged by such piracy, when a British adventurer took sides with a local Sultan and reclaimed much of his land back from local pirates and on-shore warriors, who were notable for their head-hunting. In forming an alliance with these warriors, James Brooke eventually carved out his own empire, which was finally reinforced by British gunships.

Similarly in the southern Philippines, local Muslims opposed Spanish colonialism and ensured that Mindanao and the islands of the Sulu Archipelago were effectively ungovernable, until the post-Spanish colonial United States introduced a much greater level of military intervention. Even then, local resentment was not quelled, and the establishment of the independent government of the Republic of the Philippines, which unwisely attempted to displace local Muslims without due compensation, engendered a new wave of Islamic backlash, along with a communist insurgency directed more against the post-colonial exploitation of the Philippines' mestizo elite. And in the island group between Mindanao and what was once North Borneo (now Sabah), the Abu Sayyaf Group continues kidnapping and beheading practices that while shocking, are not so very different from those practiced by their forebears, even if their rationale is couched in more explicit political terms.

In what was to become Indonesia, Islamic opposition to colonialism, based on a Middle-Eastern revival of a more pure (or 'revived') form of Islam, melded with an aspiration for an Islamic state. The 'enemy', in this case, was broadly defined, although complicated by various local agendas, broken promises, betrayals and, ultimately, a lack of sufficient support for a strongly Islamic political or legal outcome. Yet the key idea of an Islamic state held sway with a core group, which continued to resurface, in the 1940s, the 1950s, the late 1970s and again from the 1990s. Drawing on global aspirations for this more 'pure' version of Islam, such groups sent recruits to fight against Soviet forces in Afghanistan and to a lesser extent, Chechniya and other sites, as well as forming links and associations that ranged from the ideologically similar to close and in some cases quite direct connections. Al Qaeda may not be formally organised in archipelagic Southeast Asia, although to say this is to define Al Qaeda in ways that give it a much more precise organisational structure than many attribute to it. In any case, while the various 'cells' or like-minded groups may not receive formal directions (or even informal requests), their basic agendas are so similar as to cast them as factions within a wider and largely agreed ideological framework.

In global terms, the rise of a militant Islam, first noted in the West with the Iranian Revolution of 1979[4], precipitated a more general awakening of Islam as a path to political emancipation. This quality has always been present in Islam, and it has informed much Islamic political activity. However, it has only been in the post-colonial period and, in particular, since the 1960s, that this explicitly emancipatory or liberationist aspect of political Islam has come to the fore. The Iranian Revolution was, arguably, its first full flowering within the contemporary context, and served as an example to Muslims elsewhere that their religious beliefs could be combined with their political aspirations to produce real political change.

A similar emancipatory quality has also informed other forms of non-state political violence. The Free Aceh Movement in Aceh, Sumatra, has a strong Islamic quality, although it is not an explicitly Islamic organisation. Rather, it is a national liberation organisation that in part defines its sense of national identity through a common religious belief, in this case being a local, if still devout, interpretation of Sunni Islam. Less as a marker of 'nation' but at least as emancipatory, communism or other Marxist-related principles operating under that name have also appealed to some of the region's dispossessed, in Indonesia, Malaysia and the Philippines. Indeed at the time of its destruction, in 1965–66, the Indonesian Communist Party was, if not militant, still the largest in the world outside a formally communist state. The Malayan Communist Party posed a direct challenge to the outcome of the emerging Malaysian state in the 1950s, and the Communist Party of the Philippines continues to wage a military campaign against the government, a tradition started in the 1940s regrouped after its almost complete demise, in the late 1980s and early 1990s. This is not so much to suggest any 'correctness' for the focus of or on the part of such militancy, as to acknowledge the profound sense of injustice and alienation that drives it.

This then turns attention to the question of the creation of an alienating environment, and the role of government and its agents as social guardian or, more darkly, as social predator or facilitator of predatory behaviour on the part of others. In most cases of political violence in the archipelago, the hand of government can be seen either in perpetrating or perpetuating violence—in Aceh and West Papua, in providing logistical support for or being disguised as various militias, through covert military intelligence engagement, throughout the Philippines but particularly in the southern regions, and not least against activists, dissenters and very often just plain ordinary people who have become fed up with corruption, incompetence, mismanagement and brutality. It is no secret that various regional governments and their agents, at various times (some more consistently than others), have been the worst perpetrators of political violence, the most profound example being the massacres of hundreds of thousands of communists and suspected communists and sympathisers in Indonesia in the mid-1960s. Yet terrible as this undoubtedly was—recorded memories of rivers clogged with bodies do not easily disappear—there have been countless other cases of government (usually military or police) massacres and other violence; the catalogue is too extensive to list, but more than 150,000 dead in East Timor between 1975 and 1999, tens of thousands in West Papua and many thousands more in Aceh, Ambon and throughout the rest of Indonesia, the Philippines and even many dead in Malaysia during the 1950s, piling horror upon horror. And, lest anyone think that such horror is in the past, the conflict in Aceh was at its most intense as this was being written, killings had recommenced in Central Sulawesi, conflict in the Philippines continued unabated and the activities of radical militias and terrorist groups now appear as a regular part of the regional political landscape.

In attempting to address the most pressing of these issues, and by way of introduction to this collection, Fernandes and Kingsbury offer an overview of the contemporary climate in relation to organisations and activities that could be conventionally defined as 'terrorist'. They note and briefly assess each of the major organisations in the region that have, or reasonably could or should have, the term 'terrorist' affixed to them. In this, Fernandes and Kingsbury are aware that the greatest perpetrators of violence, including 'terrorism' in the region have been some of the local governments and their agencies, notably the military, police and intelligence branches.

Considering how the term 'terrorism' has changed, especially since 11 September 2001, Thayer offers a further assessment of regional terrorist organisations and how they differ from those that preceded them. In particular, he considers their institutional or wider regional links, notably to the international terrorist group Al Qaeda. Thayer finds that while some of the hyperbole over more local terrorism has overstated a determinism in its links to Al Qaeda, there remains a distinct and dangerous model of terrorist organisation that continues to pose a threat to longer term regional security and stability.

The issue of the changing nature of Islam has been the focus of much attention in recent years, yet Islam in the region has always had a militant and sometimes violent aspect to it, or to some of its interpretations. After many years of observers saying how benign regional Islam is—especially in Indonesia—there is now a recognition that while some of it remains benign, elements of it range across a spectrum of activism from the social and local to the ideological and radical and militant. To distinguish, Barton refers to the religion as Islam and the ideology as 'Islamism', and discusses these as categories and streams of influence on Indonesian politics, affecting major political parties and office-holders.

The issue of multiple claims to the tiny islands of the South China Sea have also been the site of contest within the region, particularly through conflicting claims by Vietnam, China, Malaysia and the Philippines in the South China Sea. Issues of maritime security are critical in any case, but especially so to archipelagic security. Snyder considers this issue of regional territorial claims over seaways, the capacity and intentions of the competing states, and non-traditional security threats. Snyder concludes with a survey of the technical capacities of each of the regional powers to assert their interests in the South China Sea.

A traditional source of conflict, and one that appears exacerbated rather than resolved by the construction of post-colonial states, are competing visions of national identity. Kingsbury examines the construction of post-colonial states and questions their capacity or willingness to cater for non-core groups, the construction of 'national' identity and the failure, in some cases, of nationalist projects and the use of violence to compel identification, if not with the state then at least with the state's goals and objectives. Normatively, citizenship should be voluntary but, as many individuals and groups in the region have learned, it may also be a matter of compulsion.

One area where local 'nationalist' identity competes vigorously with state identity is in the southern Philippines. But as Collier argues, significant aspects of this sense of identity are not long-standing, but rather more recent and in some cases invented responses to particular political claims. The development of 'national' or collective political identity in response to an external threat is not unusual and the focus on Islam and the Islamic sense of community can contribute to this. But as Collier points out, the status of separatist claims in the southern Philippines is neither direct nor clear. Sherlock argues a similar case for Aceh, citing the polarisation of Acehnese political society due to the long-running separatist conflict as the basic problem in the creation of 'national' identity. In particular, Sherlock is critical of the imposition of what he sees as invented traditions, both of Acehnese national identity and Aceh's forced inclusion into a narrowly defined version of Indonesian nationalism.

McCulloch, on the other hand, is rather more concerned with the economic factors that led to and continue to drive the conflict in Aceh. As McCulloch notes, the Indonesian military has a long-standing economic interest in retaining a high level of presence in Aceh, which, combined with its assertion of a place in state decision-making, often leaves the Acehnese as the hapless victims of forces that are beyond their control. A sense of Acehnese nationalism, therefore, may draw on local traditions or increase the value of such traditions, but is ultimately a response to the imposition of an inequitable economic environment and criminal military activity imposed at the point of a gun.

Also reflecting changing economic and other opportunities, but in this case the result of demographic shift, population movement and government preferences, is the conflict that has torn apart Indonesia's Maluku (Moluccas) island group centred on Ambon. While the domestic conflict that focused on competing Muslim and Christian groups was destructive enough, the introduction of external groups such as Laskar Jihad and Laskar Mujahidin, radically altered the nature and scope of conflict in this once peaceful and stable part of the world. This conflict was also worsened by the introduction of government security forces, which as Najib notes, instead of quelling the conflict, in some cases exacerbated it by taking up sides (the army generally with Muslim forces, the police generally with Christians forces), selling arms to combatants and, it was widely believed, actually promoting conflict when it died down to suit a range of other agendas, perhaps the most disturbing of which was centred on competition in elite politics in Jakarta.

One point where conflict and instability in Indonesia threatened to spill across to a near neighbour was the case of Indonesia, East Timor and Australia. Australia had long tried to accommodate Indonesia's invasion, occupation and incorporation of East Timor, often through disregarding the facts of the situation there, not to mention overwhelming Australian public opinion. But when Indonesia finally agreed to allow the East Timorese to vote in a UN supervised ballot on their future, Australia's position became untenable to the point where it did a back-flip that brought it to the brink of war with Indonesia. Fernandes traces Australia's policy position on Indonesia and East Timor and details the circumstances which obliged it to reverse a 24 year old policy, which continues as a major source of tension in Australia-Indonesia bilateral relations. One significant aspect of that tension is the sense of irredentism that it has left among 'nationalists' in Indonesia and an unofficial but militarily supported policy of destabilisation of East Timor. The view among some in Indonesia is that it is not a case of if, but when, East Timor is reincorporated into the unitary state of the Republic of Indonesia. In the meantime, as Kingsbury notes, there are economic interests promoting local interest in destabilisation, as well as the Indonesian military's historic requirement to engage in business and criminal activity to survive.

In summary, archipelagic Southeast Asia now appears more violent, more potentially fragmented and more prone to seemingly random acts of political and religious violence, than at any time in its post-colonial history. In part this is true, and there is little doubt that the islands between mainland Southeast Asia and Australia are undergoing the type of troubles that have presented the region as being one of the most unstable in the world. Yet, as noted above, this region has always been relatively unstable and has a long history of conflict and violence, so it is only those with short memories who would be entirely surprised by the shift in events here. A changing global environment and the 'war on terrorism', however, have helped to shift attention to archipelagic Southeast Asia and perhaps, after a time when there was belief that the region was genuinely beginning to settle, such conflict is disheartening for the setback it presents to the regional and global community, but more importantly for the 300 or so million people who live there. This book is not intended to produce any answers to the many awkward and deeply-rooted questions that worry this region, but it is hoped that more focus on the problems that afflict it will help provide some basis for considering possible answers to the region's security problems.

Endnotes

1. The war in Iraq may have produced 'terrorist' outcomes, but has been acknowledged by US Secretary of Defense Donald Rumsfeld not to have been launched as a consequence of meaningful evidence about pre-existing terrorist links.
2. This reflected a lack of general awareness much more than any objective reality.
3. 'Islands in between' is a translation of the Indonesian/Malay term 'nusantara', which is a common informal term for the thousands of islands that sit between mainland Southeast Asia and Australia.
4. The Iranian Revolution was based on Shia Islam, and not the more common Sunni Islam, a fundamentalist Salafiyah version of which has driven most of the recent violence that is also explicitly Islamic (with the exception of Palestine and Lebanon) and which predominates in Southeast Asia.

Chapter 1

Terrorism in archipelagic Southeast Asia

Damien Kingsbury and Clinton Fernandes

Since the destruction of the World Trade Center buildings in New York on 11 September 2001, considerable international attention has been given to non-state terrorist groups in Southeast Asia, including their claimed links to Al Qaeda. The focus since '9–11' has thus been on Islamic terrorist organisations, but there has also been a renewed focus on non-Islamic terrorism, as part of the generic concerns of the 'War on Terrorism'.

One consequence of the US-led invasion of Afghanistan in response to this attack was that members of the ruling Taliban and their Al Qaeda allies fled Afghanistan. It has been claimed that a large number of Al Qaeda personnel were also dispersed to other countries, notably to Islamic countries in Southeast Asia, from where up to 1,000 recruits to their cause had earlier been drawn and to which they felt some ideological affinity (Brownfeld 2002). Some of the recruits to Afghanistan had also been from the Southeast Asia region, and had returned prior to and after the US-led attack on Afghanistan with a radical agenda, and some funding.[1] It was these returnees, linked with former members of earlier radical Islamic organisations and new recruits, that formed the basis of Indonesia's post-Suharto-era militant Islam.

This militancy has been manifested in Islamic militias being involved in sectarian violence in Maluku and Central Sulawesi and in bombings in South Sulawesi, Java and Sumatra, and the identification of Indonesia as a primary training ground for Islamic radicals. Other recruits also returned and influenced Islamic movements in Malaysia, Singapore and especially the Philippines, where pre-existing Islamist movements existed, responding to both local conditions (southern Philippines) and the opportunities provided by a supportive environment (Malaysia, Singapore).

Terrorism

In all the public discussion about terrorism and its ostensible rise ('terrorism' in the modern sense being a common feature of various political landscapes since the 1880s[2]), very little attention has been paid to what is meant by the term. Indeed, contemporary use of the term 'terrorism' implies a pejorative, antithetical position rather than a standardised descriptive quality as such. That is, it is often less the methods employed by 'terrorists' that define them, but rather whether or not they are on 'our side'. This intense subjectivity has, perforce, undermined much clarity of analysis.

The driver for terrorism, and indeed for all political claims, is (real or perceived) economic or political scarcity; that is, lack of opportunity or resources. Such scarcity is both a contributor to and manifestation of reduced security which, if not adequately addressed, can and often does call forth a reaction. While there are examples of reactions based on more or less purely ideological grounds, even in such cases there tends to be a claimed representation of the interests of people affected by scarcity (although in some instances the interests being represented are much more personal and reflect a complex of economic considerations, status and power). Recruitment to such causes, however, relies on experience of a real, lived scarcity, which can be channelled into an ideological (explanatory and prescriptive) framework.

Experience or awareness of scarcity—of a lack of political choice or economic capacity—and acceptance of an ideological explanation for this logically implies a call for political redress. Violence has been and remains a widely accepted, if politically unsophisticated method of achieving compliance to a particular ideological prescription, and within the context of imbalances of capacity for violence, terrorism can act as a persuasive shortcut.

Despite broad acceptance of the idea of 'terrorism' being intended to obtain compliance, there remains no finite definition of 'terrorism', nor are its actors limited by position. The term 'terror' within a political context usually refers to attempts to persuade others of one's own political position by the use of exemplary violence, or the threat of violence, instilling in the audience a state of heightened or absolute fear, or terror.

Terrorism can also be used to persuade others not to accept a particular political perspective but simply to engage in action in accordance with that perspective (eg the release of political prisoners or the establishment of a material 'good') or to encourage a response that in turn supports the goals of the terrorists (eg increased generalised repression leading to broad-based, anti-repressive sentiment).

The term 'terrorist' is further usually applied to individual or collective non-state actors, but state or state-sponsored actors can (and often do) also conform to either the methods or the purposes of non-state terrorists. This has particularly been the case in Indonesia, most notably with the TNI and, at its exemplary edge, Kopassus, through their involvement in and support for extremist Islamic organisations.

Origins of Indonesia's Islamic militancy[3]

During the Second World War, independent Islamic units had been fighting as the Hizbullah (Army of God) against the Japanese occupation and later against the Dutch re-occupation. These militant Islamic groups had been outside the control of the revolutionary government and were unwilling to bow to government directives after 1949, especially after earlier 'treachery'. The prime example of such 'treachery' was the fledgling government's acceptance of the compromise Renville Agreement in January 1948, whereby, to attain a qualified independence, the republic conceded territory it had lost in 1947 to the Dutch. As part of the agreement, the republican government conceded West Java to the Dutch on the condition that the Siliwangi Division based there could be removed to Central Java. However, this left behind independent Islamic guerrillas in West Java, who continued their own campaign against the Dutch, proclaiming it a *jihad* (holy war). By December 1948, disillusioned with conventional politics, the Islamic guerrillas, under the charismatic modernist Muslim scholar Sekamardji Maridjan Kartosuwirjo, proclaimed the Negara Islam Indonesia (Indonesian Islamic State—NII). Kartosuwirjo announced that the republic had ceased to exist and that the NII was the true embodiment of the revolution. After Indonesia gained independence in 1949, the Dar'ul Islam movement (formally known as the Tentara Islam Indonesia—Indonesian Islamic Army) continued to defy the central government, at times extending its influence from West Java into Central Java and over Aceh and much of South Sulawesi. The Dar'ul Islam rebellion probably had the greatest impact from 1957 until 1961, at least partly in reaction to the growing influence of the PKI in government. It also received a significant boost when rebels in South and Central Sulawesi joined the movement in 1952 and 1958 respectively. The South Sulawesi rebellion collapsed in 1961, in response to a government amnesty. With the capture of Kartosuwirjo in 1962, the movement in West Java was militarily wiped out.

However, the desire for an Islamic state that fed the Dar'ul Islam movement remained alive, especially in West Java. In what amounted to a 'sting' operation in the mid- to late 1970s, the Indonesian military intelligence agency Opsus (Special Operations) encouraged a number of radical Muslims who had links to the Dar'ul Islam movement to again press for an Islamic state (Laksamana.Net 2002a). The intention by Opsus was to increase the legitimacy of the New Order government's authoritarian capacity, and to discredit radical Islam, which it viewed as a potential threat to state order and security. This group, dubbed 'Komando Jihad' by the Indonesian government, succeeded in bombing the Borobudur Buddhist temple in Central Java, and in 1981 hijacked a Garuda aircraft to Bangkok. This hijacking was ended by a group from the Indonesian army's special forces, who boarded the plane and killed three of the hijackers, the other two being killed on the return flight to Jakarta. Remaining members of this Islamic group were arrested and jailed, disappeared or fled into exile (a number doing so after they were released from jail). It was from this group that the core of new radical Islamic groups, including Jema'ah Islamiyah (Islamic Community[4]), were drawn.

Radical Islamic ideology

The alias chosen by the alleged former Jema'ah Islamiyah chief of operations, Riduan Isamuddin—Hambali—and the version of Islam preached by Jema'ah Islamiyah's alleged spiritual leader, Abu Bakar Ba'asyir, provide important insights into the nature of radical Indonesian Islam. 'Hambali' is the Indonesian spelling of the Arabic word 'Hanbali', which refers to the most dogmatic and traditionalist of the four Sunni schools of law. The Hanbali school is based on the teachings of the legal scholar Ahmad ibn Hanbal (780–855), which minimises the private aspect of religion, rejects personal opinion and emphasises a near-total dependence on the divine in the establishment of legal theory. Legal decisions are heavily reliant on a literal reading of the Qur'an and Hadith (narratives relating to the Prophet's life and sayings) and modernist re-interpretations are treated with hostility. The most well-known aspect of Ibn Hanbal's life is the suffering he endured during an inquisition, known as *al-mithnah,* ordered by the caliph, al-Mamun. The unflinching spirit shown by Ibn Hanbal in the face of floggings and imprisonment, as well as his intellectual work on the Hadith, ensured his stature as one of the most venerated fathers of Islam and a staunch upholder of Muslim orthodoxy. It would appear that Riduan Isamuddin identified with Ibn Hanbal's stoicism, militancy and uncompromising attitudes. Although the Hanbali school is the smallest of the four Sunni schools of law, its importance and that of Ibn Hanbal derive from their impact on the development of Islamic religious history. In the Middle Ages the school acted as a spearhead of traditionalist orthodoxy in its struggle against rationalism. One of Ibn Hanbal's greatest followers, Ibn Taymiyah (1263–1328), was claimed by both the Wahhabiyah, a reform movement founded in the mid-18th century, and the modern Salafiyah movement, which arose in Egypt and advocated the continued supremacy of Islamic law, but with fresh interpretations to meet the community's changing needs (Fakhry 1983:ch 11).

The Wahhabi version of Islam originated from the teachings and actions of Muhammad Ibn-Abd-al-Wahhab (1703–1792), who preached an austere doctrine rejecting Arabian folk Islam and Sufi beliefs and practices (Fakhry 1983:ch 11; Robinson 1999:43–4). This version of Islam is the prevailing state religion of Saudi Arabia and is highly influential in Yemen, with numerous followers across North Africa and the Middle East. Wahhabist Islam gained influence in Indonesia during the 1970s (Van Bruinessen 2002a; 2002c), and this influence is reflected in the organisation Majelis Mujahidin Indonesia (Indonesian Mujahidin Council—MMI) (*Suara Pembaruan* 2002a; 2002b). A range of radical Indonesian organisations are inspired by Wahhabist Islam. It should be noted that adherents of 'Wahhabism' strongly disapprove of the term, preferring instead to call themselves *Muwahhidun* (Unitarians). *Sunnah* means a 'well-trodden path'. In the religious terminology of Islam it normally signifies 'the example set by the Prophet' or the 'traditional and well-defined way'. The term *sunnah* is usually accompanied by the appendage *al-jama'ah* (together meaning 'the consolidated majority' or 'community'), indicating that the traditional way is the way of the consolidated majority of the community as distinct from peripheral or 'wayward' positions of sectarians, who by definition must be erroneous. Wahhabism accentuates the distinction between the consolidated majority's 'well-defined way' and the wayward path of the 'sectarians'. It is said to be a revival of Salafiya puritanism (from *as-salaf as-salih*—'pious forefathers', or the community of believers in the early Muslim state of Muhammad and his companions) (Robinson 1999:48). The Wahhabist movement identifies with an ideal time in history, and deliberately advocates atavistic practices in order to bring present-day Muslims to the standards of an earlier ideal. For the Wahhabists, early Islam has an unsullied purity with none of the accretions and later innovations like saint worship and superstition. In general terms, most movements committed to radical Islamic reorganisation have two consistent themes: the hope for a single international community undivided by ethnic or linguistic factors; and the recovery of past traditions. There is a major contradiction with the realities of the modern world, however.

The issue of modernity is a crucial one for the Muslim world in general and the traditionalists within it in particular. The most influential and enduring aspects of Islamic knowledge were completed and consolidated in the first five hundred years of the faith. The knowledge developed during this period, along with all the doctrinal controversies and clarifications that resulted, ensured the importance of the first five Islamic centuries. Subsequent centuries saw the same doctrinal issues arise, but there have been few significant challenges within Islamic knowledge. For example, traditional Muslim scholars still continue to draw upon the texts and legal precedents developed by earlier scholars, with few major changes to the original body of knowledge. The influence of the first five centuries can be traced to the manner in which Islamic knowledge was produced at the time—it occurred as a result of Islam's first interaction with the outside world, during the Arab conquests which began in the seventh century CE. Early Arab conquests of the territories of the Mediterranean basin and Asia were matched by the knowledge produced as a result of the mingling of Semitic, Hellenistic, Iranian and Indian cultural streams. When the Islamic world was presented with Hellenistic rational and philosophical challenges, it was able to confront them from a position of Muslim political dominance. By contrast, today's Islamic world has been presented with Western challenges from a position of relative political weakness.

Robinson (1998:241) points out that the material success of the West and the expansion of its authority over much of the Muslim world transformed the context in which Islamic knowledge existed. The secular, scientific outlook of the Enlightenment posed a serious challenge to the theological worldview of Islamic knowledge. As a consequence of colonial rule, Western knowledge had the further advantage of state support while by contrast, Islamic knowledge was separated from state power. These difficult circumstances for Islamic knowledge were intensified by the economic, social and technological penetration of Islamic societies by the West. As a consequence, Western knowledge became more accessible to the population, and could compete, often successfully, with Islamic knowledge. Muslims therefore found that they had to review the inherited body of Islamic knowledge to see how they might make it relevant to the present. Robinson (1998:243) notes that there were three broad strands of response: reformism, which re-evaluated but did not change inherited essential Islamic knowledge; modernism, which aimed to reconstruct that knowledge in light of Western knowledge and new economic and political realities; and Islamism, which was no less respectful of the new economic and political realities but wished to make them, and Western knowledge, subordinate to their utopian understanding of revelation. It is this last strand, Islamism, which has had most impact on militant Islam in Indonesia.

While Muslim revivalist programs are often labelled 'fundamentalist', as Ansari notes, the label is 'often applied inaccurately to anything Muslim which challenges what the West assumes to be progress'. 'Islamism' is therefore a more accurate term, highlighting the importance of activism in 'creating a new religio-political order while preserving orthodox religious observances. It therefore appeals for reinterpretation of the sources of doctrine rather than the reassertion of traditional values'. Islamism is a 20th century phenomenon which has developed within the context of its times. It centres around demands for the establishment of an Islamic system (*nizam*) in contrast to the materially based systems of Western state capitalism and (what used to be) East European bureaucratic collectivism. The Islamist phenomenon is a direct response to the vicissitudes of modern life inside Muslim societies, confronted by Western ideas and dramatic social and political changes. Islamism therefore does not represent a return to the past, when the traditional Islamic view of government was limited to creating and maintaining the right conditions for Islam to flourish. Instead, Islamists usually hold the view that government, with the enhanced power of the modernised state at its disposal, should exercise much greater responsibility for the people. This difference gives a distinctly modernist look to the relationship between Islam and the state (Ansari 1998:112), and has been characterised as reflecting more a resemblance to the structure and goals of European fascist parties and Marxist-Leninist organisations than to Islam as it is inscribed in the Qur'an (Robinson 1999:57). Such a perspective is exemplified by the Ikhwan al-Muslimin (Muslim Brotherhood[5]), the leading Islamist force in the Middle East, founded in Egypt in 1928 by Hassan al-Banna (1906–49) with the intention of liberating Egypt and the rest of the Muslim world from foreign control and establishing Islamic states (Robinson 1999:50). Beginning as an orthodox reformist movement and growing into a militant mass organisation, it reinterpreted modernisation to fit an Islamic model. Revivalist Islam was therefore a means of overcoming social and economic injustice imposed by the secular controllers of the state, who were, according to al-Banna, 'parrots of the pulpit', out of touch with reality. The Ikhwan al-Muslimin was further radicalised after it was suppressed in 1954, with its leading ideologue, Sayyid Qutb (1906–1966), hanged after being implicated in a plot to kill Egypt's President Nasser. Qutb developed the doctrine that it was permissible to engage in *jihad* against the government, a view that still underpins anti-state Islamism in Southeast Asia.

The Islamist movement is therefore not dogmatically opposed to most Western knowledge. However, its adherents tend to have a combative stance towards secular nationalists, who they believe have surrendered to secular Western culture in its entirety. Much of their efforts are therefore designed to counter the dominance of such secular nationalists, who have great influence over the educational systems of most Muslim states, including Indonesia. Islamists start from the principle that all human life, and therefore all knowledge, must be subordinated to the guidance sent by God to human beings. The essence of that guidance, according to one Islamist, is that the *syariah* offers a complete scheme of life 'where nothing is superfluous and nothing is wanting' (Robinson 1998:245). When Sukarno was president, he tried to balance the tensions between Islamists and secular nationalists by affirming his faith in *Nasakom*, to which he declared that he was 'a convinced nationalist, a convinced Muslim, a convinced Marxist'. However, no amount of rhetoric could overcome the realities of incompatible positions.

In contrast to Sukarno, the New Order regime was suspicious of political Islam, with much of his career coinciding with the Darul Islam rebellion. Suharto therefore appointed few pious Muslims to important positions, preferring to take advice from Christians, or more nominally Islamic (*abangan*) Javanese like himself. Under Suharto, the various political streams of Islam and their sometimes competing agendas were combined into one organisation, the United Development Party (Partai Persatuan Pembangunan—PPP), functionally depoliticised under the state rubric of *pancasila* (five principles) and which drove underground genuine Islamic political opposition. After Suharto, political Islam divided into a range of camps, mostly covered by political parties but, in some cases, acting outside the formal political process. The rise of Jema'ah Islamiyah and other radicalised Islamic groups in Indonesia was already implicit in the dynamics of this political system.

Few expressions of political Islam that had their gestation during the New Order followed a radical path, and even fewer chose a militant or violent method of expression. But those that drew on or were inspired by earlier militant legacies harboured grievances that increasingly found violent expression. Added to this was the New Order's more generalised repression, and the turning to Islam by young Indonesians as a means of steering away from its excesses and corruption. The corrupt repression of the New Order, the growth of Islamism among young Indonesians, and the appeal of a zealous, proselytising Islamism contributed another stream of recruits to a radical Islamic agenda, particularly from the 1970s.[6] Following the effective destruction of the Indonesian Democratic Party in July 1996, political Islam increasingly appeared to be the only option for opposition to the New Order, even as the New Order was itself attempting to co-opt elements of the Indonesian Islamic community, through organisations such as the Indonesian Committee for World Muslim Solidarity (Komite Islam Solidaritas Dunia Indonesia—KISDI), established in February 1994, which was linked to Suharto's son-in-law, Lieutenant General Prabowo Subianto, and financiers such as Fuad Bawazier, who was Suharto's last Finance Minister and was linked to Suharto through his son Bambang Trihatmodo's PT Satelindo company as 'president commissioner'. From its beginnings, KISDI was set up to split the growing anti-Suharto movement among the NU and Muhammadiyah. KISDI came to the fore for the first time when there was a mass gathering in solidarity with Bosnian Muslims in front of the Al Azhar Mosque in elite Kebayoran in South Jakarta in mid-February 1994. The gathering decided to send volunteers to wage a *jihad* in Bosnia-

Herzegovina and to raise funds to build a mosque in Sarajevo, to be named the Haji Mohamad Suharto Mosque. To facilitate these two goals a committee was set up called the National Committee for Solidarity with the Bosnian Muslims (Panitia Nasional Solidaritas Muslim Bosnia or PNSM Bosnia). Its chairman was Probosutedjo, Suharto's stepbrother and often the spokesperson for the Suharto family. Fund-raising continued for three years, using an account at Probosutedjo's Bank Jakarta.

Fuad Bawazier was also the conduit for funds from the Saudi royal family to support the university-based *salafi* Tarbiyah Movement through the Suharto-owned 'charitable foundation' Yayasan Amal Bhakti Muslim Pancasila. After Suharto lost office, businessman Tomy Winata, along with the Army foundation Yayasan Kartika Eka Paksi, also supported Suharto's radical Islamist project by contributing funds to the Laskar Jihad. Other funds were diverted from the Bosnian Solidarity Fund PNSMB.

Most Indonesian Muslims remained unconvinced of the credibility of Suharto's new embrace of Islam, but some took advantage of links, especially with some military officers, to strengthen their own position. As Suharto fell from power, the lid came off the political pressure cooker that was Indonesia and the spectrum of political Islam arrayed itself to take advantage of the new opportunities available in the post-New Order era. It was in this climate of releasing repressed anger and frustration, of changes in the style and nature of aspects of political Islam, of opportunities, long-standing agendas and newfound allies, that more radical groups within political Islam discovered the will and opportunity to assert their views. These were manifested in a series of new groups, all of which had ideological links, degrees of organisational association and a close and sometimes common history.

Jema'ah Islamiyah (JI)

Indicating the importance of the Agfhanistan link to the development of radical post-Suharto Islamism, all of the senior members 'trained in Afghanistan in the late 1980s and early 1990s, before JI formally existed. It was in the camps of the Saudi-financed Afghan Mujahidin leader Abdul Rasul Sayaf that they developed *jihadist* fervour, international contacts, and deadly skills' (ICG 2003:1). The group is said to be held together by ideology, training and an intricate network of marriages that at times makes it seem like a large, extended family. Senior JI leaders often arranged the marriages of their subordinates to their sisters or sisters-in-law to retain network security' (ICG 2003:26–8; see also Murphy 2002). This inter-marriage helped give JI has a depth of leadership that provided a capacity for regeneration.

According to senior military sources,[7] JI was said to have had a formal chain of command until the arrests of numerous members following the Bali bombing on 12 October 2002. However, its structure was always that which could operate as independent cells should the chain of command be broken, as it was at that time. Hence, what was in some respects a 'led' organisation became 'leaderless', although still functional. The lack of a single leader for radical jihadism has also been reflected in the existence of multiple organisations (JI, Laskar Jundullah, Laskar Mujahidin) that have a generally shared orientation and a range of compatible goals, and that apart from personalised rivalries could be considered factions of a larger organisation that has not had a single leader as such. These organisations have a shared ideology, as reflected in a common membership of the Indonesian Mujahidin Council (Majelis Mujahidin Indonesia—MMI), but actions are planned and carried out by much smaller groups. Such networks are usually very difficult to penetrate. While there is a high degree of organisation, it is the hierarchy and bureaucratic forms that have been reduced.

JI came to public prominence after the 12 October 2002 bombing of two nightclubs in Bali, Indonesia, which killed 202 people and injured scores more. Indonesian intelligence agencies were initially slow to accept advice from other regional governments that such a threat existed, notably from the Singaporean government. They have, however, since capitalised on the 'war on terrorism' which has given them added political clout internationally (notably with Western intelligence agencies) and domestically (by providing a pretext for a greater role for TNI). Members of JI have been identified as being involved in attacks in the Philippines, bombings in Jakarta (in particular on Christmas Eve 2000) and attempted attacks in Singapore. As investigations into JI progressed through late 2002 and into 2003, dozens of alleged operatives were arrested in Indonesia in connection with the Bali bombing and a series of earlier bombing attacks, predominantly in Jakarta.

The origins of JI can be traced to the establishment of the so-called Komando Jihad (re-activated elements of Dar'ul Islam) group in 1976–77. As noted above, this group is believed to have been encouraged or founded through an Opsus operation, directed by General Ali Murtopo, to discredit political Islam and strengthen the hand of the New Order government relative to the possible emergence of the United Development Party (PPP) as a viable political opposition (ICG 2002a:7). There was a reference to Jema'ah Islamiyah in 1977, when an alleged Medan-based Komando Jihad leader, Gaos Taufiq, invited a young teacher, Abdullah Umar, to attend a meeting in Medan. According to the prosecution in the subsequent court case, Taufiq discussed how the New Order government had violated Islamic law and that those at the meeting should join an organisation called Jema'ah Islamiyah. The Indonesian government cracked down on Komando Jihad, especially in 1981, ahead of the 1982 elections and around the time of the Komando Jihad aircraft hijacking to Bangkok. Court documents from the 1980s also show that Komando Jihad referred to the establishment of an organisation, continuing from Dar'ul Islam, as Jema'ah Islamiyah (ICJ 2002:8, 12).

In 1967, a preacher named Abu Bakar Ba'asyir had helped found a proselytising radio station at Solo, and in 1971 he and another former Indonesian Muslim Youth Movement (GPII) leader, Abdullah Sungkar, established an Islamic school near the central Javanese town of Solo, Pesantren al-Mu'min, which in 1973 moved to the village of Ngruki and was thereafter widely referred to as Pondok Ngruki.[8] While neither individual was connected to Dar'ul Islam, as later claimed, in 1975 the radio station was closed for its anti-government tone, and in 1977 Sungkar was arrested for urging his followers not to vote in the 1977 elections. The following year, Sungkar and Ba'asyir were arrested, accused of being involved with Dar'ul Islam and what was referred to in court as Jema'ah Islamiyah. Sungkar admitted that he had talked of establishing a community (*jema'ah*) to oppose the regeneration of communism. A series of crimes soon after, all linked to Pondok Ngruki, strengthened the government case against Sungkar, Ba'asyir and Jema'ah Islamiyah, while also tapping into a growing ferment amongst many radical young Indonesian Muslims (ICG 2002a:12). Sugkar and Ba'asyir were jailed in 1978 for promoting an Islamic state and in 1982 they were sentenced to nine years in prison, later reduced to three years on appeal, which meant they were released for time already served. After two years of organising and awaiting the outcome of a prosecution appeal against the reduced sentences, Sungkar and Ba'asyir fled to Malaysia in 1985, only returning to Indonesia following the fall of Suharto in 1998.

While little is known of Ba'asyir's time in Malaysia, it is known that the links between the Ngruki group[9] in Indonesia and the exiles in Malaysia remained strong, through family ties, political and religious sympathies and instructions emanating from Malaysia (ICG 2002a:5). The internationalisation of this network increased, with Sungkar and Ba'asyir travelling to Saudi Arabia to raise funds, the sending of volunteers to southern Thailand, Pakistan, Afghanistan and the southern Philippines for military training, and the dispersal of other members to Germany, Spain, Holland and elsewhere.

After Ba'asyir's return, in addition to running Pondok Ngruki, he helped found the Indonesian Mujahidin Council (Majelis Mujahidin Indonesia—

MMI), formed in Yogyakarta in 2000 as an umbrella group for those wishing to build 'an Islamic state and...an Islamic leadership in the country as well as in Muslim communities throughout the world' (Sipress & Nakashima 2003). Ba'asyir was elected as the MMI's *amir*[10] of its governing council, the Ahlul Halli wal 'Aqdi (AHWA). Along with the MMI's commitment to introducing Islamic law to Indonesia, the AHWA also had the further goal of establishing a new international caliphate, which also arose in alleged JI intentions for maritime Southeast Asia (for discussion about the origins and intentions of the caliphate movement (see Ba'asyir 2000; Baraja 2000; Khilafah 2004).

In 2003, Ba'asyir was convicted by a court in Jakarta and received a four-year jail sentence for subversion (with a charge of treason being dismissed). Indonesia's defence minister, Matori Abdul Djalil, alleged at that time that Ba'asyir was the leader of JI and that Riduan Isamuddin, also known as Hambali, was Ba'asyir's deputy. Speaking at his trial, Ba'asyir acknowledged that 'he knew fellow Indonesian Hambali as "a good man" who was active in channelling funds to Ambon, the capital city of Maluku province, to help Muslims who were battling Christians there' (AFP 2003). Acting under guidance from Riduan Isamuddin, more than 30 people alleged to be Jema'ah Islamiyah operatives were convicted of responsibility for the bombings of the two nightclubs in Bali on 12 October 2002 and the later Marriott hotel bombing on 5 August 2003. The investigation into the Bali bombing led to the arrest of Said Sungkar, the youngest brother of the alleged founder of Jema'ah Islamiyah and co-founder of Pondok Ngruki, Abdullah Sungkar. Also arrested in connection with the Bali bombings was Ali Gufron, alias Mukhlas. Mukhlas is said to have organised the Bali bombings and to have succeeded Hambali as operations chief of JI. Hambali became the most wanted man in Asia following the arrest of Mukhlas. On 12 August 2003, Hambali was arrested in Ayuthyah, Thailand, where he was allegedly planning to bomb a forthcoming meeting of the Asia Pacific Economic Co-operation (APEC) group.

The case of Hambali is illustrative of the complex nature of 'terrorist' and military/intelligence links. Hambali was held responsible for organising the bombings of churches on Christmas Eve 2000, in which 18 people were killed, the bombing of the Marriott Hotel in August 2003, helping fund the first *jihad* to Ambon and was linked to bombings in Manila in December 2000 in which 22 people were killed, as well as a foiled bid to blow up embassies in Singapore in December 2001,[11] Hambali was also under investigation for his role in the Bali nightclub bombing of October 2000. Yet according to Laksamana.net, an 'intelligence source' revealed that in the 1970s Hambali had been a Special Operations (Opsus)°plant into JI. He was given the code-name G-8 and tasked with°building the financial structure of JI°(Laksamana.net 2002a). The aim of the operation was to discredit political Islam and to legitimise repressive action by the New Order government. A similar link was established between the TNI and Fausi Hasbi, an Acehnese whose father was a leader of the Darul Islam movement in Aceh, who had a history of links with TNI intelligence dating to 1977. Hasbi was later identified as the link between TNI intelligence and three men (one of whom, Edi Sugianto, was also associated with Kopassus) charged with a bombing on Christmas Eve 2000 in Medan[12] (*Tapol* 2003; *Tempo* 4.3.2001; *Tempo* 25.12.2001; ICG 2002a:33). On 22 February 2002, Hasbi was abducted from a hotel in Ambon and murdered. His son claimed he was taken and killed by police (which police denied). Journalist John Martinkus has noted that his killing could have been to prevent him from being investigated as a link between the TNI and Jema'ah Islamiyah (Martinkus 2004:42). As senior Jema'ah Islamiyah researcher Sidney Jones noted: 'If you scratch any radical Islamic group in Indonesia, you will find some security forces involvement' (*Associated Press* 2002).

The ICG has claimed that it was the intention of JI to establish a group of caliphates in Southeast Asia under an overarching *Daulah Islamiyah* (Islamic State), based on what it refers to as '*mantiqi*'. These *mantiqi* have a political and military application, representing distinct administrative territories. Mantiqi One is said to focus on peninsular Malaysia, southern Thailand and Singapore, and was led by Riduan Isamuddin (Hambali) until 2002. Mantiqi Two focuses on Java, Sumatra and Kalimantan, while Mantiqi Three administers operations in the southern Philippines, Sabah, Sarawak (Malaysia), Brunei and Sulawesi (Indonesia). Mantiqi Four was said to focus on West Papua and Australia, with its primary purpose being fund-raising activities (RS 2003:10; see also ICG 2003a:11). As the ICG notes, the conventional thinking on the *mantiqi* is that they comprise a territorial administrative structure equivalent to regions, with *waklah* (districts) beneath them and *fiah* (cells) at the bottom. However, an alternative explanation for the structure is military, with *mantiqi* equalling brigades, *wakalah* ballations, *khatibah* companies, *qirdas* platoons and *fiah* squads. There is also understood to be a special operations unit, Laskar Khos, held by Indonesian national police to be responsible for the Marriott Hotel bombing in Jakarta in August 2003 (ICG 2003:11). It is, however, possible that this structure reflects an organisational attempt to understand JI, rather than necessarily reflecting the structure of this otherwise informally structured group. The organisational model of JI is more likely to be that of affinity groups with regional and functional divisions of responsibility, rather than as a formal hierarchical structure with specific links and chains of command. JI therefore represents a different order and type of threat to that conventionally expressed by terrorist organisations, and arrests of 'key members' may not have permanently damaged the capacity of JI to continue to engage in religiously motivated violence.

Laskar Jihad

In marked contrast to the internationalist orientation of Jema'ah Islamiyah, Laskar Jihad (LJ) has an explicitly nationalist political agenda. In this, there is a close overlap between its goals and those of what was known as the Green (pro-Islamic) faction in the TNI. The commonality of interests is illustrated by LJ's background and reflected in the alliances between the two groups. The Green faction arose as a result of Suharto's efforts from the late 1980s to establish new sources of support outside the senior ranks of the armed forces from which he was becoming alienated. He also reached out to conservative modernist Islamic organisations, which he had previously ignored. Hardliners within these organisations attacked Suharto's opponents in return for state patronage and new freedom to carry out their activities, which included undermining more moderate Muslim rivals. Simultaneously, Suharto began to promote officers belonging to the 'Green' or Muslim faction within the Indonesian military. These officers were not necessarily pious Muslims. Rather, they were willing to use Islam as a political tool. The convergence of Green military personnel and hardline Muslim organisations led to alliances being formed, which were the precursors to the launching of Laskar Jihad. The development of Laskar Jihad also benefited from President Suharto's promotion of explicitly Islamic army officers, some of whom assisted with Laskar Jihad's training, funding and logistics (see Huang 2002).

When Suharto resigned in May 1998, the rise of conservative modernist Muslim organisations was stalled. All the newly-formed overtly Islamic parties[13] performed poorly in the elections of June 1999, and fared little better in 2004.[14] The most successful was the Crescent and Star Party (PBB), which won only 2% of the vote. The elections showed that conservative Muslims would not benefit from an open, democratic system. Their Green allies in the military had a similar aversion to the new openness of the post-Suharto era, and the two groups were seeking to reassert their influence within the Indonesian body politic. Fighting in Ambon between Christians and Muslims provided the pretext for this reassertion of influence. The fighting had begun in December 1999, with reports of a massacre by Christian militia of approximately 500 Muslims in Halmahera, North Maluku. Muslim organisations responded by organising a rally of tens of thousands of supporters in Jakarta on 7 January 2000, at which there were calls for a *jihad*. This rally was addressed by Amien Rais (then speaker of the DPR), members of Islamic parties such as the PBB and Hamzah Haz (leader of the United Development Party (PPP) and later, vice-president), who endorsed calls for a *jihad* (Davis 2002). The organisers of the rally were encouraged by the turnout and moved to capitalise on the momentum generated. The Sunni Communication Forum (Forum Kommunikasi Ahlus Sunna Wal Jamaah—FKAWJ), an organisation formed in 1998, became their vehicle. The FKAWJ is controlled by a board of 60 *dewan pembina* (patrons), who under the chairmanship of Ja'far Umar Thalib established Laskar Jihad (LJ) as its military wing and assumed its leadership. The ideology of LJ is deeply conservative, opposing democracy or a female head of state as incompatible with Islam, and is influenced by anti-Zionist and Christian conspiracy theories (Schulze 2002:59). Van Bruinessen (2002) described LJ as a disproportionately influential radical Isamic organisation being among the 'most directly influenced by contemporary Wahhabism...This was the first movement in Indonesia that rejected elections on religious grounds...'.

From the beginning there were strong indications that LJ had the backing of military and political hardliners who wished to destabilise President Abdurrahman Wahid's reformist administration, which fitted in with LJ's own belief that Abdurrahman was an unbeliever (*kafir*) who ran a strict line against the organisation he had headed prior to assuming the presidency, NU, as well as regarding syncretic (*abangan*) Muslims as targets for 'purification' (Schulze 2002:59). Unlike other violent Islamic groups, which operated in a clandestine manner, LJ revelled in shows of strength, such as rallies, demonstrations, parades and processions. Its members received military training near Bogor (West Java) and Yogyakarta from sympathetic members of the Indonesian military. In particular, training near Bogor in April 2000 was undertaken by officer cadets, members of the Army's Special Forces (Kopassus) and martial arts experts. Kopassus members, probably operating 'off-line' as *milsus* (*militer khusus*—special military),[16] were supported by sections of the TNI officer corps that were opposed to the continuing presidency of Abdurrahman Wahid. Some of these officers, such as Major General Kivlan Zen (who inherited overseeing training and logistics for LJ from former TNI Commander in Chief, General Wiranto) were previously affiliated with the TNI's 'Green' faction. When approximately 3,000[17] LJ members travelled to Maluku, they were not obstructed by the military even though the government of Abdurrahman Wahid had pledged to prevent them from leaving Java. Maluku regional governor, Saleh Latuconsina, also pointed out that LJ had powerful backers because they were not being prevented from travelling. The Washington-based Centre for Defence Information (CDI) reported that, according to Western intelligence sources, over US$ nine million was transferred from the Indonesian Army's Strategic Reserve Command (Kostrad) to LJ and further funds were diverted from the business branch of Kostrad; both the group and the military denied the accusation (Huang 2002). The seven hectares of land near Bogor on which LJ trained was owned by the Wahhabist Al-Irsyad Foundation, sponsored by among others, Fuad Bawazier. Following the closure by the police of the main camp at Munjul village, near Bogor on Java, many recruits were trained in facilities outside Yogyakarta. The group's headquarters were at the Ilhya'us Sunnah Tadribud Du'at school in Degolan, also outside Yogyakarta (IRIP 2001), where facilities include a mosque and dormitories. Most members are poor Javanese, although there are some graduates and former professional workers. The recruits were trained in *akidah* (faith/religious instruction), physical exercise and the use of traditional arms.

LJ displayed the extravagant rhetoric, quasi-military forms and Javanese-inspired symbolism usually adopted by military proxies. Maluku-based Christians were described as *kafir harbi* ('belligerent infidels'—the most dangerous category of non-Muslims), meaning that religious sanction was being claimed to kill them. LJ was divided into four battalions, named after the Four Caliphs: Batalyon Abu Bakr, Batalyon Umar bin Khattab, Batalyon Usman bin Afan and Batalyon Ali bin Abu. Each battalion had four companies, each company had four platoons and each platoon had three squads. In keeping with its quasi-military form, LJ also had special forces, intelligence and logistics units. The group's explicitly nationalist agenda also conformed closely with the TNI's strategy. Indeed, Ja'far Umar Thalib went out of his way to emphasise LJ's anti-separatist credentials, stating that the problem in Maluku was not caused by religion but by separatism (Davis 2002). LJ repeatedly opposed what it claimed was the separatism of the Republik Maluku Selatan (Republic of the South Moluccas—RMS), which first appeared and was crushed in 1950, but was reinvigorated (if with limited appeal) in response to the Laskar Jihad targeting of the Christian community, in particular the wiping out of Christian villages and enclaves. Their justifications were wrapped in the rhetoric of Muslim self-defence, making it difficult for even sceptical politicians in Jakarta to criticise them for fear of being seen as anti-Muslim. Similarly, Laskar Jihad was also active in Poso, Central Sulawesi from July 2001, where it engaged in violence against Christian groups and published a daily newsletter calling for, amongst other things, *jihad*. LJ was also active in West Papua against pro-independence activists, and attempted to become involved in the conflict in Aceh, by way of assuaging Acehnese separatists (a move which was bluntly rejected). Unlike what was understood about Jema'ah Islamiyah, LJ signalled that it was not interested in overthrowing other regimes in Southeast Asia.

The military strategy of Laskar Jihad in Ambon was, in the first instance, to centralise command of the Muslim forces, co-ordinating with local and Laskar Mujahidin fighters (see below). Prior to its entry into the conflict in mid-2000, indigenous Muslim fighters had been conducting a makeshift defence of their villages and zones by using a combination of improvised and traditional weapons. Some LJ members brought automatic weapons with them; others were supplied with automatic weapons on arrival. In the beginning, most weapons were of the home-made type, although there were some conventional small arms such as AK47s and mortars obtained from the Indonesian military. In July 2000 there were reports that the Indonesian Navy had intercepted two boats containing hundreds of home-made weapons including machetes and firearms. The boats had been heading for Ternate, in northern Maluku. The boats had been sent from Galela, north of Halmahera island, an area where fierce fighting between Christians and Muslims had previously occurred. Raiders who attacked Soya village on Ambon island on 28 April 2002 were reported as having used M-16 assault rifles, swords and machetes. There were also reports that the Soya church was destroyed by mortar fire (Laksamana.net 2002a). Based on video footage of soldiers fighting with LJ, the arrest of a number of soldiers at the LJ stronghold at Hotel Wijaya II and LJ's access to standard TNI weapons and uniforms, it was clearly established that elements within the Indonesian armed forces worked with and on behalf of the group.

LJ combined military activities with social welfare and education, with much of the work to promote LJ being carried out through non-military programs such as education, health and welfare. In this respect, it attempted in some cases to fulfil roles that had been undetaken by the government prior to the political and economic crisis of the late 1990s. In keeping with the FKAWJ's welfare function, LJ's entry into the conflict in Maluku initially came through its despatch of healthcare workers and teachers to the region. This followed a breakdown of relations between the Islamic and Christian communities, based on shifting patterns of demography, patronage and legal and criminal economic opportunities, in which Christians had lost their traditional regional dominance during the New Order. In an environment of reduced central control following the collapse of the New Order and with local allegations of external provocation (according to Ambonese one of the authors spoke to in February 2002), in December 1998 tensions spilled over into communal violence in the Maluku capital of Ambon. In the following two months, the religiously mixed city and surrounding island was sharply divided through a policy of 'cleansing', creating religiously contiguous areas. More widely in Maluku, other regional tensions, some with long histories, were also defined along religious lines, spreading the conflict. Christian communities generally ended up in the stronger military position, but within months and with the introduction of troops, the conflict had begun to settle. However, a heightened sense of Islamic community, especially in Java but also in Sumatra and Sulawesi, encouraged political leaders such as Amien Rais to start talking about *jihad* in Maluku.

Laskar Jihad commander Umar Thalib was arrested in Ambon on 4 May 2002 on charges of inciting violence. However, indicative of the high level of official acceptance accorded to Laskar Jihad at this time, Thalib was visited in prison by vice-president Hamzah Has, who, until he found it politically unsustainable to do so in late 2002, also retained a public relationship with the 'spiritual' head of Jema'ah Islamiyah, Abu Bakar Ba'asyir.

LJ was formally closed around the time of the 2002 Bali bombing (it claims a few days before, but the announcement was made the day after the bombing). However, it continued to operate in West Papua at Fak-Fak, Sorong and near the border with Papua-New Guinea, at the transmigration camps of Imunda, Amanat, Green River and Waris. The US State Department noted that Laskar Jihad had 'active organisations in at least half of the province's 14 districts' (USA 2002a). Here, LJ members, including some indigenous Papuans (members of or recruited by the pro-integrationist militia Satgas Merah-Putih), were said to be armed and trained by Kopassus (Martinkus 2002; 2003). LJ members openly sold their publications, t-shirts, DVDs and books on Osama bin Laden (Barnabasfund.org 5.3.2003). In August 2003, external and locally recruited members of a group that appeared to be an off-shoot or locally recruited version of LJ, Laskar Tabligh (Missionary Troops), clashed with pro-independence protesters at Wamena over government plans to divide the province into three, in contravention of the province's 'special autonomy' status. In April 2004, Laskar Jihad leader Ja'far Umar Thalib announced that the organisation would again send its 'troops' to Ambon to protect Muslims following a renewed outbreak of sectarian violence (Laksamana.net 2002b). As Davis (2002) has noted, Laskar Jihad was unlikely to continue to receive TNI support once it had 'outlived its usefulness'. Here, one can reflect on a range of precedents for the TNI assembling and/or co-operating with paramilitary or criminal groups, before later discarding them.

Laskar Mujahidin

Laskar Mujahidin (LM) was the military wing of the MMI (Van Bruinessen 2002b). The first contingent of around 50 LM recruits arrived in Ambon in February 1999, soon after the first wave of sectarian violence. These recruits, initially called themselves Laskar Jundullah (not connected with the group referred to below—this is a largely generic name), and many of them had been active with the MILF in the southern Philippines (Van Bruinessen 2002b:19-20). By July 1999 several hundred LM members had become active in Maluku in operations against Christian militias and civilians, and later briefly in Poso, Central Sulawesi.

LM was said, at its peak in 2001, to have about 2,000 active members, who were better armed and more highly trained than LJ. However, LM probably fielded no more than 500 fighters in Maluku (and briefly, central Sulawesi) at any one time (ICGb 2002:19). From July 1999, it is believed that LM forces had access to professional military arms, including mortars, hand grenades, Stinger-5 rockets and AK47 assault rifles, delivered in bubble wrap from Surabaya in Java (ICG 2002b:20) (indicating they had come direct from military sources). LM tended to favour guerrilla-style tactics over the more set-piece battles often engaged in by LJ.

According to independent observers in Ambon in early 2002, while LM was linked to LJ through the MMI, they maintained separate operations in and around Ambon (pers comm.) and Poso, and were known to clash with soldiers and the police, whose authority they did not recognise. In part, hostilities between LJ and LM reflected personal animosities between LM leader Haris Fadillah (aka Abu Dzar) and LJ leader Ja'far Umar Thalib, who were known to have clashed on three occasions, in the Middle East, Afghanistan and Ambon. However, LM did operate together with a local Islamic force known as Laskar Hitu in attacks on the Christian villages of Hitu, Mamala, Morela and others in the area (ICG 2002b:20). In late October 2002, uniformed LM members were deployed to guard the hospital where Abu Bakar Ba'asyir was taken for treatment after being arrested in the wake of the 2002 Bali bombing.

LM leader Haris Fadillah was killed fighting Christians in Ambon on 23 October 2000. Fadillah was father-in-law of Omar al-Faruq, a Kuwaiti who is claimed to have been 'Al Qaeda's principal relationship manager in Southeast Asia' (Murphy 2003a), initially as a key conduit between Al Qaeda and Filipino Islamic militants and—since the fall of Suharto—Indonesian militants. Al-Faruq was initially trained at Al Qaeda's Camp Khalden in Afghanistan. He fought in Ambon and was being held in detention in the United States. A video-tape featuring Fadillah encouraging young Muslims to tale up arms was distributed throughout Indonesia, Malaysia and the southern Philippines, and was shown during informal religious classes by clerics with alleged ties to Jema'ah Islamiyah. This and other videos, said to have been financed by Agus Dwikarna (who first met Faruq in Makassar in 1999 through another Camp Khalden trainee, Syawai Yassin), were produced by Aris Munandar, also said to be the 'right-hand man' to Abu Bakar Ba'asyir (Murphy 2003b). In 2000, Dwikarna founded the Laskar Jundullah and in 2001 established a training camp near Poso, the site of heavy Muslim-Christian fighting in Central Sulawesi, where the training of recruits was undertaken by Faruq.

Laskar Jundullah

The aim of Laskar Jundullah (Army of God), based in Sulawesi, is the imposition of Syariah law throughout Sulawesi. It has been prepared to use violence to serve this cause and in 2003 and 2004, appeared to have devolved the use of violence to sub-units not immediately connected to it. It is important to note that there have been at least two 'Laskar Jundullahs' operating in the Poso region of Central Sulawesi, which appeared to have had links to the separatist Moro Islamic Liberation Front (MILF) in Mindanao. This group, formed on an ad hoc basis, first appeared in Poso in July 2000 in response to religious violence in June 2000, in which 200 Muslims were killed.[18] Based on earlier, sporadic religious conflict in the Poso area (dating to the 1980s and more substantially from around 1995), it is possible there may have been other ad hoc Laskar Jundullah groups before the establishment of the group that currently carries that name, which was founded in September 2000.

The existing Laskar Jundullah was established as the military wing of the Preparatory Committee for Upholding Islamic Law (Komite Persiapan Penegakan Syariat Islam—KPPSI), originally conceived of as a kind of religious police intended to enforce Islamic law among KPPSI members. The Poso region leader of Laskar Jundullah was Amno Dai, who had been a follower of Kahar Muzakkar during the Dar'ul Islam rebellion. Laskar Jundullah was believed to have drawn its members from three sources; descendants, relatives and supporters of the Dar'ul Islam rebellion, a faction of the Indonesian Islamic student organisation Himpunan Mahasiswa Islam, and Muslims from the Poso area, in particular, the Poso Committee for Islamic Struggle (Komite Perjuangan Mulsim Poso) (ICG 2002b:20).

One of the co-founders of this more permanent Laskar Jundullah, Agus Dwikarna, was arrested in the Philippines in March 2002 and sentenced to prison for illegal possession of firearms and explosives. Dwikarna was said to have close links to the head of the Spanish branch of Al Qaeda, Imad Eddin Barakat Yarbas, who in turn was closely associated with Mohammad Atta, the alleged leader of the 11 September 2001 attack against the World Trade Center and the Pentagon. In June 2000, Dwikarna allegedly acted as a guide for Al Qaeda figures visiting Indonesia, including Osama bin Laden's former second in command, Ayman al-Zawahiri, and former Al Qaeda military chief

Mohammad Atef. A series of bombings occurred in December 2002 in Makassar (South Sulawesi). Four Laskar Jundullah members were arrested on charges relating to these bombings, while two others who had not been caught were named as suspects. One of those charged, Muchtar Daeng Lau, was claimed to have trained earlier in Afghanistan and the southern Philippines. Subsequently, Central Sulawesi police discovered two separate, large caches of bomb-making chemicals. The next month, South Sulawesi police found a number of military-style camps north of Makassar, claiming that they were linked to a senior Laskar Jundullah figure[19] linked to the Makassar bombings. In 2001, the head of the Indonesian National Intelligence Agency (BIN), AM Hendropriyono, claimed he had evidence that Al Qaeda had established a training base in central Sulawesi. However, under significant domestic criticism and his failure to produce such evidence, Hendropriyono withdrew his claim, saying that Al Qaeda did not have any cells in Indonesia. In January 2003, after links between Islamic extremists and Al Qaeda had been more publicly explored, Indonesian intelligence confirmed that there had, in fact, been a number of camps operating in the Central Sulawesi district and that they had received funds, logistics and trainers from Al Qaeda (Agencies 2003).

To date, Indonesian police have arrested 18 people in connection with the Makassar bombings. Some of those arrested have reportedly claimed that they underwent paramilitary training in the camps under the guidance of instructors from the MILF. Police investigations have been complicated by the potential for a backlash from the strongly Islamic populace of South Sulawesi. Despite a common religio-ideological background and membership of the MMI, Laskar Jundullah had poor relations with Laskar Jihad in the Poso area, where it preceded the latter organisation and also had poor relations with Laskar Mujahidin.

Front Pembela Islam

Front Pembela Islam (Islamic Defenders Front—FPI) is a civilian militia that was founded on 17 August 1998 to coincide with Independence Day celebrations. At the time, the TNI was being criticised for its heavy-handed role in suppressing pro-democracy protests a few months earlier. Accordingly, it needed to sub-contract its repressive role to a more acceptable entity, which the precursor organisation to the FPI (Pam Swakarsa) undertook. The purpose of the initial group, organised and paid for at the request of General Wiranto by the 'green' officer Major-General Kivlan Zen, was the intimidation of pro-democracy protesters, although it was publicly created to provide security during the special session of the People's Consultative Assembly (MPR)

(Kivlan 2004:121–2). The group's nationalist-religious outlook was exploited by President Habibie,[20] who used it as a counterweight against his political opponents. The FPI vehemently opposes communism and has denounced the People's Democratic Party (Partai Rakyat Demokrasi—PRD), the Student Forum for Reform and Democracy and the City Forum, which it claims are neo-communist organisations. Initial support for FPI came from General Wiranto via Kivaln Zen, who personally financed the organisation of the Pam Swakarsa[21] and, later, the former Defence Minister and Armed Forces Commander. Djaja Suparman, the then Jakarta-based Military Commander, and Nugroho Jayusman, the then Jakarta Police Commander, are also alleged to have provided organisation and logistical support to the FPI. Senior FPI leader Habib Ali Baagil, who was accused by President Wahid of involvement in the Jakarta Stock exchange bombing in September 2000, admitted that he had close relations with General Wiranto and Lieutenant-General Djaja Suparman.

The second source of FPI funding was Muchsin Mochdar, husband of Habibie's youngest sister, Sri Rahayu. Mochdar and his wife control the Citra Harapan Abadi Group, the third financial arm of the Habibie clan's significant business empire. Their financial support for Muslim vigilantes dates back to November 1998, when their family charity, Yayasan Al-Kautsar, organised transportation and provided financial rewards for West Java villagers recruited to form Pam Swakarsa and demonstrate against the students in Jakarta. Two of Mochdar's brothers, Aziz and Hamid, were commissioners in several companies belonging to Bambang Trihatmodjo's Bimantara Group, increasing the likelihood that the Suharto family had also been contributing to the activities of FPI. Fuad Bawazier, a former Director-General of Taxes and then Finance Minister in Suharto's last cabinets, was believed to be another supporter. Bawazier was close to Suharto's family, in business through his job as president commissioner of PT Satelindo, the telecommunications company partly owned by Bambang Trihatmodjo, TNI-linked businessman Tomy Winata and the army charity Yayasan Kartika Eka Paksi. Fuad Bawazier was also allegedly instrumental in financing LJ through Suharto's Yayasan Amal Bhakti Muslim Pancasila foundation.

Although the FPI began as a civilian militia organisation, it later began to carry out raids on what it considered to be 'anti-Islamic' establishments, notably bars, pool halls, gambling venues, nightclubs and brothels. It typically raided entertainment venues with little or no warning, ripped up 'offensive' posters, damaged property and assaulted patrons and bystanders. Its raids were generally timed to occur during the month of Ramadan. FPI had a modicum of success in revoking by-laws that permit entertainment centres to operate during

Ramadan. For instance, after it had provided 'security' at the MPR, the FPI flexed its muscles in a street fight in central Jakarta against Christian Ambonese security guards in November 1998. Soon after, FPI members stormed Jakarta City Hall, demanding its closure during Ramadan. They then proceeded to raid bars and nightclubs in Sumatra and in other neighbourhoods in Jakarta. Their weaponry tends to be improvised: stones, bamboo sticks, sharpened poles, machetes and knives.

While the FPI was mostly active in Java and to a lesser extent Sumatra, the organisation did have a presence in Central Sulawesi, particularly around the town of Morowali, during fighting between Muslim and Christian groups. While FPI literature could be found in the more conflict-ridden town of Poso in early 2002, the less well-known (and possibly related) organisation Forum Silaturrahim dan Perjuangan Muslim Umat Islam (FSPUI, Defence Forum and Indonesian Muslim Struggle Community) was believed to be more active there.

Attacks on venues that are considered *haram* were carried out by its paramilitary wing, whose members wear white robes and green sashes. It appeared that there was also a protection racket involved: security forces are said to demand a protection fee from proprietors of entertainment venues, in return for being spared from FPI raids. In addition, the FPI has itself been accused of extorting bribes in return for allowing some venues to remain open. It has survived the presidencies of Habibie, Wahid and Megawati by co-operating with, and receiving the backing of, powerful segments of the Indonesian military. Rather than campaign on behalf of a particular party, it focused on specific issues like alcohol, drugs, prostitution and gambling. Unlike other radical Islamic groups, the FPI did not call for an Islamic state. Rather, it demanded that Indonesia's constitution be changed to include a clause that calls on citizens to adhere to Islamic law. The clause was dropped from the constitution in 1945 because of opposition from Christian and Buddhist communities and in the interests of promoting the more religiously inclusive state doctrine of *Pancasila*.

The FPI has an extensive network of Islamic religious schools and organisations as well as numerous councils. It has a formal leadership hierarchy, with five components: the Syariat Council, the Advocacy Council, the Honorary Council and the Council of advisers. Each council advises on matters within its purview and reports to the chairman and Secretary General. The FPI's leader is Al-Habib Muhammad Rizieq bin Hussein (Habib Rizieq), born in 1965 of Jakarta (Betawi) and Arab descent. He studied at King Saud University in Riyadh, Saudi Arabia in the 1980s. While FPI had an Islamic leadership, most of its members came from the lower-middle classes in Java and Sumatra. Most Jakarta-based members were ethnic Betawi, and were predominantly characterised as 'thugs'. The FPI was formally closed in November 2002 following the 2002 Bali bombing, although it was announced in March 2003 that the organisation had resumed its activities.

Prospects for the future

While these organisations tended to be secretive, most intelligence analysts believed that despite the crackdown in Indonesia and elsewhere, Jema'ah Islamiyah in particular remained active, if damaged, and was likely to strike again against what it perceived to be symbols of US hegemony, Westernism and Christianity. However, within JI there were also indications of internal dissent, with some members being unhappy with later choices of targets, including the Marriott hotel bombing that killed mostly Indonesian workers. There was also disagreement about the appropriate focus for *jihad* and over the use of a practice known as *fa'i*—robbery of non-Muslims to support Islamic struggle (ICG 2003c:31). In addition, Hambali was reported to have told his interrogators that the crackdowns and disruptive operations undertaken by the Indonesian security forces had seriously weakened Jema'ah Islamiyah (ICG 2003a).

Interestingly, there was a strong belief by some researchers that there were links between Indonesia's national Intelligence Agency (BIN) and elements of JI, the origins of which pre-dated both organisations. These links were also reflected in the TNI's association with former Darul Islam members, as noted above, and in the TNI's special forces intelligence function, which in turn links it back to BIN. This alleged association, which recalled the Opsus-Komando Jihad link of the 1970s, was intended to strengthen the relative position of the security forces in the state and to create further pressure for the resumption of external military support for the TNI (which, based on the Australian government response of announcing renewed training links with Kopassus and the Bush administration's support for renewing military ties, looked to be successful). However, Indonesian politics is at least as dirty as elsewhere and such claims must be regarded with a high degree of scepticism, regardless of their neat logic.

Laskar Jihad, meanwhile, appeared to be increasingly transparently an arm of the TNI in its efforts to suppress local separatist movements, especially along with its offshoot Laskar Tabligh, in West Papua. This in turn fell neatly into the TNI's long-standing policy of 'Total People's Defence' as 'Rakyat Terlatih' ('Trained People'). Its dissolution immediately after the JI bombing in Bali on 12 October 2002 (or before, if one believes its claim) was clearly in response to its need to reorganise following the reduction of tensions in Maluku and the poor publicity it was bringing Indonesia in the eyes of the international community. However, its resurrection in a smaller, modified form also showed the usefulness of such militia to the TNI and reinforced the nexus between the state and unofficial violence in Indonesia that had been so pronounced during the Suharto era.

Laskar Jundullah appeared to have become inactive in 2002, but in October 2003 and into 2004 there was a renewed spate of killings of Christians in the Poso area of Central Sulawesi. Following arrests, there were official reports that elements of Laskar Jundullah were still active and had co-ordinated its attacks with representatives of Jema'ah Islamiyah; the latter were said to have become resident in Central Sulawesi. These attacks were also linked to individuals linked to the TNI who had large and expanding economic interests in the region. So too, Laskar Mujahidin had reduced its public presence to (unarmed) displays of solidarity for Abu Bakar Ba'asyir. Despite sharing similar goals, a basic ideology and membership of the MMI, relations between Laskar Jihad, Laskar Jundullah and Laskar Mujahidin were poor and not immune from degenerating into violence, primarily reflecting animosities between leaders and, to some extent, conflict over control in particular regions. FPI, meanwhile, remained active, if not also somewhat more subdued, no doubt in response to the pressure being brought to bear on radical Islamic groups predominantly by Indonesia's national police.

While the Indonesian economy continued to languish under the crippling impact of international debt and sluggish growth, there was likely to continue to be a steady stream of disaffected and often desperate potential recruits for the above and similar types of organisations. The heightened security environment in Indonesia that such organisations had engendered, at least in part as a consequence of semi-official policy, had begun to challenge the democratic reforms of the post-Suharto era. As with corruption and poor economic performance, religious extremism and its consequent political instability contributed to an environment in which there would continue to be limited opportunities for many Indonesians, in which many would turn to religion for answers that contained messages of intolerance, extremism and violence.

Singapore and Malaysia

While militant and terrorist Islam has been concentrated within Indonesia, militant Muslims have long found a supportive environment in Malaysia and among radical elements of the Malay community in Singapore. Prior to colonialism, the Malayan Peninsula and Sumatra in particular were part of a common Malay world, sharing a generally common language (*Bahasa Melayau*), common religion (Sunni Islam) and at various times, common or intersecting histories. Islam is the state religion for Malaysian ethnic Malays and *Syiariah* applies to them, which has reflected and helped develop a strong sense of Islamic identity. Malaysian Islam has also been radicalised, particularly in the north, by its historical association with the Malay Muslim communities of southern Thailand, which have been engaged in a sporadic campaign for independence (or joining with Malaysia) since they were formally incorporated into the Thai state in 1893.

Kampulan Militan Malaysia

The best known (and perhaps only) militant Islamic group in Malaysia is Kampulan Militan Malaysia (KMM—Malaysian Militant Community), which is the name given to this group by the Malaysian government, rather than identifying it as Jema'ah Islamiyah, which is a more organisationally correct nomenclature.[22] JI had established a business and commercial network in Malaysia in the 1990s in order to help fund its various projects, and at this time also established a full administrative structure, fitting in with JI's wider and somewhat less formal regional structure. Among the early targets of KMM were selected Western embassies in Singapore, Changi Airport and Singaporean defence facilities, visiting US military personnel and Western warships in the Straits of Malacca (Apdal & Thayer 2003:21; see also RS 2003:11, 14).

Although local contacts with notable JI figures such as Abu Bakar Ba'asyir dated back several years, JI Malaysia and JI Singapore were probably founded around 1994–95 by Hambali and Abu Jibril, who focused their efforts on Indonesian migrants, students and lecturers at the Universiti Tecknologi Malaysia, as well as among local Islamic schools. Ali Ghufron (Muklas) and Imam Samudra, who were central to the Bali bombing, came from the same school in Johor Baru. KMM's local founding member was by an Afghan war veteran, Zainon Ismail, who promoted the violent overthrow of the Malaysian government and the creation of a pan-archipelagic Islamic state (in keeping with the JI 'caliphate' model).

Under the tutelage of Hambali, Abu Jibril and Zainon, militant young Malaysian and Singaporeans were sent for religious indoctrination in Pakistan, while about 50 others were sent to Al Qaeda training camps in Afghanistan, while others went to MILF camps in Mindanao. Total membership probably did not exceed 70 to 80 people at any one time. Around 1999–2000, JI groups in Malaysia and Singapore were converted into operational cells, with leadership of the KMM passing to Nik Adli Aziz. The Singapore branch, referred to by the Singaporean government as Jema'ah Islamiyah, dated to 1988–89, with the induction of Ibrahim Maidin by Abu Jibril. Maidin, subsequently appointed to JI's consultative council, while remaining a spiritual adviser, was replaced by Mas Selamat bin Kastari as JI Singapore leader in 1999 (RS 2003:10).

The Malaysian and Singaporean JI network was damaged in 1999 after a series of arrests by Malaysian police (Jibril was arrested in June 2000) and Singapore's Internal Security Department. A further 21 suspects were arrested in Singapore in 2001 and 2002, 19 of whom were identified as JI members, thwarting a bombing campaign against Western embassies and ending JI operations in Singapore from that time. However, KMM members did carry out a number of attacks, including the murder of a Kedah politician in 2000, after which Malaysian police arrested a further 60 members.

KMM/JI had been able to operate in Malaysia and Singapore because of a high level of sympathy for anti-Western views, especially after the US-led attack on Afghanistan. Protest against the attack was led by the religiously-oriented but mainstream Partai Islam se-Maaysia (PAS—Malaysian Islamic Party), which had called for 'jihad' against the US. Most of the 16 detainees the Malaysian government had claimed were members of KMM were also affiliated with PAS, including PAS youth committee member Mohamad Lotfi Ariffin, and KMM leader Nik Adli Aziz, who was the son of PAS spiritual leader and senior minister of Malaysia's Kelantan state, Nik Aziz (HRW 2004). Nik Adli Aziz had been named as one of those present at a meeting of 20 people called by Abu Bakar Ba'asyir and Hambali in 1999, which discussed the establishment of a Mujahidin International (*Rabitatul Mujahidin*). The meeting included representatives from the MILF, the Rohingya Solidarity Organisation, the Arakanese Rohingya Nationalist Organisation, the Pattani United Liberation Organisation, Front Mujahidin and the Republik Islam Aceh[23] (Wong and Lourdes 2003). In late 2001, the Malaysian Government arrested former Philippines Moro National Liberation Front leader and ex-governor of the Autonomous Region of Muslim Mindanao, Nur Misuari, for illegal entry into Malaysia.

Southern Thailand

Islamic separatism has long troubled Thailand's southern provinces of Pattani, Yala and Narathiwat, and to a lesser extent Songkhla and Satun, and the actions of various organisations claiming to represent separatist movements has been characterised by the Thai Government as 'terrorism'. These are primarily murders of Thai officials working in rural Pattani, but also attacks on symbols of the Thai state, such as the railway.

Pattani was established as a trading port by Muslim Malays probably as early as the 13th century, marking as it did the narrowest point of the Isthmus of Kra and being a generally flat crossing just north of a difficult mountain range. This crossing point, which focused on a well-sheltered bay and wide river, was used by Arabic, Indian and Chinese traders who wished to avoid traversing the sometimes dangerous Malacca Straits and especially trading with Malacca after its fall to the Portuguese. The principality forged alliances with other regional Malay states, but succumbed to the Thais in the 18th century. Despite numerous rebellions, which led to the principality's dismemberment into a number of provinces, Pattani was not formally incorporated into the Thai state until 1902, which was recognised by the British in 1909. Since then, the 1.2 million Malay Muslims of the region have objected to the assimilationist policies of the Thai Government and have struggled in various ways to either become an independent state (Negeri Patani Raya[24]) or to assert a claim to incorporation with Malaysia (Pattanti Darussalam), which the Malaysian Government has been sympathetic towards but careful to never formally endorse.

The primary separatist organisation in this region is now the Pattani United Liberation Organisation (PULO), which has been said to act as an umbrella organisation for a number of smaller separatist groups. Despite occasional flare-ups of tension, PULO had been relatively quiet until 2002, when the more forceful assimilationist policies of the Thai Prime Minister, Thaksin Shinawatra, and the arrest of more outspoken Muslim clerics, alienated many local Muslims. In 2002, 15 police were killed in separate attacks throughout the southern provinces. The Thai Government response was to crack down on separatism, which led to a more forceful backlash culminating in an attack by Malay Muslim youths on military strong points. On 4 January 2004, around 30 men attacked a Thai military depot in Narathiwat, killing four soldiers and taking more than 100 weapons. Around 18 schools were also burned in Narathiwat and Yala on the same day, while on the following day, two policemen were killed while trying to defuse a bomb in Pattani province (Raman 2004). In response, the Thai Government declared martial law in Pattani, Narathiwat and Yala provinces.

In June 2003, Thai police arrested three Thai Muslims, as well as one from Singapore, some of whom later admitted they were members of JI. Police later claimed that the Thai branch of JI was known as Gerakan Mujahideen

Islam Pattani (GMIP—Pattani Islamic Holy Struggle Organisation), and was alleged to have links with Al Qaeda and JI (Raman 2004). Thai police also claimed that PULO was linked to the Free Aceh Movement and had supplied arms to it, which the latter vehemently denied.

On 28 April 2004, more than 100 poorly-armed Muslim youths were killed along with two soldiers and three police officers when the youths attacked Thai army and police posts in southern Thailand. After being defeated, many of the youths fled to Pattani's Krue Se mosque, where soldiers killed 32 of them. Killings of civilians and alleged PULO members, as well as police, soldiers and Thai Government officials, continued at a regular and gruesome pace in the following months, with much of the Pattani and surrounding areas becoming a region of active guerrilla warfare.

The Philippines

The Philippines has long been troubled by insurgencies and dominated by a small clique of wealthy families that control the country's businesses and political process. These two factors are intimately linked. The ruling families include the Cojuangcos, who dominate Tarlac province north of Manila; the Osmenas, who control central Cebu province; the Macapagals, who dominate Pampanga (the second-largest province of vote-rich Central Luzon); the Bagatsings, whose land holdings underpin their authority in Manila; and the Lopezes, who dominate in central Iloilo province and nearby Guimaras Island. They have retained their influence and wealth, despite the reforms enacted since the overthrow of former President Marcos. While reformists have gradually gained some influence, changes have been slow and few, and political violence has remained.

Undermining of civil authority and civil society

The disturbances in the Philippines date as far back as the resistance of the inhabitants of the southern islands to the Spanish colonisers, with a history of piracy in the south-west islands pre-dating that. The Spaniards were unable to pacify, much less to govern the 'Moros' (named by the Spanish after the Muslim 'Moors' of Morocco) that inhabited the islands of Basilan, Jolo and Mindanao.

The Philippines was ceded to the US in the Treaty of Paris, which ended the Spanish–American War in 1898. Local resistance against the new rulers was quickly crushed in the north, while the Islamic south was more slowly brought under control. During the Japanese occupation (1942–45), and while many Filipinos collaborated with the Japanese, the southern islands functioned under de facto self-government. The Japanese also used a system of semi-private guards in order to assist its occupation forces in the maintenance of agricultural production and local security. The Japanese and their collaborators were opposed by pro-communist guerrillas. However, when the Japanese were driven from the islands, many of the collaborators were reincorporated into government under the returning US, and were set up to inherit the machinery of state when independence was granted in 1946.

This period was characterised by economic and political domination by US administrators and a local and US-based economic elite. The local elite was largely made up of major landlords, established under Spanish rule, whose interests were cemented to those of the US by the privileged market position of Philippine sugar, though there was also a business class, partly independent but much of it servicing predominant US economic interests. Administrative and bureaucratic positions were filled by Filipinos drawn almost exclusively from the ranks of the *ilustrados*.[25]

After the defeat of Japan in the Second World War, the Philippines were granted technical independence under a conservative oligarchy closely linked to the US, with the pre-war colonial economy restored. Economic and political power was concentrated in the hands of a powerful landlord and business class (the famous '400' families) and enormous US influence based on a nearly two billion dollar investment and a network of business, financial and military linkages. The first president was Japanese collaborator Manuel Roxas, a cabinet minister during the occupation and a director of the wartime rice procurement agency that had supplied the Japanese. The anti-Japanese Hukbong Mapagpalaya Laban sa Hapon (People's Army Against Japan) had drawn their forces from the militant peasant movement which had been approaching revolution in the 1930s, and hence were regarded as the enemy by the US and its domestic client. Huk representatives standing under the banner of the Democratic Alliance stood for election in 1946. Manuel Roxas prevented successful DA candidates from assuming their seats in the legislature and declared the Hukbalahap to be an illegal organisation, following which army and police units launched a brutal crackdown against the Huks.

Terror was used as an instrument of state policy during this crackdown, which lasted from 1946 to 1954. Paramilitary militias were recruited for the purpose of political thuggery and the imposition of ideological conformity. In the 1950s, the civilian guards system was re-instituted in order to serve large landlords and local government officials. The guards were an important part of the counter-insurgency structure. The US Army and the Philippines' military learned valuable lessons in counter-insurgency as a result of these terror tactics, which continue to be cited in US Army psychological warfare training materials. The Department of the Army's 1976 psychological warfare publication, DA Pamphlet 525-7-1, refers to some of the classic counter-terror techniques and accounts of the practical application of terror. These include the capture and murder of suspected guerrillas in a manner suggesting it was done by legendary vampires (*asuang*); and a prototypical 'Eye of God' technique in which a stylised eye would be painted opposite the house of a suspect (see Lansdale 1976:770).

In the southern islands of Mindanao and Sulu, there were calls for greater self-government or independence. The new Filipino administration responded by encouraging the resettlement of Christians from the 'over-populated' north to these islands in order to subdue pro-independence sentiment. There was no recognition of traditional land ownership, with many Muslim farmers losing their land without compensation. This created a sense of grievance that would re-emerge with a vengeance.

The US-backed Filipino rulers maintained the broad character of the economy as a US colony: extreme disparities in income levels, preferential treatment for US investments in the Philippines, enormous power of private US capital, dominance of a few Filipino family corporations, and corruption in government. The democratic façade of the Philippines was brittle in this society dominated by external interests and a small, very wealthy elite.

The 1965 presidential election was won by Senate president and US favourite Ferdinand Marcos. Under the Marcos administration, the guard system was updated, becoming the Barrio Self-Defence Forces. These paramilitary forces were much more organisationally sophisticated than the guard system; local detachments were formally integrated into the armed forces command structure through local constabulary forces. Marcos' first term saw an increase in government expenditure, financed by foreign loans. By the end of the 1960s, the principal and interest payments fell due. These debt servicing requirements, as well as rising imports and massive election spending, threatened a balance-of-payments crisis. In addition, there was a rising tide of nationalism, fuelled by hostility to the Vietnam War and resentment at continued US economic dominance. There was increased student activism and an increasing challenge to central authority from the Moro National Liberation Front. In 1968, the Partido Kommunista ng Pilipinas (PKP—Communist Party of the Philippines) split and Jose Maria Sison led a Maoist breakaway group to form the Communist Party of the Philippines (CPP), of which the military wing, the New People's Army (NPA), frequently clashed with government military forces.

At this time, there were widespread reports of corruption by Marcos and his wife Imelda, who were trying to subvert the constitutional requirement that he end his term of office in 1973. The number and size of student demonstrations escalated and they were violently dispersed by government forces, leaving scores of students dead. In August 1971 an opposition rally was bombed; many died and a number of senatorial candidates were seriously injured. In 1972 the Supreme Court of the Philippines ruled that the US could no longer maintain its privileged position in land ownership and that US citizens and corporations were subject to the general ban on foreign ownership of Philippine land. This brought the situation to a head. Marcos declared martial law in September 1972 and followed this with widespread arrests of opposition figures, intellectuals and journalists. He suspended the Supreme Court ruling against US land ownership and imposed tight control of the press. Later, he put forward new constitutional proposals favourable to US business interests.

Paramilitary terror was used against opponents of the regime. The Barrio Self-Defence Forces were re-constituted as the Civilian Home Defence Forces (CHDF). Their purpose was, as before, to use violence against the civilian population in order to achieve a political goal. The CHDF were also organisationally integrated into the armed forces command structure. The composition of the forces tended to exacerbate existing conflict situations. Recruits were drawn from elites and their employees. The net result was to create, and further set apart, an armed elite aloof from the majority of the population. Provided with modern weaponry and sharing the regular armed forces' discretionary powers of life and death, the new paramilitaries acted out ancestral conflicts and pursued private group interests under the guise of counter-insurgency, all of which was in accord with US military doctrine (McClintock 1992).

State-backed terror against domestic opponents was an essential component of Marcos' rule. This terror was necessary to defeat domestic opposition to a program that allowed multinationals to dominate the economy, buy out or destroy domestic enterprises, dispossess large numbers of peasants in a rapid development of export-oriented agriculture, and implement the deflationary unemployment-generating policies required by the international banking fraternity.

After the fall of Marcos, the Civilian Home Defence Forces system was modified to include the reinforcement of an elaborate command and control structure and the mobilisation and deployment of vast new forces as so-called 'vigilantes'. The Philippines' system then moved towards the system of *de facto* obligatory participation, where refusal to join military-controlled paramilitary organisations could result in reprisals.

The Communist Party of the Philippines

In 1967–68, Sino–Soviet tensions were reflected in a split within the Philippines Communist Party (Partido Kommunista ng Pilipinas—PKP). The pro-Chinese faction became the Communist Party of the Philippines (CPP), led by Jose Maria Sison. Its military wing, formed in 1969, was called the New People's Army (NPA) and employed a strategy derived from Maoist doctrines of protracted peoples' wars. The NPA focused its efforts in central Luzon, first around the key agrarian centre of Tarlac and then around Isabella. Later, its area of operations spread to other rural areas. A commander in the early years was Victor Corpus, an army officer who seized the military academy's arsenal in Manila in 1970 and defected to the NPA with the weapons. Bernabe Buscayno, an experienced resistance leader, was another commander. In the early years, China was a source of weapons and expertise. However, Chinese support ended after 1977.

As the corruption and repression of the Marcos regime continued, many mainstream—which is to say non-communist—Filipinos came to view the CPP-NPA as the only viable force for overthrowing the dictator. In the mid-1980s, the NPA was believed to have some 25,000 fighters and it operated in 63 of the country's 73 provinces. A well-organised political coalition operated alongside the NPA; there was an alliance of underground groups known as the National Democratic Front (NDF) and a range of legal organisations including peasant groups, labour unions, other sectoral organisations, political parties and development groups. Many anti-Marcos activists worked with the CPP-NPA, but did not subscribe to its ideological program. As a result, once Marcos was overthrown in 1986, the ranks of the NPA began to diminish.

Until the early 1980s, the NPA was renowned for its tight, disciplined command structure that was highly centralised. Two factors have eroded this: doctrinal differences between leaders and the distance between those on the ground, who are seen as hardliners, and those in exile or the CPP leadership, who are more conciliatory in the peace process. Breakaway factions emerged, further compromising the command structure and it was estimated that at one time there were at least 33 companies in Mindanao alone, each operating under the name of the NPA but with a very high degree of autonomy. The forces based in Luzon are traditionally more dominant, particularly over doctrine and strategy. Central command in Luzon issues orders to units under the leadership of a local commander. The guerrillas work in small units and it is unusual for the NPA to risk committing more than 100 guerrillas to an action or offensive.

The NPA numbered around 18,000 guerrillas by 1992, but following purges, splits and defections, it fell to around 1,000 cadres by the end of 1998, along with a number of splinter groups operating as quasi-bandits on particular islands. In a bid to finally end the rebellion, in 1994, President Fidel Ramos legalised the CPP, allowed it to enter the parliamentary political process and pardoned most of its leaders. The government also began a peace process with the group. But in 1999, the government re-established a military training relationship with the US and the NPA once again resumed armed activities, whilst the CPP broke off negotiations. Anti-US sentiment, continued economic difficulties, the disastrous presidency of Joseph Estrada and the failure of land reform combined to once again swell the NPA's ranks to an estimated 12,000 guerrillas (IDP 2002).

Alex Boncayao Brigade (ABB)

The ABB was formed in the mid-1980s as a break-away movement from the New People's Army (NPA, the armed wing of the CPP) and had its origins in the establishment of two Armed City Partisans (ACPs) in 1972 by the NPA. When President Marcos imposed martial law these cells were smashed. The project was relaunched in 1975, despite the grave misgivings of senior members of the NPA and the lack of support from the CPP, which doubted the effectiveness of urban revolutionary structures. In 1976 and 1977, Victor Corpus, Bernabe Buscayno and Jose Maria Sison—three senior figures within the NPA—were arrested and imprisoned. This gave the advocates of the ACPs a large degree of autonomy since the three arrested leaders were considered doctrinal hardliners. Under the leadership of Filemon 'Popoy' Lagman, the ACPs put pressure on the Marcos regime but formed relationships with other anti-government organizations, irrespective of their own political allegiances.

The Manila-Rizal committee supported candidates for the Interim Batasang Pambansa elections in April 1978. The candidates included Benigno Aquino Jr, Aquilino Pimentel Jr, Charito Planas and Alex Boncayao. On the day before polling the Manila-Rizal committee organised a noisy barrage—thousands took to the streets of Manila shouting and banging implements, with motorists leaning on car horns. The results of the poll claimed victory for the Kilusang Bagong Lipuanan, led by President Marcos' wife Imelda, but allegations of poll rigging were widespread and the state-controlled media refused to cover the demonstration. The election candidates fled into hiding or exile. Alex Boncayao returned to the countryside where he was killed fighting alongside the NPA. Popoy was disciplined by the party for undertaking such a strategy without consultation and sent to serve as a guerrilla in Bicol, while he underwent a process of 'rehabilitation' from the party's discipline committee. He returned to Manila in the early 1980s and quickly re-established his position within the Manila-Rizal committee.

In 1984, the committee renamed itself the Alex Boncayao Brigade (ABB) after its fallen comrade and declared a campaign of urban warfare against the Marcos administration. In 1984 the ABB shot and killed a police general, Tomas Karingal, at a social function in Quezon City. The relationship between the ABB and the central authority remained strained, particularly following the murder of Ninoy Aquino in 1983 by the Marcos government.

Whilst the NPA was gaining success in the countryside the CPP leadership again warned the ABB of making alliances with non-communist political organisations. The CPP became convinced that peasant revolution would be sufficient to oust Marcos and that the ABB's role was marginal in the group's strategy. In 1986 when Ferdinand Marcos called a snap election, the radical left movement advocated a policy of boycott. Popoy argued against this, claiming that a mass show of support for the opposition would put pressure on Marcos' allies, chiefly the US, to stop supporting the regime. The boycott remained in place and when Marcos lost control following attempts to rig the elections and Corazon Aquino became president, the left wing groups found themselves increasingly marginalised. Worse for the ABB, fears over government infiltration of the group had led to an extensive purge.

The end of the Marcos era left the ABB isolated and increasingly frustrated at the diktats of the CPP Central Committee. By 1992 the NPA was at war with itself, between those loyal to the leader Jose Maria Sison and several rejectionist factions. Matters were not eased by the alleged 'witch hunt' within the party for doctrinal deviancy. Popoy was labelled a rejectionist and broke away from the NPA, although the ABB continued to be described in the media as the urban wing of the CPP.

In 1994, Popoy was arrested on a murder charge. He was released after insufficient evidence was found linking him to the group. In 1996, Popoy was rearrested on the orders of President Ramos, who feared ABB activity during the APEC summit hosted by Manila.

Following Popoy's release the ABB itself divided with a faction under the leadership of Nilo de la Cruz, breaking away from the old Manila-Rizal committee. In March 1997, the ABB formed an alliance with the Revolutionary Proletarian Army (RPA), led by Arturo Tabara, another former NPA leader. The group was henceforth known as the Revolutionary Proletarian Army— Alex Boncayao Brigade (RPA-ABB). In 2000 Popoy retired, claiming that the breakaway leader, Nilo de la Cruz, was guilty of misrepresentation in calling his organisation by the ABB name. In 2001, Popoy was shot dead by an unidentified gunman.

The main RPA-ABB groups are on Luzon, Negros and the Visayas Islands. The group originated as a Manila faction of the NPA and has retained operations within the city. The RPA-ABB is highly de-centralised and is largely believed to have broken up into small criminal gangs, most of which scarcely bother with political rhetoric. The group had a policy of assassinating officials in Manila, and between 1985 and 1989 was responsible for the deaths of over 200 policemen. The group's usual tactic is to just kill one person, but in 1995 it apologised for the deaths of innocent bystanders, including a five-year-old boy, when it murdered a leading ethnic Chinese industrialist. They have also bombed large companies including three oil concerns in Manila in the space of one day. The group also sends faxes to newspapers in the name of the RPA-ABB, particularly the *Manila Times*, which has published letters from the group protesting about articles which have appeared in the newspaper. The group's weapons include AK-47 assault rifles, machine-guns, M-16 rifles, pistols and knives, which are mostly stolen or purchased on the black market in Luzon. There are indications that the police are either directly involved in the local arms market or indirectly profit from it.

Secessionist terror

Secessionism in the southern Philippines dates to the establishment of the state and focuses on the Islamic identity of many of the region's inhabitants. In more recent times, separatist conflict has been dominated by the Moro National Liberation Front, the Moro Islamic Liberation Front, the Abu Sayyaf Group and links to external terrorists, including Al Qaeda and Jema'ah Islamiyah.

The Moro National Liberation Front was formed in the late 1960s by a small group of students and intellectuals, becoming the largest grouping of armed separatists, fighting a war with the Armed Forces of the Philippines (AFP) that ended in a stalemate in the mid-1970s. Under the auspices of the Organisation of Islamic Conference, the Marcos administration conducted negotiations with the insurgents, reaching a settlement known as the 'Tripoli Agreement' in December 1976, sponsored by Colonel Muammar al-Qaddafi of Libya. According to this agreement, the fighting would stop and an autonomous Muslim region in the southern Philippines, consisting of 14 provinces, would be established. This Agreement was never honoured by the Marcos regime.

The Mindanao Christian population strongly opposed the settlement, especially its endorsement of a legal Islamic framework. Fighting broke out again at the end of 1977, although it was less intense than earlier conflict. At this time, the separatist movement began to fragment. Hashim Salamat broke away from the MNLF in 1977 over a leadership dispute and ideological differences with Nur Misuari, the Chairman of the MNLF. Salamat established the Moro Islamic Liberation Front (MILF) in 1977, attracting many supporters from Mindanao. Misuari remained in control of the MNLF, whose membership was dominated by partisans from Misuari's Tausung tribe and other Sulu-based ethnic groups. Further factionalism followed. Another breakaway group, the Bangsamoro Liberation Organisation (BLO), initially compounded the MNLF's decline. Having faltered under pressure of leadership disputes, the BLO later emerged as the MNLF-Reformist Movement, which by the late 1980s was better known as the Moro Islamist Reformist Group (MIRG). While the MNLF and its off-shoots were products of local conditions, they were increasingly contacted and influenced by external groups wishing to harness their role in Islamic revolution, with the first contacts with Al Qaeda dating back to 1988 (the year before Al Qaeda was formally founded) (Apdal and Thayer 2003:17).

The greatly weakened MNLF agreed to another ceasefire when Marcos was ousted from power. Following a 1989 plebiscite, an Autonomous Region in Muslim Mindanao (ARMM) was established, based in Cotabato, consisting of the four provinces of Tawi-Tawi, Sulu, Maguindanao and Lanao del Sur. In 2001, this province was expanded to include the island of Basilan and Marawai City in central Mindanao. Many of the ex-MNLF leaders joined the political institutions of this body, but the MILF rejected the ARMM, believing it to be riddled with corruption and unable to promote complete Muslim independence.

Nur Misuari led the MNLF into peace negotiations with the Manila government in 1996 and, as a result, was installed as governor of the ARMM on 30 September 1997. The armed wing of the MNLF, the Bangsamoro Army, was disarmed and gradually integrated into the national armed forces and security services. In the years since the 1996 accord, the MNLF's record of running the ARMM failed to satisfy even its supporters. Erratic and authoritarian, Misuari consistently performed badly as an administrator and was finally shunted aside as MNLF chairman in April 2001. He was replaced by a 'committee of 15' and his position as ARMM governor was later taken by Parouk Hussin, a member of that committee. Angered by this dismissal, Misuari and his loyalists launched a short-lived armed revolt in November 2001 on his home island of Jolo that was swiftly put down. He later fled to Malaysia's

Sabah state where he was arrested and repatriated to the Philippines at the behest of Malaysian Prime Minister, Mahathir Mohammed. He remains in custody, while on Jolo his hardcore supporters have joined the Abu Sayyaf Group (ASG).

Moro Islamic Liberation Front (MILF)

The MILF has a stronger religious component than the MNLF, with its leaders drawn from a group of Muslims educated in religious academies in the Middle East, primarily Egypt. Despite their reputation, MILF leaders typically follow a brand of Islam that is more moderate than that of the Islamic fundamentalists of the Middle East. They refuse to publicly criticise the US and remain officially committed to negotiations with the Philippines Government.

The MILF has an estimated armed strength of between 10,000 to 11,000 (according to the Philippines Government) and 40,000 (according to various Western estimates) and has been held responsible for highly visible terrorist bombings in Manila (in 2000 and 2001) and Davao City (2003). In contrast to the Abu Sayyaf Group, the MILF is a political movement with an Islamist ideology and secessionist ambitions that fields a substantial guerrilla army. The MILF maintains contacts with international jihadist groups, including Jema'ah Islamiyah, which used MILF bases as its own training camps, in particular, Camp Abubakar on Mindanao. Activists from JI have been implicated in a number of attacks in the Philippines. In 2002, Indonesian senior JI member and link to MILF (USA 2002a:21), Fathur Rahman Al-Ghozi was arrested, although he managed to escape from custody in July 2003. Al-Ghozi was killed the following October in a shoot-out with police and soldiers in North Cotabato, Mindanao.

The MILF distinguishes itself from other revolutionary organisations in the Philippines by supporting development efforts in its area of operation and by refusing to describe the US as an enemy. The MILF supported meetings between USAID and the Bangsa Moro Development Agency, an NGO supported by the MILF. It vowed not to launch sympathy attacks during the Iraq War and has not taken a public stance on joint US–Philippines exercises in Sulu. This is one reason the US has not added the MILF to its list of international terrorist organisations (the other being the lack of a request from the Philippines Government). Sporadic negotiations between the government and the MILF have taken place and a ceasefire put in place.

In May 2003, talks broke off after three months of fighting between government and MILF forces. In June 2003, both sides focused anew on the politics of the conflict with the MILF, declaring a temporary cessation of offensive operations and the government countering with an informal offer of a permanent ceasefire. Each side expressed scepticism about the other's offer, and some fighting continued. In June 2003, the US continued to express public support for peace negotiations between the Philippines and the MILF. The MILF has consistently rejected the ARMM as a vehicle for addressing grassroots Muslim grievances. While acknowledging that the ARMM has provided the MNLF with opportunities, the MILF is wary of being co-opted.

Abu Sayyaf Group (ASG)

'Abu Sayyaf' means 'Father of the Sword' in Arabic. The Abu Sayyaf Group was originally known as the Mujahideen Commando Freedom Fighters (MCFF), founded in the mid-1980s, when it was known as Al Harakat-ul Al Islamiyya (AHAI), and was renamed Abu Sayyaf Group in the late 1980s, formally 1991). The founders were Ustad Abdurazak Abubakar Janjalani, who studied Islamic law and fought in Afghanistan during the 1980s, Wahab Akbar, who studied in Iran and Syria, Amilhussin Jumaani, and ten other former members of the Moro National Liberation Front. Janjalani drew his two younger brothers—Hector and Qadaffi—into the group. Later, the two underwent explosives training in Pakistan. Hector was arrested and is currently held by the authorities. But Qadaffi went on to become Amir, or spiritual leader, of ASG after Janjalani's death during a clash with Philippine police on 18 December 1998. ASG has had active links with Al Qaeda since 1992, and is claimed as one of Al Qaeda's training and development 'success stories' in the region.

ASG fighters operate in small units under a single commander. Those with experience gained in Afghanistan are accredited with greater seniority and respect. Recruits come from the southern Philippines in particular Patikul, Sulu, Lebak, Sultan Kudarat, Malapatan, Sarangani and Zamboanga City. ASG members use the dialect Tausung for communication within the group. All volunteers are given instructions on explosives and jungle guerrilla warfare tactics at camps run by Abu Sayyaf in remote locations. Some are trained for sabotage, kidnapping and urban guerrilla activities. The most valued recruits were singled out for training in Pakistan and Afghanistan. Weapons include the AK-47 rifle and recent acquisitions are believed to include more sophisticated weapons such as mortars, heavy machine guns and grenade launchers. Weapons are smuggled into the country, brought from central and southern Asia, Burma (Myanmar) and there are accusations that arms dealers in Vietnam and Malaysia are involved in supplying ASG. The group is no longer thought to receive assistance, in the form of weapons and explosives, from Libya.

ASG's first recorded action was the 1991 attack on a military checkpoint in Sumagadang near Isabela. Wahab, the ASG leader who commanded the attack, fled to Malaysia only to return a few years later to campaign for governor. After the 1991 action, wider bomb attacks followed in 1992. These attacks targeted locations in Zamboanga and Davao and resulted in an increasing public awareness of ASG. Also in 1992, ASG member Edwin Angeles abducted a businesswoman in Davao and hid her at a residence in Basilan. She was released after paying a ransom. In April 1993, Angeles abducted the owner of a bus company in Basilan and his five-year-old grandson. The grandfather was released three days later but the grandson remained in custody. In a press conference soon after the grandfather's release, ASG member Ashmad announced that the group would continue to hold the grandson until its demands were met. The demands included: the removal of all Catholic symbols in Muslim communities; the imposition of a ban on all foreign fishing vessels in the Sulu and Basilan seas; and the involvement of Muslim leadership in the negotiations. Later in 1993, ASG abducted an American language scholar, Charles Walton, from his home on Pangutaran Island. Following the intercession of the Libyan Ambassador, Walton was released a few weeks later without ransom.

In 1994, Ramzi Yousef visited the Philippines and is alleged to have made contact with ASG members to discuss plans for an assassination attempt on the Pope, who was scheduled to visit Manila. In April 1995, ASG attacked the town of Ipil on Mindanao along with guerrillas from the Moro Islamic Liberation Front (MILF). The attack resulted in 54 deaths and hundreds of wounded. A dozen Christian villagers were taken hostage and later killed. Following the attack on Ipil, the ASG clashed with Philippine security forces throughout 1996 and 1997. Between 1991 and 1997, ASG conducted a total of 67 terrorist attacks (Apdal & Thayer 2003:19). In August 1998, ASG announced its intentions to target foreigners as well as Philippines security forces personnel. In July 2000, ASG abducted three French journalists, who were released after ransoms were paid. Later that month, ASG abducted 21 people from a dive resort on Pandanan Island, and a ransom of several million dollars was paid in exchange for the prisoners' release.

In August 2000, ASG abducted Jeffrey Schilling, a US citizen who had met with a senior guerrilla leader, accusing him of being a member of the CIA. A US$2 million ransom was set for his release. In May 2001, ASG abducted 17 tourists. When Philippines government forces attempted to pursue the kidnappers, 200 more hostages were seized from a nearby church and hospital.

In January 2002, in the wake of the US 'war on terror', some 1,200 US troops arrived in the Philippines to support the government's operations against ASG. Many of these were Special Forces personnel who were sent to train Philippine forces. In June 2002, a group of US-trained Philippine troops stormed an Abu Sayyaf jungle camp in an effort to rescue two Americans and a Filipino nurse being held hostage. During the rescue attempt, the nurse and one of the Americans were killed but the third hostage—US missionary Gracia Burnham—was freed, suffering only minor injuries. In July 2002, many US Special Forces personnel departed. Several hundred support personnel remained on the island of Basilan to carry out infrastructure projects and medical assistance.

In August 2002, ASG abducted six hostages, with two later beheaded. In December 2002, Philippine soldiers captured one of the ASG members believed to be involved in the executions. Also in December 2002, approximately 150 US Special Forces troops were deployed to the Philippines in order to train government forces in counter-terrorism and anti-terrorism operations. After heavy fighting on Basilan island, ASG members were reported to be fleeing to Malaysia by means of fast watercraft. In January 2003, Merang Abante, reportedly a senior member of ASG, was captured. This was followed by the capture of Maid Sampang, another ASG member. Also in January 2003, an additional 200 US soldiers were reported to have arrived in the Philippines to support the government's military operations.

As a result of the intense fighting in Basilan, ASG forces were reported to be regrouping on the island of Sulu. The Sulu area is commanded by Abu Jumdail (Dr Abu), Galib Andang and Mujid Susukan. The group has become increasingly factionalised; the Basilan group was greatly influenced by Janjalani and was more religiously motivated. The Sulu group has been criticised by the Basilan faction for concentrating on criminal activity at the expense of strategic goals.

As can be seen from the NPA and various Islamic separatists groups, ideological division, shifting agendas and in many cases confusion and a lack of coherence, have reduced their efficacy. Tactics have varied from outright military offensive to conventional guerrilla struggle, urban warfare and activities that might more readily be characterised as organised crime, if at a low and local level. In part, this reflects the localised nature of much of the grievance or alienation that has led to such activities, to a more generalised sense of disconnectedness and echoes of a traditional type of local control over local affairs, which fluctuates according to circumstances. The exception was, for a few years, the highly organised and centralised structure of the NPA that, however, eventually fell foul of its own internal rigidities.

If this seems to reflect a functional inability, the fact that various insurgent organisations continue to operate at varying levels of efficacy indicates that they have a regenerative capacity, that they continue to undermine the authority of the state, and that the circumstances giving rise to them have not been ameliorated. Similarly, the incapacity of the government to address the underlying concerns that continue to prompt such dissent, or to militarily crush such movements, equally indicates a low level of organisation, commitment, perhaps coherence and almost certainly lack of focus of purpose. The circumstances that give rise to insurgency and 'terrorist' organisations in Indonesia, Southern Thailand, Malaysia, Singapore and the Philippines, and to other violent non-state actors, and that allow them to continue, do not only seem unresolvable in the foreseeable future, but may be implicit in the structure of the types of states and polities that characterise the region.

Endnotes

1. Al Qaeda has reportedly helped fund, without reciprocal obligations, five regional militant Islamic organisations, including FPI, MMI, the Islamic Youth Movement and Laskar Jihad (Asmarani 2002). Al Qaeda was also confirmed as having provided some funds to the Moro Islamic Liberation Front in the Philippines (*Manila Times* 2003).
2. Of course, the use of 'terror' for political purposes is as old as politics itself.
3. This section will not consider the Free Aceh Movement (Gerakan Aceh Merdeka, or GAM, formally the Aceh–Sumatra National Liberation Front) as it does not engage in attacks outside its own immediate region, and does not engage in what might be conventionally defined as 'terrorist' practices. It is for this reason that GAM is not listed by either the USA or the UN as a terrorist organisation.
4. While Jema'ah Islamiyah has its own origins, it has parallels with not only the *Ikhwan al-Mulsimin,* but also the similarly named *Jamaat-I Islami* founded in India in 1941. Like Jema'ah Islamiyah, both organisations understand Islam as a totalising religio-political system that is incompatible with secular ideologies (Robinson 1999:51).
5. This organisation has a number of ideological parallels with the MMI.
6. Wahhabism converged with the Indonesian *Persatuan Islam* (Islamic Unity) from the 1970s at which time it developed its 'strict Salafi ideas' (Van Bruinessen 2002).
7. These sources cannot be identified. Discussion on this matter was by way of background briefing.
8. 'Pondok' usually means 'hut', but is also colloquially used to denote an Islamic boarding school.
9. A number of graduates of Pondok Ngruki have been identified with various terrorist acts, including the Bali bombing of 2002, and Fathur Rohman al-Ghozi, a bomb-making expert arrested in the Philippines (studied 198289).
10. Arabic for 'leader' or 'commander'.
11. Indonesian police claimed that Hambali was involved in 39 separate bombing incidents (*Jakarta Post* 22.8.2003).
12. Similar links were established between military intelligence and more than 30 other ostensibly Islamic bombings against churches and other targets in 2000, in which 19 people were killed and 120 injured (see Tapol 2003).
13. Not including PPP, which was an established party, or PKB and PAN, which were based on Islamic organisations but were not explicitly Islamic themselves.
14. Partai Keadlina Sejhatera (PKS) was the surprise success of the Islamic parties, achieving just over 8% of the vote, almost the same as the PPP and ahead of PAN on 6%. PKS subsequently endorsed the secular (but avowedly pious Muslim) Susilo Bambang Yudhoyono as president. PPP's presidential candidate, Hamzah Has, polled just 3% of the vote in the first presidential round, with no other explicitly Islamic candidates standing.

16   *Milsus* were either predominantly members of Kopassus Groups IV and V (later reverting to its original name, Detasemen 81) who conducted covert operations, including the training and leading of local militia groups in places like East and West Timor, Maluku and Aceh. In a number of cases, such *milsus* were also believed to include numbers of former Kopassus members who had come back on the pay-roll for special operations.

17   LJ's strength reached up to 10,000–13,000 fighters by 2001, with up to 6,000 deployed to Ambon and environs, although some estimates suggest that it had no more than 7,000 fighters, with 1-2,000 deployed to Maluku (Schulze 2002:60).

18   Van Klinken (2003) notes that sectarian violence in Poso began as early as December 1998.

19   He was in hiding at the time of writing.

20   Kivlan said he later learned the request to organise the Pam Swakarsa had originated with Habibie (*Kompas* 28.6.2004).

21   Kivlan claimed that Wiranto has promised to pay him back for financing the organisation and to give him a new job after he had been removed as chief of staff of Kostrad. Kivlan claimed that Wiranto did not honour either promise (*Suara Merdeka* 17.6.2004).

22   The Malaysian Government had previously called KMM Kampulan Mujahidin Malaysia, although this was thought to be too explicitly Islamic in orientation, hence the change.

23   The Republik Islam Aceh was originally formed in the early 1960s after the collapse of the Darul Islam revolt. However, that movement ended soon after. The version referred to here is regarded by the Free Aceh Movement (Gerakan Aceh Merdeka—GAM, formally Aceh-Sumatra National Liberation Front) as a fake organisation fronting on behalf of the Indonesian Army's Special Forces (Kopassus).

24   During the Second World War, there were two separate independence movements, one fighting with the Japanese and wanting a republic, the other fighting with the British and wanting a sultanate.

25   Children of *mestizos* who derived their wealth and influence from land ownership. The *ilustrados*, or enlightened ones, had been sent to universities in Manila and Europe.

Chapter 2

New terrorism in Southeast Asia

Carlyle Thayer

Introduction

The terrorist attacks on a disco and pub at Kuta Beach, Bali in October 2002 served as a wake up call, if one were needed, that 'new terrorism' had made its appearance in Southeast Asia[1] New terrorism is a term used to describe high-profile mass causality (or apocalyptic) attacks against civilians by internationally networked terrorist groups (Babbage 2002). 'Old terrorism' focused on selective political violence committed by anti-government insurgents and ethno-nationalist separatists, usually acting in isolation, and was confined in geographic scope (Stevenson 2003).

The emerging phenomenon of new terrorism in post-Bali Southeast Asia generated a huge demand by the world's mass media for commentary and analysis. The media immediately turned to international terrorism experts and regional security analysts for their views. Quite quickly the discourse on new terrorism in Southeast Asia became dominated by what might be termed the Al Qaeda-centric paradigm. This provided the primary framework for analysis through which the activities of militant Islamic groups in Southeast Asia were viewed. An alternative, or 'bottom up', view was offered by country studies specialists that stressed the importance of local factors and the agency of local leaders.

This chapter examines three distinct approaches to the study of new terrorism in Southeast Asia: the international, regional and country specific. The framework for each approach is critically evaluated to determine its contribution to our understanding of new terrorism in Southeast Asia.

Approaches to the study of new terrorism

Three distinct approaches to the study of new terrorism in Southeast Asia may be identified: international terrorism, regional security, and country specific. Each of these approaches should be viewed as a general tendency and not a distinct school of thought. They overlap and are not mutually exclusive. Specialists identified with one approach may differ from their colleagues over matters of historical interpretation and how to classify particular groups and their leaders. The first approach to the study of new terrorism in

Southeast Asia is that adopted by international terrorism experts.[2] Generally, these experts are not Southeast Asia studies specialists. The foremost representative of the international terrorism approach, Rohan Gunaratna, was primarily a specialist on the Tiger Tamils of Sri Lanka before turning to the study of new terrorism. Gunaratna first began writing about Al Qaeda in Southeast Asia in 2001. He wrote an influential book, *Inside Al Qaeda: global network of terror*, that offered an overview of Al Qaeda and its international network (only one chapter was devoted to Al Qaeda in Asia). According to Gunaratna (2002:1), 'Al Qaeda has moved terrorism beyond the status of a technique of protest and resistance and turned it into a global instrument with which to compete with and challenge Western influence in the Muslim world'.

Gunaratna became so prominent in the global media that he succeeded in colonising the discourse and analysis of new terrorism in Southeast Asia. Whenever a major terrorist incident occurred, Gunaratna was invariably quoted in media interviews saying there was only one organisation with the capability and intention of conducting such an act—Al Qaeda. In Gunaratna's view, Al Qaeda was the independent variable that explained new terrorism in Southeast Asia.

International terrorism experts argue that the phenomenon of new terrorism in Southeast Asia can be explained by the prime leadership role of Osama bin Laden and his organisation. The Soviet invasion and occupation of Afghanistan (December 1979–February 1989) was the key formative period for the terrorist group that took the name Al Qaeda. During the Soviet occupation, Muslim militants from the Arab world and elsewhere arrived in Pakistan eager to fight alongside the *mujihadeen* against the Soviet occupiers.[3] As early as 1980, the first volunteers from Southeast Asia arrived in Pakistan for religious indoctrination and military training. A few actively participated in combat.[4] During this period personal ties were forged between leaders of the *mujihadeen* and key Southeast Asian leaders such as: Hashim Salamat, leader of the Moro Islamic Liberation Front (MILF); Abdurajak Abubakar Janjalani, the founder of the Abu Sayyaf Group (ASG); and Abdullah Sungkar, one of the co-founders of Jema'ah Islamiyah (JI) (Gunaratna 2002:2, 5, 174, 187). Personal ties were also forged between all three Southeast Asian leaders and Osama bin Laden and his band of associates.

Al Qaeda grew out of the Arab Service Bureau founded in Peshawar, Pakistan by Abdullah Azzam and Osama bin Laden in 1984. The Arab Service Bureau was set up to recruit and train mainly Arab Muslims for service in Afghanistan. In 1988, Azzam and bin Laden fell out and bin Laden moved to form his own separate organisation. In late 1989, a few trusted colleagues joined Al Qaeda ('the base') by taking an oath of loyalty (*bayat*) to bin Laden. Al Qaeda's initial purpose was to keep track of the global network of Muslim recruits who came to Pakistan and Afghanistan (Gunaratna 2002:144). Al Qaeda set up a biographical database so relief could be sent to the families of those who were martyred or went missing in combat. After the Soviet withdrawal from Afghanistan, Southeast Asian volunteers were urged to return home and continue *jihad*. Thus, the foundation was laid for future co-operation.

In the early 1990s, Al Qaeda re-orientated itself and began offering financial assistance and support to Muslim struggles mainly in the Kashmir and Chechnya, but also Algeria, Azerbaijan, Egypt, Georgia, Indonesia, Malaysia, Mindanao, Nargo-Karabakh, Somalia, Tajikistan, Uzbekistan and Yemen (Gunaratna 2002:5). It was in this formative period in the late 1980s and early 1990s that Al Qaeda's first representatives reportedly made their appearance in Southeast Asia and provided finance and training assistance to Muslim militants in the Philippines. According to international and regional terrorism experts, this led to the co-option of the ASG and the MILF into Al Qaeda's global network. In the 1990s, Al Qaeda's influence also spread to Indonesia, Malaysia and Singapore, where Al Qaeda provided finance and training assistance to militant Muslims, most notably the JI. All major Al Qaeda terrorist plots directed against the United States in the 1990s up to 2001 were planned in part by Al Qaeda using safe havens in the Philippines and Malaysia (Abuza 2002:435, 444; Ressa 2003).

The second approach to the study of new terrorism in Southeast Asia is that adopted by regional terrorism analysts.[5] Prior to the Bali bombings, regional security analysts focused on 'old terrorism', which is political violence committed by local insurgents and ethno-nationalist separatists. It is notable that the research conducted by these specialists prior to 2001 generally overlooked or downplayed the importance of linkages between Al Qaeda and politically violent Southeast Asian groups forged during the previous twelve years. For example, in a detailed account of Islamic separatism in the southern Philippines, Andrew Tan (2000) only mentions briefly that Al Qaeda provided finance and training in explosives to the ASG.

After the events of 11 September 2001 and the Bali bombings a year later, regional security analysts all too readily adopted the Al Qaeda-centric paradigm in their analysis of Southeast Asia's politically violent groups. As a consequence, their analysis tended to become homogenised. Regional security specialists invariably concluded that any international linkage between Al Qaeda and a local militant Islamic group was evidence that the latter had become an Al Qaeda franchise or affiliate. When regional security analysts canvassed terrorism in Southeast Asia, they included in their discussion not only the ASG and JI, but the Moro Islamic Liberation Front, Kumpulan Mujahidin Malaysia (KMM), Majelis Mujahidin Indonesia (MMI, *Mujihadeen* Council of Indonesia), Laskar Jihad, Laskar Jundullah, Laskar Mujihadin, Islamic Defenders Front, Pattani United Liberation Organisation (PULO), New PULO and other organisations.[6] This approach was akin to fitting round Islamic militant pegs into square terrorist holes. These groups varied enormously in motivations, ideology, objectives and autonomy (Barton 2003; Hefner 2003).

Regional security analysts, however, did make one important contribution to our understanding of new terrorism in Southeast Asia. They correctly identified the emergence of a regional network centred on JI. JI established a five-member Regional Advisory Council or *shura* to oversee JI cells in Malaysia, Singapore, Indonesia, the Philippines and elsewhere in the region. In 1999, JI attempted to forge a regional coalition of like-minded groups under the name of Rabitatul Mujahidin. Representatives from JI, MILF and militant groups from Aceh, Sulawesi and Myanmar reportedly attended the first meeting. Rabitatul Mujahidin met three times in Malaysia between 1999 and late 2000.

The third approach to the study of new terrorism in Southeast Asia is that adopted by country studies specialists.[7] Country specialists bring a different set of skills to their analysis of new terrorism, including language(s) and a deep knowledge of history, culture, religion, society and politics of the country of their expertise. In the immediate aftermath of the Bali bombings, country specialists were put on the defensive. Their specialist skills had not alerted them to the emergence of internationally and regionally networked terrorist groups prior to 2001–02. Initially, several prominent country specialists, such as Greg Fealy, 'went into denial'. They were highly sceptical about, if not dismissive of, claims that organised international terrorism had arrived on Southeast Asia's doorstep and had made common cause with local, militant Islamic groups. They were in good local company. National leaders in Indonesia, Malaysia, the Philippines and Thailand also dismissed such claims.

Country specialists were also put on the defensive because the mainstream international media was not interested in detailed analysis about new terrorism that resulted in highly qualified assessments. The media was after the big story—the global war on terrorism. International terrorism experts and regional security analysts obliged with sound bites that were clear and simple: terrorism in Southeast Asia was part of Al Qaeda's international network headed by Osama bin Laden, America's most wanted man.

Country studies specialists do not deny the importance of international linkages between Southeast Asian groups and Al Qaeda, particularly the Pakistan/Afghan alumni connection. Nor do these specialists deny the emergence of a regional terrorist network. Where these specialists differ from international and regional terrorism experts is over the question of agency. That is, country studies specialists critically question the Al Qaeda-centric paradigm. Their focus is 'bottom up', that is, on the ability of Southeast Asians to act independently and to leverage their association with bin Laden and Al Qaeda to pursue their own agendas and objectives.

To sum up: international terrorism experts have assisted in our understanding of the emergence of new terrorism in Southeast Asia by focusing on its international dimensions. International terrorism experts generally argue that linkages between Al Qaeda and Southeast Asian militants and their organisations is evidence of the latter's co-option and/or subordination. This conclusion is inevitably derived from a lengthy analysis of the personal contacts (including records of phone contacts) between Al Qaeda members and leaders of Southeast Asian militant Islamic groups. Osama bin Laden is portrayed as a chief executive officer presiding over a global terrorist organisation composed of Al Qaeda franchises and associates. In some cases, elaborate organisational charts or wiring diagrams are drawn up to illustrate this pattern of subordination (Rabasa 2003:62). In one amusing case, a terrorist expert's wiring diagram was described as being like a 'plate of spaghetti' (Abuza 2002).

Regional security specialists have also contributed to our understanding of new terrorism by exposing the network of regional linkages forged by JI with the MILF (particularly the provision of training camps). But regional security specialists have uncritically adopted the Al Qaeda-centric paradigm as their main framework of analysis. They view not only the Abu Sayyaf Group and Jema'ah Islamiyah as Al Qaeda affiliates, but many of the region's prominent militant Islamic groups as well. This approach denies agency to local actors, as nearly every act of terrorism in Southeast Asia is described as being carried out by an Al Qaeda-affiliated or Al Qaeda-linked group.

Country studies specialists are now coming into their own after an initial period of denial and scepticism about the international linkages between local militant groups and Al Qaeda. Using their multidisciplinary research skills and deep knowledge of specific Southeast Asian countries, they have been able to produce a more nuanced and fully rounded analysis of the motives and objectives of local actors. They are also better able to provide the social and cultural context in which Southeast Asian terrorist and militant groups have emerged. This 'bottom up' view directly challenges key assumptions of international and regional terrorist experts. The Al Qaeda-centric approach over-exaggerates the role of Osama bin Laden and Al Qaeda, to the virtual exclusion of other international terrorist leaders and organisations. It also undervalues the agency of Southeast Asian actors in leveraging their association with Al Qaeda to pursue their own aims and objectives. These issues will be explored in greater depth in part three below.

Defining terrorism

One key methodological problem associated with the study of political violence is the lack of an agreed definition of what constitutes terrorism (Hoffman 1998:13–44). As long ago as 1937, the League of Nations failed to reach consensus on a draft convention that defined terrorism. The United Nations General Assembly has also unsuccessfully grappled with this question. A resolution defining terrorism has been on its books since 1999. At present, the General Assembly's Sixth Committee is considering a draft Comprehensive Convention on International Terrorism that would include a definition of terrorism if adopted.

Other international organisations have fared no better. For example, the Organisation of Islamic Conference (OIC) has been unable to reach agreement on a definition of terrorism as well. At the OIC extraordinary session held in Kuala Lumpur in April 2002, Malaysia's Prime Minister Mahathir proposed that any deliberate attack on civilians, including those by Palestinian suicide bombers, should be classified as acts of terror. Delegates disagreed. In their final OIC Declaration on Terrorism they stated *inter alia*:

> We reject any attempt to link Islam and Muslims to terrorism as terrorism has no association with any religion, civilisation or nationality;
>
> We unequivocally condemn acts of international terrorism in all its forms and manifestations, including state terrorism, irrespective of motives, perpetrators and victims as terrorism poses a serious threat to international peace and security and is a grave violation of human rights;
>
> We reiterate the principled position under international law and the Charter of the United Nations of the legitimacy of resistance to foreign aggression and the struggle of peoples under colonial or alien domination and foreign occupation for national liberation and self-determination. In this context, *we underline the urgency for an internationally agreed definition of terrorism, which differentiates such legitimate struggles from acts of terrorism* [emphasis added].[8]

Unable to reach consensus, the OIC quickly threw this contentious issue to the United Nations for consideration. Surprisingly, the United States Government, the leader in the global war on terrorism, had not adopted a single comprehensive definition of terrorism. Terrorism is defined in the US Code of Federal Regulations,[9] but the State Department,[10] Defense Department[11] and Federal Bureau of Investigation[12] all have their own separate definitions. President George Bush added yet another when he issued an Executive Order on terrorist financing in the wake of September 11.[13]

In summary, the international community has been unable to agree on an acceptable definition of terrorism. Because of the widely divergent views on what constitutes terrorism (or acts of terrorism), international and regional terrorism experts have been free to pick and choose which Islamic militant groups to include in their analysis. In most cases little or no justification is given for their inclusion of a particular group as a terrorist organisation.

It appears that if a militant Islamic group engages in political violence and has linkages to Al Qaeda, it is uncritically classified as part of Al Qaeda's international network. Defining what constitutes a militant Islamic group is problematic as well. The security literature that discusses terrorism and Islam in Southeast Asia employs a number of descriptors such as fundamentalist, deviationist, radical, militant and extremist. Often these terms are undefined and used interchangeably. Militancy is often equated with terrorism. Quite often too, analysts fail to distinguish between Islamic fundamentalism, extremist religious views and terrorism.

As noted above, international terrorism experts and regional security analysts view the activities of militant Islamic organisations in Southeast Asia through an Al Qaeda-centric paradigm. This approach is methodologically unsound for two reasons. First, in the absence of a definition of terrorism, the basis of classification is arbitrary. Second, the term 'Al Qaeda' is highly ambiguous. When experts and analysts use the term 'Al Qaeda' are they referring to an inner leadership hardcore grouped around bin Laden, the myriad associations of militant Islamic groups found around the world or the much larger modern radical Islam movement itself?

The approach adopted in this chapter is to sidestep the vexed question of how to define terrorism. For purposes of analysis a terrorist or terrorist organisation will be defined as those individuals and groups that have been proscribed by the international community through the United Nations. In the aftermath of September 11, the UN adopted Resolution 1267, which made provision for the United Nations Monitoring Group to maintain a consolidated list of entities and individuals that were part of, or associated with, the Taliban and Al Qaeda. The UN resolution is binding on all members. The current list contains the names of 272 persons associated with Al Qaeda and the Taliban.[14]

The United Nations identifies only three terrorist organisations currently operating in Southeast Asia: Al Qaeda, Abu Sayyaf Group and Jema'ah Islamiyah. The UN list is not a comprehensive database of terrorists or terrorist organisations found across the globe. In 2003, a UN monitoring committee found that 108 states failed in their responsibility to report the names of suspected terrorists to the UN

What is Al Qaeda?

There are three key methodological problems in discussing the role of Al Qaeda in Southeast Asia. The first is how to best characterise Al Qaeda as an organisation. The second problem is how to account for change over time. The third is how to assess the question of agency in Al Qaeda's relationship with the ASG, JI and other militant Islamic groups in Southeast Asia.

International terrorism experts and regional security analysts differ in their characterisation of Al Qaeda as an organisation. Zachary Abuza (2002:429–30) argues that Al Qaeda is composed of a central leadership of around 30 individuals, an international network of 24 constituent groups, 80 front companies operating in 50 countries, and a membership of between 5,000 and 12,000 organised into cells in 60 different countries. Finally, Abuza argues that 'Al Qaeda was brilliant in its co-optation of other groups, those with a narrow domestic agenda, and in bringing them into Al Qaeda's structure' (Abuza 2002:431).

Jane Corbin and Peter Bergin,[15] argue that Al Qaeda was run like a business conglomerate or multinational corporation under the directorship of Osama bin Laden. Bergin (2001:31) writes that Al Qaeda was an analogue of the Saudi bin Laden Group, the large construction company founded by Osama bin Laden's father:

> [Osama] Bin Laden organised Al Qaeda in a businesslike manner—he formulates the general policies of Al Qaeda in consultation with his *shura* council. The *shura* makes executive decisions for the group. Subordinate to that council are other committees responsible for military affairs and the business interests of the group, as well as a *fatwa* committee, which issues rulings on Islamic law, and a media group.

Rohan Gunaratna's characterisation of Al Qaeda's organisation is less precise and more equivocal. On the one hand, he portrays Al Qaeda in much the same terms as Corbin and Bergin. He notes that:

In 1998 Al Qaeda was reorganised into four distinct but interrelated entities. The first was a pyramidal structure to facilitate strategic and tactical direction; the second was a global terrorist network; the third was a base force for guerrilla warfare inside Afghanistan; and the fourth was a loose coalition of transnational terrorist and guerrilla groups (Gunaratna 2002:57).

The first entity, the hierarchical leadership structure, consisted of an Emir-General, a consultative council (*shura majlis*), four operational committees (military, finance and business, *fatwa* and Islamic study; and media and publicity) and dispersed regional 'nodes'. Gunaratna further notes that bin Laden directed the core inner group and that the operational committees ensured the smooth day-to-day running of the organisation. An emir and a deputy headed each committee. The military committee, for example, was responsible for recruiting, training, procuring, transporting and launching terrorist operations (Gunaratna 2002:58). Al Qaeda also ran its own internal security service and an extensive financial and business empire (Gunaratna 2002:60–69). In Gunaratna's (2002:54) assessment: 'Al Qaeda became the first terrorist group to control a state'. On the other hand, he asserts that Al Qaeda 'is neither a single group nor a coalition of groups: it comprised a core base or bases in Afghanistan, satellite terrorist cells worldwide, a conglomerate of Islamist political parties, and other largely independent terrorist groups that it draws on for offensive actions and other responsibilities' (Gunaratna 2002:54). This amorphous portrayal of Al Qaeda permits Gunaratna to include virtually all Islamic terrorist groups and militant Muslims into his definition of what constitutes Al Qaeda. This is the main methodological weakness of the Al Qaeda-centric paradigm.

Jason Burke (2003) presents a powerful critique of the Al Qaeda-centric paradigm adopted by Bergin, Colvin, Gunaratna and other international terrorism experts. Burke dismisses the notion that Al Qaeda was 'a coherent and tight-knit organisation, with 'tentacles everywhere', with a defined ideology and personnel, that had emerged as early as the late 1980s' (Burke 2003:12). He argues that to accept such a view 'is to misunderstand not only its true nature but also the nature of Islamic radicalism then and now. The contingent, dynamic and local elements of what is a broad and ill-defined movement rooted in historical trends of great complexity are lost' (Burke 2003:12).

According to Burke, Al Qaeda, as it is popularly conceived, 'consisted of three elements. This tripartite division is essential to understanding the nature of both the "Al Qaeda" phenomenon and of modern Islamic militancy' (Burke 2003:13). The first of these elements composed the 'Al Qaeda hardcore', numbering around 100 active 'pre-eminent militants', including a dozen close, long-term associates of Osama bin Laden, many of whom had sworn an oath of loyalty to him. This inner core were all veterans of the Afghan war or veterans of the conflicts in Bosnia or Chechnya. They acted as trainers and administrators in Afghanistan and on occasion were sent overseas to recruit, act as emissaries or, more rarely, to conduct specific terrorist operations. But, Burke (2003:14) cautions, 'it is a mistake to see even this hardcore as monolithic in any way'.

The second element comprises the scores of other militant Islamic groups operating around the world. But, injecting another note of caution, Burke argues 'a careful examination of the situation shows that the idea that there is an international network of active groups answering to bin Laden is wrong'. To label groups included in this second element 'Al Qaeda' is 'to denigrate the particular local factors that led to their emergence' (Burke 2003:14). Burke explains why this second element should not be included as constituting part of Al Qaeda:

> But, though they may see bin Laden as a heroic figure, symbolic of their collective struggle, individuals and groups have their own leaders and their own agenda, often ones that are deeply parochial and which they will not subordinate to those of bin Laden or his close associates. Until very recently many were deeply antipathetic to bin Laden. As many remain rivals of bin Laden as have become allies (Burke 2003:14).

The cases of Indonesia's Laskar Jihad and Free Aceh Movement are instructive. Both groups received and held discussions with Al Qaeda representatives and rejected offers of support in order to retain their operational autonomy. Yet, some regional security analysts continue to characterise Laskar Jihad as Al Qaeda-linked if not an Al Qaeda affiliate. The Free Aceh Movement is held suspect because several of its members reportedly have received training at 'Al Qaeda-affiliated' MILF camps in the southern Philippines.[16]

The third element composing Al Qaeda consists of those individuals who subscribe to 'the idea, worldview, ideology of Al Qaeda'; in other words, 'the vast, amorphous movement of modern radical Islam, with its myriad cells, domestic groups, "groupuscules" and splinters...' (Burke 2003:207). Burke rejects the Al Qaeda-centric paradigm that characterises Al Qaeda as an organisation incorporating all three elements into its organisational structure. In his view, it is the hard core alone that constitutes Al Qaeda (Burke 2003:207).

The second methodological problem in discussing Al Qaeda's role in Southeast Asia is how to account for change over time. International and regional terrorism experts adopt an approach that can be characterised as 'back to the future'. In other words, their analysis of Al Qaeda's operations in Southeast Asia in the late 1980s and 1990s begins with the events of 11 September 2001 and works backwards in an ahistorical manner. Al Qaeda is portrayed as a purposive organisation, endowed with virtually unlimited resources, from the very start. It is as if Osama bin Laden's announcement of the formation of the World Islamic Front for the Jihad Against Jews and his call to international *jihad* against Americans (military and civilians anywhere) and their allies was made in 1988, not February 1998. But, as Reeve (1999:170) notes, 'for many years al Qaeda was little more than an umbrella organisation for various bin Laden projects'.

Burke (2003:208) argues that Al Qaeda as an organisation was limited in time and space:

> Something that can be labeled 'Al Qaeda' did exist between 1996 and 2001. It was composed of a small number of experienced militants who were able to access resources of a scale and with an ease that was hitherto unknown in Islamic militancy, largely by virtue of their position in Afghanistan and the sympathy of so many wealthy, and not so wealthy, Muslims across the Islamic world, though particularly in the Gulf.

In other words, it was only after bin Laden returned to Afghanistan in May 1996 that Al Qaeda as an organisation really came into being. According to Burke (2003:16), '[t]hey even had a country they could virtually call their own. There were thus able to offer everything a state could offer to a militant group by way of support'. Al Qaeda played the role of 'the state' by projecting its power and influence globally by using the huge financial resources and human capital available. In summary, Al Qaeda facilitated a global terrorist network through funding, services and facilities but did not control or direct local agents.[17]

It is important to note that militants from Southeast Asia first journeyed to Pakistan/Afghanistan in 1980, at least eight years before Al Qaeda was founded and 18 years before bin Laden launched his global *jihad*. It was during this early period that Southeast Asians forged personal links with leading figures in the *mujihadeen*. One particularly influential figure was Abdul Rasul Sayyaf, a Pushtun warlord and leader of one of the *mujihadeen* factions, who headed the Islamic Union for the Liberation of Afghanistan. Sayyaf was an ally of bin Laden.

It was under Sayyaf's patronage that key future leaders of the ASG and JI were trained at his camp in Afghanistan. Sayyaf provided training facilities to the bulk of Southeast Asia's Muslim militants while bin Laden, along with the bulk of his supporters, was in exile in the Sudan (1991–96). There, bin Laden built up his international network of contacts while pursuing his prime objective of opposing the regime in Saudia Arabia and its American military allies. As a result of international pressure the Sudanese Government forced bin Laden to leave. By the time bin Laden returned to Afghanistan in May 1996 the country was embroiled in a civil war as the Taliban initiated its drive to power. Simon

Reeve (1999:192) notes that bin Laden was 'a powerful figure funding many Islamic militants, but his level of day-to-day control over Al Qaeda must be questioned'. Given the uncertainty of this period, Southeast Asia's militants had already decided to relocate their training camps to the southern Philippines. Thus, the Al Qaeda-Southeast Asia relationship may be viewed as having passed through at least three distinct periods and phases: (1) 1980–89 (anti-Soviet resistance); (2) 1990–96 (Abdul Rasul Sayyaf influential, bin Laden in exile in the Sudan); and (3) 1996–2001 (continuing yet diminished Al Qaeda relations with Southeast Asia's militant groups).

The period after 2001 marks a fourth distinctive phase. The US led attack on the Taliban regime and Al Qaeda camps in Afghanistan in the final quarter of 2001, resulted in the death or capture of key Al Qaeda leaders and greatly degraded and disrupted Al Qaeda's international command and control structures. Al Qaeda members were forced to seek refuge in remote areas of eastern Afghanistan and in Pakistan's North West Frontier. Other Al Qaeda members dispersed overseas, including Yemen, Chechnya, Iran (Stern 2003:27–40) and also in Southeast Asia. Since late 2001, the initiative for political terrorism in Southeast Asia has mainly rested in the hands of indigenous organisations with some collaboration with Al Qaeda remnants left stranded in the region.

The third methodological problem is how to assess the question of agency in Al Qaeda's relationship with the Abu Sayyaf Group and Jema'ah Islamiyah. This is a particularly difficult question to answer during the period from the late 1980s until 1996. International terrorism experts and regional security analysts are often ambiguous when they use the term 'Al Qaeda'. Who or what represented 'Al Qaeda' in its dealings with Southeast Asian militant groups in these formative years? This is a particularly pertinent question for the period 1991 to 1996, when bin Laden was in the Sudan and Southeast Asia's militant leaders were in contact with *mujihadeen* leaders in Pakistan and Afghanistan.

The same question can be asked about the Abu Sayyaf Group and JI. Who or what represented these groups in their relations with Al Qaeda prior to their formation in 1992 and 1993, respectively. There is a third aspect to the question of agency: how to avoid the 'back to the future' framework of analysis in our assessment of the objectives of Al Qaeda, ASG and JI in different historical periods of development. This question will now be addressed in greater detail.

The Abu Sayyaf group

This section critically examines the applicability of the Osama bin Laden/Al Qaeda-centric paradigm to analysis of Al Qaeda-ASG relations. As noted above, the Soviet invasion of Afghanistan sparked a movement throughout the Islamic world in support of the Afghan resistance movement. An estimated 1,000 Southeast Asians, mainly Filipinos and Indonesians, flocked to Pakistan to render support to the *mujihadeen* cause. With few exceptions, most Southeast Asians were grouped in one training camp where, as Islamic militants embarked on holy war, they formed enduring personal bonds. This laid the basis for later co-operation between the ASG, the MILF and JI.

The Abu Sayyaf Group is a breakaway faction of the MILF, which itself is a break away faction of the Moro National Liberation Front (MNLF). The MNLF was the major Islamic group leading the struggle for an independent Moro Republic in the southern Philippines in the 1970s. In December 1977, a faction led by Salamat Hashim, split from the MNLF and established an external headquarters in Pakistan. In 1984, Salamat Hashim formally named his organisation the Moro Islamic Liberation Front. Hashim's group played a prominent role in the recruitment of Filipino volunteers to join the *jihad* against the Soviet Union in Afghanistan in the 1980s. Among this number was Abdurajak Abubakar Janjalani, a native of Basilan province.

Janjalani was educated in Libya and reportedly studied in the Middle East under the sponsorship of Muhammed Jamal Khalifa. Janjalani and his brother, Khaddafi, underwent paramilitary training at a *mujihadeen* camp near Khost in Afghanistan in the late 1980s. This camp was run by the Afghan warlord Abdul Rasul Sayaaf, with the support of financiers in Saudia Arabia. Sayyaf's camp promoted Wahhabism and this was in accord with Janjalani's religious beliefs. Janjalani advocated creating an independent Moro Islamic Republic in the southern Philippines.

International terrorism and regional security analysts argue that Al Qaeda's first penetration of Southeast Asia took place in 1988 when Muhammed Jamal Khalifa, Osama bin Laden's brother-in-law, arrived in the southern Philippines to start up the operations of several international Islamic charities. According to Maria Ressa (2003:10) this marked the first phase of Al Qaeda's expansionist plans. Khalifa is portrayed as a key Al Qaeda official and operational planner acting under instructions from Osama bin Laden. Al Qaeda did not exist in 1988. When it was formed it was initially concerned with providing assistance to the families of Muslim martyrs and supporting like-minded Muslim groups in their struggle against state oppression. It is entirely plausible that during his first visit, Khalifa was primarily acting as an agent for Islamic charities that were interested in donating money for the construction of orphanages, hospitals and mosques and in providing relief to the families of Filipino Afghan war martyrs.

Far more important were the initiatives of Janjalani. During his time with the *mujihadeen* in Pakistan/Afghanistan, he met and was befriended by Osama bin Laden. After the Soviet withdrawal from Afghanistan in early 1989, Janjalani travelled back and forth between Basilan and Peshawar soliciting assistance from his *mujihadeen* mentors and Al Qaeda. According to Simon Reeve (1999:136), 'Osama bin Laden, either directly or indirectly, offered him financial backing for his attempts to create an independent Islamic state'. Janjalani also recruited supporters from the MILF camp in Afghanistan for his Islamic movement. Thus, the personal bonds forged in struggle against the Soviets formed the basis for co-operation between Janjalani and his followers and Al Qaeda. The year 1991 was pivotal: Osama bin Laden left Saudi Arabia for Pakistan, and Janjalani was also visiting the country. Khalifa met Ramzi Yousef in Peshawar in the summer of 1991 and 'it all came together' (Reeve 1999:156). Yousef agreed to visit the Philippines in the company of Janjalani. They did so between December 1991 and May 1992. During this trip Yousef offered instruction in bomb making techniques to Islamic militants at a camp in Basilan. It was at this time that Janjalani renamed his militant band the Abu Sayyaf Group.[18] Other accounts suggest that Yousef encouraged the formation of the ASF (Abuza 2002:430).[19]

Khalifa returned to the Philippines in October 1991 to resume his charitable work, set up business interests and provide funding to support the activities of Janjalani's group. The importance of Khalifa's status as bin Laden's brother-in-law has been over exaggerated in accounts of this period. As Burke (2003:263 nb27) points out, bin Laden had nearly 50 siblings and, according to a senior Saudi diplomat, 'a brother-in-law...in Saudia Arabia [is] not even considered part of the family'. According to Burke (2003:101), 'there is nothing to indicate that those monies [provided by Khalifa's Islamic charities] included funds from bin Laden himself. There would have been no need for Khalifa to be in touch with bin Laden. His own connections were broad-ranging'. Janjalani was also receiving funding from Libya at this time. These new sources of funds enabled the ASG to embark on a new wave of political terrorism.

The next phase of Al Qaeda's penetration of the Philippines came in 1994, when Ramzi Yousef returned after unsuccessfully trying to blow up the World Trade Center in New York in December the previous year. Yousef stopped first in Basilan where he trained nearly two dozen Abu Sayyaf Group members in explosive techniques. Yousef then moved to Manila where he met up with Khalifa. They were joined shortly after by members of Al Qaeda's inner core, Wali Khan Amin Shah and Khalid Sheik Mohammad. With a small group of colleagues they planned a series of high-profile terrorist actions which took the code-name Operation Bojinka. These plotters considered and rejected a number of options such as killing the Pope, assassinating President Bill Clinton and crashing a plane into the headquarters of the Central Intelligence Agency. They finally latched on to a plan to simultaneously blow up eleven American commercial airliners over the Asia Pacific.

In January 1995, a mishap resulted in the exposure of the Operation Bojinka cell and the eventual arrest of its main plotters.[20] It is not altogether clear that Operation Bojinka was an Al Qaeda-sanctioned operation. Throughout his career as an international terrorist Ramzi Yousef has shown himself to be the consummate, professional, 'evil genius'. He slept with the Al Qaeda devil and took the devil's money but he remained a true freelancer and not a disciplined member of the hard core (Reeve 1999:71–155). Yousef planned and executed the 1993 World Trade Center attack on his own initiative, on a shoestring budget. After fleeing New York, Yousef eagerly undertook a number of freelance assignments in Pakistan at the behest of extremist Islamic groups (Reeve 1999:47–70). Operation Bojinka clearly falls into this pattern of independently planned terrorist actions. It is important to note that Bojinka was not a joint Al Qaeda—Abu Sayyaf Group operation. It was a self-contained operation from which the ASG had been excluded by Yousef because he did not think them competent enough to carry it out (Ressa 2003:25–6; Abuza 2002:443).

In 1991, Janjalani's militant group initiated its first terrorist act by killing two American evangelists in Zamboanga city. Another attack resulted in the murder of a Catholic Bishop. As a result of ASG's growing notoriety it attracted the support of a number of criminal gangs active in the Sulu Archipelago. An analysis of 67 terrorist attacks ascribed to the ASG between 1991 and 1997 reveals that about half were indiscriminate killings and massacres with no apparent religious motivation. Clearly the ASG only gave occasional lip service to its pretension of establishing an independent Islamic state in western Mindanao and the Sulu Archipelago.

There is evidence that as Janjalani's domestic program of wanton terrorism unfolded, Al Qaeda decided to downgrade its ties and develop relations with the MILF (Davis 2003). According to Abuza (2002:443), 'by 1996, bin Laden had lessened his interest in the Philippines…Cells continued to be developed in the Philippines and elsewhere in Southeast Asia, but the region became secondary to Al Qaeda'. As noted above, in 1995–96, Southeast Asia's militants moved their training camps from Afghanistan to Mindanao under the sponsorship of the MILF.

The character of the ASG changed markedly with the death of Janjalani in late 1998. It degenerated into a number of semi-autonomous criminal factions whose stock in trade consisted of terror bombings, assassinations, extortion and kidnapping for ransom (USA 2002b). In April 2000, the ASG kidnapped foreign tourists from a resort on the Malaysian island of Sipadan, and the following year kidnapped a number of foreign tourists in Palawan. The ASG's resort to ransom and extortion were sure signs that it was not receiving significant covert external funding. After the US-led coalition occupied former Taliban-ruled Afghanistan, the United States and the Philippines government joined forces against the Abu Sayyaf Group as part of the global war on terrorism. ASG forces on Basilan were initially targeted and nearly decimated (Fargo 2003). The ASG still lives on, however, with a presence on Sulu and Tawi-Tawi islands as well as a foothold on the Zamboanga Peninsula. The ASG still retains the capacity for conducting terrorist attacks.

Jema'ah Islamiyah

Jema'ah Islamiyah is the second terrorist group in Southeast Asia to be proscribed by the United Nations[21]. Australia's Defence Minister, Senator Robert Hill (2003:2), noted in a recent speech, '[i]t should go without saying that in referring to "Jema'ah Islamiyah" I am talking about the terrorist organisation that has been listed by the United Nations, not about the peaceful "community of Islam" that the term traditionally denotes'. Jema'ah Islamiyah, the terrorist organisation, has its origins in *jema'ah islamiyah* (community of Islam), which in turn has deep roots in contemporary Indonesian society.

The origins of the contemporary JI organisation may be traced to 1967 (if not earlier) when remnants of the Darul Islam movement[22] revived under the name Dewan Dakwah Islamiayah Indonesia (DDII). DDII engaged in religious proselytising and worked closely with the Saudi-funded World Islamic League to promote Wahhabi fundamentalist beliefs.

Two key Islamic clerics played a key role—Abdullah Sungkar and Abu Bakar Ba'asyir. They first met in 1963, and two years later began campaigning for the establishment of an Islamic state. In 1967 they set up an unregistered radio station in Central Java to broadcast their views. In 1972, Sungkar and Ba'asyir founded the Pesantren Al Mukmin in Ngruki village in Central Java in order to promote Wahhabi fundamentalist teachings (ICG 2003c). Graduates of this school would later form the extremist hard core of the terrorist organisation JI.[23] During the 1970s and 1980s, Sungkar and Ba'asyir promoted *jema'ah islamiyah* in the sense of an 'Islamic community'. It was in this context that the *Jema'ah Islamiyah* organisation gradually emerged as an extremist group of Muslim scholars and students that identified with the Wahhabi religious teachings. Towards the end of the 1970s, Sungkar and Ba'asyir got caught up in a covert operation conducted by Ali Murtopo, the Indonesian intelligence chief (ICG 2003c:5-9). Murtopo cultivated remnants of the Dar'ul Islam movement ostensibly for use as a weapon against the Indonesian Communist Party. In 1978, Murtopo moved to clip the wings of the very organisation he had encouraged. Sungkar and Ba'asyir were detained, tried and sentenced to jail in 1982. They were released on appeal but when threatened by further legal action, they fled to Malaysia in 1985.

In Malaysia, Sungkar and Ba'asyir re-established themselves and founded a religious school in Johor which propagated their extremist views. Their school attracted several of the Ngruki alumni. Sungar and Ba'asyir actively recruited volunteers in Malaysia, Singapore and Indonesia to study in Pakistan and to undertake paramilitary training in Afghanistan. All senior members of JI's future leadership trained in Afghanistan at a camp run under the auspices of Adbul Rasul Sayyaf at this time. The first class commenced in 1985 and the last class completed its three-year course in 1994. A few Indonesians also attended short training courses between 1993–95 (ICG 2003c:2).

During the 1980s the revived Dar'ul Islam movement formed part of *Jema'ah Islamiyah* and was virtually indistinguishable from it. In 1992 a rift occurred and Sungkar led a breakaway faction that 'resulted directly in JI's creation as an organisation separate and distinct from Darul Islam' (ICG 2003c:6).[24] This point is collaborated by a JI detainee who revealed that '[in 1993] Sungkar and Ba'asyir announced that they would be known as Jema'ah Islamiyah and a new structure began to take place' (Barton 2003:4).

In 1994, the last class recruited by Sungkar and Ba'asyir completed its course. The following year, Southeast Asian Islamic militants in Afghanistan made the decision to relocate their training facility to Camp Abu Bakar, run by the MILF in Mindanao. Students at Camp Abu Bakar were trained mainly by Indonesian Afghan veterans, as well as Arab and other foreign specialists associated with Al Qaeda. After the fall of Suharto, Sungkar and Ba'asyir returned to Central Java in 1999 and resumed teaching at their school in Ngruki. Whatever personal bonds may have linked Sungkar to bin Laden, they were terminated in November 1999 with Sungkar's death. Jema'ah Islamiyah, as it emerged on peninsular Malaysia, took a different form from that in Indonesia. The Singapore branch of JI was probably founded around 1993 when Ibrahim Maidin, a Singaporean religious teacher, returned from Afghanistan after completing a short paramilitary training course. He facilitated the travel of other Singaporeans to Pakistan and Afghanistan. Maidin first met Ba'asyir in the late 1980s.

JI's Malaysia branch was founded sometime in 1994–95 under the leadership of Hambali, JI's operational chief (Barton 2003:4). Recruitment was conducted primarily among the Indonesian migrant community. Hambali also sought out promising recruits from university lecturers and students at the Universiti Tecknologi Malaysia and students at Islamic schools. Approximately fifty militants were dispatched to religious schools in Pakistan for ideological indoctrination and Afghanistan for paramilitary training. Others were sent to MILF camps in Mindanao.

A distinct split began to emerge in JI with the death of Sungkar in late 1999. According to an investigation by the International Crisis Group, 'many of Sungkar's Indonesian recruits, particularly the more militant younger ones, were very unhappy with the idea of Ba'syir [sic] taking over...They saw Ba'asyir as too weak, too accommodating, and too easily influenced by others'. The military core included Hambali, Imam Samudra and Muchlas (Ali Gufron). Hambali began to take on a more proactive role in JI and eroded Ba'asyir's ability to exert control (Hefner 2002:7). In 1999, Hambali issued instructions for the activation of operational cells in Malaysia. These cells were then ordered to begin planning for a series of high-profile terrorist attacks against selected Western diplomatic missions in Singapore, US military personnel in transit on shore leave, US warships in the Straits of Malacca, Changi airport and Singaporean defence facilities. JI emissaries went to Afghanistan to present their terrorist prospective before Al Qaeda, but Al Qaeda took no action. Hambali initiated JI's first terrorist action in late 2000 with a series of church bombings.

Hambali's ambitious terrorist plans came to an abrupt end in 1991, when Malaysian police and Singapore's Internal Security Department (ISD) separately carried out arrests of a number of JI suspects.[25] In August 2002, the ISD arrested another 21 suspects, of whom 19 were identified as members of JI. As a result of these roundups it is believed that most members of JI's branches in Malaysia and Singapore fled abroad or went underground in Malaysia. Hambali reacted to JI's set back by ordering a change in tactics to so-called soft targets. This resulted in the Bali bombings in October 2002. Ever since, it has become commonplace to refer to Jema'ah Islamiyah as an Al Qaeda affiliate, as well as Southeast Asia's most potent terrorist group. However, according to Clive Williams (2003), one of Australia's leading counter-terrorism experts, '[t]here is, as far as I'm aware, no evidence of Al Qaeda involvement [in the Bali bombings]'.

Recent Australian intelligence reports indicate 'a clear split between some JI cells strongly pushing for a return to political agitation and propaganda and others that advocate nothing less than increased militancy' (Chulov & Walters 2003). JI has become an organisation in disarray. According to a senior member of Australia's counter-terrorism effort, 'JI has become a bit fractured from within' with a disparate collection of cells working at cross purposes due to deep divisions over strategy and no clear leader (Chulov & Walters 2003). This assessment is supported by a growing number of Western and Asian government analysts who now view JI as 'a stand-alone regional operation, with its own camps, recruiting, financing and agenda' (Bonner 2003).

Conclusion

This chapter has offered a critique of the Al Qaeda-centric paradigm as a useful framework for analysing the emergence of new terrorism in Southeast Asia. Part one reviewed the three main approaches to this subject. It noted that international terrorism experts contributed to our understanding of new terrorism by drawing attention to linkages between Al Qaeda and militant Islamic groups in Southeast Asia. However, this approach over-exaggerated the role of Osama bin Laden and Al Qaeda itself. Regional security analysts contributed to our understanding of new terrorism by drawing attention to the regional networks created by militant Islamic groups. But a major shortcoming of their approach was their uncritical acceptance of the Al Qaeda-centric paradigm as a key variable in explaining new terrorism. Country studies specialists failed to identify the international and regional character of new terrorism when it first emerged. Their major contribution has been to focus on the question of agency—the ability of local groups to leverage their association with Al Qaeda for their own ends.

This chapter also explored various methodological problems associated with the use of such terms as terrorism and militant Islam. It argued that in the absence of an agreed definition, the classification of a group as terrorist was highly arbitrary. Quite often, international and regional terrorism experts equated terrorism with the actions of militant Islamic groups. Such an approach failed to make a distinction between religious beliefs and politically motivated actions.

Next, the chapter focused on three methodological problems associated with the usage of Al Qaeda: its characterisation, change over time and the question of agency. The chapter noted that international and regional terrorism experts used the term 'Al Qaeda' in a highly ambiguous manner, usually referring to Al Qaeda as the 'network of networks'. The chapter argued that Al Qaeda was best conceived as a small hard-core whose influence globally and in Southeast Asia was limited in time (1996–2001) and space (Afghanistan).

The chapter described various phases in the development of relations between Al Qaeda and Southeast Asia when developments were influenced by a plurality of actors and organisations. Finally, parts four and five addressed the question of agency with two case studies, one focusing on the Abu Sayyaf Group, and the other focusing on Jema'ah Islamiyah. It concluded that neither could properly be classified as an Al Qaeda franchise or affiliate.

What assessment can be offered about the prospects of new terrorism in Southeast Asia today? The original definition of new terrorism—high profile mass casualty (or apocalyptic) attacks on civilian targets—must be reconsidered. Al Qaeda's international organisation has been gravely disrupted by the overthrow of the Taliban regime and the global war on terrorism (Denny 2003). The main threat posed by new terrorism in Southeast Asia today is not high-profile apocalyptic attacks against civilians directed by Al Qaeda through its regional affiliates. Southeast Asia's terrorist groups do not appear to have the capability to carry out a successful mass casualty attack involving biological, chemical or radiological weapons. Today, the main threat of new terrorism resides with Jema'ah Islamiyah and its core of trained professionals. JI has the ability to replace losses through continued recruitment from its network of Islamic schools and its growing linkages with domestic criminal gangs and other extremist groups. What is 'new' about JI is its regional network which includes access to training facilities in the southern Philippines. If this assessment is accurate, new terrorism in Southeast Asia must be redefined to refer to any terrorist group that is regionally networked, with intermittent international linkages, capable of conducting high profile attacks using conventional explosives resulting in scores, if not hundreds, of casualties. This is a radically different view of the threat of new terrorism from that offered by international and regional experts who declared that Southeast Asia had become Al Qaeda's second front, if not the epicentre, of global terrorism.

Endnotes

1. Some specialists argue that new terrorism first appeared in Asia seven years earlier when the Aum Shinrikyo sect launched a sarin gas attack on Tokyo's subway system. For background see Mangold & Goldberg (1999:335–1).

2. Representatives of this approach include: Babbage (2002); Bergin (2001); Corbin (2002); Gunaratna (2002); (2003); and Hirschkornet al (2001).

3. Abuza (2002) states that up to 1,000 Southeast Asians fought with the *mujihadeen* in the 1980s; of this number 700 were Filipinos.

4. Gunaratna (2002:175) refers to a Moro sub-brigade in Afghanistan.

5. Representatives of this approach include Abuza (2002); Chalk (2002); Manyin, Cronin & Niksch (2002:1–13); Ressa (2002); and Tan (2002).

6. Such as the Barisan Revolusi Nasional (BRN) and the Barisan Nasional Pembebasan Patani (BNP).

7. This group includes Greg Barton, Michael Davis, Greg Fealy, Robert Hefner, Paul Nitze, the International Crisis Group and Martin van Bruinessen.

8. 'Kuala Lumpur Declaration on International Terrorism', adopted at the Extraordinary Session of the Islamic Conference of Foreign Ministers on Terrorism, 1–3 April 2002.

9. The US Code of Federal Regulations defines terrorism as 'the unlawful use of force and violence against persons or property to intimidate or coerce a government, the civilian population, or any segment thereof, in furtherance of political or social objectives' (28 CFR Section 0.85).

10. The US Department of State defines terrorism as 'premeditated, politically motivated violence perpetrated against noncombatant targets by sub-national groups or clandestine agents, usually intended to influence an audience'.

11. The US Department of Defense defines terrorism as 'the calculated use of violence or the threat of violence to inculcate fear; intended to coerce or to intimidate governments or societies in the pursuit of goals that are generally political, religious, or ideological'.

12. The US Federal Bureau of Investigation defines terrorism as 'the unlawful use of force or violence against persons or property to intimidate or coerce a government, the civilian population, or any segment thereof, in furtherance of political or social objectives'.

13. According to the Executive Order on Financing Terrorism (24 September 2001), terrorism '(i) involves a violent act or an act dangerous to human life, property, or infrastructure; and (ii) appears to be intended—(a) to intimidate or coerce a civilian population; –(b) to influence the policy of a government by intimidation or coercion; or –(c) to affect the conduct of a government by mass destruction, assassination, kidnapping, or hostage-taking'.

14 Second Report of the Monitoring Group, pursuant to resolution 1363 (2001) and as extended by resolutions 1390 (2002) and 1455 (2003) on sanctions against Al Qaida, the Taliban and their associates and associated entities, 2003.

15 They both rely on the testimony of Jamal al-Fadl, a Sudanese defector.

16 Editor's note: The Free Aceh Movement says that none of its members has been trained in the Philippines nor has any connection with the MILF or other religiously-inspired political organisations. Many GAM members were, however, trained in Libya.

17 Burke suggests that three models characterise Al Qaeda's organisational structure: a wealthy research university, a venture capitalist firm and a publishing house. In each of these cases individuals, small companies and freelancers approach the institution to seek support and facilities for their ideas and proposals. Some are accepted and funded, others are not (Burke 2003:208–9).

18 Abu Sayyaf was Janjalani's *nom d'guerre*. Some sources say the ASG took its name from Abdul Rasul Sayaaf, their benefactor.

19 Abuza quotes Philippine National Police intelligence documents.

20 Ramzi Yousef was apprehended in February 1995 in Islamabad and deported to the United States. Wali Khan Amin Shah, who was arrested, escaped, and was re-arrested, was deported to the US in December 1995. Khalifa fled the Philippines. He was arrested in the US and deported to Saudia Arabia to stand trial for treason. He was acquitted. Thereafter Khalifa denounced bin Laden's terrorist tactics and severed all family connections.

21 The discussion in this section relies in part on ICG (2202b) and RS (2003).

22 The Darul Islam movement emerged in the 1940s advocating the creation of an Islamic state based on *syariah* and opposition to Dutch colonialism. In August 1949, Darul Islam leaders proclaimed the formation of an Indonesian Islamic State in opposition to the secular Republic of Indonesia. Darul Islam continued its resistance to the Indonesian republic until it was crushed in 1962 with the capture and execution of its leader.

23 For example, Fathur Rahman al-Ghozi, Hambali (Riduan Isamuddin), Abu Jabril and Agus Dwikarna.

24 *Jema'ah Islamiyah in South East Asia: Damaged But Still Dangerous*, 6.

25 Malaysia designates its domestic terrorists as members of Kumpulan Militan Malaysia (KMM) after initially identifying them as members of Kumpulan Mujihaddin Malaysia.

Chapter 3
Islam, Islamism and politics in Indonesia
Greg Barton

In the wake of September 11, Islam and Muslim societies are receiving more critical attention from the West than they have in decades. In this heated environment scholars of Islam have a responsibility to shed light, encourage understanding, and as much as they can, defuse prejudice. Nevertheless, it is also important that scholarship neither retreats from critical analysis nor shirks its responsibility to advise on policy responses.

This paper represents an attempt at a contextualised understanding of political Islam and Islamist radicalism in Indonesia and attempts an objective assessment of the risk that Islamist radicalism represents to the social and political stability of the region now and into the future. It argues for a global and holistic approach to understanding Islam and Islamism—an approach that pays equal attention to ideas and ideologies, to actions and activities, and to context and circumstances. It reviews the changes that have taken place in Indonesian Islam over the past three decades, and examines their social and political context, in order to assess the extent to which radical Islamists and progressive liberals, representing as they do small minorities at each end of the broad spectrum of Indonesian Islam, are able to act as catalysts for social and political change. And while it counsels against undue alarmism, it also argues against complacency and for the need to take radical Islamism, and Islam itself, more seriously. It concludes with a discussion of the domestic and international policy implications for dealing with radical Islamist movements in Indonesia and the importance of assisting moderate Islamic groups in strengthening civil society.

Threat perception and radical Islamism in Southeast Asia

The Al Qaeda attacks on America caused Western observers to begin to observe Southeast Asian Islam afresh and have conferred on the region's small bands of radical Islamists a prominence out of all proportion to their limited domestic appeal. Rightly or wrongly, many have assumed a link between militant Islamism in the Malay world or archipelagic Southeast Asia and extremist movements in the Arab world and in South and West Asia. In Indonesia especially, observers are divided on how to assess the threat of Islamist radicalism and how to respond. Some see the unfettered existence of vigilante groups such as Laskar Jihad, apparently with the support of elements within the military elite and the involvement of such militia in fatal violence in Maluku and Central Sulawesi, as deeply troubling developments that may represent portents of things to come. At the very least, they argue that Indonesia's current chronic state of disarray and the dysfunctional nature of much of the state apparatus, especially outside Java, leaves Indonesia so dangerously vulnerable that the possibility of international, radical Islamist networks operating within the archipelago cannot be dismissed out of hand. Other observers, however, argue that, in general, the threat of radical Islamism in Indonesia is greatly overrated and that, in particular, little hard evidence exists to sustain the charge of international engagement by radical elements and terrorist networks in local affairs. And virtually all observers agree that the vast majority of Indonesian Muslims are personally tolerant and moderate in their outlook and are generally opposed to militant radicalism.

What, then are we to make of concerns about radical Islamism in Indonesia? Certainly, the essentially moderate nature of Indonesia's two mass-based Islamic organisations, Nahdlatul Ulama (NU) and Muhammadiyah (which together represent a major portion of all Indonesian Muslims and the great majority of all *santri* Muslims), is widely seen as evidence of the quiescent and tolerant nature of Indonesian Islam. At the same time, however, completely denying the influence of globalised radical Islamism in Southeast Asian society would be almost as foolish as succumbing to essentialism. Radical Islamism might only enjoy a very limited following in Indonesia but that does not mean that we should not give it serious attention.

Al-Qaeda in Southeast Asia?

The most recent scholarly report to tackle the question of Islamist radicalism in Indonesia and possible links with international terrorism, is a report released in early August 2002 by the Brussels-based International Crisis Group (ICG 2002a; see also ICG 2001c). The report represents an exhaustive review of reliable, public domain data about Al Qaeda's links in Indonesia. It identifies a handful of individuals with possible direct or indirect links with Al Qaeda, but finds no evidence of extensive Al Qaeda links with radical Islamists in Indonesia. For this, we should be grateful. Had this careful study uncovered an active Al Qaeda network in Indonesia it would have been a matter of enormous concern. The report should put a brake on the kind of wild speculation that has flared in some corners of the media that suggest Indonesia is a hotbed of Islamist terrorism. Nevertheless, its findings do not mean that Indonesia has nothing to worry about. The ICG report was narrowly conceived and intended to focus on a single issue, namely the evidence for an Al Qaeda presence in Indonesia.

The ICG report focuses on the loose network of radical Islamists associated with the Pondok Ngruki *pesantren*, led by the outspoken preacher Abu Bakar Ba'asyir, and situated in the village of Ngruki near Solo in Central Java. Abu Bakar Ba'asyir, who is also Commander of the Majelis Mujahidin Indonesia (MMI—the Indonesian Mujahidin Council), the radical organisation founded in Yogyakarta in 2000 and to which many Pondonk Ngruki graduates belong, draws inspiration from the Darul Islam (abode of Islam) rebellion led by Sekarmadji Maridjan Kartosuwirjo in West Java in the 1950s.

Active in the pre-Second World War nationalist movement, Kartosuwirjo was one of the principal organisers of Hizbullah, a militia set up during Japanese occupation by the peak Islamic organisation Masyumi and later marshalled to fight the Dutch. Although he played a significant role in Masyumi's post-war transition to become a political party he became unhappy with the moderate direction being taken by the new party. In January 1948, Kartosuwirjo established the Tentara Islam Indonesia (TII—the Islamic Army of Indonesia) in West Java, refusing to go along with an agreement arrived at by other nationalists with the Dutch that would have required the withdrawal of revolutionary forces from parts of Java. One and a half years later, in the final months before the Dutch withdrawal on 7 August 1949, he proclaimed the creation of Negara Islam Indonesia (NII—The Islamic State of Indonesia), in districts controlled by his TTI troops as being Darul Islam—the Abode of Islam—a move which brought him into direct conflict with the nationalist forces. Kartosuwirjo's TTI forces engaged in periodic skirmishes with the Indonesian military (Tentara Nasional Indonesia—TNI) until 1962, when Kartosuwirjo was finally arrested. In South Sulawesi another former Hizbullah leader and respected nationalist, Kahar Muzakkar, upset with the refusal of TNI officers to grant places within TNI to members of his militia, refused orders to demobilise his men and instead declared that they would fight for the rights of the people of Sulawesi. In 1952 he made contact with Kartosuwirjo and the next year, inspired by the success of Kartosuwirjo's Darul Islam in West Java, he proclaimed that Sulawesi was part of the Negara Republik Islam Indonesia (NRII—Indonesian Islamic Republic). Kahar Muzakkar's rebellion, which began as a regional rights dispute (he felt that his Sulawesi Hizbullah fighters were being discriminated against by the Javanese/Sumatran leadership of TNI) and only later became radicalised along Islamist lines, continued to fight the TNI up until the time of his death at the hands of the TNI in 1965.

After the collapse of the West Java and South Sulawesi rebellions relatively little was heard about Darul Islam style radical Islamism in Indonesia until the late 1970s. In mid-1977 the Suharto regime arrested 185 people, many with

Darul Islam connections, accused of belonging to an organisation it referred to as Komando Jihad. It is not clear whether this fresh crack-down on radical Islamism was precipitated by a genuine, grass-roots resurgence of interest in Darul Islam radicalism or whether the Indonesian military (known at this time as ABRI—Angkatan Bersenjata Republik Indonesia, the Armed Forces of the Republic of Indonesia) was simply attempting to 'flush-out' and make an example of radical Islamists ahead of the 1977 general elections. What has long been suspected, and what the ICG was able to verify, was that General Ali Murtopo, Suharto's notorious 'Special Operations' manager, and his officers within BAKIN, the ABRI intelligence agency, engaged in a elaborate 'sting' operation that lured hundreds of former Darul Islam fighters out of hiding (ICG 2002a:5). Selling the line that the fall of Saigon in 1975 heralded the danger of Communist advances throughout Southeast Asia, and represented a challenge that required the forces of the right to work together (and possibly also offering financial inducements) Murtopo's men were able to persuade key former Darul Islam members to contact their colleagues and reactivate their movement. This resulted in the establishment of Jema'ah Islamiyah (the term, which was to be commonly invoked by the Indonesian military in subsequent decades, is very non-specific and simply means Community/ies of Islam) as a precursor for establishing a new Darul Islam movement. While Murtopo appeared to have nothing more extensive in mind than a sting operation (there being no suggestion that Murtopo's group contained anyone with Islamist sympathies, or that Murtopo was seeking to co-opt Islamist activists to use against rivals within the regime) the ploy had significant unintended consequences, as the ICG (2002a:9) report observes:

> The operation set in motion by Ali Murtopo and the Indonesian intelligence in the 1970s had several unintended consequences. It renewed or forged bonds amongst Muslim radicals in South Sulawesi, Sumatra, and Java. It promoted the idea of an Islamic state in a way that the original Darul Islam leaders had perhaps not intended, and in doing so tapped an intellectual ferment that was particularly pronounced in university-based mosques. That ferment was only beginning when Komando Jihad was created, but through the late 1970s and early 1980s, its was fuelled by the Iranian revolution, the availability of Indonesian translations of writings on political Islam from the Middle East and Pakistan; and anger over Soeharto government policies.

Together with Abu Bakar Ba'asyir, the other key leader of the so-called Komando Jihad or Jema'ah Islamiyah, identified by Indonesian intelligence when they were arrested in November 1978, was Abdullah Sungkar, from Brebes, Central Java. Like Ba'asyir, Sungkar, a former officer in Kartosuwirjo's TII, was born in Java in the late 1930s of Yemeni descent. Both men had long careers as Islamic activists, beginning with years spent in the Masyumi affiliated

Gerakan Pemuda Islam Indonesia (GPII—Indonesian Muslim Youth Movement), followed by periods of *dakwah* (missionary) activism that saw Ba'asyir join al-Irsyad and Sungkar Masyumi. The two men first began to work together in 1967 when they founded first Radio Dakwah Islamiyah Surakata in Solo in 1967, and then Pesantren al-Mu'min (later to be known as Pondok Ngruki) in Ngruki in 1973 (ICG 2002a:7).

Abu Bakar Ba'asyir and Abdullah Sungkar were finally tried in 1982 and were initially sentenced to nine years in prison. These sentences were overturned on appeal, however, and the pair were released with their sentences being reduced to the three years and ten months that they had already served prior to their trial. Returning to Pondok Ngruki they worked hard to build up a network of supporters. If the alleged Jema'ah Islamiyah network of the 1970s was substantially a fiction created by BAKIN, then during the mid-1980s it was made a reality by Ba'asyir and Sungkar and their followers, newly radicalised by the experience of military repression. Ba'asyir and Sungkar encouraged their followers to return to their villages and establish *usroh* cells of around a dozen members, to live communally and to avoid all non-Islamic institutions. As well as in Solo, Islamist discussion groups and cells also emerged in nearby Yogyakarta. In this city of universities and colleges many students who were angry with the increasingly corrupt and repressive Suharto regime, and disillusioned with the West that supported it, found inspiration in the 1979 Islamic revolution in Iran. They translated and published, read and discussed, the writings of Islamist intellectuals such as Ali Shariati of Iran, Hasan al-Banna and Sayyid Qutb of Egypt's Islamic Brotherhood (Ikwan al-Muslimun) and Maulana Maududi of Pakistan's Jamaat-i-Islami.

Adding to the radicalisation of the young men drawn to Ngruki was the bitter experience of the September 1984 riots in Jakarta's port district of Tandjung Priok. The Tandjung Priok incident, which saw dozens (possibly many more) members of local mosque communities and *usroh* activist cells shot dead by troops under the command of Catholic general Benny Murdani, was clearly intended to intimidate the Islamists. This it did, but it also radicalised many more and hardened their resolve to work for change.

In February 1985, a prosecution appeal was lodged with the Supreme Court challenging the reduced sentences awarded to Ba'asyir and Sungkar. Faced with the possibility of a further period of detention the pair decided to flee (*hijrah*) to Malaysia. In the wake of the Tandjung Priok killings and the arrest of a former Pondok Ngruki lecturer, Abdul Qadir Baraja, over the January 1985 bombing of the Buddhist Stupa of Borobudur, outside Yogyakarta, and then the flight of Ba'asyir and Sungkar to Malaysia, the *usroh*/Jema'ah Islamiah network in Central Java began to break up, or at least go to ground.

On his way to Malaysia in 1985 Abdullah Sungkar stopped briefly in Lampung, South Sumatra, an area that was home to tens of thousands of transmigrants from Central and East Java. He quickly established a local following which came to coalesce around *Jema'ah Islamiyah* community established on donated land in the district of Way Jepara. In time, the community attracted members fleeing persecution in Central and East Java, some of whom had links with the earlier Darul Islam movements in West Java and Aceh and with Abdul Qadir Baraja, who was by this time serving a 15-year jail sentence. By 1989 the group, increasingly known for its hard-line views, had attracted adverse attention from the local authorities. Warsidi, the man who had donated the land on which the community was established, was summoned to appear before the local military commander. When he refused, nine of his followers were taken into custody. Fearing imminent attack the community armed itself and prepared for confrontation. The tense stand-off came to a violent end when the subdistrict military commander was hacked to death when he went to speak with Warsidi. Predictably, the killing was met with an overwhelming response from the military (ICG 2002a:16). The following day, when most of the men had gone into hiding in the surrounding jungle, the compound was over-run by the military. The attack, which was led by the head of the local military command, Colonel Hendropriyono, is widely regarded as representing a massive over-reaction, though probably one that was carefully calculated to send a strong message to other hard-line communities. It is thought that around 100 people, many of whom were women and children, were killed in the assault. Lieutenant General Hendropriyono went on to become head of Badan Intelijens Nasional (BIN), the national intelligence agency, and a key figure in President Megawati's cabinet.

Whilst in self-imposed exile in Malaysia Ba'asyir and Sungkar continued to actively maintain links with associates in Indonesia, not just in Central Java but also in Jakarta, West Java, North Sumatra and South Sulawesi, where they were able to recruit small numbers of volunteer *mujahidin* fighters for the struggle against the Soviets in Afghanistan. In the mid-1990s, Ba'asyir and Sungkar underwent a significant shift in their position following contact with Usama Rushdi of Gama Islami, the radical break-away faction of Ikwan al-Muslimin. Gama Islami (or al-Gama'at al-Islamiyah) closely linked to Al Qaeda and is led by Sheikh Umar Abdul Rahman, the Islamist teacher convicted in the US for his part in the 1993 World Trade Center bombing. The Gama Islami connection saw Ba'asyir and Sungkar move beyond the old Darul Islam vision of establishing an Islamic state within Indonesia, or at least making the Indonesian state more Islamic, to the more radical, pan-Islam position of calling for the re-establishment of an international Islamic caliphate. This shift was initially the cause of some dispute within the Ngruki exile community but in time came to be accepted by the network as a whole (ICG 2002a:17).

Following the resignation of President Suharto in May 1998, Ba'asyir and Sungkar returned to Java. Sungkar died soon after returning from exile, but Abu Bakar Ba'asyir was able to re-establish himself in Pondok Ngruki, from where he spear-headed a push to unite all groups concerned to implement Syari'ah in Indonesia. In August 2000, at a time when President Abdurrahman Wahid was facing overt challenges from radical Islamist groups (including the Laskar Jihad militia that had been established earlier that year and which had sent thousands of fighters to Maluku, despite his orders to block them), Ba'asyir was able to organise a three-day Mujahidin Congress in Yogyakarta. This remarkable gathering drew delegates from across the archipelago, representing virtually every Islamist group in the country. The main achievement of the congress, apart from its success as a show of strength, was the establishment of the Majelis Mujahidin Indonesia (MMI—the Indonesian Mujahidin Council), dedicated to preparing the way for the establishment of an new international caliphate. Significantly, Hizbut Tahrir, the Jordan-based militant Islamist organisation calling for the re-establishment of the caliphate, sent a number of observers to the congress in Yogyakarta, an indication of its growing influence in Indonesia. Abu Bakar Ba'asyir was declared Amir ul-Mujahidin, or commander, of MMI's governing council and Abdul Qadir Baraja was appointed head of its *fatwa* section. Other people closely linked with the Ngruki network, including a number who had fought in Afghanistan and studied in Pakistan, made up much of the leadership of MMI (ICG 2002a:17).

The reason for the ICG focusing on the Pondok Ngruki network is that it is this one network that has produced all of the known Al Qaeda links with Indonesia. The four main figures alleged to have close links with Al Qaeda are all involved with Pondok Ngruki:

- The first is Fathur Rahman al-Ghozi, who had been detained in Manila since January 2002, when he was arrested for possession of false passports and on suspicion of involvement in a series of bombings in Manila in December 2000 and a planned attack in Singapore. In court he was alleged to have been found with illegal explosives and false documents in his possession when arrested, and to have subsequently confessed to being involved in the Manila bombings, and on the strength of this evidence, was sentenced to 18 years in jail. Al-Ghozi escaped from custody in July

2002, but was killed in a shoot-out with police and soldiers in North Cotabato, Mandanao, the following October.

- Second is Hambali (who also goes under the names of Riduan Isamuddin and Nurjaman), who is said to be Al Qaeda's main contact in Indonesia and allegedly linked with bombings in Jakarta and Manila in December 2000 and a planned attack on American navy personnel in Singapore. Hambali was arrested in Ayuthaya, Thailand, in Feburary 2004 and extradited to Indonesia.

- Third is Abu Jibril (alias Fikirussind Muqti, alias Mohamed Iqbal bin Abdurrahman), who is currently under detention in Malaysia. He was said to be Al Qaeda's main financial courier in Southeast Asia and appears in a videotape recruiting fighters for Maluku).

- Fourth, Agus Dwikarna, who has been under detention in the Philippines since his arrest in March 2002. It is alleged that he was apprehended carrying a suitcase containing explosives but there are credible counter-claims that these were planted (ICG 2002a:2–3).[1] He, too, is said to be involved with the Jakarta and Manila bombings. The ICG report concludes that the evidence against Abu Jibril and Agus Dwikarna is 'unconvincing' and the links with al-Qaeda are unproven.

Some important questions that the ICG study does not really set out to address remain: Is radical Islamism ratcheting up its influence in post-Suharto Indonesia? Are elements within the military continuing to opportunistically support radical Islamist militia, as they have done in recent years? And, are elements of the political elite showing signs of exploiting the appeal of radical Islamist ideas as a way of leveraging their political power? Are moderate Islamic intellectuals facing increasing opposition?

The big question is, what does this means for the future? Although a definitive answer is impossible we do need to raise the question of whether there is a real danger, however remote, that Indonesia will follow the path of Pakistan. In other words, will a small, radical Islamist minority, aided and abetted by opportunistic elements within the civil and military elite and by deteriorating economic and social conditions at home, come to disturb the religious and political freedoms of a moderate majority, particularly in more outlying provinces?

Effective engagement with this question requires a multidimensional approach. In seeking to understand the key factors we need to consider three essential axes: ideas and ideology, actions and achievements, and context and circumstances. Too much of the commentary in the media, about Indonesia and the wider Muslim world, has been simplistic and superficial. The truth is seldom neat and simple, and if we are to apprehend it we need to move beyond reading things a face-value and to get below the surface.

Reading Islam

Judging by appearances is never a good idea. When it comes to religion, judging-by-appearances is a particularly inept strategy—we are likely either to equate difference with danger and become prejudicial, or be blinded by the exotic and become naïve and uncritical. To interpret, for example, the traditional Islamic dress and manner of the Acehnese as indicative of religious fundamentalism would be a foolish error. To then link this, as some in the international media have done, with the Acehnese struggle for self-determination, and paint it as religious conflict, is an even graver error, one that blinds us to the real issues and the underlying problem of injustice and military brutality. On the other hand it is, for example, equally misleading to dismiss the Ngruki network or Laskar Jihad as representing nothing more than religious conservatism simply because their ramshackle *pesantren*, or religious boarding school, in Central Java, looks much like the thousands of *pesantren* run by the moderate Nahdlatul Ulama.

It is important that we look beyond appearances and pay attention to ideas, to behaviour and the changing specifics of the social and political context. This, however, is precisely where we run into trouble. Traditionally, the study of ideas has been left to orientalists or text-oriented experts, whose careful scholarly approach has not generally extended to a consideration of social and political engagement and the real-world application of the documents that they are studying. At the same time, comparatively few political scientists and commentators have a deep knowledge of the thinking associated with the groups they are observing and all political parties or groups with an Islamic connection tend to get lumped in together. And, if it is rare for commentators to make an effort to understand the mind-sets and the political activism of these groups, it is even rarer to find this knowledge linked to an awareness of the changing political and social context in which the groups operate.

Ideas and ideology—Islam and Islamism

Ironically, one of the main reasons why, in the West, so little attention is paid to understanding the central ideas of Islamic groups appears to be because it is regarded as being too difficult. Much of the time we are not even sure quite what we mean by 'Islam', much less how we can objectively evaluate its various forms. Consider for a moment the way we use expressions such as:

'political Islam', 'Indonesian Islam', the 'role of Islam', the 'Islamic influence', the 'Islamic factor' and so forth, and the extent of the confusion soon becomes obvious. We understand, of course, that Islam is for many believers a deeply personal and private faith and yet others would argue that there is no separating faith and politics. In any case, regardless of one's view of secularisation and modernisation, there is a very real sense in which Islam is nothing less than the sum total of a raft of social, cultural and political norms, expectations, convictions, values, habits, traditions, outlooks, attitudes and identity markers.

Whilst there are good reasons for saying that Islam is all of these things we nevertheless become incapable of achieving meaningful progress if we only talk in generalities. Without greater precision in our language we risk endlessly groping for direction in a fog of confusion. Ludwig Wittgenstein famously observed that many philosophical problems are the result of 'language going on holidays'. The same observation could well be made concerning religion. Certainly, the absence of clear definitions and reasonably precise terminology is a certain recipe for ensuring that discussion about Islam and politics is constantly at cross-purposes.

There are many ways in which we could choose to begin to analyse and categorise Islamic movements and political parties, but it is hard to see any better point of departure than belief itself and the ideas and ideologies that these groups define themselves by.

One of the most helpful and accurate terms to emerge in recent years is that of 'Islamism'. Islamists, or those who hold to Islamism, believe that Islam can and should form the basis of political ideology. Handled with sensitivity, the term 'Islamism' is one that both 'insiders' and 'outsiders' can relate to with a reasonable degree of common understanding. Which is considerably more than can be said of terms like 'fundamentalism' and 'radicalism', both of which can be profoundly ambiguous.

If Islamists find in Islam something of a blueprint for political engagement, non-Islamist Muslims find nothing more specific than values and principles. A significant minority, however, find in these core values of Islam a counter-argument to Islamism. They argue that not only should Islam be first and foremost a personal faith, it should also accept and respect differences of opinion, commitment and practise. They embrace terms such as 'liberal' and 'progressive' fully aware of the connotations of these terms in post-enlightenment Western thought.[2]

Where Islamists tend, in varying degrees, to problematise the relationship between Islam and Western conceptions of modernity, liberal Islamic intellectuals find an essential congruity between Western Judeo-Christian thought and Islam.

Liberals are comfortable in articulating their political vision in terms of Western concepts such as democracy, human rights, modernisation and the separation of 'church' and 'state'. Islamists, on the other hand, tend to draw more selectively on such ideas and instead, argue that society will overcome the problems of modern life only when it becomes truly Islamic. To this end, Islamists tend to place great stock in legislative reforms that commit the state to taking a greater interest in the Islamisation of society and, in particular, many see the implementation of Syari'ah as a panacea for society's ills. In its most extreme form Islamism is radical, revolutionary and utopian.

Both liberals and Islamists understand themselves as minorities seeking to influence a somewhat neutral majority, but also claim to represent mainstream sentiment.

Although the term 'Islamism' is of recent coinage, the distinction between Islamists—those who want legislated recognition and a direct role for Islam in the state—and other Muslims—who are, to varying degrees, quiescent or intuitively apprehensive about the state playing a direct role in 'the affairs of the heart'—dates back to the emergence of nationalism in the colonial period. It represents an unresolved dispute of enormous importance to Indonesian politics.

When, on 17 August 1945, two days after the Japanese had surrendered to the Allies, Sukarno, Hatta and the other nationalists, under some pressure from younger nationalists, suddenly declared independence, the brief and sketchy constitution drafted for the new state was very much a rough draft, and understood as such, being nothing more than an interim measure. Nevertheless, the nationalists were not entirely unprepared for independence. In fact, in the tumultuous final months of the war they had given considerable attention to debating the form and nature of the new Indonesian state. Some proto-Islamist elements wanted the new state to be an Islamic one, though there was little clarity about exactly what that meant, others wanted the state at least to recognise Islam as its official religion, much as Malaysia was later to do, and to take some responsibility for enforcing piety and morality. Others, including some of the leading *ulama*, were deeply concerned about making Islam the state religion. In part, this was because they feared that such a move would alienate non-Muslims (who represented approximately 15% of the population) and non-*santri*, or so-called *abangan*, Muslims whose beliefs and practices did not conform with conventionally pious expectations (and who represented perhaps more than half the population).³ The consequence of this debate was reflected in two important decisions.⁴

Firstly, it was agreed that the Indonesian state would be based on Pancasila and would therefore be 'theistic' but non-sectarian. Decades later, under Suharto, Pancasila became a justly-maligned instrument of statist oppression but, in principle, it represented a compromise of no-small-genius and of far-reaching importance. Some weeks before the declaration of independence Sukarno introduced Pancasila to the people of Indonesia in a 1 June speech setting forth his vision for the new nation. Significantly, the term was derived from Sanskrit—'the Latin of Southeast Asia' the scholarly language of Indian thought and pre-Islamic civilisation—rather than from Arabic. The fifth 'sila', or principle, stated the belief in 'one God', and was therefore congruent with *tauhid* (the 'oneness' of God), the doctrinal core of Islam, without privileging any one tradition (although it did leave Buddhists and Hindus at a disadvantage they chose not to construe it as such and adopted monotheistic terminology when required).⁵

Secondly, the secular, or at least non-sectarian nature of the Indonesian state was reinforced by an 11th hour decision to drop a caveat to the first *sila* of Pancasila that would have added the words: 'with the obligation for adherents of Islam to carry out Islamic law' (*'dengan kewajiban untuk menjalankan Syari'ah Islam untuk pemeluk-pemeluknya'*). These 'seven words', as they became known, were to be part of the so-called 'Jakarta Charter' which was to form a preamble to the constitution when it was proclaimed on 18 August 1945, the day after the declaration of independence. Sukarno and his colleagues were worried that the inclusion of the 'seven words' of the Jakarta Charter would have alienated non-Muslims and *abangan* Muslims whilst pleasing only a minority of Indonesians. They were almost certainly right, but the last-minute deletion left the proto-Islamists incensed and deeply suspicious. What, exactly, the inclusion of 'the seven words' would have meant was not then, and is not now, clear. Nevertheless, the Jakarta Charter became a bone of contention and a cause-célèbre for many Muslim politicians and leaders. And the emotive campaign that developed provided a mechanism by which leaders with radical Islamist convictions could draw behind them a long tail of socially conservative, but otherwise moderate, Islamic leaders for whom the Jakarta Charter was largely a matter of symbolic importance. Unfortunately, the dispute was to have consequences that went well beyond what most of those who joined the fray could have envisaged.

By the time of Indonesia's first general elections in 1955, sociological tensions, political ambitions and wounded pride had led to the traditionalist

Muslims of NU parting company with their modernist brothers (most of whom were from Muhammadiyah, but some of whom were from the more conservative groups such as Al-Irsyad, the association of Arab Indonesians) in the peak Muslim party Masyumi.[6] Contesting the polls under its own banner, NU gained 18.4% of the 1955 vote, slightly less than Masyumi, which garnered 20.9%, and a little less than the 22.3% achieved by the Indonesia Nationalist Party (PNI) aligned with Sukarno but ahead of the 16.4% achieved by the Indonesian Communist Party (PKI). The results were a surprise to many in the four large parties—the 1955 elections representing as they did the first ever opportunity to ascertain a objective and comprehensive map of communal allegiances in Indonesia. It was clear that the *aliran*, or 'streams' of communal allegiance associated with the large parties, were surprisingly even in size. This confirmed the wisdom of Sukarno and the leading nationalists in pushing for a pluralistic and inclusivistic philosophical foundation for the new state. It did not, however, resolve the issue of the Jakarta Charter.

With the national parliamentary elections successfully concluded, the way was clear for a second round of voting at the end of the year to elect the 514 members of the Constitutional Assembly (Konstituante): the body charged with formulating a comprehensive replacement to the interim constitution of 1950. The 1950 Constitution, which emphasised parliamentary democracy, had replaced the vague and unsatisfactory 1945 Constitution, with its integralist or totalitarian vision of the state as a unified family. Although a considerable improvement over its precursor, the 1950 Constitution was also never intended to be anything more than a stop-gap measure.

Had the Constitutional Assembly been able to complete its task Indonesia would have had very likely gained a constitution of considerable sophistication and importantly, one arrived at via a transparently democratic process that gave voice to all *aliran*. Unfortunately, in July 1959, nine months before it was scheduled to conclude its deliberations, Sukarno dissolved the Constitutional Assembly arguing that as it had not been able to reach consensus on the Jakarta Charter after sitting for three and a half years, it lacked practical legitimacy and represented a failed experiment.[7] This judgement conveniently overlooked all that the Constitutional Assembly had achieved, which included significant consensus on human rights and the division of powers within government.

When Sukarno sacked the Constitutional Assembly, parliament was also dissolved (until 1960), and he announced a return to the 1945 Constitution with its strong, largely unchecked, presidential powers and weak legislative function. In this he had the support of the military who, like Sukarno himself, were disturbed by the instability of parliamentary coalitions in Indonesia's multi-party parliament and by rebellions such as Kartosuwiryo's radical Islamist Darul Islam insurgency in West Java which had the army tied up throughout the 1950s and its echoes in South Sulawesi and Aceh. The final straw for Sukarno was the PRRI rebellion of 1958 in West Sumatra, which had the support of the CIA and key Masyumi leaders. This rebellion led not just to the banning of Masyumi and the demise of democracy, but also to the long-lasting suppression of Islamism during Sukarno's 'Guided Democracy' regime of the 1960s and throughout Suharto's New Order regime in the late 1960s, 1970s and 1980s. Relief was to come only in the final decade of Suharto's New Order regime when the president, fearing the power of a restless military, embarked on a campaign of co-opting the Islamists.

The growth of Islamic liberalism and of Islamism

The four decades between Sukarno's abolition of democracy in July 1959 and the holding of free and fair elections in July 1999 saw significant developments in Indonesian Islam.

Throughout the 1960s and 1970s NU pragmatically avoided confrontation in the political arena. In politics it focused on maintaining the good relations necessary to ensure success in obtaining business contracts and, related to this, maintaining its influence within the Department of Religious Affairs and on odd issues of religious importance, such as changes to family law. For the most part, however, it focused on its social and education affairs as a religious association, which were worked out through its network of 6,000 to 7,000 *pesantren* (communal religious boarding schools) spread across Java, southern Sumatra and parts of Kalimantan. This approach was, if anything, made easier by Suharto's move in 1973 to scrap all eleven political parties except Golkar and redirect Muslim political interests to the newly-created United Development Party (PPP) and nationalist interests to the Indonesian Democratic Party (PDI). For the traditionalists the most important developments occurred outside politics and revolved largely around intellectual reform. Throughout the 1970s and 1980s, the *pesantren* system was steadily modernised and an increasing number of *pesantren* graduates went on to complete tertiary studies, either at the increasingly sophisticated State Islamic Institutes (IAIN) or at regular universities. A small but significant number also went on to obtain post-graduate qualifications abroad. For many young activists and intellectuals the combination of a modern, secular education and a rich, classical Islamic education was a very productive one. The 1970s saw the emergence of Islamic liberalism, pioneered by gifted young intellectuals from a traditionalist background such as Nurcholish Madjid and Abdurrahman Wahid who further contributed to educational reform (Barton 1996; 1997a:323–50; 1997b).

The early 1980s saw a largely liberal and youthful reform movement within NU steadily gain ground to the point where, in 1984, its leading lights, Kiai Achmad Siddiq and Abdurrahman Wahid, took charge of the national leadership. Ideological and pragmatic considerations drove this new leadership team to withdraw NU, as an organisation, from direct involvement with PPP, and to argue in favour of acquiescence to the New Order regime's campaign for the adoption of Pancasila as 'the sole ideological basis' (*asas tunggal*) by all social and community organisations, a campaign aimed at reigning-in the power of Islamist groups (van Bruinessen 1996:163–89).

Official repression of Islamism during the 1960s, 1970s and 1980s achieved curiously mixed results. In the political arena, of course, Islamism was effectively neutralised, as was every other oppositional ideology. The consistently strong electoral performance of PPP was a constant reminder to the Suharto regime that it was never going to control political Islam through force alone. Nevertheless, PPP was essentially a useful pressure-valve for political frustrations and a safe channel for political ambitions, whilst at the same time helping to maintain the fiction of democracy.

The effect of state control in the civil sphere, however, was much more mixed. On the one hand, the repression of Islamism helped provide the necessary environment for Islamic liberalism to develop into a significant social movement. It was not that pressure towards accommodation with the state produced Islamic liberalism, but rather that repression of Islamism allowed liberal ideas to be openly developed and disseminated without the sort of intimidation that had seen liberal Islamic intellectuals in other Muslim societies either silenced or forced abroad.

On the other hand, the official repression of Islamism, which because it occurred in the context of military-backed authoritarianism was often excessively violent, was also counter-productive. Driven underground, Islamism became a powerful social movement on university campuses and within certain mosque and *madrasah* (religious day school) communities. The imprisonment of movement leaders only increased their influence amongst students who were angry with the injustices and corruption of the Suharto regime, cut-off from other revolutionary ideologies and hungry for simple solutions to complex problems.

More importantly, the banning of Masyumi under Sukarno and the neutering of its logical successor, Parmusi, under Suharto, had the effect of developing within certain modernist Muslims, an unhealthy obsession with politics whilst embittering them to the point where much of the intellectual vigour and creativity that had earlier marked the modernist movement was extinguished. The obsession with political achievement and the 'Holy Grail' of the Jakarta Charter had the tragically ironic effect of ensuring that Modernism's most significant achievements were confined to the field of secular education, health care and social service, whilst intellectually significant religious thought largely failed to develop within succeeding generations of young modernists.

The impoverishment of religious thought amongst moderate modernists in Muhammadiyah and elsewhere left the growth of the underground Islamist movements and the small, officially tolerated conservative foundations funded by foreign Wahabist institutions, without effective competition for the hearts and minds of modernist youth. Moreover, the international resurgence of interest in Islam, which contributed to the steady '*santri*-fication' of Indonesian society saw many students from *abangan* families drawn to 'controversial' Islamist groups, seduced by their simple answers to complex problems.[8]

Dewan Dakwah and KISDI

Previously, as they sought to give voice to their political aspirations the hardliners within the modernist community found themselves blocked at every turn. In 1967, Suharto had engineered an internal coup within Parmusi to ensure that former Masyumi leaders did not advance and then set about making political Islam an object of ridicule and suspicion. As the danger of communism began to recede in the 1970s, Islamism and extremist Islamist politics began to replace communism in the demonology of Suharto's New Order regime. The result was that Islamist modernists found themselves blocked from opportunities for political engagement. As is so often the case, as their isolation increased so too did their determination to engage politically.

The result was the steady embitterment of many of the modernist's brightest minds. Muhammad Natsir, the great Masyumi leader of the 1950s, responded by establishing the Islamic Preaching Council (Dakwah Islamiyah Indonesia— DDII) in 1967, to act as a vehicle for advancing the interests of conservative Islamist politics and blocking Christian expansion (Hefner 2000:106–9; Liddle 1993:77–107). Unfortunately the combined effects of an obsession with politics and the failure of the modernists to provide sound theological education for their youth was to result in the rise of Islamism, the simplistic union of a narrow and limited understanding of Islam with a sectarian political agenda.

In the 1950s, Masyumi represented an eclectic bundle of widely varying streams of modernist thought, and was centred around a core of highly educated and generally cosmopolitan professionals. Many within the party did not share the conviction of leaders such as Muhammad Natsir that Islam needed to be accorded special recognition by the state in the constitution. And at the time even Natsir himself, despite belonging to the conservative Islamic organisation Persatuan Islam (Persis, Islamic Union) was regarded as being a reasonably progressive figure who enjoyed friendly relations with a wide circle of intellectuals and politicians.

In the decade after Dewan Dakwah's formation the organisation became increasingly militant in its views, which were reflected in its periodical *Media Dakwah* (which evolved from modest origins to become a glossy monthly magazine). By the 1980s, *Media Dakwah* had adopted a harsh and sectarian stance and although some of its writers and reporters were moderates, the magazine frequently carried strident critiques of liberal Islamic thinkers such as Abdurrahman and exposes of 'anti-Islamic conspiracies', often marked by strong anti-Semitism (Hefner 1997:77–103).

Nevertheless, the majority of modernists were not as attracted to Islamist ideas as was Amien Rais. Unfortunately, however, because they lacked the theological education necessary to make a direct contribution to the rethinking of Islamic thought, they tended to not get involved in theological discussions. A significant exception to this was Dawam Rahardjo.

In 1987 Ahmad Sumargono and Lukman Harun, two of the most conservative figures within Dewan Dakwah, established *Komite Indonesia untuk Solidaritas dengan Dunia Islam* (KISDI), the Indonesian Committee for Solidarity with the Islamic World. They were later to find a willing patron and rising star within ABRI, President Suharto's son-in-law, Prabowo Subianto (Hefner 1997:201). Robert Hefner explains that:

> ...KISDI was originally established to heighten Indonesian sympathy for the plight of the Palestinians. Although genuinely concerned with Palestinian suffering, the KISDI leadership knew well that the Palestinian cause could be used as a wedge to underscore differences between Muslims and the West. The campaign proved to be a brilliant recruitment strategy. Although most Muslim Youth had long lost interest in Masyumi, many were deeply moved by the Palestinian's plight. In promoting this issue, then, KISDI was able to introduce the younger generation to the senior modernist cause.
>
> In the 1990s KISDI launched other, equally effective campaigns in support of Muslims in Bosnia, Indian Kashmir, France, and Algeria. A theme in all these campaigns has been the treachery of the West (especially the United States) and Western hypocrisy in the enforcement of human rights. When Soeharto intensified his courtship of conservative Islam in the early 1990s, he borrowed directly from KISDI's critique of human rights and liberal democracy. Through his aids, Soeharto appealed to KISDI to aim its critique of human

rights not only at Western powers but at the domestic prodemocracy movement as well (Hefner 1997:109–110).

ICMI

By the time the regime decided to change tack and seek to co-opt the Islamists within the largely moderate, safe, confines of the Indonesian Association of Muslim Intellectuals (ICMI), it was too late to reverse the subversive appeal of Islamism. ICMI did, nevertheless, serve a useful purpose for the Suharto regime. For much of the 1990s it contributed to restoring a sense of legitimacy to the regime in the eyes of people who were previously its fiercest critics.

Some of the intellectuals involved with ICMI, however, such as Nurcholish Madjid, were troubled by the president's enthusiasm for the organisation. Despite having helped draft the organisation's original conceptual guidelines, Nurcholish and other moderates were not comfortable about the organisation's sudden rise. They feared that Suharto intended to make ICMI an instrument for his own political purposes. Nevertheless, others who also recognised this, such as NGO activist and development economist Dawam Rahardjo, felt that it could also be turned to their advantage. Although trained as an economist Dawam was intensely interested in the 'renewal of Islam' discourse and in many ways shared similar convictions to Nurcholish and Abdurrahman. He played a significant role in encouraging younger intellectuals through his NGO *Lembaga Studi Agama dan Filsafat* (LSAF), or the Institute for the Study of Islam. In the early to mid-1990s, as an initiative intended to promote the rethinking of Islamic thought, LSAF published the scholarly magazine *Ulumul Qur'an*.

Dawam rejected Abdurrahman's criticism of ICMI arguing that even if it was being used for the president's purposes, it might still give them an opportunity to be engaged in the institutions of government. Reinforcing this conviction was the fact that many saw ICMI as representing a superb instrument for the *santri*-fication of elite society.

For more than a decade a revival of interest in Islam had been underway in Indonesia just as it had throughout the Muslim world. During the 1980s it had become increasingly commonplace to see businessmen, bureaucrats and public servants taking time out from their work to pray at the appointed times and to fast during the main Muslim fasting month of Ramadan. Many who had previously identified with a nominal or *abangan* position made conscious efforts to become more *santri*.

The reasons for this revival are complex and difficult to delineate. They were partly the result of changes elsewhere in the Islamic world and partly the product of unique local factors. In the Middle East many intellectuals and activists turned to Islamism in the 1960s and 1970s after having found nationalism and Marxism wanting. Ironically, the more that Islamist movements were repressed, the more powerful they became to the hundreds of thousands of mostly young men who crowded into squalid shanty suburbs on the fringes of Cairo and other large cities, seeking a better life but experiencing frustration and disappointment. Islam, or better, Islamism, became a rallying cry for disaffected youth everywhere. In Indonesia many students, intellectuals and activists, facing surveillance and oppression on the campuses and in the labour movement following the Malari riots of 1974, turned to mosque-based discussion groups and the utopian vision of Islamism. This was typified by the so-called 'Salman movement' that developed around the Salman mosque at the Bandung Technological Institute (BTI—Indonesia's premier institute for engineering and technology) and which was lead by Imaduddin Abdulrahim. Imaduddin, who in the 1980s was harassed and eventually jailed by the Suharto regime, was one of the key figures in the founding of ICMI. As has already been noted above, the success of Islamist revolutionaries in bringing down the Shah of Iran in 1979 served as an inspiration to Islamists throughout the world. The rise of Islamism in Indonesia was also a reaction to the 'Westernised', decadent culture that flourished in the 1970s and early 1980s under Ali Murtopo's modernisation drive and the wealth that flowed from a surge in international oil prices (Hefner 1997:3–10, 123–7). The Islamic revival, however, went beyond Islamism and disaffected youth. In the 1980s, many middle-class, urban Indonesians began to turn to Islam not for political reasons so much as personal ones. They sought in Islam a spiritual anchor and source of meaning in their busy modern lives. And for most it was not Islamism but the liberal Islam of Nurcholish Madjid, Abdurrahman and their friends that appealed to their hearts and their heads. At the same time, thousands of *pesantren* graduates (many of whom were also IAIN graduates) and others from a traditionalist background were settling in large cities in unprecedented numbers.

Progressive Muslim intellectuals such as Dawam, Nurcholish and Abdurrahman used this Islamic revival to promote a tolerant, sophisticated, rational and well informed approach to Islam. Dawam, who was one of the prime movers in the formation of ICMI, was widely expected to become secretary general to the new organisation, but he lost to the Habibie loyalists, who quickly took charge of ICMI's upper echelons (Hefner 1997:155).[9]

Many of those most active within ICMI, however, were not wholly concerned with making Indonesians more liberal, tolerant and sophisticated in their understanding of Islam. Their prime concern was political power and influence. As liberal thinkers like Nurcholish started to draw back from ICMI others, such as Muhammadiyah firebrand Amien Rais, came to the fore.

Within a couple of years almost all of the important posts within ICMI were safely in the hands of technocrats loyal to Habibie. Muslim intellectuals and activists continued to play an important role but the resources available to them depended very much on how Suharto judged their utility. Those whom Hefner dubs the 'regimists', whose loyalty to the regime was unwavering, not surprisingly, did best (Hefner 1997:148–52). Ambitious younger activists, almost entirely from a modernist background, such as Din Syamsuddin, Muhammadiyah youth winger leader, also one of the organisers of the militant protests against *Monitor* (Hefner 1997:177) and University of Indonesia academic Amir Santoso, who made it clear where their loyalties lay, were well rewarded. Din, for example, was quickly elevated to a senior strategist position within Golkar. Others with a more intellectual bent and much less interest in political careers, such as Nurcholish Madjid and Dawam Rahardjo, were happy to be left on the periphery of the organisation.

For Suharto, one of the clear achievements of ICMI was that outspoken critics of the regime such as Muhammadiyah leader Amien Rais were persuaded, for a while, that there was virtue in attempting to reform the system from within. In the particular case of Amien Rais, however, these gains were spectacularly reversed, with it turned out exquisitely poor timing, when in early 1997 Suharto pressured ICMI patron BJ Habibie to expel Amien from the organisation's central leadership.[10]

At a time when the leading liberal Islamic intellectual, and NU chairman Abdurrahman Wahid was forced to sue for peace and seek rapprochement with Suharto after spending the decade locked in battle with the president, in part because of his opposition to ICMI and Suharto's strategy of co-opting the Islamists and with popular, then ousted, PDI leader Megawati Sukarnoputri, at home considering her political future, Amien was once more free to speak his mind.[11] Up to this point, Amien, who was widely regarded as a chauvinistic Islamist, had struggled to gain credibility outside his own community. With Megawati and Abdurrahman temporarily off the scene, and avoiding further confrontation with Suharto, Amien stepped forward to lead the students in calling for Suharto to step down.[12]

In other circumstances this might have led to Amien and the student protesters facing violent repression but as it happened, Amien was hitting his stride just when the economic crisis hit Indonesia in late 1997 and then suddenly it was Suharto who was forced to give ground. By the time that Suharto resigned in May 1998, Amiens's reputation had been transformed from Islamist firebrand to courageous democrat and statesman. The transformation caught even Amien by surprise, and was sufficiently dramatic that in the post-Suharto scramble to establish new political parties Amien was persuaded by friends to reject the opportunity to lead the Islamist PPP in favour of heading the impressive, newly-formed, National Mandate Party (PAN). In 1998 PAN, formed by Muhammadiyah moderates and progressive intellectuals such as writer Al Qaeda Goenawan Mohamad, was arguably the most impressive of all the new parties and with the high-profile Amien at the helm, looked set to fulfil its ambition to reach out to educated urbanites of all religious and ethnic backgrounds.

Ironically, for all of the changes that had occurred in the 44 years since Indonesia's only previous fair and free general election, the 1999 election results reflected a surprisingly similar breakdown of *aliran*, or communal affiliations, as had been seen in the 1955 election (Barton 2001b:244–55; Fealy 2001).

The minority appeal of Islamism was reflected in the results of the general election of June 1999. Parties with radical Islamist agendas polled poorly. The best results were achieved by the Crescent and Star Party (PBB), with 1.94% of the vote and the Justice Party (PK), with 1.36% of the vote.[13] A handful of similar parties garnered fractions of 1%. The largest Islamist party was the long-established United Development Party (PPP) of Hamzah Haz, which gained 10.72% of the vote.

The National Awakening Party (PKB) of Abdurrahman Wahid gained 12.62 of the vote and the National Mandate Party (PAN) of Peoples' Consultative Assembly Speaker, Amien Rais, gained 7.12%. These parties are Muslim parties in that they are largely supported by members of NU and Muhammadiyah respectfully but they formally reject Islamism and deliberately style themselves as non-sectarian parties open to anyone. The most successful parties in 1999 were Megawati's Indonesian Democratic Party of Struggle (PDI-P), with 33.76% of the vote and Golkar, the party of former president Suharto, with 22.46%.

In short, the results of the 1999 elections strongly suggest that relatively few Indonesians are attracted to any variety of Islamism, much less radical Islamism.[14]

The same message can be found in the civil sphere. As has already been noted, the mass-based Islamic organisations Muhammadiyah and NU are consistently and self-consciously moderate in orientation. The same is true for the vast majority of community associations and NGOs. Radical Islamist groups such as Laskar Jihad and the Islamic Defenders Front have been able to mount some frighteningly impressive rallies in recent years but their membership numbers are miniscule in a nation of 220 million people.

Why then the concern about radical Islamism? One reason is the awful sectarian violence that has wracked post-Suharto Indonesia and the apparent impunity with which groups like Laskar Jihad have been able to act. Such groups are by no means the only reason for sectarian violence in Indonesia but it does appear that they have provoked and prolonged violence in socially vulnerable areas such as Maluku and Central Sulawesi. The truly frightening thing is that it appears that such groups have been opportunistically exploited by elements within the TNI who have recruited them as militia, presumably with the intention of destabilising the Wahid presidency and maintaining pressure on the government of President Megawati (Barton 2002b).

Context and circumstances

Indonesia is still in the initial stages of regime change as the young nation attempts to break with three or four decades of military-backed authoritarianism and establish full democracy. Such transitions are not always successful (consider Pakistan), and even when they are they can take 15 years or more (think of the Philippines). Significant elements of the Suharto regime remain in power, corruption ranks amongst the worst in the world (in a comprehensive 102 nation report by Transparency International released in August 2002, Indonesia ranks as being perceived to be the seventh most corrupt nation in the world), and rule of law is incomplete at best, and non-existent at worst.[15] Meanwhile, the military, despite its commitment to withdraw from the parliament in 2004, remains outside of full civil control and continues to terrorise and abuse civilians and dominate organised criminality on every front. In short, many of the basic incentives and pressures that drove the military to exploit radical Islamist militia in recent years continue. Moreover, the West's war on terrorism seems to have had minimal impact on TNI thinking. In fact, the TNI has attempted to use it as justification for its significantly intensified military campaign in Aceh, whilst at the same time overseeing the introduction of Syari'ah law in the province, against the wishes of most Acehnese. It is a worrying development then, that TNI-controlled militia numbers have increased dramatically in Aceh at the same time as Jakarta has moved to introduce Syari'ah law to the beleaguered province, ostensibly as a concession to pious Acehnese sensibilities. Most Acehnese, however, women especially, resent this imposition and see it as an instrument of control, an impression reinforced by the fact that the government is pressuring the *ulama* to come out in support of the initiative. Consequently, there is now reason to worry that radical Islamism, imported via TNI militia, might make an appearance in this otherwise essentially secular conflict.

Despite their relatively small, absolute representation, following the 2004 elections, the Islamist parties now enjoy considerable political leverage. Their main strength lies not in a legislative majority, but in their support for President (and avowed *santri* Muslim), Susilo Bambang Yudhoyono and his Vice-President, Jusuf Kala, who has a political geneology in South Sulawesi that goes back to the Darul Islam movement. That is, the new president has done deals with the Islamist movement to achieve their support.

Once it was clear that Abdurrahman Wahid was not prepared to 'do deals' with various leaders of the political and military elite, and was instead determined to push ahead with a program of far-reaching reforms, his presidency was marked by constant criticism and attacks on all fronts. When the long-running campaign to have him impeached on trumped-up charges of corruption had run its course and failed to achieve its ends, his opponents in parliament decided simply to vote him out of office on the grounds of incompetence. The Megawati presidency was as uneventful as the Wahid presidency was tumultuous. Political commentators, domestic and foreign, have rightly observed that this was one of the greatest strengths of that administration. And whilst there were clear indications on every front, not least in her relations with the military, that Megawati was much more conservative, and considerably less reformist, than Abdurrahman, the relative absence of conflict amongst the Indonesian elite was a welcome change.

There is no doubt that this change was, in part, a product of Megawati's more cautious approach to reform and her reticence to talk. The garrulous Abdurrahman was often his own worst enemy. After decades of authoritarian rule, his openness, transparency and general willingness to engage with the media, was welcomed by many (Barton 2002b). But his lack of political capital in parliament, his extensive array of enemies desperate to scuttle his reform program and his penchant for outspoken statements, inappropriate humour and colourful exaggeration meant that he was constantly setting himself up for bad press. It would be a grave mistake, however, to believe that the political peace that Megawati enjoyed as president was primarily a product of her personal style. The main reason that Megawati did not face the same barrage of criticism and underhand attacks faced constantly by Abdurrahman was not simply a difference in personal style between her and her predecessor, but rather, a difference in circumstances.

Golkar, for example, was (and remains) more than happy to bide its time and allow the Megawati administration respite from criticism because its focus is on the 2004 elections. Golkar is still working hard on rebuilding itself from within, securing key institutional posts, such as *bupati*-ships and governoral postions and repairing its public image. Once the campaign for the 2004 elections began in earnest, however, Golkar was not gentle with Megawati. Matters about which it had earlier refrained to comment on the lack of significant achievement during her presidency—the failure to move forward with reforms and to roll back the burden of poverty—and the unsavoury and unprofessional behaviour of many within her party and her own family, formed the basis of a sustained attack on her competency as a leader and her credibility as a reformer. PPP and the smaller Islamist parties also joined the chorus of criticism although, in the end, it was Golkar that formed a legislative alliance with Megawati's PDI-P. Their political calculation was simple: as essentially conservative parties, they had more in common than not, and both opposed the presidency of Yudhoyono. PKB spoke confidently about dramatically increasing its share of the vote, but Golkar's strategists understood better than most of PKB's own leaders that the party faced enormous challenges in making grounds outside of the traditionalist Muslim, rural Javanese, NU community. Golkar already occupied a commanding position in most provinces outside of Java and PPP worked hard to ensure that NU members who had supported PPP were not tempted to stray across to PKB.

The resources that Golkar brought to the 2004 elections, in terms of financial and human capital, social networks, political savvy and technical expertise outstripped anything that any of the newer parties could muster. Consequently, Golkar retained a strong share of the legislature, while support for the PDI-P slumped. Yet when it came to the presidential election, in a three-cornered contest, Megawati managed to stay just ahead of Golkar's Wiranto, with both of them well behind the quasi-independent, Islamist-aligned Yudhoyono. Even before it was born, the debate about what role religion should play in the new nation of Indonesia was fiercely contested, and despite what the bare demographic figures might suggest, that debate is far from over.

Conclusion

What should we say about the threat of radical Islamism in Indonesia? What policy responses are appropriate, desirable or possible?

Some might question whether it is even appropriate to talk of radical Islamism representing a threat. After all, what moral basis is there for singling out radical Islamists as a threat? In response, several points need to be made.

It is not being suggested that religious conservatism—sometimes called 'fundamentalism'—is inherently bad and problematic. There are plenty of conservative religious traditions around the world that, for all their lack of appeal to outsiders, can not fairly be said to be doing harm. In fact, it could well be argued that the world is a richer place for their presence. The Amish of North America, for example, represent an extremely conservative approach to Christianity, but their conservatism does no harm to any outside their community. They are legalistic and have strong convictions but they are not about changing society to conform to their convictions. There are many conservative Muslim communities that display similar characteristics, and like the Amish they might sometimes be referred to as fundamentalist. Islamism, however, means something quite different from this sort of 'fundamentalism'. Islamism represents a particular response to modernity that has transformed the religion of Islam into a political ideology. Islamism is therefore pre-eminently concerned with changing society by political means in order to bring the state and society into conformity with a particular understanding of Islam. This involves, amongst other things, formalising the state's constitutional and legislative recognition of Islam and, for radical Islamists, the introduction of Islamic law. It is important to recognise that many who voted for Islamist parties in Indonesia, such as PPP, do not hold radical Islamist views.

The problem with radical Islamism is that it seeks to impose a 'tyranny of a minority over a majority' and is unconcerned with trespassing on the rights of others. In practice, aggressive legalism and the application of a particular understanding of Syari'ah can lead to serious erosion of human rights, especially amongst women.

Radical Islamism is anti-democratic (though it is not adverse to using democratic means where they offer an advantage) and problematic. Nevertheless, it is important to make a distinction between radical Islamism and terrorism. Strictly speaking, terrorism is not an ideology but a means, an instrument to achieve a certain ideologically determined end. Many whose ideological position could best be described as radical Islamism would argue strongly and sincerely that the 'means' of terrorism do not justify the 'ends' of their ideology. Adopting a radical Islamist position by no means determines that someone will support the use of violence and terrorism. This distinction is enormously important because there exists a very real danger that initiatives to root out terrorist networks will have unintended consequences and could even transform non-violent Islamists into militant Islamists. Already in Indonesia there is great anxiety amongst moderate leaders about the possibility of radicalisation as a direct consequence of what is perceived to be the indiscriminate demonising of Islam and of Muslims.

For this and other reasons, the most effective way to counter the threats posed by radical Islamism and militant Islamism is to strengthen the hand of Islamic liberals. They, like the radical Islamists who oppose them, represent a small but critically important minority of Indonesian Muslims. Their influence on broader Muslim society can by catalytic. But so too is the influence of radical Islamism. Each feels themselves locked in a battle to shift, as it were, the centre of gravity within Islamic society. All things being equal the liberals would probably continue to make steady gains, as they did in the 1970s and 1980s, when Suharto stayed the hand of the Islamists and hence allowed the nascent Islamic liberalism movement to develop and strike roots in Indonesian society. Today, however, all things are not equal. The global environment for one is a factor that might well work to the advantage of the radical Islamists, especially if the 'war on terrorism' sees a significant 'blow back' effect. The liberals face four other factors that serve to constrain them and limit their effectiveness:

Firstly, the radical Islamists make effective use of intimidation to stop the liberals getting their message out through the media. There have been many incidents where militant Islamists have enjoyed great success through the use of mob violence to intimidate media companies into changing course. The Chinese Catholic publishing consortium Gramedia and its publications, such as the national daily *Kompas* and the popular magazine *Monitor*, has suffered from highly effective campaigns of intimidation. More recently, prominent young liberal Islamic intellectual Ulil Abshar Abdalla and his Liberal Islamic Network group have seen their public service television advertisement proclaiming 'Islam is multi-coloured' (*Islam warna-warni*) pulled from the air in the face of pressure from the Indonesian Mujahidin Council of Abu Bakar Ba'asyir (Yates 2002).[16]

Secondly, liberal Muslims could benefit from extensive capacity building, as they tend to be less well-organised, resourced and managed than the radical Islamists. In particular, where radical Islamists have long realised the benefit of networking locally and globally, liberal Islamic activists are comparatively poorly networked.

Thirdly, certain radical Islamists enjoy strong party-political and military connections and support. In part, this has to do with their utility to elite power brokers during this period of regime change and transition.

Fourthly, whilst the radical Islamists and Islamic liberals enjoy a catalytic effect in influencing Muslim society, the related 'ratchet effect' of such influence tends to work much more strongly in favour of the radicals. In other words, gains made by radical Islamists are very difficult to reverse and over time the cumulative effect of a series of small gains can be considerable, whereas gains made by liberals are much more easily lost.

There is one other party whose influence, though difficult to delineate and quantify, is of enormous importance to the 'success' of militant Islamism. It is doubtful that militant Islamists would be able to operate in the many ways they do without the help and backing of certain sections of the Indonesian military. There is now little doubt that Islamist militia, such as Laskar Jihad and Front Pembela Islam, are used as tools of TNI and POLRI (the Indonesian police). The same may even be true of other groups such as the Indonesian Mujahidin Council. Now that TNI is once again receiving assistance from the US government it is important a 'feedback loop' is instituted, such that the continued backing of such militia results in direct pressure on TNI. For this to work it is essential that independent parties, unobstructed by TNI and POLRI, closely monitor the activities of these groups. Whilst sections of the Indonesian government and the Indonesian parliament are sadly indifferent to international opinion, TNI is presumedly not indifferent to the flow of support it hopes to receive from the US. The threat of that flow being interrupted might be the one thing that will push the leadership of TNI to reigning in their erstwhile friends.

Endnotes

1   For a sharp critique of the paucity of hard evidence against these alleged Al Qaeda operatives, see Fealy (2002), which is particularly scathing of Lieutenant General Hendropriyono and BIN, pointing to their poor track record and predilection for fabricating evidence.

2   For a discussions of Islamic liberalism from a theoretical point of view, refer to Rahman (1982; 1979:315–30); Binder (1988:399) and Kurzman (1998). For discussion of its development in Indonesia, refer to Hefner (1997b:75–127); (2000), Barton (1991:69–82); (1994); (1995); (1997b).

3   The contemporary usage of *santri* and *abangan* was popularised by Geertz (1960).

4   For a comprehensive account of the development of Islamic politics up until the late 1960s in Indonesia, refer to Boland (1971).

5   Editor's note: The order of the *Pancasila* was changed under Suharto to place 'Belief in One God' as the first principle.

6   For in introduction to Muhammadiyah and Islamic modernism, refer to Nakamura (1983).

7   For a discussion of the end of a parliamentary democracy from the point of view of NU, refer to Fealy (1994).

8   For an overview of these developments, refer to Hefner (1997a:3–40).

9   For a discussion of the political dynamics connected with ICMI and Suharto's approach to Islam in the 1990s refer to: Ramage (1995).

10   Of all Suharto's ministers, BJ Habibie enjoyed a uniquely intimate relationship with Suharto. The two had met in Southern Sulawesi in the late 1950s, when Habibie was only 13. Suharto's army unit was stationed across the road from his house, and when Habibie's father died months, later the older man became a virtual foster-father to the bereaved teenager.

For the next four decades, Suharto was to watch over the bright young man with all of the indulgence of a natural father. In the late 1960s Habibie undertook doctoral studies in the faculty of engineering at the Technical University of Aachen, West Germany, graduating *summa cum laude*. Within the space of a few years he rose to become a vice-president and Director of Applied Technology at the aircraft manufacturer Messerschmitt-Bolkow-Blohm, a truly impressive achievement, for at the time it was the highest rank obtained by a foreigner in the corporation. In 1973, Suharto sent a message to Habibie saying that he wanted him to 'return home and help his country'. In 1976 Habibie was put in charge of the newly formed Nusantara Aircraft Industry (IPTN) and in 1978 he was appointed State Minister of Research and Technology. Not long afterwards he was placed in charge of Indonesia's 'strategic industries', a series of state-owned companies involved in heavy industry, including the manufacture and procurement of armaments for the Indonesian military. Although technically brilliant in his field of aeronautics Habibie quickly established a reputation as a romantic dreamer with little aptitude for turning his ventures into profitable businesses. Nevertheless, Suharto ensured that he was supplied with hundreds of millions of dollars of capital each year to achieve his grand vision of helping Indonesia 'leapfrog' its industrial development via a series ambitious high-tech ventures.

Towards the end of the 1980s Habibie, who earlier was not known to be especially pious and whose one real passion was aircraft manufacture, was, at Suharto's instruction, touring the country touting the links between technology and Islam. By appointing Habibie to take charge of ICMI it was clear that Suharto was prepared to give the new organisation considerable backing.

11 For a discussion of Abdurrahman Wahid's struggles with the Suharto regime, refer to Fealy (1996:257–77) and Ramage (1995).

12 For a discussion of these developments, refer to Barton (2001a).

13 The results figures for the 1999 general elections are taken from Fealy (2001).

14 For a comprehensive review of what the 1999 election results mean for political Islamism in Indonesia, refer to Fealy (2001).

15 The Transparency International *Corruption Perception Index 2002* on the 102 nations for which reliable data is available place Indonesia (96th out of 102) at the very bottom of the table, just above the worst placed Bangladesh (102nd), Nigeria, Paraguay, Madagascar, Angola and Kenya, and well below the Philippines (78th), Pakistan (77th), Russia (74th), India (73rd) and Thailand (64th). The report can be found at: www.transparency.org/cpi/2002/bpi2002.en.html. For an incisive examination of the state of Indonesia's legal system, refer to Lindsey (2000).

16 Another area where the debilitating effects of this sort of censorship by force are clearly visible is in Indonesia's desultory AIDS awareness campaign, where a recent series of government-sanctioned television advertisements were pulled from the air after complaints from the Indonesian Mujahidin Council (Aglionby 2002).

Chapter 4
Maritime security in Southeast Asia

Craig Snyder

Maritime security in Southeast Asia in general, and the South China Sea in particular, is an issue that has taken on increased importance as a result of the convergence of three main factors. The first is the added importance of maritime resources and Exclusive Economic Zones as a result of the Third United Nation's Convention on the Law of the Sea (UNCLOS). The second factor is the changing nature of the security environment in the region as a result of the end of the Cold War and the fear created by a perceived decline in the US Navy's presence in the region. Finally, maritime security issues have gained in importance as the role of maritime forces moves from support for the domestic regime to protecting the state from external threats and non-traditional threats such as piracy, drugs and illegal migration. These factors have converged over the territorial disputes in the South China Sea.

The South China Sea contains three main areas of contested territory, the Spratly Islands, the Paracel Islands and Scarborough Shoal. These territorial disputes have been the spark for a modernisation and expansion program of the region's maritime forces (naval and air assets) that were only checked by the Asian Financial Crisis. While the financial crisis had significant impact on the arms modernisation programs of many of the states in Southeast Asia this has, with the exception of Indonesia, merely resulted in a delay rather than a cancellation of the modernisation programs.

The South China Sea is a particularly sensitive issue due to the widely held perception among the coastal states that in addition to the known presence of important fisheries resources, the area under dispute also boasts considerable sea bed resources, most especially hydrocarbons. The South China Sea represents a strategic waterway of global significance, providing the key maritime link between the Indian Ocean and East Asia. Furthermore, the nationalism which underlies the sovereignty claims should not be forgotten. The seemingly intractable nature of these complex jurisdictional disputes has, over the years, led coastal states to place increasing emphasis on their ability to enforce their sovereignty claims militarily. The Sino-Vietnamese clash over the Paracels in 1974 and the bloody engagement between the same foes in the Spratlys in 1988, illustrate that parties to the dispute have not been afraid to use military force to assert their respective claims. One of the problems in attaining a resolution of the territorial disputes is the fact that there is no agreement amongst the claimants in terms of a legitimate basis for a claim. China, Taiwan and Vietnam all base their claim on historic rights of sovereignty. The Philippines bases its claim on the grounds of discovery and proximity, while Malaysia and Brunei claim only those features that are within their Exclusive Economic Zones.[1]

Changes in ocean governance

One of the key factors behind the increased need for maritime military capabilities has been the changes in ocean governance legislation that gives coastal states greater sovereignty over their coastal and adjoining waters. Historically, the law of the sea has been based on two key principles. The first is the concept of state sovereignty over a territorial sea based on the concept of the 'cannon-shot' rule (that is, a state retains sovereignty over coastal areas to the range of how far its cannons could shoot a cannon ball). The second is the principle of the freedom of navigation that acknowledges the non-sovereign nature of the 'high seas' and recognises the rights of all states to access maritime resources and conduct unhindered seaborne trade (Pratt 2000:1).

Contemporary debate over the need to codify rules and regulations with regard to maritime rights and obligations commenced in 1945 following two proclamations by the US that directly challenged the historic, free access to the seas. The first proclamation claimed US ownership of the 'natural resources of the subsoil and sea bed of the Continental Shelf beneath the high seas but contiguous to the coasts of the United States' (Pratt 2000:2). The second claimed the right to 'designate fisheries conservation zones in the high seas beyond the US claimed territorial sea' (Pratt 2000:2). These proclamations claimed sovereign rights far beyond the historically established territorial seas and, unsurprisingly, other concerned coastal states soon followed suit by citing similar claims. Increasing concern with the growing tide of creeping coastal state jurisdictions led to the United Nations convening the First Conference on the Law of the Sea in Geneva in 1958. This conference led to the agreement of four Conventions relating to the determination of maritime zones and fishing and conservation on the high seas (Pratt 2000:2).

However, it was not until 24 years later at the Third UNCLOS in 1982 that agreement was finally reached on all extant matters and the Convention signed. UNCLOS subsequently came into force on 16 November 1994. The Convention provides a comprehensive legal regime covering the world's oceans and resources, including maritime zones, economic and commercial activities, scientific research, technology, environmental management and the settlement of disputes. It establishes a balance of state rights and obligations and attempts to prevent, or at least manage, conflict between competing interests. Although the Convention is not binding on non-signatory states much of it is now considered customary international law. Noting the number of national interests involved, UNCLOS is invariably a compromise agreement and this has led to some criticism of the Convention for being non-definitive and open to interpretation (see Environment Australia 1997, part 6:3; Pratt 2000:3).

UNCLOS establishes a comprehensive framework for the regulation of all ocean space and grants coastal states sovereign rights and obligations with respect to the marine and sea bed resources adjacent to their coasts. It introduces a tiered series of maritime zones over which coastal states may exercise varying degrees of sovereignty or jurisdiction. These include, internal waters or those that are contained within the defined land territory of the state. State sovereignty is paramount within these waters and UNCLOS does not apply. Beyond the coastline all states can claim a 12 nautical mile territorial sea. A state's sovereignty over its territorial sea, including the air space over and the sea bed and subsoil, has all the attributes of its sovereignty over its land territory with the sole limitation that foreign ships enjoy the right of 'innocent passage'. A further 12 nautical mile contiguous zone can also be claimed which acts as a buffer zone within which a coastal state has the right to exercise jurisdiction over matters such as customs, fiscal, immigration and pollution control (Tsamenyi & Herriman 1996:6).

An Exclusive Economic Zone (EEZ) may be claimed to a maximum distance of 200 nautical miles and within this region the coastal state may, in the exercise of its sovereign rights, take such measures as may be necessary to ensure compliance with laws and regulations, including 'hot pursuit', boarding, inspection, arrest and prosecution. Within the EEZ coastal states have sovereign rights for the purpose of exploring, exploiting and managing the natural resources in the water column, the sea bed and subsoil. They also have the rights to undertake scientific research and construct artificial structures within their claimed EEZ. These entitlements are qualified in that the freedom of navigation and over-flight remains and other states retain the right to lay submarine cables. The rights are accompanied by specific coastal state obligations to take measures, to protect the marine environment, to control sea traffic, to provide charts and maps, to ensure safe navigation, to enforce safety regulations and to provide search and rescue services (Pratt 2000:1–7). The concept of the EEZ is now generally regarded as 'a major innovation and a cornerstone of the Convention' (Tsamenyi and Herriman 1996:2).

The high seas are that part of the oceans that are outside the jurisdiction of any state, that is, beyond any claimed territorial waters or EEZ. On the high seas, all vessels have the right of unrestricted navigation or overflight and the freedom to capture marine living resources and conduct scientific research. UNCLOS directs that the 'high seas shall be reserved for peaceful purposes' and that 'no State may validly purport to subject any part of the high seas to its sovereignty' (Pratt 2000:7). International law is not static however. It is at times cumbersome, complex and seemingly impenetrable, yet it is a key driver of two powerful forces for security: legitimacy and jurisdictional boundary clarity. Sometimes the scope of international law and legal instruments changes markedly. Future developments in legislative regimes are important drivers and shapers of future security in the region. The extent to which states and non-state actors abide by these requirements or buy out or not comply, shapes the resource security threat. If the regional powers' enforcement capability is weak, then challenges to the legitimacy of their sovereignty and economic claims in these areas can be made.

Role of maritime forces in Southeast Asia

Maritime forces by their very nature have great utility and can operate in areas ranging from open oceans, over the continental shelves, archipelagos and into shoreline areas and estuaries. Maritime forces exercise naval power by the influencing or controlling of behaviour in the maritime environment; guaranteeing use of the sea and providing flexible power projection capability (Sherwood 1999:129). The adaptability and utility of maritime forces provides governments with a wide range of options to deal with conventional and non-military threats. Ken Booth (1977:15–25) argues that the roles of maritime forces fall into three categories, or a trinity of roles: military, diplomatic and policing. The military role has traditionally formed the base of the trinity, especially for Western states, because the nature of navies is their conventional military character. The diplomatic role is concerned with the attainment of political aims, and the policing role is concerned with the protection of offshore resources. Importantly, the ability of maritime forces to undertake diplomatic and policing or constabulary operations is built upon their ability to carry out their military roles. The capability to carry out these peacetime tasks is thus largely a by-product of the resources and core skills developed for war fighting although the capability match is not always easy or efficient (Sherwood 2000:26–31).

The capacity of maritime forces throughout Southeast Asia is small to medium, as is their number of ships and aircraft. The main task of maritime forces has generally not been the traditional military role of the defence of the state against external attack, although that capability has always been a consideration in force development. Rather, the main task of maritime forces has been and continues to be 'asserting sovereignty and security maritime resources, very often in disputed maritime zones' (Joon 2002:42). The role of these forces is primarily focused on the policing role of protecting resources in their exclusive economic zones and in dealing with low-level, non-traditional threats such as piracy, drug and other smuggling, and since 11 September 2001, terrorism. As a result, maritime forces in many of these countries serve more of a constabulary role than a war fighting role. In addition, the geographic realities of Southeast Asia dictate that most states in the area need relatively large forces for these constabulary roles. The large coastlines, internal archipelagic waters and EEZs require a large number of small coastal patrol vessels rather than a small number of major combatants, such as frigates or destroyers. The smaller states in the region, such as Singapore, and to a lesser extent Brunei, do not have large territorial waters and can concentrate on more forward defence force structures, but are constrained in their naval operations as a result of the proximity of their neighbours and therefore do not need to develop forces beyond brown or green water capacity (Joon 2002:43–5; IISS 2002).

This constabulary role is beginning to expand as states in Southeast Asia begin to recover from the Asian Financial Crisis and re-cast their strategic gaze on the territorial disputes with each other and progress with their military procurement in general, but air and naval procurement in particular. The rationale for this force structure and roles and responsibility can be seen in the political history of many of these states. Following independence many of the regimes struggled over issues of political legitimacy and viewed internal security threats to the regime as the most important. The army, which in many states had a critical role in the independence struggle, has tended to play an active role in the domestic politics of the state and in many cases is used by the governing regime to combat the internal threats to the regime's authority. As a result, the army in many of these states maintains a predominant position in relation to the other services. In contrast, those states with strong regime legitimacy, as demonstrated through liberal political structures and processes, are able to focus their strategic policies on external threats and can therefore pursue a more balanced force structure (Heginbotham 2002:86–125).[2]

The role of many of the Southeast Asian state's naval forces is to protect the national interests, territorial integrity, national sovereignty and to ensure the security of their nationals and property in times of war. The peacetime duties of these forces focus on training for war, protection of the state's citizens and their property, supporting the state's foreign policy and support of the air and land forces. Many of the naval forces are also involved in hydrographic surveys, assisting civilian agencies in times of emergencies, law enforcement and search and rescue and EEZ law enforcement. During the Cold War these maritime forces were equipped primarily with coastal patrol vessels armed with small calibre guns and limited maritime air-patrol capabilities. Since the end of the Cold War many have purchased modern patrol craft armed with anti-ship missiles, have increased their minewarfare and anti-submarine warfare capabilities, as well as extending their maritime air-patrol capabilities and purchasing advanced fighter aircraft for maritime strike capabilities (Joon 2002:56).

China's military capability

For the People's Liberation Army (PLA) in general and the PLA Navy (PLA-N) in particular, the South China Sea disputes proved an excellent basis on which to justify the need for modernisation of China's maritime forces. Focusing on the South China Sea rather than other alternatives had several positive elements to it. The risks and benefits on the political, economic and military level were minimal compared with other disputes with Japan, such as over the Sengakus. While the South China Sea represented the threat of foreign encroachment on Chinese territory, the threat was from small, Southeast Asian states that the PLA-N felt it could easily handle. The distance from the mainland and the 'dangerous ground' of the Spratlys meant that the naval forces would need to be of a modern, technically proficient, combat-ready, long distance navy skilled in joint operations. On the non-military front, China's political and economic ties with the other claimant countries were not as strong as those with Japan and the economic returns offered by the South China Sea could be substantial and immediate (Garver 1992:1021–22; You 1995:380).

In the 1980s the PLA leaders began to recognise that future international conflict would be of a limited nature with threats to the Chinese periphery rather than the heartland. In these conflicts victory would be dependent on high-technology weapons, electronic warfare, highly motivated and well-trained troops, ground, air and sea mobility and the ability to inflict maximum damage while not being bogged down in a protracted engagement (Shambaugh 1994:53). In 1985, the PLA-N began to identify the need to shift from a coastal defence role to offshore defence. This strategy had a dual task of supporting and protecting economic and developmental projects in the waters surrounding the mainland. In light of this strategy it was decided that the PLA-N would require a nuclear submarine capability, a mobile force capable of responding to a variety of incidents in ocean conditions, and fortified positions for the basing of troops from which combat operations could be mounted. The adoption of the offshore defence strategy had important implications for the South China Sea as well as the areas around Taiwan, as the Paracels and the Spratlys were now included in the area of operations. The new strategy also required the development of new equipment, such as surface and sub-surface combatants and aircraft capable of operating farther from the Chinese coastal areas (Wen-Chung 1995:5–8).

There is, however, some disagreement among Chinese defence analysts, as to the rationale for the changing force structure or strategic revision of the role of the PLA-N. Some believe the new strategy was only an 'update' rather than a complete revision of the strategy of the past. Others argue that the Central Military Commission (CMC) of the Chinese Communist Party's Central Committee recognised the reduced threat of the Soviet Union and that the restructuring was merely the PLA shifting to a peacetime footing. A third group argues that under the CMC's 1985 directive the PLA has been given a new task to prepare to fight small-scale limited wars around China's periphery.[3]

In 1986, the then assistant commander-in-chief of the PLA-N, Zhang Xusan, argued at an all-services seminar on campaign doctrine, that as naval operations are usually conducted far away from home bases it is important for the navy to have the capability to be able to detect and interdict an enemy invasion fleet quickly. It would therefore be necessary to concentrate on the development of highly mobile forces of high combat effectiveness in order to engage the enemy at the earliest possible time. In addition, it would be necessary for the navy to become familiar with the waters out to the 'first island chain'.[4] Over the next few years the senior Chinese PLA-N officers advocated that due to the increased threats emanating from the sea and in order to safeguard the waters inside the first islands chain, the navy would need to be modernised. This modernisation would focus on expanding the number of ships capable of combat missions at sea, including warships, submarines and mine sweepers. The PLA-N would also concentrate on developing advanced weapons systems with electronic command and control mechanisms (Wen-Chung Liao 1995:9–10).

In 1992, the Chinese President, Jiang Zemen, in a report to the 14th National People's Congress announced that the role of the PLA would be to 'ensure national unification, safeguard territorial integrity, and protect maritime rights and interests (Jiang Zemen, quoted in Wen-Chung Liao 1995:11). With this, the PLA-N would be responsible for establishing a three-ring combat strategy. In the inner ring, within 150 nautical miles of the mainland, the navy would deploy a variety of small, coastal defence vessels to protect this area. In the centre ring, between 150 nautical miles and 300 nautical miles larger vessels, such as the new multi-role frigates would be used to engage and destroy an enemy fleet. In the outer ring, beyond 300 nautical miles (from the Korean Strait to the north, Okinawa to the east and the Spratly Islands to the south), the navy would rely upon submarines and aircraft, such as the B-6 bombers and advanced fighters operating from the mainland (Wen-Chung Liao 1995:13–14). Coupled with this new role the PLA-N published a report that year calling on a readjustment to naval strategy to ensure protection of Chinese oil and gas exploration and production efforts in the South China Sea. To do this the PLA-N deputy commander-in-chief, General Zhang Xusan, told the Xinhua News Agency that China would need to develop more advanced weaponry (*NST* 1992).

You Ji argues that by 1991, the PLA started to shift its focus from using the Spratlys to justify larger naval budgets to expressing concern over the generally poor state of the navy. The PLA leadership implied that should their requests for a strong navy be addressed they might change their tactics in the Spratlys. This is an important element as it impacted on how a potential resolution to the disputes could be reached. If the PLA focused on a general modernisation program rather than on regaining Chinese territory, this might be easier to deal with in a peaceful manner (You 1995:391–2). In April 1992, General Zhang Xusan, the deputy commander-in-chief of the PLA-N, was reported by the *China Daily* as stating that China planned to develop more advanced weaponry for the navy in order to allow it to protect Chinese claims in the South China Sea. That same month, Vice-Admiral Zhang Lianzhong, commander of the PLA-N, reported that the Central Military Commission had ordered the Chinese Navy to improve its combat readiness in order to protect Chinese waters (Yeong 1992).

Limitations on Chinese power

The continuing uncertainty regarding Chinese intentions over the South China Sea is a driving factor feeding an increasing fear of Chinese actions. But what can the Chinese military actually do in the region? In the 1990s, the PLA Air Force (PLA-AF) began to update its largely obsolete fleet of combat aircraft. The rapprochement between China and Russia in the 1990s provided China with an opportunity to circumvent the US military technology sanctions imposed on China after the Tiananmen Square massacre. In recent years, the PLA-AF has procured 50 Su-27SK and 20 Su-27UBK fighter aircraft from Russia and arranged to build a further 150 under licence. China has also taken delivery of 38 advanced SU-30MKK fighter aircraft with some 78 on order (SIPRI 2002:420–1; Novichkov 2002). The PLA-AF have modified some 30 H-6 bombers to hold Exocet-type C-601 anti-ship missiles and up to 130 torpedo-equipped H-5 light bombers. China is also buying Airborne Early Warning and Control (AEW&C) technology from Israeli, Russian and British sources. However, in comparison with the size of the PLA-AF, these numbers represent the modernisation of a relatively small proportion of the force, and the pilots allocated to these modern 'fourth generation' fighter aircraft fly insufficient hours annually to gain proficiency in all air combat roles.[5] Additionally, China is reliant on Russia for the manufacture and deeper maintenance of some key aircraft systems, such as the high performance jet engines used in the latest generation fighter aircraft (Nemets & Torda 2002a). Thus, the operational significance of China's efforts to date to re-equip its air force must be considered debatable at best.

China's naval force is also in the process of modernisation focused on deploying vessels that have greater range, last longer and carry more lethal weapons systems than the current PLA-N's largely obsolete coastal defence force (Carpenter & Weincek 1999). Issues of training and maintenance will determine whether the naval component of China's power projection capability is fully realised. Over the past ten years the PLA-N has purchased or ordered a total of four *Sovremenny* class guided-missile destroyers armed with anti-ship cruise missiles, one *Luhai* class guided-missile destroyer, three *Luhu* class guided-missile destroyers and 12 *Jiangwei* class guided-missile frigates. These new warships are equipped with the HQ-61 or HQ-7 short-range air defence systems that will probably be replaced by a longer-range vertical-launch system within the next three to five years. They also have integrated tactical data systems, an improved antisubmarine warfare suite that includes embarked helicopters and diesel or gas turbine propulsion. China is also producing a new type of guided-missile Destroyer with fleet-air defence capabilities, reportedly designated as type 052B, which is currently under construction in Shanghai. The PLA-N has also purchased four *Kilo* class diesel attack submarines (two type EKM877 and two type EKM636) and has ordered an additional eight of the more advanced type EKM636 for delivery in 2007 (IISS 2002:146–7; SIPRI 2002:420–1; Nemets & Torda 2002b).

Constraints on Chinese power projection capabilities

The Chinese forces are technologically underdeveloped, and the majority of their warships possess no effective air defence; nor can they monitor attacking aircraft approaching from over the horizon. Only the *Sovremenny*, *Luhai* and *Luhu* ships can be considered effective, modern fighting ships and even these must be logistical and maintenance nightmares as many are equipped with French missiles, Italian torpedoes and American engines (Downing 1996:186; Wortzel 1994:164). While the radar systems on these ships allow for detection of airborne contacts out to 100 nautical miles the ship-to-air missiles have a range of only seven nautical miles. This would also limit the PLA-N's ability to defend against aircraft armed with the 100 nautical mile range Exocet and Harpoon anti-ship missiles (Gallager 1994:178–9; Chang 1996:365). The PLA-N submarine fleet, while currently being upgraded with the purchase of the Russian *Kilo* class submarines, is severely limited in its effectiveness as most of the fleet is not seaworthy, and those that can put to sea can only remain submerged for very short periods of time. Even the *Kilo* submarines are proving to be problematic for China as there are reports of major battery failure on the two older EKM877 types (You 1995:286).

In a 1995 article, the Hong Kong Chinese language newspaper, *Kuang Chiao Ching*, described a potential assault task-force that the PLA-N could assemble for an assault on the Spratlys. This would include one *Luhu* class destroyer, six *Luda* class destroyers, two frigates, 30 missile patrol boats, ten landing ships, ten minelayers and 18 submarines. In addition, the task force would comprise between 30 and 50 support ships and two or three battalions of marines. The task force would be supported by strike and fighter aircraft from the PLA Air Force and the naval air wing. The strike aircraft would include the H-6 bomber, armed with C-601 anti-ship cruise missiles and the new H-7 all-weather bomber, armed with C-801 sea-skimming anti-ship missiles. The 24 PLA-AF Su-27s and the J-7 and J-8 fighters would provide air cover for bombers and the fleet (Blanche 1996:189).

Even today the likelihood of such a force being assembled or effective is highly doubtful. While a similar task force could be extended to include the newer, guided-missile frigates and Su-30s, the PLA-N lacks any long-range amphibious capability and almost no effective logistical or support infrastructure to supply their forces over long distances for a protracted period of time. The Chinese only possess three tankers with replenishment at sea capabilities, which would limit the size of any task force operating far from Chinese supply bases to about 18 to 24 ships (IISS 2002:147; Wortzel 1994:167).

The PLA-N surface fleet has only a limited capability to protect itself from air attack, so it would require the naval air wing and PLA-AF aircraft to commit a great deal of its efforts to providing a combat air patrol over the fleet. The Chinese currently do not have the long-range aircraft, in-flight refuelling and airborne early warning capabilities that would be required for such a task (Fulghum 1995:26). In addition, the PLA-AF and naval air wing do not possess many all-weather fighter aircraft and only the Sukhois have the range to cover the Spratlys. The Chinese aircraft are primarily copies of older Soviet aircraft designed in the 1960s. The Chinese are trying to make modifications to the Q-5 fighter and the J-7—a copy of the Russian MiG-21—but analysis of their performance suggests they do not have the range to operate effectively over the Spratlys.[6] The PLA-N and PLA-AF have also deployed approximately 100 J-8 high-altitude interceptors that were domestically produced but are equipped with radar, fire-control and navigation systems designed by the American Grumann Aircraft Corporation and 600 Q-5 attack fighters equipped with Italian technology (Ding 1995:4–5; IISS 2002:145–8).

The limited number of Sukhois in the Chinese inventory would not guarantee them control of the sky over the South China Sea, however. Even with the latest agreement to purchase additional aircraft this does not give the Chinese enough aircraft to continuously control the skies over the Spratlys. The Sukhois have an effective combat radius of 1,400 kilometres and as the nearest Chinese airbase, on Woody Island in the Paracels, is approximately 1,000 kilometres from the main group of the Spratlys, the fighters would have very little time to patrol any potential combat area. In addition, the Sukhois are part of the PLA-AF not the naval air wing. As such, they are not equipped for naval operations; neither are the pilots trained for operations over water or to provide tactical support for naval units, which would severely restrict their effectiveness over the Spratlys (IDR 1994:10; Chang 1996:363–4). The Chinese bomber force is also limited in its combat radius as the H-6 has an effective range of just over 1,600 kilometres (Wortzel 1994:169) so while the planes can reach the Spratlys they would have only a limited amount of time to search for mobile targets, such as warships. While some reports suggest that the PLA-AF has recently modified some of its H-6 transport planes into aerial refuellers the limited size of these aircraft would only provide the Sukhois with a limited extension of their combat radius, especially in time of war when the tankers would be targets for enemy fighters. Moreover, aerial refuelling is a complex task requiring the tanker and fighters to rendezvous at specific co-ordinates, altitude, speed and direction. As the Sukhois do not train over water the pilots do not have the necessary skills to navigate effectively over such a large and featureless environment (You 1995:386; Chang 1996:361).

There have also been conflicting reports as to where the Chinese are planning to deploy the Sukhois and the *Kilo* submarines. The *Kilos* are likely to be spread among all naval commands. The Sukhois seem to have numerous deployments, as articles on the South China Sea refer to their deployment to airbases on Woody Island, while articles on China–Taiwan relations suggest their deployment to airbases near the Taiwan Strait. Indeed, during the recent military combined arms exercises that the Chinese conducted in the Taiwan Strait in the run up to the presidential election in Taiwan, numerous articles and pundits focused on the role of the Su-27s in these exercises. While air assets such as the Sukhois are highly mobile and can conceivably be deployed in each of these theatres, the ground crews and support equipment are not as mobile and would limit the Sukhoi's effectiveness in short-term conflicts, especially those initiated by other claimants or in accidental clashes. Indeed, the supply of spare parts for the new aircraft will be a major problem for the Chinese, at least until they develop the production facilities they purchased from the Russians in December 1995. Even then, the components of Russian built aircraft are not all interchangeable. The rivets in each aircraft, for example, are hand-drilled and as such, are not always in the same place. Thus, when a part is removed the aircraft does not fly until the part is replaced. In light of this problem the Chinese stockpile a one-year supply of spare parts for each aircraft at their airbases, which also severely limits their ability to re-deploy in times of crisis. The most probable, permanent deployment for the Sukhois is at the airbase in Wuhu in Anhui province where they underwent their initial training. This is where the PLA-AF has its best safety record and where it traditionally bases its most advanced fighters (Chang 1996:362–3).

China might have a large quantity of military equipment but its lacks quality, especially in aircraft and submarines. Moreover, the Chinese forces are orientated for defence and have little capability to fight overseas (Klintworth 1994/95:221). The Chinese have not yet developed the capabilities for a 'blue water' navy and it will take them ten to 15 years to do so. Given the current state of Chinese equipment and training the Chinese have no capability to pursue an expansionist maritime policy (Gallager 1994:193). There are reports from Western military officials that the Chinese are having difficulty in maintaining the new Sukhoi aircraft which is causing delays in the training program the pilots are undertaking on these fighters (Tyler 1996). Added to these problems is the general lack of flight training the Chinese are able to offer their pilots. The Chinese are attempting to address the training problem by increasing the amount of combined military exercises. Since the late 1980s the Chinese have increasingly included army, air force, naval and rapid reaction forces in their military exercises. While initial exercises were designed to respond to an invasion of the Chinese mainland, in recent years they have included training in the rapid deployment of troops by air and sea, including exercise '934' in 1993, which involved airborne and seaborne landing operations (Tyler 1995).

In 1995, Admiral Liu Huaqing, the head of the PLA, acknowledged the out-dated and near obsolescence of the PLA but stated that the Chinese do not have the economic resources to fully modernise its military force in the foreseeable future (Tyler 1995). The much speculated Chinese aircraft carrier is unlikely to be developed over the short-term as China possesses neither the technology nor the resources to build or buy one (Tyler 1995; Barber 1995). While China has long aspired to an aircraft carrier capability, there are currently no plans and even tentative proposals to introduce such a capability. China would require at least two or three carriers to maintain a single carrier on operations at any one time, the others being in refit, transit or replenishment. The cost of procuring a carrier task force of this size is significant, and China is unlikely to have sufficient defence funding in the foreseeable future. In addition, the technology necessary to develop a carrier battle group is not readily available to China. Even a modest Vertical/Short Take-Off and Landing (VSTOL) carrier would be expensive and problematic to deploy within the next 20 years, especially given the difficulty in obtaining VSTOL technology aircraft (Storey and Jou Ji 2002:36–9).

Questions about the ability of the Chinese to operate the new weapons and weapon systems they are able to purchase or acquire are due to the fact that they are buying a wide variety of off-the-shelf, high technology systems from several different suppliers. The technological leap that these systems represent for the Chinese maintenance crews and the mix of suppliers—Russian, French and American—will severely limit the ability of the Chinese to properly maintain all systems. Indeed, as mentioned above, the PLA-AF ground crews have had serious problems in maintaining the new Suhkois for flight training operations. The need for effective ground crews and general maintenance programs was demonstrated in the 1982 Falkland Islands War, when the Argentine ground crews were able to maintain the older but less effective American built A-4 fighter aircraft, but had difficulty in maintaining the newer and more advanced French-built Mirage fighters. In addition, the Argentine Navy's aircraft carrier, the *Vienticino de Mayo*, had to be kept in port because of machine failure which the Argentineans could not repair in time. Meanwhile, the British operating far from their home bases were able to send their Harrier fighter aircraft on six sorties per day at which time they were grounded due to pilot fatigue rather than mechanical breakdown (Snyder 1989). The 1991 Gulf War, however, demonstrated the need for advanced weapons systems as the Iraqi Air Force, which ranked as sixth largest in the world prior to the conflict, was defeated in short order by a technologically superior opponent (Walters 1992).

Vietnamese military capability

China's military power is restricted due to the distance its forces would have to travel to get to the Spratlys. Such restrictions, however, do not apply to the military options of other claimants. Vietnam does not possess a large naval force but the Spratlys are within range of the 12 Su-27SK fighters it has recently purchased from Russia, as well as some 120 MiG-21s and 50 Su-22s in the Vietnamese Air Force.[7] While the majority of the Vietnamese fighters are no match for the Chinese Sukhois, the Vietnamese can deploy a far greater number of fighter and attack aircraft over a potential combat area. Moreover, the Argentinean Air Force demonstrated the continued effectiveness of older aircraft in dropping gravity bombs on warships during the Falklands–Malvinas conflict.[8]

The Vietnamese Navy is very small and possesses almost no combat capability beyond its coastal waters as none of its seven frigates are combat worthy. It does have over 50 missile and coastal patrol craft and torpedo boats including Russian-built HO-A (type 124-A) corvettes equipped with anti-ship missiles. The only ships capable of operating in the farther portions of the South China Sea, however, are the new corvettes, eight *Osa-II* missile craft and 19 torpedo boats. In any clash with the PLA-N these ships would be severely out-classed and out-gunned (Cloughley 1995:22). Vietnam does have an amphibious assault capability, notably through three ex-Soviet *Polnochnyu* class medium landing ships and almost 30 smaller landing craft of limited seaworthiness. Vietnam also has a naval infantry force comprising roughly 27,000 troops (Lok 1992:19; IISS 2002:167–8)).

Malaysian military capability

Malaysia has focused its maritime capabilities on a limited number of surface combatants, such as its two *Lekiu* (*Yarrow*) guided-missile frigates, *Laksmana* (*Assad*) guided-missile Corvettes equipped with Exocet ship-to-ship missiles, and has stationed them for patrol of the South China Sea, as well as the purchase of two 'New Generation Patrol Vessels' from Germany (MEKO-A100 type Frigates) but primarily through the purchase of advanced fighter aircraft and anti-submarine warfare helicopters. In 1993 Malaysia ordered MIG-29 fighters for air-to-air combat and F/A-18 fighters as dedicated attack aircraft. In 1999 Malaysia also ordered six Super Lynx anti-submarine warfare helicopters (IISS 2002:156–7; SIPRI 1994; Joon 2002:58–9).

Malaysia also has a maritime aerial surveillance capability through its recent purchase of four Beechcraft B200Ts, which have a range of 3,200 kilometres, allowing the Malaysians to patrol a large portion of the South China Sea. While the small number of these aircraft limits the effectiveness of the patrols on a daily basis, in times of crisis the effectiveness can be increased by focusing patrols on the disputed areas of the South China Sea. Surveillance of the South China Sea is also conducted by the Royal Australian Air Force (RAAF) which operates two P-3C Orion maritime patrol aircraft from the Butterworth air base on the Malayan Peninsula. The RAAF also regularly operates a squadron of its F/A-18 fighters from the Butterworth air base during FPDA exercises.

The Malaysian Air Force pilots' skills are adequate, and benefit from training the pilots receive through the Five Power Defence Arrangement exercises. Many analysts are, however, concerned that the Malaysians are going to experience great difficulty in integrating the two radically different fighters and their support and maintenance programs into the air force. It is speculated that the Malaysians will deploy the MiGs in the Malayan Peninsula and use them for defence of western Malaysia, while the F/A-18s will be deployed in eastern Malaysia and will be used to defend Sabah and Sarawak and be available to protect Malaysian interests in the South China Sea. The F/A-18s will be equipped with air-to-air missiles and Harpoon anti-ship missiles. They have a combat radius of between 540 to 800 kilometres depending on their configuration. Malaysia also has 25 *Hawk* trainers equipped with an anti-shipping attack capability and have a combat range of 1,234 kilometres (Hassan 1993; Lambert 1993:338; Taylor & Munson 1995; Cloughley 1995:22). These will allow the Malaysian Air Force either a significant amount of time to patrol their claim area, which extends only 350 kilometres offshore, or the ability to strike at potential enemy forces before they threaten Malaysian interests.

Malaysia has also recently announced that it is purchasing two *Scorpene* submarines from the French and Italian manufacturers DCN International and Izar. Malaysia has expressed interest in acquiring submarines since 1988 when it was offered two upgraded ex-Royal Navy *Oberon* and *Porpoise* class submarines as part of an arms package it had signed with Britain, and in 1991 Malaysia contemplated the procurement of two Swedish submarines (JNI 2002; Joon p 58). The Malaysian maritime force projection capabilities are hampered by a lack of funding to the Royal Malaysian Navy (RMN) as well as its dual role of war fighting and resource protection. While the RMN desires greater Sea Lane of Communication (SLOC) protection capabilities its resource protection functions have dictated the purchase of a larger number of smaller surface ships. While these surface ships are armed with anti-ship and anti-air missiles, they maintain a limited anti-submarine capability that hampers their ability to project power outside the range of the land-based strike fighter combat range.

Taiwanese military capability

Taiwan's power projection capability is severely limited due to its primary concern of defence against invasion from the communist mainland. The

Taiwanese Air Force is relatively large and has recently upgraded its fighter squadrons with modern F-16, *Ching Kuo* and Mirage 2000-5 fighters. But Taiwan does not possess any in-air refuelling capabilities, so these modern fighters would be of limited use over the Spratlys. The Republic's naval forces are, however, capable of operating farther from shore. Taiwan has a relatively modern naval force equipped with American, Israeli and domestically produced ships and weapon systems. The fleet is designed more to combat Chinese submarines and warships close to home and to support an invasion of the mainland than to protect distant outposts. The Chinese navy has deployed one combat support vessel capable of replenishment at sea allowing the Taiwanese naval forces to operate farther from home (IISS1995:192–3). The navy is also familiar with the South China Sea because Taiwanese ships regularly sail through the waters in order to conduct port visits in Singapore and the Philippines. The force responsible for patrolling the South China Sea is not the navy, however, but the coastal police force equipped with lightly armed patrol vessels.

Philippines military capability

The Philippines does not possess any real capability to fight in the disputed area. In the past, the government of the Philippines has not committed large amounts of resources to defend its claims to sovereignty over the Islands. Instead it relied on its Mutual Defence Treaty (MDT) with the United States to protect Filipino interests in the area. While the MDT does not specifically cover the Spratlys, the Filipino decision-makers relied upon the unwillingness of any rival to risk a potential clash with the US should it attack Filipino positions in the Spratlys. With the withdrawal of the US Navy and Air Force from their bases in the Philippines in the 1990s, there was a great concern that the level of American interest in the South China Sea had also diminished, and with it much of the Philippines' ability to defend its sovereignty in the area. The Philippine Navy and Air Force are small and equipped with outdated equipment and weapon systems. The Philippine Air Force has less than 15 F-5 fighters. The navy has almost no ability to patrol the disputed area as its ships are all of Second World War vintage. In 1995 following the Chinese occupation of Mischief Reef, the Philippines Navy transported members of the international media to the vicinity of Mischief Reef, but the warship carrying these reporters broke down on the return voyage and had to be towed into port. The Philippines has only a limited maritime surveillance capability in one Fokker F-27M aircraft. Inshore surveillance is conducted by 34 search-and-rescue fixed-wing BN-2A and HU-16 aircraft and some 30 helicopters (Cloughley 1995:22).

Following the Chinese occupation of Mischief Reef the Philippines Parliament passed a law authorising the spending of 50 billion pesos (about US$2 billion) to upgrade the armed forces. The law calls for the development of the Navy's war fighting capabilities, including surface, amphibious, anti-air and anti-submarine warfare capabilities. In addition the Navy's sealift, transport and maritime surveillance capabilities are to be upgraded. The Air Force was also allotted funds to purchase surveillance aircraft as well as multi-purpose fighter/attack aircraft. The 50 billion pesos will not be enough to totally modernise the Philippine Navy and Air Force but the military leaders have indicated that initial funding will be focused on purchasing fast patrol craft, surveillance aircraft and modern fighter interceptors to protect the 200 nautical mile EEZ (AFP 1995; Carranza 1995). In December 1996, a second bill was passed in the Congress allotting a further 164.5 billion pesos (US$6.3 billion) to modernise the military in the ensuing 15 years. The Congress, in passing the bill, issued a statement that it hoped this would increase the capability of the Philippine armed forces to a level where it can effectively and fully perform its mandate to uphold the sovereignty and preserve the patrimony of the nation. To date not much has come from the arms modernisation bills as the need to fight the Abu Sayyaf Group in the south has drained much of the Defence spending in the Philippines (AFP 1996).

In 1994, the chief-of-staff of the Armed Forces of the Philippines, General Arturo Enrile, estimated that the military would need 370 billion pesos (US$14 billion) for a basic military modernisation program. This program would centre around the purchase of a squadron of interceptors and a radar system for the Air Force, gunboats armed with ship-to-ship missiles to patrol the Philippine EEZ for the Navy and improved communications and artillery for the Army (Ghosh 1994). The chief of the Air Force, Lieutenant General Nicasio Rodriguez, has echoed a similar warning that the Air Force will require 100 billion pesos itself to purchase new fighters and train its air and ground crews on these advanced fighters (Ghosh 1994).

In the short term, the Philippines has also tried to garner direct American support. The foreign secretary of the Philippines, Raul Manglapus, argued in a press conference following a meeting with the American Ambassador to the Philippines, Frank Wisner, that the Americans were obliged to defend the Philippines if it was attacked in the Spratly islands. He stated that the Mutual Defence Treaty provides that a Philippine ship is an extension of Philippine territory and...[therefore] the United States is obligated to defend our ships. The US rejects this stating that the treaty only covers the territorial limits of the Philippines as they existed when the treaty was signed. Moreover, the treaty does not bind the Americans to use military force to defend the Philippines in any case (RLR 1992; AFP 1996).

Brunei military capability

The Royal Brunei Armed Forces have begun to extend their role in the South China Sea from coastal enforcement to protection of their offshore oil platforms and economic zones. While the Brunei military possesses no fighter aircraft, it has three missile patrol craft equipped with Exocet ship-to-ship missiles. It has also ordered three *Yarrow* Class guided-missile frigates from Britain (IISS 2202:143–4).

Singapore military capability

Singapore, while not a claimant to the territorial disputes in the South China Sea, is included as it is perhaps the most advanced in Southeast Asia in developing a balanced force designed for the protection of its sea-lanes of communications (SLOC). To this end, it has purchased *Challenger* (*Sjoormen*) coastal submarines, *Victory* class corvettes armed with Harpoon anti-ship missiles, *Bedok* (*Landsort*) coastal mine hunters and advanced F-16 fighters. In 2000, Singapore also ordered six *La Fayette* class multipurpose Project Delta Stealth Frigates to be delivered in 2009. It has also adopted appropriate doctrinal approaches for a comprehensive maritime strategy incorporating surface, sub-surface and air components (Joon 2002:49–53; SIPRI 2002:162–3; JDW 2002).

Indonesian military capability

Although Indonesia is not directly involved in the Spratlys dispute, there is potential for maritime conflict with Beijing in the South China Sea. There has been some speculation that the Chinese 'Historic Waters' dashed line would overlap with the Indonesian continental shelf boundary, which was delimited between Malaysia and Indonesia in 1969 and which contains the large Natuna natural gas fields. Indeed, following the Chinese occupation of Mischief Reef Indonesia raised, with the Chinese authorities, a map made public by Chinese officials in which the nine dashed lines demarking Chinese 'historic waters' appeared to overlap the Indonesian 200 nautical mile EEZ off Natuna Island. In response to Indonesian protests the two foreign ministers met in Beijing in July 1995. Upon his return to Jakarta, Ali Alatas, the Indonesian foreign minister, reported on his conversations with the Chinese foreign minister, Qian Qichen, who reassured Alatas that while China had sovereignty over the

Spratlys and while the sea border line is not certain, China had no dispute with Indonesia. Alatas said that Qian had told him that China recognised Indonesian sovereignty over Natuna and that they recognised that Indonesia and China did not have any overlapping claims (RWS 1995; Sinaga 1995).

Indonesia, like the Philippines, however has not been able to adequately modernise its maritime forces. Indonesia was particularly hard hit by the Asian financial crisis and many of its procurement projects were postponed or cancelled outright. Its naval forces consist mainly of patrol and coastal ships, most of which are ships from the former East German navy. The Indonesian military has also been concentrating on the political implications of the *refomasi* process and on dealing with secessionist movements. As a result the army has maintained its position as the senior service and its share of defence procurement budgets.

Implications of the military balance in the South China Sea

The arms modernisation programs of the various rival claimants in the South China Sea have been seen by many analysts as evidence of a trend by Southeast Asian states to strengthen their military in an attempt to increase their security in an area made jittery by the apparent withdrawal of American commitments to the region and the presence of an expansionist neighbour. The ASEAN states are, however, merely attempting to secure a minimum level of control over their adjacent seas. While the above list of military hardware stockpiles and acquisitions seems impressive, the Southeast Asians suffer many similar problems in providing effective maintenance and logistical support as do the Chinese. Joon Num Mak argues that there is not a sufficient 'maintenance culture' developing in the ASEAN states to guarantee effective operation of these assets during times of crisis. As the most recent purchases have involved off-the-shelf, sophisticated, high-technology weapons and weapon systems, there is a great deal of uncertainty as to how these will be integrated into the existing military systems (Joon 1994:20).

None of the claimants are, therefore, likely to attempt a military occupation of the entire Spratly group. Any military conflict that does occur is likely to be restricted to sporadic, low intensity conflict. While this limited military capability has not prevented armed clashes in the past, the claimants have tended to act with some self-restraint. Each claimant has sought to demonstrate its sovereign control over the disputed areas and this, at times, has led to an increase in tensions. In 1974 and 1988 these tensions erupted into brief military conflicts. In 1974, China took advantage of the Vietnam War to forcibly evict the South Vietnamese troops occupying the Western Paracel Islands. In 1988,

China also took advantage of a UNESCO Oceanography Commission project to occupy several features in the Spratlys. This led to a brief naval battle between China and Vietnam in which two Vietnamese ships were sunk and over 70 sailors and marines killed (Milovojevi 1989:71; Holley 1988). These incidents are more the exception rather than the rule as the claimants have restricted their military deployments to unoccupied features in the Spratlys.

Given the level of uncertainty over the legality of any of the littoral states' claims to the disputed area and the intermixed pattern of occupation, crises will inevitably arise from time to time, as any demonstration of sovereignty exercised by one claimant will have a direct impact on the claim of the others. The Chinese occupation of Mischief Reef is probably best seen in this light and not as foreshadowing future Chinese military aggression in the Spratlys. In this incident the Chinese acted against a previously unoccupied reef. Given the weakness of the Philippines military the Chinese could have easily overwhelmed a Philippines garrison. Of course, this probably would have sparked a more militant response from the Philippines and the other claimants. What the Chinese occupation did spark was the Philippine Senate's approval for an arms modernisation law. Following the approval of the legislation, many international arms merchants descended on Manila to flog their goods, including representatives of the Chinese arms manufacturer, North Industries Corporation (Norinco), an enterprise controlled by the PLA. Norinco offered the Filipinos shipboard arms, missiles and an air defence system. The question that needs to be asked by those concerned with Chinese intentions in the Spratlys is, why are the Chinese willing to sell the Filipinos weapons if they expect a military confrontation with them?

The likelihood of military confrontation arising from any of these actions is limited as many do not represent a direct challenge to the other claimants' positions. The improvements to military garrisons or the development of civilian structures on many of the features do nothing to threaten the activity of the other claimants. Moreover, the claimants have tended to act with some self-restraint. While the Vietnamese and Chinese have been the most belligerent in their activities, especially with respect to oil exploration, they have recognised the danger of military confrontation and have looked to diplomacy to downplay the crises. In light of these activities the commonly held image of China as a regional bully bent on hegemonic domination of the region appears to be difficult to justify. While the Chinese have been active in pursuing their sovereignty claim, so have most of the others. With the sole exception of Brunei, all the claimants have deployed military troops to various features and have taken steps that not only increase their own claim to sovereignty over the Spratlys but *ipso facto*, impinge on the claims of the others.

Conclusion

The perceived threat from China is likely to spur the development of maritime capabilities of the regional states. How far this development will go and the implications of this on the role, composition, strategic concepts and strategic culture of the regional maritime forces in particular, and their armed forces in general, has been the focus of this chapter. Moreover, changes in ocean governance legislation has raised the importance of maritime resources and the increased maritime power projection capability of the various states may also result in creating greater tension among the Southeast Asian states who, until now, have been unable to conduct military operations far from their shorelines or for any sustained period. Since the end of the Cold War and the decline in the US naval presence in the region, coupled with an increase in the Chinese power projection capability, the perception by many in Southeast Asia is that there is a need to modernise and expand their own maritime forces to defend their maritime boundaries and to effectively administer and control their EEZ and territorial claims in the South China Sea.

Endnotes

1. For a survey of the various claims, see Snyder (1982), Shiying (1993); Heinzig (1976).
2. Eric Heginbotham argues that the political ideology of naval officers had a particular impact on the rise of navies in those countries where liberal political leaders held power as these leaders were not beholden to the more conservative army officers.
3. This debate is cited in Jun Zhan (1994:180).
4. The first island chain comprises Japan, Taiwan and the Philippines (see Wen-Chung Liao 1995).
5. Reports vary as to the amount of flying hours flown by Chinese fighter pilots, but the PLA-AF is quoted as indicating an average of 100 flying hours, compared with 180 to 200 for Western air forces. This was reported at Reuters, 'China's Arms Shopping Spree Alarms Washington',www.rense.com/general27/chnew.htm. The 'Annual Report on the Military Power of the PRC', 2000 Report to Congress, also indicates that PRC 'pilot proficiency is improving, but China's best pilots lag behind their Taiwan counterparts in terms of capabilities'. This report can be accessed at www.defenselink.mil/news/Jun2000/china06222000.htm.
6. The J-7 and J-8 fighters have combat ranges of less than 1,000 kilometres. While both can carry external fuel tanks that would extend their ranges, this would come at the cost of armaments and ordnance carried on these flights (see Lambert 1993:46, 56).
7. The MiG-21 and Su-22 have a combat radius of approximately 500 kilometres, which can be extended with external fuel tanks, while Vietnamese airbases are located approximately 400–500 kilometres from the main group of Spratly Islands (see Chang 1996:360; IISS 2002:168).
8. While the Argentinean Air Force was not successful in preventing a British landing on East Falkland Island, their pilots flying ageing A-4 attack fighters were able to score a large number of 'hits' to British warships. The Argentinean Naval Air Corps also demonstrated the effectiveness of air-launched missiles against naval forces not adequately protected by air cover. For a more detailed assessment of the air war in the Falklands, see Menaul (1982:84–85) and Snyder (1989:112–20).

Chapter 5
Instability in archipelagic Southeast Asia

Damien Kingsbury

Of the many conflicts that exist within archipelagic Southeast Asia, a number refer to divisions within existing states. These divisions include 'vertical' challenges to the state, that have the capacity to split the state into geographic divisions based on proto-nationalist identity, and 'horizontal' challenges to the state, defined by ethnic and communal rivalry and conflict. This chapter will canvass some of these issues. In doing so, it will address state formation in the region, 'national' identities, the role of *ethnie*[1] as a pre-existing challenge to the 'nation' and the development of communal rivalry. It will therefore consider the extent to which the archipelagic region is governable in a conventional, modernist sense, and the challenges the geography and ethnicity of the region present to notions of cohesion and security.

Divisions within the archipelago can be said to exist within particular states, notably violence between indigenous Dayaks and Madurese transmigrants in West and Central Kalimantan, and between religious groups (Christians and Muslims) in the southern Philippines, in Maluku (Moluccas) and in Central Sulawesi. There has also been racial violence against ethnic Chinese in Indonesia, notably in 1998, but with longer lasting consequences, especially to the economy, and between religious, regional and political groups in Java. All of this is set against a backdrop of continuing economic lethargy and state weakness in Indonesia and the Philippines.

Yet problems do not just exist in Indonesia or the Philippines. Malaysia's racial violence has been relatively quiet since the late 1960s, although there have been increasing clashes between ethnic Malays (about 50% of the population) and ethnic Chinese (about 35% of the population). Resentment towards peninsular Malays by the inhabitants of northern Borneo (Sarawak and Sabah) have also been noted, in particular by the indigenous 'Dayak' groups towards exploitation of natural resources, in particular the clear felling of tropical rainforests, without compensation.

Further to the east, the Philippines continues to be wracked by a corrupt and self-serving elite, a weak state and the reduction of the once powerful New People's Army into a number of ideologically divided bands that, in some cases, operate more as highly organised bandits than as revolutionary forces. In the southern Philippines, in response to northern/Christian colonisation (Collier 2002:1–2) and the failure of the government to meet cease-fire promises, the Moro National Liberation Front (MNLF)[2] and Moro Islamic Liberation Front (MILF)[3] stand in military opposition to the central government, while the islands of the Sulu Archipelago, always a haven for pirates and banditry, have succumbed to the Abu Sayyef[4] and other bandit groups operating under an Islamic umbrella.

Interest

Any discussion of competing political identities must address the issue of 'interest'. Within politics generally and in particular the idea of the state, interest is the defining characteristic of political identity. Interest can be manifested as 'self-interest', which is primarily aimed at securing the fortunes of oneself and one's immediate family or group; 'shared interest', which sees one's fortune as concurrent with the wider group; 'enlightened self-interest', which identifies the securing of the fortune of oneself through helping secure the fortunes of others; and 'altruism', which is primarily to benefit others. Of these types of interest, self-interest and shared interest tend to dominate most societies, although aspects of the latter two types of interest are also notable and are often held up as the public ideal, especially in mythology (hagiography of national heroes being a prime example). Shared or aggregate interest is the basis of joint claims. As such, it is the foundation of political groupings (groups acting out of shared interest), and it has the capacity to define political groups not just in their own terms, but in opposition to each other (competing interest).

These types of interest fall into further sets of categories within the context of the Southeast Asian archipelago. Interest within the archipelago can be defined as vertical interest and horizontal interest, the former ascribing to communal or bonded cultural group interest, expressed as a distinct political identity (such as in Aceh, West Papua and Islamic southern Philippines) in competition with the state, and the latter ascribing to local interest vis-à-vis other local groups. Modernist, political conceptions locate aggregate interest as the most common in industrially developed, literate and contiguous political communities, identifying interest across communities similarly located within an economic framework (factory workers, 'middle-class', and so on) but who are unlikely to personally know each other. This corresponds to Anderson's 'imagined communities', which refers to a sense of common bond through the use of a common language and the modernist communications medium of print despite no direct knowledge or contact (Anderson 1991). Such communities, which express their aggregate interest as policy preference, are the basis of modern political parties, are identified with more 'advanced' or modernist conceptions of political development,[5] and are usually regarded as necessary for the functioning of a modernist national polity (Kingsbury 2004).

In Indonesia, aggregate interest is limited, as a consequence of the relatively recent trend towards industrialisation, because of the logistical difficulties in establishing communication and common interest across the archipelago, not least because of the success of the New Order in severely limiting the development of interest groups and genuine political parties and its reification of local identity. In particular, the Indonesian Communist Party (PKI), which was organised on the basis of aggregate economic rather than communal interest and which identified 'nation building' as essential to a successful state (McVey 1990:5–27; 1997:96–117), was destroyed in 1965–66, limiting the possibility of growth of non-communal political organisations and helping to cement the legitimacy of communal difference.

When there are few social stresses, political societies based on communalism can function in a relatively cohesive manner. However, most societies experience competing interest within them, and in times of such tension, communally-based political societies tend to retreat to ethnic or community group loyalty, despite what might otherwise be an underlying material commonality of interest between groups, or division of interest within a particular group. Distinctions between communal groups tend to be made on grounds of social or cultural identification and indeed, their primary focus may well not be political; hence, they are sometimes not well equipped to address complex policy issues.[6] This is because the inherent tension between aggregate communal interest and sub-aggregate interest based on competing interest does not allow the development of coherent or internally consistent policy positions. Political parties can and often do retain aspects of communalism, and indeed, in many less politically developed societies, political parties may be based on communal identity, but, in theory at least, they aim to address issues that extend beyond the immediate tribal or communal group and may distinguish within such a group fundamental differences of interest.

Malaysia has most successfully combined communal and modernist political considerations, in large part by adopting a relatively authoritarian political structure in which decisions made at the top are predicated on modernist development assumptions (see Crouch 1996; Milne & Mauzy 1999). In the Philippines the tensions are between the narrowly defined interests of a self-serving elite and appeals to populism within a nominally democratic framework. This divided focus again produces a lack of internal coherence in policy making (Hutchcroft 1998), which has been reflected in the Philippines political history (see Wurfel 1988). Indonesian politics has been characterised by political parties based on direct communal interest (notably the Islamic parties) or perceived loyalty descending from cascading systems of patronage

(PDI-P, Golkar). Within such a system, political elites are defined as the (usually) charismatic head of a party in which loyalty is primarily to the individual and not to the institution. Elite interests include ensuring the wellbeing of their particular patronage networks, but are otherwise similar in fundamental orientation. As with the Philippines, political appeal is otherwise based on populism, but of perhaps an even less well developed policy variety.

Vertical or proto-nationalist interest tends to have pre-colonial foundations, some of which were enhanced or exacerbated by colonial and post-colonial processes. These could be said to include the encouragement of regional identity for the purposes of divide and rule, the use of soldiers from one area against the peoples of another (such as Dutch local troops from Ambon and Sulawasi used in Java and Sumatra), and through the relocation of 'loyalists' to areas where loyalty is suspect (for example, East Timor, Maluku, Aceh, West Papua, Mindanao and Sarawak), sometimes under the guise of relieving population pressure in loyalist heartlands.

Regional state formation

A state is defined for this purpose in the modernist sense of being a sovereign territory that has the capacity to exist beyond the change of government, has a functioning bureaucracy and institutions of state (capacity for generating income such as taxes, a judiciary, communications infrastructure, and so on), has fixed and delineated borders and exercises its legal authority to those borders (see Morris 1998; Krader 1976; Laski 1934). No state or nationalist group defines its appeal to solidarity in other than modernist terms, at least insofar as it claims a defined territory and sovereignty within it. Appeals to 'post-modernism' (itself sometimes said to be a sub-category of modernism) are reflected in claims to both global and local challenges to the state. However, globalisation still regards the state as the basic unit of international relations and with the capacity to make law, wage war and so on, while localism is expressed either as claims to a new statehood or for greater recognition within existing states.[7]

As a definitional quality of the modernist state, the territory of the state may not necessarily be contiguous, although if it is not there usually needs to be some national or historical precedent for the existence of the state. A state also does not have to be based on a single national group, although without a core national group, or the identification of a set of common 'nationalist' values around which a core can cohere, a state would be subject to significant and possibly destructive internal tensions.

Earlier models of the state were, globally, significantly different from the modern state form, notably in the ambiguity of earlier state boundaries and the extent of their authority. The model of the Hindu-Buddhist *mandala* has been used to describe pre-colonial Southeast Asian states (see Coedes 1968; Wolters 1999), with the state in this case focusing on the centre and receding in the assertion of its authority towards the periphery. In such a model, authority is greatest at the centre and at the margins it was sustained through local alliances that were never permanent and often shifting, according to the strength of central power at any given time. At some distant point of the state, authority would effectively disappear into some uncontrolled territory or begin to run up against the margins of territory controlled by a neighbouring state. The logic of this state model was that if its authority was not growing and by definition its territory expanding, its authority diminished, along with the capacity to control territory. As a consequence, expansionism and conflict was a defining characteristic of this type of state. The ebb and flow of state authority was nowhere more pronounced than in archipelagic Southeast Asia where, beyond specific island states, claims to sovereignty were rarely unchallenged[8] and often fanciful.[9] We read some of the claims of the Majapahit (such as in the *Nagarakertaagama*) and Sri Vijaya empires, but little of the thoughts of their more distant subjects.[10]

The lack of physical contiguity of numerous state claims meant that, beyond (and often within) the single island, ethnic groups understood themselves as distinct rather than as common, and relations between the administrative centre of the state and the periphery were fraught with even more tension than usual, not least because of problems with transport and communication. That is to say, numerous communities within the archipelago have some pre-colonial history of regional political relations. While this type of state ceased to exist with the advent of colonialism in the region, ideas informing state construction (as in Indonesia and the Philippines) and the physical make-up and intrastate relations (for example, Jakarta and Aceh, Manila and the Sulu Archipelago) of some regional states continue to echo this model.

The introduction of colonialism to the archipelago initially operated on a not dissimilar theme to that of established states (or in the case of the Philippines, attempted to construct a state from a largely pre-state society). That is, the colonial powers established bases of authority from which they initially asserted a claim to economic advantage. It was only when there was a shift from trade with existing states to controlling those states and then developing other forms of economic endeavour (e.g, plantations, mineral extraction), that colonialism began to replicate a European/modernist understanding of state authority, complete with territorial boundaries, assertions of legal sovereignty and the structures of the modern state, such as bureaucracy.

Legitimacy of the state

Given the relatively recent construction of the archipelagic states of the region, their basis as constituent parts of colonial empires and the dissent that derived from that, it is necessary to consider the claims of these states as a legitimate expression of the will of their peoples. This is the counterpoint to considering the legitimacy of emerging separatist claims based on ethnic (or the redundant proto-nationalist) identity[11] (see Gellner 1983; Connor 1993; Conversi 2002). The legitimacy of the state rests on whether or not it has the capacity or desire to represent the aspirations of its constituent groups; that is, whether it is a legitimate representative and whether it has functional capacity (Morris 1998). The legitimacy of a state tends to be derived from the legality of its appeal to a right to exist, such as Indonesia as the successor state to the Netherlands East Indies (NEI), external recognition of that claim, and whether or not it reflects the territorial aspirations of its inhabitants. That is, the state can claim legitimacy as a successor to a pre-existing state or states, and as the (romanticised) embodiment of the aspirations of its citizens.[12] However, where the claim as a successor state is open to challenge (East Timor, West Papua, Aceh) or where the precursor state was itself understood as illegitimate (like the NEI), this claim to legitimacy is difficult to sustain in the minds of the particular proto-nationalist groups concerned.

If the legitimacy of the state is in question, the territorial integrity or ideology of the state can be maintained through force, and this has at different times been the case throughout the archipelago. Military force to guarantee territorial integrity has been applied in the southern Philippines, from one end of Indonesia to the other, and throughout Indonesia, the Philippines, Malaysia, Brunei and East Timor (or the proto-state existing there in August 1975) to guarantee ideological compliance. However, this use of force does not imply stability, but rather the freezing of hostility. In such a context, it is possible for a state to re-legitimise itself, through economic growth, the proper functioning of the institutions of state (the judiciary and so on), and political participation. However, the experience of the archipelago has been that that freezing of hostility has been used more to advantage more favourably placed individuals and groups at the expense of indigenous inhabitants. Thus, region tensions remain and indeed build.

This situation of continuing unmet political claims is not able to be contained forever in a strong (assertive) state, but faces real problems in a weak (disorganised) state, in which central authority has reduced coherence. Indeed, the necessity for the imposition of state power rather than the voluntary acceptance of state authority implies an inherent weakness in state structure, which only requires changed circumstances to reveal. A weak state, then, is a strong state that has become disorganised and therefore had diminished its capacity for assertion. In such circumstances, local or proto-nationalist claims, usually defined as territorial, are increasingly asserted.

'National' and communal legitimacy

The legitimacy of the proto-nationalist or communal aspiration is both easier and more difficult to substantiate. In a qualitative sense, the legitimacy of a local claim can be relatively easy to gauge. No-one who had spent any time in East Timor prior to its 1999 ballot and had even a passingly frank conversation with its inhabitants at that time could have been left in any doubt as to the outcome of the ballot. While this was hardly a quantitative ('scientific') assessment, it proved to be a remarkably accurate gauge of public sentiment. Even ahead of East Timor's elections for a new legislature, it was clear that Fretilin was by far the most popular party and would almost certainly receive an outright majority of votes. But it was also clear that this majority would not be of the order anticipated by Fretilin cadres. There were simply too many people, anecdotally, who supported other political parties, and again this proved accurate. Similarly in Aceh, the extent of popular support for the Free Aceh Movement (Gerakan Aceh Merdeka—GAM[13]), at least among ethnic Acehnese, is very high, indicating why the Indonesian government has been so reluctant to agree to a referendum on autonomy or independence in the province. A similar situation is found in West Papua, where the ratio of support for independence is perhaps not quite as high as Aceh, but is significant and undoubtedly in the majority with ethnic Melanesians ('Papuans'). One might even suggest that among some other of Indonesia's ethnically defined communities there is a high degree of support for separation based on some proto-nationalist ideal, while similar sentiments are held, perhaps less forcefully, by many 'Dayaks'[14] of northern Borneo. More strongly again, popular support for a separate 'national' identity could be said to be high among the Islamic population of the southern Philippines.

Legitimacy of a claim does not, of course, imply legitimacy of its expression. The use of violence in support of locally perceived legitimate claims does not always enjoy total support, not least for the grief it has the capacity to bring on all. An economic grievance might warrant a protest, for instance, but few would accept as a trade-off their home destroyed or family members killed in support of it. However, the dynamics of political violence are rarely this simple, and are usually incremental. When otherwise legitimate protests are met with a high degree of belligerence or use of force, a whole range of other factors come into play. To illustrate, GAM's legitimisation of its own methods relies on the far greater violence of the Indonesian army (Tentara Nasional Indonesia-Angkatan Darat—TNI-AD[15]), a history of violence in support of economic exploitation and a history and mythology of (the sanctity) of the struggle. Here altruism and (heroics) violence are easy mixed and violence is easily rationalised.

As discussed elsewhere (Kingsbury 2001:ch2), the idea of 'nation' is understood here as distinct from the state, the nation being a bonded cultural group that identifies itself through the expression of a common political aspiration or manifestation. Frequent although not limiting characteristics of such a nation include the use of a shared language (the vehicle for cultural signification and mutual intelligibility), shared values, a common history or shared set of myths, other cultural markers such as a common religion, often a common territory or identified 'homeland' and sometimes a common enemy.

Nationalist claims in the archipelago that do not coincide with existing states reflect the relatively arbitrary post-colonial demarcation of the region, the imperial character of multiple incorporations and the fluidity of pre-colonial boundaries. For example, claims by separatists in Aceh are based upon a conventional nationalist identification of pre-colonial history, a separate language and a relatively high degree of ethnic homogeneity.[16]

Some scholars have used the term *ethnie* to describe the 'pre-national' community (Smith 1986; 1991), in which the defining characteristic is cultural commonality but not yet defined in terms of territory. A common method of self-identification of *ethnie* is along extended village lines, in which the identifying community is restricted to the personally known or local (for example, in Indonesian: *suku*). There may be some more broad associations, most notably in times of common external threat, but these have tended to be short-lived and have often not formed the basis of a wider political grouping. The OPM is perhaps a contemporary case in point, being based on a number of ethnic clans that have a relatively low level of mutual organisation. However, Connor (in Conversi 2002:24–41), argues that ethnic groups are indeed 'nations' in the correct sense of the term.

This idea of *ethnie* (or ethnic group) resonates throughout the Southeast Asian archipelago, being dominated as it is by scores of such *ethnie*, only some of which have more recently begun to define themselves in terms of a coherent 'nation' (in Indonesian: *bangsa*) and even then only as a component cultural group of 'state' (Indonesian: *negara*, Acehnese: *neugara*). The

Philippines, for instance, could be said to comprise more than 70 such *ethnie* and arguably it also contains two nations although, in formal terms, only one state. The Philippine *barangay* could be said to accord to this model of *ethnie*, as could the greater long-house communities of Borneo/Kalimantan and a number of smaller communities especially in eastern Indonesia. The 'nation', however, usually implies a territorial identification and being a wider territory than just the immediately local, suggests a more developed set of social and political arrangements throughout a wider group association.

East Timor stands as a good illustration of comprising *ethnie* and state and the problems of becoming a nation. East Timor contains three broad racial groups—along the northern coast, the mountains and the southern coast, further divided into 16 linguistic groups, not including Indonesian, Portuguese, English and Chinese, and some 18 further dialects. These *ethnie* understood themselves in a pre-colonial territorial *national* context and could be identified as small nations with their own local kings (*liuri*). Portuguese colonialism left local distinctions relatively intact, while removing practical political power. As Portugal moved towards decolonisation in 1974, East Timorese elites began to develop options for a post-colonial state. The effective formation of a new state was cut short by Indonesia's invasion in December 1975, although this event had the converse effect of creating among the disparate *ethnie* a broader 'national' identity constructed around the unity of resistance. Since 1999 and the advent of the process of independence and state formation (formally from 2002), without a common enemy and with many internal pressures (not least of which is a high level of unemployment and relatively low level of infrastructure), East Timor has experienced a partial political devolution to local identification,[17] indicating that the process of nation creation is not complete. The success or otherwise of the state will depend largely on the extent to which its (mostly Portuguese influenced) leaders can subsume unrealistic economic aspirations, frustration with which has the potential to drive its citizens back to pre-national or communal identification.

In the Philippines, the multiple *ethnie* that have broadly accepted Christianity as their dominant faith could be said to comprise a nation, in that they have a wider social and political identity that is attached to territory. The other Filipino 'nation', in this sense, could be said to be the Islamic *Moro*[18] communities of Mindanao and the southern islands, incorporating a range of other *ethnie* under a 'nationalist' banner developed first in response to American colonialism and then to exclusion by the Christian-dominated government. Although inhabiting part of the state of the Republic of the Philippines, the Islamic political organisations, bringing together various *ethnie*, have organised a political identity based on territoriality in response to the twin threats of external aggression, notably under the Spanish and American colonial regimes, and the loss of territory to Christian settlers from the north, supported by the Philippines military. As with numerous other claims, some Filipino Muslims also claim an historical precedent to their 'national' identity, basing it upon the Sulu Sultanate. The Sulu Sultanate's claimed statehood was predicated on harnessing the region's well-developed tendency towards piracy. This orientation appears to continue to underpin some of the logic of organisations such as the Abu Sayyaf of Basilan, Jolo and Tawi-Tawi islands in the Sulu Sea. However, the Abu Sayyef's more pronounced Islam, its association with some other Islamic organisations and, not least its very public methods, leads external agents to ignore this version of an age-old (though never externally acceptable) tradition of piracy[19] in favour of the international phenomena of 'terrorism'. This analysis prompted the United States to send 160 Special Forces soldiers and 500 support personnel to the Philippines to assist the Filipino army in pursuing the group. It was the first time since 1975 that US soldiers had been actively engaged in military operations in Southeast Asia.[20]

Conversely, organisations such as the MNLF and the MILF have a more conventional orientation, to establish an Islamic homeland (*Bangsa Moro*— Moro Nation) for the Islamic groups of the southern Philippines.[21] Because of their more conventional military tactics, the MNLF[22] and the MILF have not been regarded outside of the Philippines as terrorist organisations[23] as such, although they do present a threat to regional security. However, it would be naïve to suggest that in a religion that espouses its unity across 'nations' there were no links between these groups and external Islamic 'terrorist' organizations.[24]

Combined with the Philippines' Islamic challenge is that of 'communism'. Since 1969, more than 40,000 people have been killed in fighting between the communist New People's Army (NPA) and the Armed Forces of the Philippines (AFP). However, as a consequence of lack of ideological clarity, internal purges (see Weekly 1996:35–7) and the collapse of international communism, the NPA in the 1990s divided into a number of ideologically distinct anti-government groups, notably on the islands of Luzon, Negros, Cebu and Mindanao, but also operating in urban centres. It was not until the late 1990s that the NPA began to rebuild itself as the clearly dominant armed force of the Philippines communist movement. The primary characteristic of these groups is their geographic location, their ethnic identity and their tendency at times to act more as well-organised bandits than as guerrillas. In this, class conflict was divided vertically by ethnic identification and geographic location. From little more than 6,000 in the mid-1990s, the NPA has grown to field a force of around 12,000 guerrillas (Collier 2002:1).

Across from the Sulu Straights, in northern Borneo, no such violent assertion of local identity exists, although in the 1950s until the early 1960s there were causes that combined ideology and ethnicity. The predominantly ethnic-Chinese Malayan Communist Party was active in Sarawak and the Malay Peninsula throughout the 1950s and into the early 1960s and until the 1970s on the peninsula. The Sarawak branch, the predominantly Chinese Sarawak People's Guerrilla Force (SPGF) was relatively distinct from the peninsula branch, having somewhat different origins and in the early 1960s being supported by the Indonesian Government and precipitating its 'Confrontation' with Malaysia. Similarly in Brunei in 1962, the Tentara Nasional Kalimantan Utara (TNKU—North Borneo National Army), an expression of the Partai Ra'kyat (Peoples' Party) in favour of democratising the sultanate and uniting Sarawak, Brunei and Sabah, was trained and supplied by the Indonesian army (Kingsbury 2003:ch3). The TNKU and SPGF groups were defeated by the British and Commonwealth army and removed to Indonesian West Kalimantan, from where Indonesian military cross-border raids continued. After Indonesia's anti-communist purges of 1965, the SPGF and TNKU were destroyed by the Indonesian army.

In the period since the 1960s, and notably since the 1970s, in North Borneo there has been a different type of political distinction based on ethnic identity, economic exploitation and political representation. Ethnic distinctions existed between the five major ethno-linguistic groups on Sarawak and Sabah[25] and along lines of kinship and class (Harris 1956:37), but more importantly continue between them and the coastal Malays[26] and Chinese,[27] with whom they are somewhat closer.[28] Since the 1980s, a high level of rainforest logging in Sarawak has displaced numerous Dayak communities and engendered a high level of local resentment and, in some cases, physical opposition. However, blocking logging tracks and staging protests, which began in the 1980s and continued into the new millennium (Rengah Sarawak 2002; Jalong 2002), falls into the category of peaceful protest or, at worst, low level civil disobedience and while it caused considerable bitterness it had not spilled over into greater conflict.

Development of communal rivalry

Within particular states in the region, internal divisions reflect the somewhat arbitrary delineation of the region based on the colonial division of the archipelago. The colonial division necessarily incorporated European notions of fixed and delineated boundaries and full sovereign control to the extent of the boundaries. This did not evenly match the region's relatively fluid population, the competing regional and historical claims to various areas and what was in many cases the patchwork settlement of people from differing ethnic groups. As a consequence, people from single ethnic backgrounds were in some cases divided. These tensions or clashes between such ethnic groups constitute the aforementioned 'vertical' challenges to the state. That is, they have the capacity to split the state into geographic divisions based on ethnic origin.

Where communal rivalry has become conflict it has primarily been where one ethnic group has moved into an area and displaced another. This has been most notable in programs of government sponsored migration, which have had a marked tendency not to adequately consider, or to ignore, the impact of such migration on indigenous communities. Such migration programs can be seen at work in Mindanao, West Kalimantan, Maluku, West Papua, East Timor and throughout Sumatra, including Aceh. Not surprisingly, these areas have been the sites of dispute and considerable violence, both inter-ethnic and between local communities and the state. In part, such migration has been intended to ease population pressure in more densely populated areas. However, in each case there has also been a marked government agenda of introducing to these areas colonies of people representing the 'core' of the state. Regardless of the rhetoric involved, this represents colonialism in its pure form, whereby the colonial power (in this case Java) sends its own inhabitants to an area inhabited by people of a distinctly different ethnic background, primarily for economic purposes, and to a lesser extent, for strategic reasons (see Roberts 1971:35).

East Timor

In the case of East Timor, migrants from around Indonesia but in particular Nusa Tenggara and Java, were encouraged to settle in the recently acquired territory to assist its 'development'. However, this policy of 'Indonesianisation' through colonisation—assisted by education and enhanced communication primarily—served to cement in the territory the ideas of the greater state conceived of as empire and an external population to manifest such an idea. When the people of East Timor were given the opportunity to vote on their own political future, these recent settlers and some co-opted East Timorese violently opposed the idea of independence. This violence was not surprising in that many of them were protecting their recently acquired interests. But this violence was also encouraged by the Indonesian army and sections of the Indonesian political elite who were deeply ideologically opposed to the idea of an independent East Timor (see McDonald et al 2002; Bartu 2000; Kingsbury 2000; 2003:ch3; Davies 1999).

Notably in East Timor, pro-integration militias were portrayed as variously protecting themselves from attacks by pro-independence guerrillas and as a legitimate expression of internal political difference. That is, representatives of the Indonesian Government claimed that the violent conflict in East Timor in 1999 was essentially between pro-independence East Timorese and pro-integration East Timorese and that it was a local domestic affair that was beyond the control of the police and the military. This would have categorised the East Timor violence as essentially communal and hence open to a 'police'-type action. However, there was overwhelming evidence to show that the East Timor militias were not entirely or in some cases even largely comprised of East Timorese[29], that they were trained, armed and led by members of the Indonesian army[30] with the connivance of the police as part of a larger plan to subvert the ballot process and its result (see Ganardi 1999). With the outcome of the referendum effectively a foregone conclusion, the colonial population of East Timor left *en masse*, while the TNI with the help of militias encouraged or forced more than 200,000 people—about a third of the population—to leave for West Timor, from where most were only slowly repatriated.

East Timor remains a strategically troubled area and although the Indonesian armed forces, the TNI, have reduced militia attacks across the border into East Timor, they have also established a 'strategic command centre' in the West Timor capital of Kupang, in response to the foreign military presence across the border, while maintaining more than 2,000 specialist (Kostrad) troops along the border (until some of that number were drawn away to assist with new military operations in Aceh from May 2003). While the Indonesian Government has formally recognised East Timor's independence, there are some among Indonesia's elite, not least among the TNI, who continue to harbour irredentist claims to the territory. This has the potential, in the period after May 2005 when the UN has formally left the fledgling state, to develop into another, probably covert, intervention.[31] West Timor also remains a politically sensitive area, with hundreds of former militia bitter about their loss in East Timor and expressing a generally high level of aggression towards non-Indonesians.

Kalimantan

In West Kalimantan in the late 1990s, officially sponsored migration by ethnic Madurese[32] led to clashes with indigenous Dayaks and resulted in horrific communal violence. These clashes, which were sporadic in their intensity, reflected long standing grievances between indigenous peoples and outsiders. The most recent and widespread round of anti-Madurese violence started in early 1997 (after a fight between Dayak and Madurese youths in December

1996) and continued sporadically up until 2000.[33] This was attributable to a number of connected causes. In the first instance, Dayaks had been politically marginalised since the beginning of the New Order period, because of their alleged sympathy for Sukarno and/or leftist leanings. Many Dayaks claim they were intentionally excluded from official positions, tilting the balance of power against them as the province's largest ethnic group. The economic displacement of the local Dayak people by the Madurese also led to Dayak resentment. Land leased to Madurese transmigrants was not returned to Dayaks when the leases expired, and this was a major cause of economic displacement. The Dayaks also claim that the education system discriminated against them; there were few teachers for large classes. Dayak education and qualifications were consequently poor, and Dayals were increasingly pushed out of jobs in gold, tin and coal mines and on rubber and palm plantations. The traditional Dayak swidden, or shifting dry rice cultivation, was also disrupted by the establishment of plantations and logging on a scale greater than anywhere else in Indonesia.

In the first few weeks of 1997, officially more than 300 people were killed in Dayak raids on Madurese homes, predominantly in the north of West Kalimantan. Unofficial though widely reported sources put the number of dead at up to 3,000, with more than 30,000 Madurese refugees sheltering in the provincial capital, Pontianak. This killing continued spasmodically thereafter, occasionally flaring into a multi-province conflict. In early 2001, this violence spread to Central Kalimantan where a local conflict between two minor government officials over job security led to an outbreak of ethnic fighting. In this, well over 1,000 Madurese, including women and children, were reported killed in less than 10 days. Most Madurese in Central Kalimantan were turned into internal refugees or forced to flee to Madura or East Java, with less than a quarter of the population remaining only a few weeks after the violence first broke out. One disturbing aspect of this already worrying situation was that in the later clashes between Dayaks and Madurese, in one instance in West Kalimantan in 2000, the majority ethnic Malays joined the Dayaks in their attacks on Madurese.

While the Kalimantan violence had real, local causes, there was also widespread belief that senior officers in the army encouraged the violence for wider political purposes, including a bid to destabilise the presidency of Abdurrahman Wahid, especially given that he was overseas during the Central Kalimantan killings. However, the Dayak attacks on the Madurese did continue to tap into a long-held sense of territorial ownership, and reflected ways in which distinct ethnic communities identified advantage as being allocated along communal lines.

Maluku

In Maluku, after four decades of what appeared to be stability and order following an abortive attempt at secession, the island group's two provinces descended into high-level sectarian violence. The sources of this violence were various, but the most commonly identified cause was again a result of inter-provincial migration. This transplanted people who were regarded as being loyal to the state to areas where the loyalty of the indigenous populations was believed to be suspect.

Maluku had been a predominantly Protestant region and, during the colonial period, loyal to the Dutch. The Dutch indigenous forces, the Royal Netherlands Indies Army (Koninklijk Nederlands-Indisch Leger—KNIL), primarily from Maluku and to a lesser extent South Sulawesi, were largely opposed to Indonesian independence and fought a brief separatist war in 1950. However, the influx of Muslim migrants from Sulawesi from the mid-1960s altered the religious and ethnic balance of the islands, which in 2001 was about 43% Muslim and 57% Christian (Ambon Information Website). Perhaps more importantly, however, was that as the religious mix changed so too did land ownership and local political representation. As a result of the shift in ethnic and religious balance, and reflecting patronage from Jakarta, the political leaders of Maluku shifted from being predominantly Christian to predominantly Muslim, with the provincial governor being a Muslim from 1992. In particular, Maluku's governor, Mohamad Saleh Latuconsina, a Muslim, was claimed to have replaced all of the province's senior civil servants with Muslims.[34] While some redistribution of political and economic power was to have been expected with a shift in population, longer standing residents of the province believed this was to ensure that separatist aspirations in Maluku (dating from 1950) were substantially diluted, if not extinguished, and in part to assuage the aspirations of Indonesia's increasingly vocal militant Muslims. Beyond this, many of the more recent immigrants to Maluku lived on land acquired through forced 'land reform' projects, thus displacing the original inhabitants. And, adding insult to injury, former President Suharto's son Tommy was given monopoly control of the clove trade, which employed many indigenous Malukuns. Not only did Tommy impoverish clove farmers through his monopoly control, but the massive debts racked up by his business were ultimately paid for by the clove farmers themselves.

Another shift in economic power was between criminal gangs more or less religiously differentiated. The gangs had links to competing religiously identified factions in Maluku politics, and competed for the spoils of illegal businesses. One version of events was that a Christian Ambonese gang had been working in Jakarta, but had lost a local turf war and had retreated to Ambon and, based on their existing bitterness, intended to move out competing Muslim gangs, in particular those connected with the Moluccan Muslim Student Movement, which was linked to the predominantly Islamic PAM Swarkasa (civil guards) (van Klinken 1999). In East Timor these PAM Swarkasa were the basis of the pro-Jakarta militias that wrought havoc on the territory before and after the referendum of August 1999. This rise of antagonistic but politically connected gangs was set against a backdrop of historical antipathy towards Jakarta, political and economic communal tension and a lower level of official authority and control.

With political weakness at the centre, on 19 January 1999, a fight between a Muslim youth and a Christian bus driver tapped into tensions that had been rising between Christians and Muslims and spilled over into communal violence, quickly escalating into what effectively amounted to provincial civil war and an official state of emergency. While local resentment was real enough, spurred on by somewhat subterranean local feuds, there was also a widespread and probably valid belief that external forces were pushing along the violence. As with some other issues, it was not uncommon for elite rivalries to be played out in theatres other than Jakarta, and in early to mid-1999 elite rivalries, in particular between the army and other 'nationalists' and President Habibie, were at a high level. Instability in the provinces could be used as a means of destabilising the presidency.

Within two years, the conflict in Maluku had spread from Ambon throughout the province and into Halmahera, leaving thousands dead, with more than 3,000 killed in North Maluku alone and more than 5,000 in Ambon and the southern Moluccas, with the creation of around a quarter of a million internal refugees, or one in ten of the provincial population. Serious human rights violations, including the genital mutilation of Christian girls, was also documented. Destruction of homes, businesses and religious buildings was widespread.

Initially, Christian militias had the upper hand in the conflict, and the involvement of more than 10,000 soldiers and the national police, often on either side of the conflict and sometimes against each other, only deepened divisions. The balance in the conflict was tipped by the arrival of more than 3,000 Islamic 'warriors' (Laskar Jihad Ahlus Sunnah) from Java and South Sulawesi in 2000. It helped little that, on their arrival in Ambon, the Laskar Jihad, members were greeted by Governor Latuconsina and then regional military commander Brigadier General Max Tamaela. The Laskar Jihad were openly tolerated and in some cases supported by the army, although by late

2001 the army had begun to crack down on their activities. In this there can be seen Jakarta politics at work, in which the Laskar Jihad was supported or not discouraged to help destablise the presidency of Abdurrahman Wahid, with whom the army was deeply uncomfortable, but was quickly brought back under control after Megawati Sukarnoputri, who had a close relationship with the army, had attained office.

Although violence in Maluku became more sporadic in 2001, one notable turn was the formal declaration of a separatist movement in April. Although southern Maluku had been home to the Republik Maluku Selatan (RMS— South Maluku Republic) rebellion against the state in 1950, the more recent violence had been widely perceived to be more communal. But in late April 2001, an organisation referring to itself as the Front Kedaulatan Maluku (FKM—Maluku Sovereignty Front), hoisted its red, white, blue and green separatist flag in the Kudamati area of Nusaniwe district. At the flag raising, about 100 supporters sang *Hena Masawaya* (Mother of Nation) and read out the 1950 declaration of independence of the RMS.

Central Sulawesi

As with large parts of Maluku, parts of North and Central Sulawesi have been Christianised as a consequence of Dutch colonialism. However, parts of Sulawesi are also home to some of Indonesia's most fervent Muslims,[35] and since the late 1960s they have moved into some traditionally Christian areas, notably around the Central Sulawesi towns of Poso and Tentena. Poso is a largely Muslim town, although a large Christian population lived on one side of the river that divided it.[36] There had been tension between Christians and Muslims in Central Sulawesi since the 1980s, following Muslim migration from Java and the economic and subsequent political displacement of indigenous Christians. In 1998–99 antagonism between the two groups escalated into a full-scale conflict, with hundreds of people being killed, in part related to and paralleling similar violence in Maluku.

This violence reached new heights with the arrival in Poso of some 3,000 Laskar Jihad fighters returning from Maluku in October 2001, with hundreds more people being killed and several villages destroyed. Although the military eventually restored relative peace to the region by December 2001, there have been continued outbreaks of violence, often undertaken by the group Laskar Jundullah, which was led by Agus Dwikarna who in turn was linked to Al Qaeda through Omar Al-Faruq,[37] Al Qaeda's senior representative in Southeast Asia, and Ayam Al-Zawahiri, Al Qaeda's second-in-charge. Ressa cited leaked intelligence documents that claimed that Dwikarna acted as a guide for Al-

Zawahiri and Mohammed Atef, Al Qaeda's former military chief in Indonesia, in June 2001 (Ressa 2002). Sporadic sectarian attacks continued in Central Sulawesi throughout 2003 and 2004, indicating that there continued to be more subterranean agendas at work in the conflict, some of which were said to be linked to various business interests, the military and religious interests.

Aceh

Conflict in Aceh was and is primarily defined along vertical lines, as a challenge to the state that claims sovereignty over the territory. There are Javanese transmigrants in Aceh, predominantly Central Aceh, who have become involved in the conflict, often as military-supported militias. And there are a small number of other Acehnese who have also chosen to stand with the wider state, again often as militias. However, this has been within the context of taking sides of the vertical conflict and does not represent communal conflict as such. Aceh has been in a state of restiveness and often rebellion since the first invasion of the modern era, by the Dutch in 1873. The Dutch invasion was intended to consolidate their control over the island of Sumatra, and to guarantee control of the strategically and economically vital Malacca Straits. However, the invasion was strongly contested, and it was not until 1903 (Nazaruddin 1985:16) that the Dutch managed to occupy the capital, Kuta Radja (now Banda Aceh), and not until around 1913 that the Dutch could claim that they more or less had control of the former sultanate.

Though employing a divide and conquer technique similar to that used in Java, the Dutch never completely suppressed *ulama*-led[38] guerrilla activity in the region. The Dutch were still engaged in security operations in Aceh when Japan invaded in 1942, providing a new focus for Acehnese attacks. The Dutch did not return to Aceh after 1945, although the Acehnese participated in Indonesia's war of independence against the Dutch, particularly in North Sumatra. From the Acehnese perspective, it was as a part of their more specifically focused campaign against Dutch colonialism. The Achenese agreed to join Indonesia in federation, but when the central government failed to acknowledge Aceh's provincial status and unilaterally established a unitary state in 1950, Aceh opposed this move and in 1953 joined the Darul Islam rebellion, nominally for an Islamic state (Negara Islam Indonesia—NII) but more to assert its independent status. Because of Darul Islam's unitary claims, the Acehnese movement broke with the Dar'ul Islam–NII in 1958, and linked with the remnants of the PRRI rebellion, finally agreeing to 'special' provincial status in 1962 (Nazaruddin 1985). However, promises of Acehnese 'special' status were not fulfilled while the province underwent considerable economic exploitation by Jakarta. As a consequence, the Aceh Sumatra National Liberation Front, more commonly known as the Free Aceh Movement (Gerakan Aceh Merdeka—GAM), came into being in 1976.

Since 1976, the Aceh conflict has had three decisive phases—1976 to the Military Operations Region period (Daerah Operasi Militer—DOM, or martial law), from 1989 to 1998, which came close to finishing GAM, and a significant upsurge in activity from 1999, followed by a high level military[39] crack-down from late 2001 and the re-launching of military operations and the declaration of martial law from May 2003, which ended with a 'state of emergency' from May 2004. By mid-2004, there were some 58,000 TNI troops and paramilitary police in Aceh, along with around 10,000 fully armed and trained, predominantly Javanese, militia in the central highlands,[40] the base of Acehnese resistance in the 1950s. By mid-2002, GAM had around 6,500 guerrillas and an active and armed support base of around 10,000, although by late 2004 the government offensive had pushed the guerrillas away from coastal areas and back into pockets of the central mountains, and cut the force to around 4,500 active fighters. It was this remoteness that saved GAM from the devastating effects of the Boxing Day 2004 tsunami, which killed at least 100,000 people in Aceh and was believed to have wiped out at least two TNI battalions (near Banda Aceh and Meulaboh on the west coast).

The government's strategy in securing Aceh was twofold. On one hand, at the beginning of 2002, it proclaimed special autonomy status for Aceh, including a relatively high level of political and economic autonomy (including an initial 70% of receipts from locally generated revenue) under the Aceh State of Peace (Nanggroe Aceh Darussalam—NAD) and imposed Syariah (Islamic law), which was thought would diffuse some of GAM's claims. It also appointed an Acehnese governor (who turned out to be notoriously corrupt and hence unpopular). On the other hand, Aceh was proclaimed as a separate Military Command Area (Komando Daerah Militer—Kodam), as Kodam I Iskandar Muda under an ethnic Acehnese commander. The effect of this twofold strategy was simple. GAM rejected the imposition of Syariah and the status of NAD, while the heightened military operations led to widespread killings of villagers and the destruction of villages thought to support GAM.[41] Despite formal dialogue,[42] the Indonesian government had clearly opted for a military solution to the problem, but appeared to further radicalise the Acehnese and drive most away from the Indonesian cause. As such, although the military balance might have come down in favor of the Indonesian Government, this strategy appeared to have alienated most Acehnese from the Indonesian cause for the foreseeable future, and sowed the seeds of future conflict.

At the time of writing, GAM had declared a unilateral ceasefire to allow an unimpeded international relief effort that had focused on Aceh following the 2004 tsunami. In response, the TNI escalated its operations against GAM. However, there appeared to be a divide between the recently elected President, Susilo Bambang Yudhoyono, and his Cabinet on one hand, and the TNI and a handful of 'nationalists' on the other, as to how to address Aceh's post-tsunami future. As GAM made overtures to the government to re-enter peace talks, it appeared there was some possibility of a return to a ceasefire. However, this was far from certain, and if it was achieved it was not clear that it could be sustained.

West Papua

Again, as with Aceh and East Timor, conflict in West Papua is predominantly vertical, reflecting a widespread desire on the part of many Papuans to separate from Indonesia. There are also elements of horizontal conflict within West Papua, between ethnic Papuans and non-Papuans (transmigrants) and a small number of West Papuans. But as with Aceh, this can essentially be understood as elements of the vertical conflict rather than as horizontal conflict properly defined.

West Papuan discontent towards Indonesia has existed since 1962, when the Netherlands acceded to Indonesia's demands for it to hand over the territory of Dutch New Guinea (West Papua). The Indonesian claim was based on Indonesia's assertion that it was the legitimate successor state to the Dutch East Indies and, as such, had a right to include all Dutch territories in the region. This claim was linked to the attachment some early independence leaders had to the territory when they were imprisoned in the remote Bovun Digul camp in West Papua. Yet the reluctance of the Dutch to give up the territory was based on a number of considerations.

In the first instance, the Dutch considered West Papua to be an administratively separate part of its regional colonial empire. They recognised a significant cultural and historical distinction between the Melanesian Papuans and the predominantly Malay Indonesians. This has been compounded by the vast majority of West Papuans professing a Christian faith, as opposed to Indonesia's Islamic majority, and incorporating that into their understanding of their separate identity. By 1961, aware that Indonesia was pressing its claims, members of the *Nationaal Comite*, led by members of the New Guinea Council, sought to have West Papua and its people identified as such. Chauvel identified the nationalist aspiration expressed at this time as being linked to more recent expressions of nationalist aspiration, most recently supported by the Papuan Executive Council (Presidium Dewan Papua—PDP) (Chauvel 2002).

In the interim, West Papua's claims for independence have been carried forth by the Free Papua Organisation (Organisasi Papua Merdeka—OPM). The OPM was founded in 1963, when the Netherlands acceded to international pressure and Indonesian claims and Indonesia formally occupied West Papua. The OPM received further support after the 'Act of Free Choice' of 1969, in which a carefully selected group of 1,022 West Papuan 'representatives' voted on behalf of 'their people' to formally join Indonesia.

The OPM has never represented a real military threat to the Indonesian presence in West Papua, being fragmented along tribal lines and rarely, if ever, numbering more than several hundred poorly-armed men. However, the OPM has harassed Indonesians in West Papua, attacking Indonesian sites and occasionally killing or kidnapping non-Papuan people. It has, more importantly, also engaged in public awareness campaigns, mostly through ceremonies around the raising of the West Papuan Morning Star flag, which have in many cases brought about a high level of retribution. As with a number of separatist organisations, the functional nature of the OPM is to sustain a manifestation of the claim for independence.

Indonesian heavy-handedness, including the arbitrary and at times widespread killing of civilians and dispossession, has ensured that there is a significant sense of West Papuan alienation from their Indonesian counterparts. Such heavy handedness has also ensured that the PDP and the OPM have become a more cohesive political force, while helping to legitimise a claim to international intervention in the territory. Having overseen and formally endorsed the 'Act of Free Choice', the United Nations is unlikely to intervene in West Papua. However, there is significant and growing international support for legally revisiting the 'Act of Free Choice', and this could provide a mechanism for a vote on self-determination, should Indonesia be otherwise pressured into accepting such a reconsideration (as per East Timor).

Chinese

The issue of ethnic Chinese throughout the archipelago has long been a contentious one, although the Chinese managed to merge with Filipino society much more successfully than elsewhere. Descended primarily from labourers brought to the region during the colonial era, ethnic Chinese quickly established themselves as the region's merchant class and, in some cases, dominated parts of local economies. Because of their history of being a go-between for colonial powers and a perceived tendency to exclude non-Chinese from business, considerable resentment has grown on the part of indigenous communities. This resentment spilled over into widespread racial violence on the Malay Peninsula in May 1969, between the majority Malays (about half the population) and the minority Chinese (about a third of the population, the rest being Indian and of mixed descent). This prompted Mahatir Mohammad to formulate what was to become Malaysia's 'New Economic Policy', implemented under his later prime ministership, which discriminated in favour of ethnic Malays. There have been subsequent racial tensions, notably in 2001. However, these have not threatened the relatively cohesive social fabric of the state in the way that the 1969 riots threatened to do.

Racial violence was also pronounced in Indonesia in 1997 and 1998, culminating in the rape of hundreds of ethnic Chinese women and the burning of hundreds of Chinese homes, businesses and churches. These attacks, which fed into a long-standing history of anti-Chinese sentiment, especially in Java, were clearly politically motivated and probably politically orchestrated. There is a high degree of religious resentment towards ethnic Chinese by formal (*santri*) Muslims,[43] and of general resentment towards what many indigenous (*pribumi*) Indonesians believe is the excessive wealth of many Indonesian Chinese. There has been some evidence to support such resentment, such as a 1984 report by the magazine *Expo* that, in a list of Indonesia's 100 wealthiest people, had ethnic Chinese occupying 39 of the first 44 places. But Chinese have been scapegoated in Indonesia since colonial times. Jakarta's Chinese quarter of Glodok was originally established outside the city walls after anti-Chinese riots, while there were anti-Chinese attacks in West Java in the 1950s, and a number of ethic Chinese were killed by Muslims in the Tanjung Priok riot of 1984. Thousands of ethnic Chinese were also killed during the anti-communist purges after October 1965, even though many of them had no association with the Indonesian Communist Party or its front organisations. President Abdurrahman Wahid made some amends to Indonesia's ethnic Chinese by recognising Chinese holidays and allowing the use of Chinese written characters and medicines. However, many Indonesian Chinese fled in 1998 and remain fearful of returning. They took with them what wealth they could salvage, and their loss has remained a significant impediment to Indonesia's economic recovery.

Cohesion and the state

Economic underperformance and occasional economic chaos in Indonesia and the Philippines have been a factor, and probably the primary contributing factor, in regional instability. In simple terms, the elites of both countries have been corrupt and self-serving and there has been a marked lack of cohesion around notions such as a social contract. This has created tensions among under-classes whose desperation has driven them into identifying a range of culprits for their problems, even though in many cases the alleged culprits are themselves hapless victims.

In this, economic exploitation of particular regions has perhaps demonstrated the greatest capacity for regional instability, accounting for chronic violence in the Philippines, social unrest in northern Borneo and protest and often violence throughout Indonesia. There is a sense that the high level of artificiality in archipelagic state creation has created opportunities for metropolitan elites to exploit the resources traditionally belonging to the inhabitants of the region from which they are derived. It could be argued that there are no states that in some senses are not artificial (Aspinall 2002), and indeed as all political communities beyond the local require some degree of imaginative understanding they are all 'created' to some degree. However, this calls forth the distinction between an 'organic' construction and one that is 'artificial'. The combination of peoples who do not share contiguity of territory, an original common language, a common culture or common histories and myths does detract from the capacity for a 'natural' or 'organic' self-selection of political communities. That is, political communities that come together more or less voluntarily, and that stay together because of a perceived common good (usually based to some degree on reality), are much more likely to enjoy cohesion and not be disrupted by violence bred from competing claims.

Conversely, colonial empires were constructed and maintained through violence or the threat of violence were necessarily coercive and did not, according to the claims of independence, enjoy local legitimacy. The successor states to such colonial empires inherited the same coercively defined boundaries and faced, as a first challenge, the issue of their own legitimacy. Liberation may have been a legitimising factor, but liberation may apply as much to a locally defined empire as to one defined over a greater distance. It could be argued that in most cases legitimacy can be won if the parties to the claim reach a mutually satisfactory arrangement, usually through some form of social contract or agreement about the appropriate distribution of the benefits of belonging to the state. This implies that the state and its elites have the capacity and the will to share the benefits of belonging to the state. But where such a social contract does not exist, or exists in the breach, and where benefits of belonging to the state are not shared upon an agreed or agreeable basis, there will necessarily be dissent. That is, the capacity or the will of the state and its elites are, in some instances, disinclined to consider all citizens as equally deserving of state benefit.

Assuming no other change, such consequent dissent requires coercion to ensure the continuing viability of the state. This then creates a cycle of repression and further dissent, the only outcome of which can be instability and, inevitably, weakness. This weakness plays upon and exacerbates the already significant institutional weakness of the state. A state that holds itself together through repression may have little internal movement, at least if the repression is successful, as it has been from time to time in Indonesia and the Philippines, but it will not be stable and it will remain riven by internal flaws and weaknesses.

The questions remain, then, to what extent is the archipelago governable in a conventional, modernist sense, and how far do the geography and ethnicity of the region challenge notions of cohesion and security? It was probably possible to construct 'national' identities from diverse *ethnie* based on colonial constructions if there was a genuine commitment to sharing the benefits of the state under regularised, institutional arrangements. However, the failure to do this and the repression used to control subsequent dissent has meant, in some cases, that what were once dissident voices that could be satisfied are now beyond the point of being brought back into the 'national' fold. This could be said to be the case in Aceh, West Papua and in and around Mindanao. This does not mean these areas will necessarily be able to break away from the state. But it does imply that there will be a high level of dissent in these areas, that they will remain unstable and insecure, and that there will probably be a relatively high level of violence for the foreseeable future.

Endnotes

1. The term *ethnie* is used to describe a proto-nationalist group that coheres around a common political identity. It is distinct, in common usage, from the term 'ethnic group' in that the latter describes a cultural but not necessarily a political group identity.
2. In 2002 the MNLF abandoned its 1996 ceasefire, following what it claimed were attacks by government forces (MNLF 2002).
3. Formed in 1977 as a breakaway group from the MNLF, which conceded its claim for total independence to one of autonomy.
4. Abu Sayyef, a more militant Islamic group, broke away from the MNLF in 1991.
5. 'Advanced' political development could be said to include participatory and representative government, the stability of state institutions despite change of governments, and a separation of powers between state institutions (such as the judiciary, the military) and government.
6. One might note here the quasi-communal basis of most parties contesting Indonesia's 1999 elections, and the almost complete absence of policy as a point of political appeal.
7. This approach corresponds approximately to what is sometimes referred to as 'neo-realism'.
8. Imperial control was usually by coercion.
9. The chroniclers of empires such as the Majapahit were keen to extol the glories of their rulers, both as an assertion of the expanding quality of the mandala and to satisfy the conceits of the emperor.
10. There are limited references to the Javanese Sailendra dynasty in what became Cambodia, but these are almost entirely expressed in terms of casting off Sailendra hegemony and establishing the first true Khmer state.
11. The etymology of 'ethnic' is the Greek word *ethnos*, meaning nation.
12. Another expression is 'will of the people', although this implies both a singularity of expression and a unity of self-identification, which is rarely accurate and leads towards an organicist type of political system that has rarely enjoyed more than short-lived and quite localised legitimacy (for example, Nazi Germany).
13. The formal name of GAM, since July 2002, has been the Government of the State of Aceh (Pemerintah Neugarah Aceh—PNA), and that of its military force State of Aceh Army (Teuntra Neugarah Aceh—TNA).
14. The term 'Dayak' is regarded by some so-identified people as pejorative, and they prefer to be identified by their specific ethnic identity, such as Iban. This is particularly the case with those groups that share ethnic identities across the Malaysian border in the states of Sarawak and Sabah.
15. Most commonly referred to as the TNI, although formally this incorporates all three armed services.

16 About two-thirds of Acehnese residents speak the Acehnese language (Aspinall 2002:139). There are also two significant minority indigenous groups, the Gayo and Alas of the central highlands, who have varying degrees of loyalty to the idea of an independent Aceh.

17 Political affiliation has traditionally been based on personal local group loyalty, a consequence of which is that whole villages tend to identify themselves politically in common. Political parties in East Timor are surprisingly well-developed in terms of ideology and policy positions, given their communal bases, perhaps reflecting European influence in the ideological positions of the elite.

18 The name *Moro* derives from the Spanish term for 'Moor', or Muslim, from Morocco, a people who occupied significant parts of the Iberian Peninsula between 711 and 1492.

19 Although the young Maranao may have replaced his curve-bladed *kris* with a modern pistol, he still learns to sing the *darangan* or ancient ballad and memorises the Koran in Arabic. Smuggling and piracy in the waters around Sulu and cattle rustling on Mindanao are considered semi-legitimate professions by many young Moros (Ravenholt 1962:16).

20 There was a brief show of force by US Marines in East Timor in late 1999, when they distributed aid supplies near the then troubled border region, but this was technically not part of an active US military campaign.

21 The Abu Sayyaf also claims that as its rationale, but with far less likelihood of success.

22 The MNLF reached a cessation of hostilities with the Philippine Government in 1996, but briefly resumed hostilities in 2001.

23 Neither the US nor Australia lists these organisations as terrorist.

24 Collier notes links between Abu Sayyaf and Al Qaeda, and between the MILF and the brother-in-law of Al Qaeda head Osama bin Laden, Mohmman Jamal Khalifa, and between MILF and the Al Qaeda-sponsored regional network Jema'ah Islamiah (Collier 2002:2)

25 Iban, Bajau, Dusun (two dialect groups), Murut and Kayan.

26 Malays may be from the rest of the archipelago (and some are converted Dayak Melanau), in particular, the Malayan Peninsula, but are predominantly identified by their Islamic faith. Islamic Malays have politically dominated the coastal regions for some centuries, setting up a conflict of interest between the largely inland Dayaks and the coastal Malays, especially as the former moved towards the coast during the 19th century.

27 There were four Chinese dialect groups: Hakka, Foochow, Cantonese and Hokkienese (Harris 1956:56)

28 I was told, in Sibut and Kuching, that a mutual taste for pork and a dislike of Islam were unifying criteria between Dayaks and Chinese.

29 Based on conversations at that time with numerous militia members; many could not speak and did not understand the East Timor lingua franca, Tetum Praca.

INSTABILITY IN ARCHIPELAGIC SOUTHEAST ASIA 153

30   Predominantly by members of the Special Forces (Kopassus). The author also witnessed the hand-over of new weapons from TNI members to militia members in Maliana, East Timor, at the time of the ballot, and witnessed several instances where police failed to respond to militia attacks, even though they were within metres of them. Such eye-witness reports were commonplace among UN officials and accredited observers to the ballot at that time.

31   Indonesia's original intervention in East Timor was covert, both through the formation and support of political parties, through fomenting discord between the major parties, and through infiltrating Special Forces soldiers into East Timor in the three months prior to the formal invasion of December 1975.

32   Madura is an island next to Central Java.

33   There were more than eight clashes between Dayaks and Madurese reported between the early 1980s and the late 1990s. There were about four million people in West Kalimantan, just over 40% of whom were Dayaks, Muslim coastal Malays 34%, Chinese 14%, Javanese 3%, Buginese 5% and Madurese about 2.5%.

34   This claim was recognised by then President, Abdurrahman Wahid, himself an Islamic religious leader.

35   South Sulawesi was involved in the Dar'ul Islam Rebellion from 1950 until 1963.

36   That part of Poso was almost completely destroyed by Laskar Jihad fighters in November 2001. Information based on a visit to Tentena and Poso by the author in December 2002.

37   Al-Faruq was arrested and held in the US prison at Guantanamo Bay in Cuba.

38   Religious scholar.

39   Although the national Police Mobile Brigade (Brimob) are not formally soldiers, their function is as an internal military, they undergo military training, are armed with military weapons and operate in conflict areas under the same line of command and control as the TNI.

40   Armed and trained by TNI Kopassus (Special Forces) Covert Operations Detachment, Sandi Yudha.

41   GAM claimed that around 6,000 people were killed in Aceh in 2001, and at least a similar number in 2002. Killings were also widespread in 2003–04, but restrictions placed on foreign access and movement meant that reports of deaths and other atrocities were sporadic. Other reports cited the deaths of 1,000 or 2,000 people each year.

42   The various meetings were accompanied by increased military activity against GAM, a Cessation of Hostilities Agreement in December 2002, and its cancellation and full-scale military assault in May 2003.

43   Leaders of Indonesia's second largest Islamic organisation, the 30 million strong Muhammadiyah, have been openly critical of ethnic Chinese living in rural areas, and of Chinese business practices.

Chapter 6

Dynamics of Muslim Separatism in the Philippines

Kit Collier

> Perhaps the Bangsamoro struggle for freedom and self-determination is the longest and bloodiest in the entire history of mankind.
>
> Hashim Salamat, 1998

The myth of Morohood

Do these sentiments, expressed by the founding chairman of the Moro Islamic Liberation Front (MILF), represent a statement of historical fact or the 'invention of tradition' in the service of an 'imagined community'?[1] There can be no question that what is commonly referred to as the 'Moro' conflict has, since the beginning of the 1970s, been immensely costly in (mostly Muslim) lives lost—estimates range from 50,000 to more than 120,000. According to Salamat, however, this is only the most recent phase of a continuous struggle that dates back to 1521, 'when Spain invaded the Bangsamoro homeland' (Salamat 1998).

This 'modern myth of Morohood'—the idea that a single, transcendent identity was forged among Philippine Muslims in the course of a 'four-centuries old history of Muslim–Christian hostility' in the archipelago—finds widespread support among scholars of the Southern Philippines,[2] as well as partisans of the Bangsamoro cause, and resonates strongly with primordialist notions of 'cleft countries' and 'civilisational fault lines' (Huntington 1997).[3] As Thomas McKenna (1998:85) cogently observes, however, it also 'obviates any need for the social analysis of present-day political mobilization for Muslim separatism'.[4] Acting on primordial ethno-nationalist impulses, rank-and-file secessionists rally behind contemporary leaders like *Amir* Salamat in defense of faith and homeland just as spontaneously as their forebears fought Spanish cross and sword.

Intriguingly, the appeal of the myth of Morohood also extends to the most entrenched opponents of Muslim self-determination. At the height of the civil war in Mindanao in May 1973, Cesar Adib Majul's monumental volume *Muslims in the Philippines* was launched by President Ferdinand Marcos' Executive Secretary, Alejandro Melchor, who declared the book 'useful and timely' in the 'building of our New Society'—Marcos' martial law regime that had been imposed eight months earlier. By 'lay[ing] bare the roots of enmity between our peoples' in 'the foreign wars of foreign peoples' (the

Spaniards), Majul's work contributed to 'the happy effects of martial law...breaking down the many tribalistic enclaves' of the Philippines 'and merging all of them...into one single, unitary society' (Melchor 1973:x-xii). The 1973 Miss Universe, Margarita Moran, daughter-in-law of prominent Marcos crony, banana baron and former New Society Movement regional kingpin Antonio Floirendo, has likewise popularised more recent culturological readings of the Mindanao conflict.[5]

The significance of primordialist myths lies as much in what they obscure as what they highlight in the constitution of identity. For McKenna, the myth of a 'deeply rooted cultural homogeneity among Philippine Muslims' bridges social distance within, as well as geographic and linguistic barriers between, the diverse Moro tribes. This is because the myth of an ancient, unified and self-conscious Moro oppositional identity is coupled with, and premised upon, another myth of 'sanctified inequality' that entitles a Muslim aristocracy—the *datus*—to rule on the basis of ancestral ties to the Prophet. Historical narratives of the 'Moro Wars' against Spain bolster the nobility's claims to an illustrious as well as sacred bloodline, so that culture, community and *datu*ship become inextricably linked.

Contrary to the twin myths of Morohood and sanctified inequality, Thomas McKenna argues that the 'Moro Wars' were less a clash of civilisations than an assortment of isolated and relatively brief armed collisions, punctuating a mostly peaceful co-existence. While the Spaniards indeed laced their mercenary aggression with religious rhetoric, and imparted the singular denomination 'Moro' (Moor) to their plural antagonists in the Philippine south, McKenna (1998:80–5) finds little evidence of a unified or even explicitly Islamic response. Instead, he locates the origins of the Moro identity in the colonial state-building project of the United States, which ruled the Philippines from 1898 to 1946. And rather than emerging from the crucible of anti-colonial resistance, he finds that 'a new transcendent ethno-religious identity as "Moros"' developed gradually under American auspices, 'with the active encouragement of colonial agents' (McKenna 1998:88). Patricio Abinales concurs that the politics of identity in Mindanao, rather than serving anti-colonial ends, have 'long been used...for precisely the opposite purpose: to keep the Muslims 'integrated' into the larger Philippine body politic through the co-option of 'brokering' Muslim elites' (Abinales 2000:3).

Primordialist accounts of the Mindanao conflict, which assume a direct correlation between ethnic consciousness and Muslim–Christian confrontation—invariable across the centuries—fail to capture the complexity of the dialectic between collaboration and resistance. The crucial question that is obscured by the myth of Morohood and related culturological accounts is why secessionist conflict should only have erupted in the early 1970s, after six decades of relative stability in the southern Philippines. These six decades encompassed seismic shifts in the relationship between Mindanao and the rest of the archipelago, into which, for the first time in history, it was politically and economically integrated. Yet these shifts produced only the weakest of tremors along the 'civilisational fault line' dividing Muslims and Christians.

As political brokers mediating the worlds of Muslim populace on the periphery and (post)colonial metropole, the *datus* were an invaluable instrument of control for state-builders in Manila, and a reassuring buffer between Muslim indigenes and the massive influx of Christian migrants to the southern frontier in the 1950s and 1960s (Abinales 1998:81–94). Rather than inspiring aristocratic resistance, notions of 'sanctified inequality' and a distinctive Moro identity were pandered to by American and Filipino state-builders who sought to draw the Muslim population into the new nation through the medium of its nobility. For their part, the *datus* played upon Orientalist preconceptions of a 'potent and exotic' Muslim nobility to parlay (often tenuous) aristocratic bloodlines into the tangible benefits of the 'policy of attraction': political office, and lucrative new sources of wealth (McKenna 1998:101–3).

In a pattern replicated across the colonial world, Muslim elites pursued the expanded opportunities for self-advancement presented by state formation and economic integration by means of—and simultaneously at the expense of— traditional clientelistic ties with their mass following, or *sakup*. As political economy became increasingly disembedded from traditional social institutions, ordinary Muslims found themselves abandoned by patrons acting as 'gatekeepers for an alien central authority' (McKenna 1992:2).[6] Colonial administrators valued good relations with the *datus* to the extent that they could 'control' their subjects, who, unlike Christian Filipinos in the later years of American rule, were deemed unfit for direct participation in electoral politics. By encouraging the myths of Morohood, the Americans hoped to reinforce the bonds of aristocratic control over a potentially turbulent population.

Until the early 1970s, notes Jeremy Beckett, Cotabato province, which was at the forefront of Christian in-migration to Mindanao, 'saw little in the way of agrarian conflict'. Although Muslim peasants were steadily displaced by Christian settlers, local conflicts were defused by *datus* who often favoured the newcomers over their traditional clients, regarding the settlers as 'better and more progressive' farmers. Christian voters, in return, supported Muslim elite candidates for mayoral, gubernatorial and congressional office in the belief that they could best keep ordinary Muslims in line, and Christians remained junior partners in politics until the elections of 1971 (Beckett 1993:293).

The breakdown of interethnic brokerage between 1967 and 1971 flowed from a complex concatenation of pressures from above and below that defies analysis in purely ethnic or religious terms. Prominent among these were intensifying competition between the two national political parties, Liberal and Nacionalista, as the centralising regime of Ferdinand Marcos sought to tighten its grip on a rapidly expanding, vote-rich constituency in the South; the concurrent eclipse of key *datus* whose captive Muslim votes were no longer as prized in the changing demographic environment; and the emergence of a new Muslim counter-elite who, for the first time, articulated a nationalist ideal of Morohood:

> From this very moment there shall be no stressing the fact that one is a Tausug, a Samal, a Yakan, a Subanon, a Kalagan, a Maguindanao, a Maranao, or a Badjao. He is only a Moro. Indeed, even those of other faith who have long-established residence in the Bangsa Moro homeland and whose goodwill and sympathy are with the Bangsa Moro Revolution shall, for purposes of national identification, be considered Moros. In other words, the term Moro is a national concept that must be understood as all embracing for all Bangsa Moro people within the length and breadth of our national boundaries (Noble 1976:418).

This call to unity from the first issue of the Moro National Liberation Front (MNLF) newsletter, *Maharlika* (Freedom) illustrates just the 'vagueness and lack of programmatic content' that gives nationalism 'potentially universal support within its own community', according to Eric Hobsbawm (Hutchinson and Smith 1996:357). The absence of any serious attention to 'issues of internal social transformation' (McKenna 1992:9) in the emerging Bangsamoro project enabled a coalition as broad in scope as it was shallow in substance. Prominent *datus*, smarting from their exclusion from power in the elections of 1967–71, embraced the symbols of a new form of ethnic politics championed by young radicals like Nur Misuari and Hashim Salamat.

True to their role as political brokers, *datus* like Udtog Matalam and Rashid Lucman provided the social prestige and external connections, including diplomatic and material support from the wider Muslim world, that the new militant counter-elite needed to launch their Bangsamoro 'revolution'. But true also to the long-standing pattern of Muslim elite collaboration with the Philippine state, most alienated *datus* saw the mobilisation of the Bangsamoro myth in similar terms to their earlier control of *sakup* voting blocs: as a resource for gaining greater leverage *within* the state, not for breaking away from it.

This pattern revealed itself in the responses of Muslim notables to the declaration of martial law in September 1972 and the eruption of full-scale secessionist conflict in the following months. Many expressed immediate support for the authoritarian regime, or co-operated more discreetly, and were rewarded with the customary perquisites: offices, sinecures, licences. Among the minority who continued to support rebellion, 'the most notable feature...was its rapid rate of defection. Datu commanders surrendered earlier and in greater numbers than any other rebel leaders' (McKenna 1998:162–3). Rank-and-file insurgents drawn through clientelistic ties with these *datus* into the loosely structured coalition that was the MNLF often surrendered *en masse* with them. Much as during the colonial period and pre-martial law days of brokerage politics, these followings represented a form of human capital to be leveraged into generous settlements with the state. Recognition and reward based on the size of one's *sakup* reflected, in fact, an even deeper continuity with the precolonial past. A case in point is Datu Guiwan Mastura, who, being a 'direct descendant' of the legendary Sultan Kudarat, held the Muslims of three strategic Cotabato towns 'indisputably in sway'. When he surrendered to General Fortunato Abat in April 1973, he was accompanied by a 'coterie...of nearly a thousand people composed of able-bodied fighters, their wives and children' (Abat 1993:98–100).

Rather than articulating a clearly revolutionary program for the empowerment of ordinary Muslims, marginalised by decades of *datu* collaboration with (post)colonial authorities and Christian settlers, the MNLF placed 'renewed emphasis on traditional Philippine Muslim political institutions', retaining 'aristocratic, autocratic leadership...as an intrinsic component of Moro political culture' (McKenna 1998:165). Instead of looking to the mass constituency of the embryonic Bangsamoro nation as the source of real, institutionalised—as well as merely symbolic, captive—legitimacy from below, separatist leaders have perpetuated upward- and outward-regarding attitudes to power. Access to external patronage, especially diplomatic backing from rival Muslim states in the Middle East, and to arms supplies smuggled through Sabah, has been the primary measure of Moro leaders' prowess, and has interacted with enduring, less-than-national loyalties to produce recurrent cycles of factionalism, co-option, and renewed revolt.

After providing further background on state formation and the antecedents of conflict in the Southern Philippines, this chapter traces these cycles through the rise of the MNLF and MILF, to the key junctures of the 1976 Tripoli and 1996 Jakarta peace agreements. It examines the gradual breakdown of these agreements in the context of the longstanding pattern of instrumentalist rebellion and elite–state collaboration described above, relates this pattern to contemporary debates on the 'banality of ethnic war', and finally suggests that the cycle is unlikely to be broken in the absence of the direct democratic empowerment of ordinary Muslims, who remain invisible in most accounts of the Southern Philippines conflict.

State formation and the antecedents of conflict

Unlike nearby Southeast Asian neighbours like Indonesia, Malaysia, Vietnam or Cambodia, the Philippines has no recorded history of classical pre-colonial state formation akin to the legacies of Majapahit or Angkor.[7] The influence of Hindu civilisation was attenuated at the eastern margins of the region, but is plainly present, as in Java, as an underlay in contemporary Islam, combined with prototypical Austronesian elements.[8] Islam appears to have first reached the Sulu archipelago in the late 14th century by way of the extensive trade networks of the Malay 'lands below the winds', with a Muslim Sultanate becoming established in Sulu by about 1450 (Reid 1988).

There are conventionally 13 Muslim ethnolinguistic groups, comprising between four and 7% of the Philippine population of 82 million, concentrated in southwest Mindanao and the Sulu archipelago. Three groups—the Maguindanao of the Cotabato region, the Maranao-Iranun of the Lanao region and the Tausug of Sulu—are considered major tribes of between one and two million persons. The Tausug (or People of the Current) were the first to undergo Islamisation, and look to a single Sultanate at Jolo that was once a significant force in the South Seas, sending intermittent tribute missions to China. Tausug *tarsilas* (genealogies) trace the ancestry of their present-day nobility through the 15th-century Arab, Sayyid Abu Bakr, to the Prophet Muhammad (Gowing 1979:18–19).[9]

The Maguindanao (People of the Flood Plain) have a similar aristocratic founder-figure in Sarip Kabungsuan, also said to be descended from the Prophet through the Sultanate of Johor, and a refugee from the Portuguese conquest of Melaka in 1511. The Maguindanao did not achieve the same degree of political centralisation as the Tausug, however, since two rival 'upriver' (Buayan) and 'down-river' (Maguindanao) Sultanates based on separate descent lines vied for influence in Cotabato from the 16th century, alternately feuding and allying with the Spaniards in their efforts to gain ascendancy over each other.

State formation was least marked amongst the Maranao (People of the Lake) and closely related Iranun. Here in the Lanao region, 'the Islamization process, which began late in the sixteenth or early in the seventeenth century, was by no means completed' by the time the Spaniards made their first, unsuccessful incursions in 1639–40 (they did not return until the final years of Spanish rule two-and-a-half centuries later) (Gowing 1979:23). The Maranao heartland of Lake Lanao then comprised about 50 settlements totalling 8,000 people under four *datus* (Majul 1973:155–6). There has traditionally been no supreme Sultan among the Maranao, but a confederation of 'four lakeside encampments' (*pat a pangampong ko ranao*) under the *datus* or *rajas* of Balo-i, Bayabao, Masiu and Unay (Gonzales 1999:99).

These modest polities, particularly the maritime Sultanates of Maguindanao and Sulu, represented the most highly organised forms of political association in what Spanish navigator Ruy Lopez de Villalobos named the Philippines, in honour of his future King Philip II, in 1543. As segmentary states, they in no way resembled the Weberian ideal-type of monopolised coercion exercised uniformly over a clearly delineated territory. On the contrary, Sultans were merely 'datus among datus' (Gowing 1979:45), *primus inter pares*, with no unique powers of war-making, and their influence waxed and waned in classical Southeast Asian fashion in accordance with personal charisma and shifting polycentric alliance networks.[10] 'Territory', notes Thomas Kiefer (1981:68), 'was not an important element in the Tausug polity: power was always over men, and only secondarily over the territory on which they lived'. The term *datu*, indeed, signifies 'he who has vassals' (Tarling 1999:78) and until the (post)colonial demographic explosion and commercialisation of agriculture fundamentally altered the relative value of land and manpower, *datus* engaged in unending competition to maximise their followings.

It would be difficult, as Gowing (1979:45) does on the basis of their shared Islamic identity, 'to speak of Moros constituting a single society and a single nationality' during the Spanish period—there is no evidence that Muslims did so themselves—and this anachronism may well misrepresent the reasons for the Southern peoples' relative resilience in maintaining their independence from Spanish rule. Until the advent of the steam-powered gunboat in the mid-19th century, at least, conflict in the Southern Philippines would be more accurately characterised as reflecting a multi-polar 'anarchical society' (Bull 1977) than a bipolar 'clash of civilisations'. The petty powers of the region, including Spain, which lacked decisive technological or organisational advantage, treated, traded and waged war on each other in turn in pursuit of their individual advantage, like *datus* writ large. Only after 1851 did the balance of power begin shifting decisively in Spain's favour, and the campaign launched that year, inspired by colonial rivalries with the British and Dutch, not crusading religious fervour, proceeded along familiar lines of *divide et impera*.[11]

The US, after seizing the archipelago in 1898 as a prize of the Spanish–American War, saw the disunity and fractiousness of the Muslim polities, rather than any oppositional solidarity among them, as the obstacle to their integration into a new 'civilised' body politic. Accordingly, ruthless 'pacification' was accompanied by paternalistic accommodation. As Najeeb Saleeby argued in his influential essay *The Moro problem*, it was in the Americans' interest to 'unite the Moros' under their traditional leaders in order to initiate development, and to 'encourage and promote' Islam, for it was Islam that bound the Muslims to their leaders, who were inclined, for the most part, towards co-operation (McKenna 1998:105–6).

The establishment of the Moro Province in 1903 marked the first effective unitary state authority in the history of the Southern Philippines, and as a 'regime-within-a-regime', its 'singular characteristic...was the autonomy its administrators sought to maintain from Manila on the basis of Muslim difference' (Abinales 2000:17–18). While the United States Army, which governed the province until 1914, laid down the basic infrastructure of the colonial 'administrative grid'[12]—roads, telegraph lines, outposts and a system of tribal wards, whereby pliant headmen were supervised by district governors—American officials fended off pressures from Christian Filipinos for an end to the region's special status. As civil rule and a limited franchise were introduced elsewhere in the colony, and the national legislature and civil service were gradually Filipinised, some Americans doubted the Filipinos' ability to govern Moros justly, or the 'benighted' Moros' ability to compete on an equal footing with Christians. Others eyed the region's export potential and proposed its separation as a permanent United States Territory to be known as the 'Mindanao Plantations'. Ultimately, however, domestic US agricultural interests, a shortage of American administrative personnel and a powerful nationalist lobby led by Senator and later Commonwealth President Manuel Quezon, ensured that when the Philippines gained independence in July 1946, it was as a unitary Republic under Christian domination.[13]

By this time, 40 years of American patronage had wrought what three centuries of Spanish hostility could not: 'a shared and self-conscious [Philippine Muslim] ethnoreligious identity that transcend[ed] ethnolinguistic and geographical boundaries' (McKenna 1998:109). Military rule under the Moro Province had ended in January 1914, to be replaced by the Department of Mindanao and Sulu (1914–20) and the Bureau of Non-Christian Tribes (1920–36), which continued to insulate the South from full integration into the rest of the country. American officialdom displayed no awareness of the distinctions among the various Muslim tribes, adopting the collective term 'Moro' from the Spanish as the exclusive referent for policies, particularly in the field of education, which had the effect of 'rationalising' and 'objectifying' the Islamic identities of a generation of Muslim leaders. This laid the basis for a newly 'ethnicised' Islam as national integration accelerated after independence (McKenna 1997:53).

Christian migration to Muslim Mindanao, a steady but restrained flow until the inauguration of the Commonwealth (1935), grew exponentially from 1946.

As the new Republic grappled with post-war reconstruction and a potent communist-led 'Huk' insurgency in the tenancy-wracked provinces of Central Luzon, Mindanao's 'Land of Promise' beckoned.[14] Millions responded to the lure of the homestead in a monumental movement that Abinales justly describes as 'the most important social change in the [post-war Philippines]', in which 90% of the island's ten million hectares was classified as 'public land', unalienated and disposable for settlement once released by the Bureau of Forestry (Abinales 2000:96–9). Amongst Muslims, only *datus* had sufficient grasp of the Torrens titling system to benefit from the influx. 'It seems to have been common for *datus* to title in their own names the land then occupied by their followers' under traditional arrangements, then 'sell parcels of this land...with the effect of displacing or dispossessing their own followers'. Some *datus* even donated large tracts to the government 'to encourage Christian settlement' and thus 'greatly increase the value of the adjacent holdings of these same datus'. Many less-educated Muslims saw the cadastral survey as a government device for imposing taxes on them, and moved away to unsurveyed areas while the frontier remained open. As long as land remained available, ordinary Muslims often failed to see its value as a commodity, and gambled it away or sold it for a pittance. When they later came to realise what had been lost, they felt 'cheated out of land which was rightfully theirs' (Stewart 1972:39–40).

Between 1918 and 1970, the Christian influx reduced Muslims from 60% to 28% of the population of the Cotabato region; from 91% to 61% of the Lanao region (and just 23% in Lanao del Norte province); and from 62% to just 13% in the Zamboanga region.[15]

> For some years, Maguindanaon peasants had been fighting a rear-guard action against Christian encroachment. Maguindanaon politicians had largely ignored the fact, being more concerned with maintaining good relations with Christian voters'. Political developments between 1967 and 1971, however, already touched upon in the first section of the chapter, 'made it clear that this game was over. The politician, too, would be fighting a rear-guard action (Beckett 1993:301).

The key figures in these developments were Ferdinand Marcos, Salipada Pendatun and Datu Udtog Matalam. Marcos, elected president under the Nacionalista banner in 1965 and facing re-election in 1969, looked covetously at Cotabato's burgeoning bailiwicks,[16] and determined to unseat the long-standing Liberal partnership of brothers-in-law Pendatun (in Congress) and Matalam (as Governor). In a series of complicated manoeuvres, Matalam found himself forced into 'involuntary retirement', and with his sense of personal honour (*maratabat*) further piqued by the death of his son in a shooting incident, made 'a dramatic gesture to seek renewed respect and recognition'. In May

1968, Matalam announced the formation of a 'Muslim Independence Movement', with the formal aim of Muslim secession from the Republic of the Philippines 'in order to establish an Islamic state'.[17]

Matalam's MIM was 'never a popular secessionist movement', and largely stemmed from personal motivations (McKenna 1998:146–7; George 1980:ch8). It provided a fulcrum, however, upon which a range of other powerful social forces converged. Two months earlier, the 'Jabidah Massacre' of dozens of Muslim army recruits in an ill-fated plot to destabilise Sabah provoked outrage among youthful Muslim activists. Educated in Manila on scholarships from the government's Commission on National Integration (CNI) or at Cairo's Al-Azhar University, this new generation of self-identifying Philippine Muslims immediately gravitated around the alienated Liberalista elder statesmen of traditional brokerage politics. The latter saw the creation of an armed force under the rubric of the MIM as a 'useful new resource in a mixed political strategy' in the face of an aggressive Nacionalista drive to wrest control of Cotabato and Lanao, and in 1969, sponsored a guerrilla training program in Sabah for the young Muslim militants (McKenna 1998:148–9).

The primary concern of Congressmen Salipada Pendatun (L-Cotabato) and Rashid Lucman (L-Lanao del Sur) in adopting this strategy was the threat posed by their increasingly well-funded (and well-armed) Nacionalista rivals, the Sinsuat-Ampatuan clan in Cotabato, and Ali and Macacuna Dimaporo in Lanao—who were also Muslims.[18] But rumors of MIM training camps and arms smuggling generated increasing Christian anxiety in Cotabato, which coincided with the appearance of the *Ilaga*, an armed band of upland tribal Tiruray led by a Christian Ilonggo settler, known as 'Commander Toothpick'.[19]

The *Ilaga* appear to have arisen as a response to localised land-grabbing and extortion by Muslim gangs in the employ of Maguindanao and Christian elites (Gomez 2000:163–8; McKenna 1998:150–1), but in a spiral of sectarian polarisation between March 1970 and November 1971, scattered local conflicts across Cotabato and Lanao with multiple, complex causes, taking on an increasingly transcendent, ethno-religious colour as *Ilaga* bands fought Maguindanao 'Blackshirts' and Maranao 'Barracudas'. As the interethnic bargain broke down, politicians sought to consolidate core voting blocs by provoking mass evacuations of Muslims or Christians in the run-up to the November 8, 1971 elections. Armed gangs proliferated as opportunities for land-grabbing and cattle-rustling multiplied, carried out in the guise of 'ethnic war'.[20] Although the violence had subsided by mid-1972, Marcos, facing a two-term limit on the presidency the following year, used the disorder in the south to justify the imposition of martial law on 21 September.

Cycles of factionalism, co-optation and renewed revolt

Rather than restoring order, the further concentration of powers in the executive, heightened militarisation in Mindanao and the demand that all loose weapons be surrendered to the state, cemented the ethnic alliance of Muslim traditional politicians and militant youth. The Sabah trainees, under the leadership of Nur Misuari and known as the 'Top 90,' became the core commanders of a well-funded Moro National Liberation Front, formally established in 1971. The MNLF's Bangsa Moro Army (BMA) unleashed a devastating series of offensives against government forces in Jolo (November 1972) and Cotabato (February 1973), with full-scale positional warfare reaching a crescendo at the two-month long siege of Tran (June–August 1973) and the bombardment of Jolo town (February 1974).[21]

It seems certain that many ordinary Muslims were drawn to the MNLF by a sense of desperation at the escalating violence of the early 1970s, which left them dispossessed and defenseless. Yet community-based organisation building, which might have provided supportive material and ideological structures for a sustainable Bangsamoro 'revolution,' appears never to have been an MNLF priority, in striking contrast to the communist New People's Army (NPA), also in revolt against the martial law regime. Virtually the entire political leadership was overseas-based after martial law, working to secure the external assistance upon which the loyalty of military commanders on the ground depended. These commanders' own authority over rebel fighters was likewise contingent on their ability to deliver critical resources, especially weapons, to the rank-and-file, many of who 'appeared to have only tenuous loyalty to the MNLF as an organisation' (Cline 2000:123). The boundaries of this 'loosely knit' organisation were themselves problematic, with many local commanders only 'marginally connected with the MNLF's program' (Noble 1976:413).[22]

Thomas Kiefer's study of Tausug social structure provides some insight into the nature of the 'organisational looseness' that continues to characterise the MNLF (Fuentes 1998:105–6), with important implications for the dynamics of conflict in the Southern Philippines. Tausug society, Kiefer argues, 'almost wholly lacks any development of corporate groups'—bounded and perpetual social units with unambiguous membership, fixed ways of choosing leaders, internal solidarity and collective will—but defines groups 'in terms of their leader,' with composition becoming 'vague at the periphery'. The size and membership of these 'ego-centred networks' varies with the nature of the specific task at hand, as well as the leader's personal influence, while the benefits of group involvement are expressed by Tausug as 'highly individual advantages with little emphasis on larger group objectives'.

Each participant in a very large alliance has his own private reasons for being there; he has little conception of the group's overall needs...Extended rebellion would require...commitment to generalized ideological objectives, as well as permanent coalitions between the many splinter groups of armed men (Kiefer 1986:105–6).

Although originally written in the late 1960s, before the emergence of the MNLF, and largely concerned with feuding patterns internal to Tausug society rather than organised ethnonationalist secessionism, Kiefer's abstractions capture an essential characteristic of the Bangsamoro 'revolution' since 1972. 'If Misuari succeeded in holding disparate elements together as long as he did', notes TJS George (1980:231), 'the prime reason was his status as the most effective link with foreign supply sources, without which the fighting in Mindanao could not have continued'. These disparate elements included 'former outlaws,' 'social bandits' and 'former cigarette smugglers,' as well as 'junior members of *datu* families' (McKenna 1998:160–2), all greater or lesser 'power centres in themselves' with their own backgrounds, motivations, and personal, local and provincial loyalties (George 1980:230; Noble 1976:412).[23] A complicating factor beyond Kiefer's analysis is that in addition to the Tausug, who have formed its primary following, the MNLF has also, of course, attempted to encompass the Maguindanao, Maranao and others in its national project.

The fall from power of Sabah's Chief Minister, Tun Mustapha, in 1975 turned the MNLF's greatest strength into a weakness and exposed the fragility of that project. Mustapha's direct aid to the Moro rebels and his willingness to use the Eastern Malaysian state as a conduit for Libyan assistance had been 'critical in sustaining the scope and intensity of the fighting'. These resources were drastically curtailed by late 1975 so that 'groups which had joined the MNLF primarily to secure their weapons supply had little incentive to remain loyal' (Noble 1987:195). While the Marcos regime pursued a policy of attraction at home to induce a reported 30,000 insurgent surrenders between 1974 and 1978 (Cline 2000:123), its adept diplomacy abroad undermined Arab support for secession, pressuring Misuari to accept a reduced offer of autonomy for 13 southern provinces and nine cities under the Libyan and Islamic Conference-sponsored Tripoli Agreement of December 1976.

The subsequent fragmentation of the MNLF reflected the movement's lack of ideological cohesion as well as the personalistic and tribal dynamics identified above. Three broad factional 'streams' emerged in the aftermath of Tripoli: 'traditional' (aristocratic), 'secular,' and 'religious,' which corresponded very roughly with the ego-centred tribal networks of the Maranao Abulkhayr Alonto, the Tausug/Sama Nur Misuari and the Maguindanao/Iranun Hashim

Salamat (Fuentes 1998:15–18). With diplomatic pressure diffused by Tripoli, Marcos proceeded to 'implement' its terms unilaterally, creating two 'Regional Autonomous Governments' (RAGs) for Regions IX (Western Mindanao) and XII (Central Mindanao). Alonto, vice-chairman of the MNLF, succumbed to these blandishments, surrendering in December 1977 to become Speaker of the Region XII assembly (Marohomsalic 2001:284). At an MNLF Central Committee meeting in Jeddah, Saudi Arabia, in the same month, Salamat challenged Misuari's leadership with the support of the traditionalists; Misuari refused to recognise the vote, and expelled Salamat and Alonto (Fuentes 1998:16–17).

As traditionalist, secular and religious wings jockeyed for patronage in Jeddah, Damascus, Teheran, Cairo and Islamabad, armed struggle in the Philippine South, which had resumed in a fragmentary way after the breakdown of negotiations in April 1977, sputtered on desultorily, punctuated by further mass surrenders. A 'significant number of defectors received large cash payments, special export licenses, or government positions', notes Cline (2000:123–4). The Salamat faction, known as the 'New MNLF' from 1978–84, suffered a 'stunning political blow' when the chairman of the Kutawato Revolutionary Committee (KRC), Amelil 'Commander Ronnie' Malaguiok, defected to the government with several of his field commanders in 1980. The KRC had been the MNLF's largest regional unit and the only one under Salamat's effective control. As his 'prize', Malaguiok received the 'premier position' in the Region XII Autonomous Government and, along with Jamil 'Commander Jungle Fox' Lucman, his 'Top 90' batch-mate, obtained licences 'to import sardines, cut logs and export *bangus* [milkfish] fry or fingerlings' (Gutierrez 1999:264–5).

In remarkably similar fashion to the American colonial regime, then, Marcos combined repression with attraction by flattering the new Moro leadership with symbolic political concessions, and real economic opportunities, playing on their readiness to sacrifice 'group objectives' for 'individual advantage' (Kiefer 1986). The Regional Autonomous Governments, like the Presidential Task Force for the Rehabilitation and Development of Mindanao (PTF-RAD) and Southern Philippines Development Authority (SPDA) before them, were 'cosmetic creations' that nevertheless provided substantial opportunities for prestige, patronage and personal profit. Very little of this state largess trickled down to the ordinary Muslims who had followed their leaders into battle against the dictatorship. The 'collaborating datus...provided few, if any, discernible services to ordinary Muslims between 1980 and 1986,' writes McKenna. 'The [RAGs] had no power of taxation and little government money to spend. Most of what budget it had was spent on itself,' providing jobs and junkets for a favoured few (McKenna 1998:218).

A second attempt to implement the autonomy provisions of the Tripoli agreement followed after another decade of sporadic fighting, diplomatic manoeuvrings and the overthrow of the Marcos regime in 1986. The new government of Corazon Aquino (1986–92) signed the Jeddah Accord with Misuari's MNLF in January 1987. The basic issue of contention remained the scope of a revised autonomous region. Like Marcos, the Aquino government insisted that the 13-province and nine-city Tripoli arrangement be subjected to a plebiscite in the affected areas, and when this took place in November 1989, only four provinces (and no cities) voted for inclusion in the Autonomous Region of Muslim Mindanao (ARMM).[24]

Officially inaugurated in November 1990, the ARMM, under its first two governors, Zacaria Candao (1990–93) and Liningding Pangandaman (1993–96), quickly became 'a massive and inept bureaucracy, a hindrance to, rather than an effective tool for, the delivery of services' (Guetierrez and Danguilan-Vitug 1999:189). An additional layer of government between Manila and the existing provincial structure, it serves primarily as an 'employment agency...for relatives of top officials,' with about 20,000 employees on the payroll, many lacking appropriate qualifications. Salary arrears often extend to months as funds are diverted, or allegedly even held back for lending at usurious rates of interest to the very same employees (Guetierrez and Danguilan-Vitug1999:194). Like the *datus* of old, the ARMM's contemporary powerbrokers are not above despoiling their own clients.

Despite its manifest shortcomings, the ARMM remained the cornerstone of the third attempt to implement the Tripoli formula under the government of Fidel Ramos (1992–98). Three rounds of formal negotiations between 1993 and 1996, accompanied by 'backroom talks' on the perennially thorny question of a plebiscite (mandated by the Philippine Constitution) culminated in the 'Davao Consensus' of June 1996. This compromise skirted the issue by providing for a three-year transition period, during which a new Southern Philippines Council for Peace and Development (SPCPD) would oversee peace and development efforts in the 'Special Zone of Peace and Development' (SZOPAD), comprising the (now) 14 provinces and nine cities agreed at Tripoli.[25] The SPCPD consisted essentially of yet another employment-generating layer of bureaucracy parallel to the ARMM, with a 'Consultative Assembly' mirroring the latter's Regional Legislative Assembly. The ostensible rationale was that this 'pre-autonomous' transition period would provide an opportunity for the MNLF to enhance its capacity for governance and secure a more favourable outcome in the eventual plebiscite. Accordingly, on 2 September 1996, the 'Final Agreement on the Implementation of the Tripoli Agreement' was signed with much fanfare in Jakarta by Ramos and Misuari (Fuentes 1998:20–4).[26]

As an informal corollary to the new pact, Misuari ran for Governor of the ARMM under Ramos' *Lakas* party and was simultaneously appointed Chairman of the SPCPD. He was elected a week after the agreement, and although previously a critic of ARMM corruption, now set about increasing the number of employees 'to absorb some of his former rebel colleagues'. Some 84% of the body's budget was spent on 'personnel services' in 1997, and 14% on 'operating expenditures,' leaving just 1%—fewer than a million dollars—for capital outlays (Bertrand 2000:45). The SPCPD, meanwhile, with no revenue-raising or administrative powers independent of the Office of the President, could not initiate nor implement policies, and likewise, devoted most of its budget to salaries, maintenance and operating expenses. 'SPCPD is functioning much like the ARMM and the defunct [RAGs]', concluded Macapado Muslim—'as a mechanism for co-optation and conflict regulation, not conflict resolution' (Muslim 1999).

The effect has been quite the opposite of that supposedly intended in 1996. Rather than boosting confidence in the New Regional Autonomous Government (NRAG) to be initiated after the transitional phase, the SPCPD experience heightened opposition to autonomy in Christian Mindanao, and produced further fragmentation of the MNLF. Apathy in Congress delayed passage of the Organic Act required to establish the NRAG. Finally, three years behind schedule, the plebiscite was held on 14 August 2001, resulting in the addition of Basilan province and Marawi City (both with Muslim majorities) to the autonomous region, and the ratification of the Organic Act. Voter turnout was low.

Increasingly isolated after his ouster as MNLF Chairman by its 'Executive Council of Fifteen' on 29 April 2001, Nur Misuari opposed the plebiscite and subsequent ARMM elections set for 26 November. In a final act of desperation to forestall the elections and 'preserve his power and privilege' (Rodell 2002:232–3) and, following a series of government attacks on MNLF bases, several hundred of Misuari's followers rose up in Jolo and Zamboanga City just days before the polls. The insurrection failed, the leader of the Council of Fifteen, Parouk Hussin, was elected ARMM Governor, and Misuari was captured and extradited after fleeing to Malaysia. He has remained under detention south of Manila ever since (Musuari 2003).

Hashim Salamat's Moro Islamic Liberation Front (as the 'New MNLF' was renamed in 1984) was not a party to the 1987 and 1996 treaties, and continued to wage a low-level insurgency throughout the 1980s and 1990s. As disillusionment with the ARMM mounted, a steady stream of MNLF defectors shifted their support to the MILF, which by 2000 had established some 46 base camps across Mindanao, with about 15,000 men under arms. Repeated clashes with government troops around the primary base camp, Abubakar as-Siddique, and the Narciso Ramos Highway connecting Cotabato and Marawi cities, where MILF fighters imposed road tolls, escalated dramatically in early 2000. The government of President Joseph Estrada (1998–2001) launched a full-scale offensive against the MILF, overrunning Camp Abubakar in July 2000 and dispersing the rebels' regularised formations into a potentially more volatile, decentralised guerrilla force (Vitug 2002:5–7; Davis 1998:30–5).[27]

The most visible expression of the Philippine South's continuing volatility, as far as the outside world is concerned, is the rise of the Abu Sayyaf Group and Jema'ah Islamiyah, both with suspected ties to the MILF. In the wake of the September 11 attacks on New York and Washington, the US is taking a renewed interest in Southeast Asia's 'Second Front' in the War on Terror, declaring Abu Sayyaf a Foreign Terrorist Organisation with links to Al Qaeda, deploying its own armed forces in Mindanao for the first time since the colonial era, and potentially reprising its catalysing role in Bangsamoro ethnogenesis. As the anthropologist Charles Frake (1998:49–50) observes in an unusually thoughtful article on the Abu Sayyaf:

> ...when disparate local conflicts [that are typically quite parochial in origin] produce eruptions of violence sufficiently impressive to receive regional and national attention, they are subject to interpretations that, even though uninformed as to local causes, provide a new context for framing 'what happened.' This new context, in turn, becomes a frame that shapes local interpretations of subsequent events. Interpreting what happened requires identifying agents and victims. It requires identity ascription. Repeated cycles of contested interpretation and reinterpretation foster identity proliferation.

'What happened' on 11 September 2001? Or during the 'Jabidah Massacre'? Is the Southern Philippines the site of a 'civilisational fault line' that explains an unbroken history of Muslim–Christian hostility since 1521? If so, can anything be done, other than to pray piously for a 'Culture of Peace'—or kill our enemies before they kill us? The way we answer these questions will have profound implications for the human condition in Mindanao and beyond. This chapter has argued that the politics of ethnic identity, as constituted in the Southern Philippines, has served not only (or even primarily) as a vehicle of popular Muslim emancipation, but rather, to obscure the mechanisms of class and ethnic domination, which are intertwined in the 'brokering' function of the *datu* and his modern 'sultanistic' counterpart.[28] Muslim elites and (post)colonial authorities have shared an interest in perpetuating the myths of Morohood because, by displacing the 'parochial' or 'banal' dynamics of conflict from view—in crude terms, by misrepresenting 'greed' as 'grievance' (Mueller 2000:42–70; Collier and Hoeffler 2001)—their collusive partnership is elided, agents and victims are misidentified in everyday notions of 'what happened' and 'issues of democratisation and development are glossed over' in visions of autonomy (or *jihad*) devoid of significance to ordinary people's lives (Gutierrez & Vitug 1999).

Endnotes

1. These terms are Eric Hobsbawm's and Benedict Anderson's respectively. See Hobsbawm & Ranger (1983).
2. In this case, Peter Gowing (1979:199). See also Majul (1973) and George (1980).
3. 'Primordialist' approaches to ethnicity tend to view social bonds of religion, blood, race, language and custom as 'given', 'overpowering' and 'ineffable', in contrast to 'instrumentalists', notably Hobsbawm & Ranger (1983) and Anderson (1983), who emphasise the socially constructed, or 'taken', nature of these ties. For further discussion, see Hutchinson and Smith (1996).
4. The term 'modern myth of Morohood' is McKenna's.
5. Moran Floirendo has produced a video documentary, 'Mindanao: Healing the Past, Building the Future', which calls for a 'Culture of Peace' as the solution to the armed conflicts that have wracked Mindanao 'for well over 300 years'. The New Society Movement (*Kilusang Bagong Lipunan*—KBL) was Marcos' ruling party during the dictatorship of 1972–86.
6. On the significance of social disembedding, see Polanyi (1957).
7. I am fully aware that the legacies of Majapahit and Angkor are themselves in part 'invented traditions' in the service of state-building; nevertheless, these pre-colonial states exceeded in power, cohesion and reach any proto-state entities existing in the Philippines prior to the 16th century.
8. Core elements of what is considered archetypically 'Muslim' culture (by Christian Filipinos as well as Muslims themselves) are actually pre-Muslim and common to much of the Austronesian world. The word *datu* is shared with non-Muslim, animist tribes (or *Lumad*) in Mindanao, and indeed is cognate with the Malay *datuk*, the Malukan *latu* and Fijian and Tongan *ratu*. *Adat* law and the *kulintang* gong ensemble have similarly ancient roots. Hindu influence is apparent in the Maranao epics *Raja Indarapatra* and *Darangen*.
9. *Tarsila* is from the Arabic *silsila*, 'name-chain' or 'link'. Gowing, like most scholars of Tausug history, draws heavily on the early, definitive work of Najeeb Saleeby, American colonial Chief-in-Charge on Moro Affairs. Saleeby's impressive corpus of work is a powerful testament to the American interest in helping construct Philippine Muslim identity (see Saleeby 1963).
10. For classic statements on the 'man of prowess' (*orang besar*) and the polycentric polity, much of which apply to Moro politics, see Anderson (1990:17–77; 1983).
11. For details of this sixth and final 'stage' of the 'Moro Wars', see Majul (1973:Ch VIII). The Spaniards finally instituted the framework of a 'politico-military government' composed of six districts in Mindanao and Basilan in 1860, and subdued the Maguindanao Sultanate in 1861, Sulu in 1878 and Buayan in 1890. Lanao remained restive despite Maranao defeats in 1895. This consolidation resembles equivalent colonial 'forward movements' in Southeast Asia by the British, French and Dutch in the second half of the century.

12 I owe this term to Gerard Finin, who details similar processes of colonial identity formation in the Northern Philippines' Mountain Province (see Finin 1991).

13 Pressures for separation crested under Philippines Governor-General Leonard Wood (1921–26), also first Governor of the Moro Province (1903–06), when Muslim leaders petitioned Manila and Washington for Territorial status, and New York Senator Robert Bacon filed a supporting Bill in the US Congress.

14 For a remarkable Cold War manifesto on the significance of frontier resettlement in nation-building and combatting the Huk rebellion, without recourse to land reform, see Scaff (1955).

15 Calculated from figures in Rodil (1994:99, 102–3) and Majul (1985:31). Rodil provides a detailed picture of (post)colonial land laws and their impact on Muslim and *Lumad* communities.

16 For detail on the growing electoral significance of the frontier 'special provinces', where the franchise was only fully extended in 1955, see Abinales (2000:Ch 6).

17 McKenna (1998:144–6) provides the specifics of this key sequence of events, which cannot be elaborated here.

18 Lucman lost the November 1969 Congressional race to Macacuna Dimaporo, who had the support of Marcos and the provincial Philippine Constabulary. Lucman, like Matalam, responded by 'playing the ethnic card', forming the *Ansar el-Islam*.

19 The Tiruray are the largest animist-Christian *Lumad* tribe of the Cotabato highlands, traditionally a source of slaves and tribute for the Maguindanao Sultanate. The Ilonggos are the largest Christian migrant group in Cotabato, originating in the western Visayan islands of Panay and Negros. *Ilaga* is Visayan for 'rats', but was widely represented as signifying 'Ilonggo Land Grabbers' Association'.

20 For an incisive analysis of how 'small bands of opportunistic marauders' similarly spawned violent 'ethnic' conflict in the contemporary Balkans, see Mueller (2000:42–70).

21 For a detailed account of the war from a government perspective, see Abat (1993).

22 Cline (2000:122), summarises the MNLF manifesto, issued in March 1974, as follows: 1) An independent state for the Moro people; 2) Armed struggle is necessary to establish such a state; 3) The MNLF would never agree to anything short of the goal of independence; 4) Democracy in the new state; 5) Christian Filipinos who want to remain in the Muslim state would have their rights protected as long as they renounce their Philippine citizenship; 6) The MNLF is committed to the growth of Islam in its homeland, but other religions and 'indigenous cultures' would be permitted; 7) The MNLF shares the general goals of 'oppressed colonised humanity' everywhere; 8) Freedom of the press; 9) Foreign investment in the Moro state would be welcomed and encouraged. The full text is reproduced in Majul (1985:117–19), and reveals further commitments to the UN charter and Universal Declaration of Human Rights, and 'the preservation and enhancement of world peace'.

23 The parallels with Kiefer's description of the 'segmentary state' should be obvious.
24 For details, see Madale (1992:169–84). The four provinces were Maguindanao, Lanao del Sur, Sulu and Tawi-Tawi; only one other province, Basilan, has a Muslim majority, and with Marawi City voted to join the ARMM in August 2001.
25 The partition of South Cotabato created an additional province, Sarangani, in 1992.
26 The full text of the agreement is appended in CR (1999).
27 Following the installation of Gloria Macapagal Arroyo as President in a civil–military uprising in Manila in January 2001, talks with the MILF in Kuala Lumpur have produced a formal ceasefire, a framework for negotiation and an agreement on relief, rehabilitation and development which would channel government funds directly to the MILF through a Bangsamoro Development Agency.
28 For Max Weber's original formulation of 'sultanism' as an extreme form of patrimonial rule, see Weber (1978:231–2). Weber's approach has strongly influenced recent work on (Christian) Philippine politics by John Sidel, Paul Hutchcroft and Mark Thompson, but, remarkably, has yet to be systematically applied to Muslim politics in the Philippines.

Chapter 7
The tyranny of invented traditions: Aceh

Stephen Sherlock

A period of relative peace in the Indonesian province of Aceh ended on 19 May 2003, when the Indonesian security forces launched an all-out military offensive against the pro-independence Free Aceh Movement (*Gerakan Aceh Merdeka*—GAM[1]) in Indonesia's western-most province of Aceh. The renewed offensive followed the final collapse of a ceasefire agreement that had commenced in December 2002. President Megawati Sukarnoputri issued a decree declaring a state of emergency in the province for six months, authorising the military to take responsibility for security and beginning an operation involving up to 50,000 military forces and police against a few thousand GAM guerrillas.[2]

The offensive marked the failure of a series of efforts by successive Indonesian governments since the fall of Suharto in 1998 to reach a negotiated settlement to the problem of Acehnese separatism. It was also a victory for the Indonesian military (*Tentara Nasional Indonesia*—TNI), which consistently opposed any policy of conciliation towards GAM. Despite TNI's failure to defeat the separatist movement, it has continued to argue that it could achieve victory if only it were allowed a free hand. As widely predicted, however, renewed military action has failed to change the situation in Aceh in either a military or political sense.

TNI has been unable to capture the frontline leadership of GAM or to produce any convincing evidence that many Acehnese are abandoning their opposition to the policies emanating from Jakarta. The military's admission of failure was eloquently expressed by the government's renewal of the state of emergency for a further six months in November 2003.

Critics of the Megawati administration's policy, with its implicit 'blank cheque' for the military, have emphasised the continuities with Suharto's approach to the issue of Acehnese separatism during the New Order regime of 1965–98. Such critics are correct, in my opinion, to argue that the return to a 'security approach' to Aceh is a relapse into the failed policies of the New Order that exacerbated anti-Jakarta resentment in the province and that the policy represents a capitulation by Megawati and her Cabinet to pressure from the Indonesian military (TNI) (ICG 2003b). There is also a clear historical pattern of organised military resistance in Aceh, led by powerful elements of

Acehnese society who have contested the ideological foundations, policies or very legitimacy of successive regimes that have sought to rule the Indonesian archipelago.

The argument developed in this chapter, however, is that a tyranny of assumed or invented continuities has grown up around the question of Aceh and that, for very different reasons, participants and observers of the Acehnese tragedy have tended to project these continuities far into the past. While the state of emergency is clearly a continuation of Suharto's incapacity to respond to Acehnese demands except by force, there is a temptation to assume a line of logical development between the upsurge of support for autonomy or independence in Aceh since 1998, the declaration of independence by Acehnese separatists in 1976, earlier insurgencies against the government in Jakarta that merged into the Dar'ul Islam movement of the 1950s, even to the struggle against the Dutch after 1873. In fact, the idea that the Acehnese have, as a people, been continuously involved in some kind of unique struggle is part of a mythology shared by the TNI and the ideologues of GAM.

This chapter also argues that the transformation of Aceh into a war zone from 1989 and the consequent creation of separatist sentiment with possibly majority popular support in the province were intimately connected with the political economy of the New Order regime. The patrimonial developmentalism of the New Order allowed for sustained economic growth in Indonesia as a whole for three decades, but it had a particularly perverse social and political impact in Aceh. When Acehnese reacted negatively to the change being imposed on them, the TNI's tendency to see all Acehnese as congenital separatists led to a violent crack-down that allowed projections of a martial and rebellious Acehnese identity to become self-fulfilling. This fed the nationalist myth making that is apparently appealing to increasing numbers of Acehnese.

The fact that the Megawati government has been unable to pursue a new policy in Aceh is not just a failure of security policy-making, but is symptomatic of its failure to challenge the fundamentals of power relations in Indonesia, despite an apparent regime change in 1998–99. The government is locked into the patrimonial relationships of the New Order (especially the central role of TNI in those networks) and therefore has been unable to break from the patterns of thinking and policy that reigned under Suharto. Security policy in Aceh is not just repeating history because of personal failings or institutional weakness (though that is part of the story), but because of the continuing reality of domination by interests who cannot relinquish the control they have established in Aceh.

History, continuities and invented traditions

There has been repeated conflict in Aceh since the 1870s, but the origins and nature of this conflict have varied greatly and easy assumptions about the repetition of history have led to critical misrepresentations. Aceh was one of the first regions in the archipelago to be converted to Islam (from at least the 13th century) and the Sultanate of Aceh had a long history of commercial and cultural links with the Islamic world of the Middle East and India. The independence of the Sultanate of Aceh had been protected by the 1824 Treaty of London, under which Britain and the Netherlands divided their spheres of influence in the Indies. In 1873, however, this tenuous autonomy gave way in the face of common British and Dutch concerns about the growing influence of the United States in the area. In that year, Britain agreed to a new treaty that allowed for the Netherlands to expand its sphere of influence, thus beginning a long and violent Dutch campaign to complete its subjugation of northern Sumatra. The Sultanate held out for 30 years, until Sultan Muhammad Daud's final surrender in 1903, after which time the Dutch faced episodic resistance right up to the time of their surrender to the Japanese in 1942 (Reid 1979).

The special difficulties faced by the Dutch imperialists in Aceh tended to be explained by the Dutch in exceptionalist cultural terms, with strong emphasis on the role of religious fanaticism. This tradition was continued into the post-colonial era, by commentators, including scholars of Indonesian history who, in Morris's words, have tended 'to focus on the ethnic distinctiveness and Islamic fervour of the Acehnese' (Morris 1985:83).

But persistent localised resistance to colonialism was not unique to Aceh. Although the modern Republic of Indonesia covers the entire territory of the former Dutch East Indies, the history of which extends back to the 16th century, Dutch control over parts of the archipelago was in many cases only quite brief. The Balinese, for example, were not conquered until 1908 after a long and bitter struggle. As a result of that struggle, the Balinese were seen in the Dutch imagination as a race of particularly fierce and brutal warriors, given to fits of uncontrollable and unpredictable rage, 'a fierce, savage, perfidious and bellicose people', as described by one 19th-century Dutch visitor.[3] The Dutch and the Portuguese also faced repeated uprisings on the island of Timor, right up to the eve of the First World War, and a final border between the two colonial territories on Timor was not delineated until 1912 (Dunn 1983:17–19).

But despite long histories of resistance to occupation, other areas of Indonesia have not retained an association with bellicosity. The image of Bali was transformed in the years following its final incorporation into Dutch territory. Bali was re-created as an island Eden, the relaxed and friendly tropical paradise promoted in Dutch tourist campaigns, an idea taken up with enthusiasm by European artists and bohemians in the 1920s and 1930s and built upon in later years by successive post-independence governments. In Vickers' (1996:11) words, 'there is much that has been forgotten' in current perceptions of Balinese traditions, even though the selective amnesia began setting in little more than a decade after the crushing of anti-colonial resistance. Vickers (1996:199) himself, though developing an historicised critique of the creation and recreation of traditions, seems to suggest that contemporary Balinese have imbibed or become imbued with traditions of tranquility, proposing [in 1989] that 'the majority of Balinese are more loyally committed to Suharto's New Order and are less likely to express dissent than many other Indonesians, including Javanese'.

It is clearly the case that many Acehnese do maintain a sense of an historical distinctiveness, including a separation from the colonial experience of other regions, such as Java and the 'spice islands' of eastern Indonesia. But over the six decades since the independence struggle, that sense has arguably been no stronger than that felt in many other regions of the diverse Indonesian archipelago. The argument developed below is that the crucial difference in Aceh was that the province came to play a particular role in the economic foundations of the New Order and that the nature of that regime prevented it from coming to a political settlement with the Acehnese that could have accommodated local traditions. In fact, the New Order reneged on the deal that had been made with the centre in the 1960s, following the defeat of the *Da'rul Islam* movement.

Attachment to a certain idea of Acehnese identity was no impediment to anti-Dutch forces in Aceh committing themselves enthusiastically to the vision of a united, independent Indonesian republic encompassing the entire East Indies. Acehnese leaders were a critical element of republican strength, a fact celebrated in street names throughout central Jakarta and many other Indonesian cities today. Equally, although anti-Jakarta sentiment began to develop in Aceh in the post-independence period, it was not linked to a desire for separation from Indonesia but was motivated by disappointment with particular features of the independent Indonesian state as it was envisioned and shaped by secularist, non-Islamist leaders such as Sukarno. Many Acehnese nationalists (that is, Indonesian nationalists in Aceh) had a different, more Islamic-inspired ideal of a post-independence Indonesia from the Java-based leaders who dominated politics after 1949. The Acehnese wanted 'to claim for themselves the national revolutionary legacy' (Morris 1985:105). The central government managed to antagonise Islamic and non-Islamist elements in Aceh when the separate province of Aceh was abolished and merged into North Sumatra immediately after independence from the Netherlands. This flowed into generalised opposition to the constitutional and political character of the Indonesian state that reached a peak when Sukarno began to ally himself with the Indonesian Communist Party (PKI) in the latter part of the 1950s.

The fact that discontent with Sukarno's Republic of Indonesia was not peculiar to Aceh was demonstrated by the fact that anti-Jakarta sentiment manifested itself within the *Dar'ul Islam* rebellion, a diverse collection of insurrectionist Islamic groups that emerged from 1953 in West Java and South and Central Sulawesi, as well as in Aceh. The leaders of this rebellion had their origins in Islamic military units during the war of independence, autonomous from the central republican leadership in different areas of the country, who had opposed various compromises (such as the Renville Agreement of 1948) with the Dutch and who continued to oppose the secular policies of the central government after independence. None of these groups explicitly wanted to break up Indonesia but to change it. The Acehnese had no wish to separate their region from Indonesia but looked to a greater degree of autonomy within an Islamic Republic of Indonesia.[4] They 'only wanted to be part of an alternative unitary state of [the Republic of Indonesia]: an Islamic state and/or a federal state—but *not* as a separate nation' (Abdullah 2003:15).

By 1962, *Dar'ul Islam*, within and outside Aceh, had been defeated by central government military campaigns. In the case of Aceh, the movement had been politically undermined when the central government granted Aceh 'special region' (*daerah istimewa*) status in 1959, providing for local autonomy over religion, customary law and education. Sjamsuddin (1985:286–94) has shown that the central government's motives in compromising with the Acehnese were complex, but the critical point was that a negotiated solution was possible as long as Jakarta was willing to provide for a degree of special autonomy for the region and to recognise its separate identity. Local ruling groups not only agreed to remain within the Republic of Indonesia, but were happy to be seen as having a special role in the creation of the Republic and in shaping its identity.

Aceh and the political economy of the New Order

Following the end of the *Dar'ul Islam* movement, Aceh was free of open conflict for several years, but new problems emerged when President Suharto's New Order regime began to intensify centralised rule from Jakarta from the end of the 1960s. As part of the regime's consolidation and its elimination of potential centres of opposition, Islamic organisations across Indonesia were subject to suspicion or outright repression and there was little room for local political forces in any of the country's provinces. Military officers were imposed as provincial governors throughout the country and the only possible expression of political opinion was through the ritual of five-yearly votes for officially sanctioned national-level parties.

Signs of discontent with the New Order and the emergence of separatist feelings in some quarters led to the foundation of the Free Aceh Movement (*Gerakan Aceh Merdeka*—GAM) in 1976 by Hasan M di Tiro, a member of a family of *ulama* (Islamic religious leaders). At another level, Acehnese voters took the limited opportunity offered by the sham New Order elections, defied pressure to vote for Golkar and recorded high levels of support for the United Development Party (PPP), the forced amalgam of existing Islamic parties created in 1973, even scoring more votes than Golkar in the 1977 and 1982 elections (Evans 2003:57). Golkar was forced to make special efforts in Aceh to reverse this trend and achieve majority support in subsequent elections (King & Rasjid 1988).

Aspinall (2002a:11) observes that there has been 'an inverse relationship between Aceh's economic and administrative integration into the state and the level of popular support for such integration'. But the rise of Acehnese resentment about the policies of the Suharto regime cannot be understood simply in terms of the general loss of regional autonomy that affected all Indonesians. Aceh became a special case because the discovery of large natural gas resources in North Aceh in 1971 made the province crucially important to the economic underpinnings of the New Order. As Dawood and Sjafrizal note, 'one of the most staunchly independent regions, long in conflict with the central government, [was] now subsidising that government and the rest of the country' (1989:115). Oil and gas made Aceh into an instructive and extreme example of the dynamics of the political economy of Suharto's Indonesia.

Suharto's hold on power was based on his position at the apex of a network of patronage that made domestic and foreign investors dependent on his favour for commercial success. In addition to the 'bureaucrat-capitalists', mainly serving and retired military officers, who controlled state-owned industries (including those inherited from the time of Sukarno), Suharto sponsored a class of ethnic Chinese business people whose ethnicity made them personally dependent on himself.[5] The institutions of state were dominated by Suharto and the military (in a complex and sometimes rocky relationship of interdependence and competition), and the state, in turn, maintained a direct controlling interest in large sectors of the economy and a tight political grip on the owners of private capital through privileged access to contracts, investment capital and concessional deals. McLeod (2000:101) uses the apt metaphor of "franchises" to describe the replication of these arrangements at successive levels of the state and the economy. At the provincial level in Aceh, the New Order fostered what Kell (1995:29) called a 'local coalition consisting of the all-powerful and ubiquitous army, and the civilian provincial government led by the technocrats'.

The windfall of petroleum earnings, both from Aceh and elsewhere in Indonesia, provided the basis for the twin New Order objectives of centralised political control and national economic development. The continuing flow of oil and gas revenue provided capital for new developmental investment and the revenue's ease of control through the all-important mechanism of the state-owned oil corporation, Pertamina, ensured that the main benefits could be kept in the hands of a select few with privileged access to the state.

The corollary of mobilising resources in this way was a ruthless concentration of power and wealth in Jakarta. All key investment decisions were made by individuals and institutions located at the centre of power. Thus Aceh's sudden rise to economic prominence meant that the province had to be kept under particularly close political control. The LNG boom of the 1970s and 1980s brought an even tighter grip over the local economy and politics by outside elements. Although Aceh began recording one of the highest nominal rates of provincial GDP per capita and some downstream manufacturing investment occurred (most notably, the ASEAN Aceh Fertiliser plant and other manufacturing around Lhokseumawe), the main effect was to create 'enclave development' with little perceived general improvement (Dawood & Sjafrizal 1989). Many Acehnese felt they received no benefit or were even worse off when they lost land and forest resources to make way for industrial, plantation and forestry developments. Newcomers from other regions of the country were seen as taking most new jobs, while generals, politicians and well-connected businessmen from Java creamed off all the profits.

For many years after its formation in 1976, GAM was fairly ineffective as a political or military force, and the exiled leadership gained little attention on the international stage. In the absence of any meaningful data about how people in Aceh regarded the economic and political situation from the 1970s to the 1990s, one can only speculate about how much sympathy came to be felt for the idea of increased autonomy or independence, or how much GAM was regarded as the legitimate and most effective expression of such sentiments. The fact that political activism in Aceh grew rapidly to prominence after the lid of repression was removed in 1998 suggests that opposition to the governing regime and support for GAM was steadily growing. It is generally thought that repressive actions by TNI gradually led more Acehnese to the banner of autonomy or independence. In 1989, GAM re-emerged with a campaign of attacks on police and military installations and government facilities, even though this was 'a time when the New Order leadership had reason to believe that the brutal methods it had used in East Timor, Irian Jaya, Java, Lampung and other "trouble spots" had worked' (Robinson 1998:147).

The Suharto government's response to the resurgence of separatist activities was to repeat the usual formula of repression and launch a military offensive. From 1989, Aceh was declared a Military Operations Zone (*Daerah Operasi Militer*—DOM), an acronym which became synonymous with violence and unrestrained and unaccountable military actions. During the ten years of the declaration of a DOM, from 1989 to 1998, most estimates put the number of people killed in the conflict between 2,000 and 10,000, most of whom were civilians. Reports of intimidation, beatings, rapes and torture were numerous, and an unknown number of people 'disappeared' or were otherwise unaccounted for (HRW 2001:8). The population of Aceh was left traumatised and desperate for some sort of solution (Saad 2003).

Peace efforts after Suharto

When Suharto resigned in May 1998, there was a general tide of sentiment that the abuses of his New Order regime should be exposed and recompense made. Suharto's successor, President BJ Habibie, lifted the DOM in August 1998. Both Habibie and the then Minister of Defence and head of TNI, General Wiranto, apologised for abuses committed by members of the security forces. The new democratically elected President, Abdurrahman Wahid, called for a fresh approach of reconciliation and negotiation, although in response to contrary pressures from Acehnese for an immediate referendum and from TNI for a renewed offensive, Wahid 'fudged the issue' and 'repeatedly failed to explain what he was doing' (Barton 2002:292).[6] Wahid's off-hand remarks— that he supported a referendum at some unspecified time—swelled expectations amongst the Acehnese public and amongst his political enemies (O'Rourke 2002:332–4). Soon after he came to office in October 1999, Wahid established an Independent Commission to Investigate Violence in Aceh and a number of junior officers and soldiers were convicted over some cases of killings of civilians. Megawati Sukarnoputri, both as Vice President and President (from July 2001), also made statements suggesting she strongly supported a new approach to the Aceh problem, once famously declaring that 'not one drop of the people's blood' should be shed in the province.

On the Acehnese side, the end of the New Order and the sentiments being expressed by leading figures in Jakarta created expectations not only that they would be freed from the heavy hand of TNI but that they would be given an opportunity to express their true feelings about the future of their province. In November 1999, a huge rally in Banda Aceh, the capital of Aceh, claimed to comprise over a million people, called for a referendum on independence and an end to military violence.[7] The referendum on autonomy or independence in East Timor in August 1999 was taken up as a precedent for Aceh. This freer political environment also led to the growth of non-government organisations (NGOs), campaigning for a referendum, and others taking up human rights, humanitarian and developmental issues in the province. The mass movement for a referendum was largely led by student organisations, without any initial connection with GAM in either an organisational or ideological sense. Indeed, many of the new NGOs and student groups entered into direct competition with GAM, showing that opposition to the central government and TNI was not necessarily the same as support for GAM.

The 'Humanitarian Pause' and 'Special Autonomy'

President Wahid's government undertook two important initiatives in 2000 and 2001: the 'Humanitarian Pause' of June 2000 and the passing of a law for 'special Autonomy' for Aceh in July 2001. The Humanitarian Pause was a ceasefire, a three-month accord designed to break the cycle of fighting and allow the distribution of humanitarian assistance to the people of Aceh, and was extended several times in different forms over the next year. The Special Autonomy law provided for the introduction of certain elements of *syariah* law in local courts,[8] increased oil and gas revenues for the province and direct election of the province's Governor and district heads in 2004.

The ceasefire, together with the Special Autonomy law, created an impression outside the province that progress was being made. The reality on the ground, however, was that most Acehnese concluded that little had changed. Although the Humanitarian Pause initially brought a lull in fighting, TNI and GAM seemed to regard it as little more than an opportunity to re-group and re-arm. Outside observers and local NGOs reported that violence had returned to pre-Pause levels by the end of 2001 (ICG 2003a:2).

Special Autonomy, at least as it was structured under the 2001 law, garnered little support because the law did not provide for immediate provincial and gubernatorial elections, thus denying the much called for expression of Acehnese opinion. Instead, it allowed the increased resource revenue to pass into the hands of the corrupt provincial government still dominated by pro-

Jakarta elements from Golkar, the old ruling party. The law did not clarify how *syariah* would be implemented or how Special Autonomy would be implemented in conjunction with the decentralisation of government that was occurring across Indonesia. Critically, the law did not allow for the establishment of local political parties, thus providing no incentive for GAM to participate in a legal political process or for new non-GAM elements to emerge (ICG 2003a:4). Under the electoral laws for the 1999 elections, and under the new laws passed in 2003, political parties could not contest either national or provincial elections unless they were organised at a national level, with members and branches in a majority of provinces. This provision was specifically designed to prevent the emergence of provincial and regional parties, the argument being that such parties would fan separatist sentiment.

The Cessation of Hostilities Agreement

The gradual disintegration of the Humanitarian Pause and the failure of efforts to revive the peace process during 2001 and 2002 came about because neither side appeared to be committed to a negotiated settlement. Nevertheless, through the mediation of the Geneva-based Henri Dunant Centre for Humanitarian Dialogue (HDC), the parties were brought together again for a series of talks during 2002. With the assistance of foreign 'wise men'[9] a Cessation of Hostilities Agreement (COHA) was signed in Geneva on 9 December 2002. The first intention of the COHA was to bring about another ceasefire, but the two parties also agreed to a framework that was designed to lead to disengagement and disarmament and to negotiation over the issues of principle at stake.

After a two-month confidence-building stage, a series of 'peace zones' was to be established, where GAM would 'begin a phased placement' of its arms and from which TNI would be 'relocated' (ICG 2003a:8–10). A team of monitors (50 nominated by the Indonesian Government, 50 by GAM and 50 from overseas by HDC—principally from the Philippines and Thailand) would oversee the process. A so-called All-Inclusive Dialogue of all elements of Acehnese society would 'review' the law on Special Autonomy. The elections in 2004 would then lead to a democratically elected provincial assembly and provincial government. Most reports indicate that the COHA was greeted with enthusiasm and relief amongst the population in Aceh and the level of violence dropped dramatically (ICG 2003a:10). By the end of January 2003, the first 'peace zone' was established and more were being planned. Many of the peace monitors had been deployed throughout the province and their reports on violations of the ceasefire placed pressure on both parties to keep to the Agreement.

Despite initial enthusiasm, the vagueness of most of the terms of the agreement soon became an obstacle to implementation. The two sides proved to have a different understanding of what was meant by terms such as 'placement' of arms by GAM, 'relocation' of TNI and whether the 'review' of the Special Autonomy law could involve discussion about the principles of autonomy or independence, including public debate and campaigning. By February 2003, Indonesian military leaders began accusing GAM of failing to meet the deadline for the 'placement' of arms and of using the ceasefire to strengthen their forces. They also claimed that rallies in support of independence or a referendum violated the principle of acceptance of the law on Special Autonomy. Armed clashes between the two sides began to increase again, with each side blaming the other for violations of the ceasefire. GAM was accused of recommencing their attacks on government facilities and personnel and TNI was accused of attacking alleged GAM supporters, either directly or through armed militias. In April 2003, 50 people were reportedly killed during that month alone and most of the monitors had withdrawn from the field into the provincial capital due to threats to their security.

By the end of April the situation was reaching a crisis, both on the ground in Aceh and in negotiations in Geneva. When talks planned to take place in Geneva on 28 April failed to materialise, the Indonesian government gave GAM a two-week deadline to initiate negotiations or face a renewed military offensive. The Security Co-ordinating Minister, Susilo Bambang Yudhoyono, declared that peace talks could continue only if GAM accepted the law on Special Autonomy and guaranteed to surrender its weapons. Last minute talks in Tokyo on 18 May failed to produce a compromise and the next day Megawati signed an emergency decree and TNI began an all-out operation against GAM.

Why did the ceasefire collapse?

The COHA of December 2002 was seen by many observers as the last chance for a peaceful resolution to the Aceh conflict. Given the gravity of what was at stake for all sides, why did they seem to treat the Agreement so lightly? What were the motivations and calculations of the three main parties—TNI, GAM and the Indonesia Government—in signing the COHA and in their subsequent actions? When progress in the COHA faltered in March 2003 and GAM stuck to its determination to push for independence rather than autonomy, TNI began to undermine the agreement by orchestrating demonstrations against the international monitors and by making preparations for renewed military action. There were a number of attacks on monitors, their vehicles and offices, attacks which were linked to anti-independence militias organised by the military (Aspinall & Crouch 2003:28). As the military began moving reinforcements into Aceh, with Megawati's apparent approval, it became clear that proponents of a negotiated solution were being 'overwhelmed by the demands of the military hardliners for a military offensive' (Aspinall & Crouch 2003:20).

In the eyes of most TNI officers, the COHA was a first step along the road to legitimacy and recognition for GAM and ultimately, to a repetition of the disaster and humiliation of East Timor. For them, the last time civilian politicians were allowed to handle a problem of separatism was in East Timor in 1999, and in that case, Indonesia lost a province for which the military had shed its blood to defend. The resumption of military operations was thus, for the generals, a return to the 'proper way' to deal with threats to the country's territorial integrity.

Leading elements in the Indonesian military have consistently argued for a forcible solution to the problem of Aceh and were opposed to the COHA because they saw the Agreement as implicit recognition of forces which threatened the territorial integrity of Indonesia and which threatened the political and financial viability of the military in the Indonesian state. As suggested above, TNI's opposition to a negotiated settlement goes to the heart of the military's efforts to maintain a key role for itself in the political economy of post-Suharto Indonesia.

The granting of real autonomy to Aceh would undermine TNI's pretensions to be the sole guarantor of the unity and integrity of Indonesia. It would be a blow to TNI's prestige as a military force and to the primacy of what is usually called the 'security approach' as the only appropriate response to separatism, whether in Aceh, East Timor, West Papua or elsewhere. One senior officer, Lieutenant General Kiki Syahnakri, attacked the COHA as allowing GAM a 'golden opportunity' to campaign 'nakedly and freely'. He said that unless negotiations were strengthened by 'military action and security operations' they would fail to reach a final solution (*Kompas* 2003).[10] The rigid operational doctrine of the TNI says that any easing of military pressure is an invitation to those elements intent on disturbing the security and integrity of the state. The experience of the post-1998 period, when efforts to find a negotiated solution were accompanied by a rapid growth of public support for GAM, is seen as vindication of this position. The recent period is contrasted with the early 1990s when GAM was marginalised by the use of military use.[11]

It is simply denied that the attraction of the people of Aceh to the ideas of autonomy and independence and to GAM itself is mainly the result of past military actions. Rather, any explanations for the persistence of separatist sentiment are couched in terms of the inherent character of the Acehnese.

Such explanations revolve around the putatively troublesome and rebellious nature of the Acehnese as an ethnic group, with the history of the anti-colonial struggle and post-independence movements posited as evidence. In this construction of reality, even the prominent role of Acehnese in the independence war becomes justification for treating Aceh as especially formidable. Secondly, the greater adherence to a doctrinal version of Islam amongst the Acehnese, in contrast to the syncretic Javanese who have predominated amongst the military leadership since independence (and especially since the rebellions of the 1950s), is seen as temperamentally inclining the Acehnese people to extremist intrepretations of the role of Islam in politics and society (Crouch 1978:36–7). For the Indonesian military, with a long history of antagonism to political Islam, this makes any expression of Acehnese identity potentially threatening (Lowry 1996:199–200). For many years 'the New Order regime utilised depictions of Acehnese Islamic "fanaticism" to legitimate repression against the GAM insurgency' (Aspinall 2002c:22).

But TNI also has direct material interests in maintaining a presence in Aceh. The official budget for TNI has never covered more than about a third of the military's real operating costs (Liddle 2003; Lowry 1998–9). The remainder is made up through officers' official and unofficial involvement in private and military-owned business activities and by contributions from wealthy business people. These activities also include illegal trade, unofficial levies on local interests and sheer extortion. Regions of conflict like Aceh have regularly provided the best cover for the more lucrative (and usually corrupt and illegal) fund-raising activities. An operational posting is highly desirable for many TNI officers because it presents the best opportunities for personal enrichment. It is an open secret that TNI officers have been involved in illegal logging, drug smuggling, extortion and other illegal activities in Aceh (Lowry 1996:168; Van Zorge 2003).

The public image of TNI suffered a major blow from perceptions of human rights abuses before and during the fall of Suharto in 1998. Since that time its formal political power has been reduced, including the removal of its representation in parliament (to take effect after the 2004 election) and a greatly diminished role of military officers in the civil administration at all levels of government, particularly its near-monopoly of control in 'sensitive' provinces. Separation of the police from the military was also a setback for TNI because it meant that responsibility for internal security was officially transferred from the army to the police. The President's declaration of a state of emergency, in which the military took back the internal security role in Aceh, was seen as demonstrating that only TNI had the operational capability to deal with internal disturbances and to defend the unity of the nation.

Many leading political figures who had been critical of the actions of the military during 1998 and who have advocated a diminution of TNI's role in politics and governmental affairs, including Amien Rais and Abdurrahman Wahid, have tacitly accepted the military's return to centre stage in Aceh since May 2003. While the generally independent official human rights monitoring organisation, the National Commission for Human Rights (KomnasHAM) has sent missions to Aceh since the declaration of emergency, its reports have been quite muted and some ambiguity has been created about whether the armed forces or GAM have been primarily responsible for human rights violations. Even human rights NGOs have found it difficult to generate public interest in military violence in Aceh, as well as issues such as the displacement of thousands of Acehnese due to fighting and arson. By apparently convincing the majority of Indonesians to view the issue of Aceh as a question of national unity, the TNI has succeeded in silencing or drowning out those who would otherwise see current government policy of perpetuating the military's undemocratic place in Indonesian politics as rolling back progress in civil–military relations achieved since 1998.

GAM's quest for legitimacy

GAM and its insurrectionary strategy for independence has only become a leading force in the province's politics since the fall of Suharto in 1998. As argued above, the idea of a sense of separate identity amongst the Acehnese is a far more complex and contingent story than is presented by the ideologues of GAM, or as it is echoed in TNI propaganda. The spectrum of opinion within Aceh ranges from opposition to the presence of TNI and to the current division of the benefits from natural resources, to support for a particular recognition of the place of Islam, to sentiment in favour of some sort of special status for Aceh, through to advocacy of full independence and statehood. None of these positions necessarily translates into support for GAM itself, although heavy-handed repression by TNI, the corrupt reputation of its officers and the sense of crisis the armed forces have created, have been GAM's best source of recruitment.

The military's pursuit of a one-track strategy of armed conflict has also had the paradoxical effect of making it impossible for non-GAM political parties or NGOs, including human rights groups, to operate in Aceh. As mentioned above, there was a flowering of NGOs during the relatively peaceful period after the fall of Suharto in 1998, but the resurgence of conflict has provided a cover for TNI and GAM violence against non-aligned organisations. While the military regards any independent Acehnese activist as subversive, GAM often regards them in a hostile way as competitors for the loyalty of the

Acehnese population. The polarisation of Acehnese politics has played directly into GAM's hands, helping it to position itself as the only voice of the people of Aceh.

From GAM's point of view, the COHA relieved the intense pressure of TNI repression, while providing an opportunity to strengthen the movement's domestic and international legitimacy. GAM has never been a very effective military force, and while TNI has never been able to eliminate it completely, open armed confrontation has always left GAM on the defensive and confined to scattered and remote areas. GAM has also faced the problem that its ill-disciplined and factionalised membership has sometimes been indistinguishable from the bandits and stand-over men who have exploited the chaos and weakened GAM's standing.

The official leadership of GAM is a group of exiles centred around its founder, di Tiro, who have lived in Sweden for many years and taken out Swedish residency or citizenship.[12] But the exiled leadership has not always been able to make Aceh-based supporters implement agreements the leaders make in Geneva. Some members of GAM seem to have given only half-hearted support to the COHA, while other splinter factions[13] have carried on with their normal activities of attacking the operations of the central government, clashing with the security forces and levying 'taxes' on local and foreign businesses.

GAM's implicit strategy seems to have been to provoke an ill-disciplined TNI into atrocities that would rally the Acehnese population to its banner and bring international attention to the struggle. The military's behaviour has certainly hardened attitudes towards the central government and roused support for a referendum on independence, but GAM's confrontational policies and a record of human rights abuses by some of its members raises questions about whether the majority of Acehnese see it as fit to be an alternative government. GAM was in effective control of large parts of Aceh from 1999 to 2001, but circumstances have obviously not permitted an open democratic expression of opinion. One of the arguments of the mainly student-led movement for a referendum is that a vote could settle the issue once and for all. The central government's refusal to allow such a vote reflects its lack of confidence that a majority would opt to stay in Indonesia (especially with the experience of East Timor in mind), and the fact that the very act of conceding to this demand would extend legitimacy to the idea of the right of Aceh, or any other province of the Republic of Indonesia, to secede at will.

Nevertheless, GAM's efforts to propagate an historicised view of a sense of Acehnese national identity seem to have borne fruit in the context of central government-sponsored repression. And it is the actions of TNI that have, paradoxically, been the critical instrument of that success. In Aspinall's (2001:3) words, 'contemporary Acehnese nationalism emerged...in direct response to the activities of the Indonesian state'. Not only are GAM and TNI clinched together in a military sense, like two evenly matched boxers unable to land a killing blow on the other, they are also locked together in an ideological contest where the actions of one become the justification for the actions of the other. If, as Aspinall (2001:3–4) argues, 'Acehnese nationalism emerged primarily as a reaction against the Indonesian state's modernising, nation-building project', it is also the case that the New Order's principal instrument in that project was the military. Because Aceh's petroleum became critically important to the nation-building project as it was pursued by the New Order, it became certain that Aceh would fall into the vice-like grip of military control. The violent, intolerant and rapacious hold of the military on the resources and politics of the province—especially a province that had a history of rebelliousness upon which its nationalist mythmakers could draw—ensured that GAM's re-creation of Acehnese traditions would find a receptive audience. This myth making has, in turn, made it less likely that the TNI would see any Acehnese reaction against the effects of the New Order's policies in the province as anything less than a full-scale assault on the Indonesian state. As Robinson (1998:132) observed: 'one might even argue that in the absence of the presumed "tradition" of Acehnese resistance, New Order authorities would have paid far less attention to the movement'.

The second element of GAM's efforts to establish itself as the leading, if not sole, advocate of true Acehnese aspirations has been on the world stage. The reasons for this are not hard to discern. In practical political terms, 'the only secessionist movements that have proven successful are those that have benefited from international support' (Aspinall 2002c:9), either militarily or diplomatically. The combination of UN non-recognition of Indonesia's claim to East Timor and Australia's willingness to risk political capital to act as a vanguard for international military force was critical for East Timor's achievement of independence. Similarly, Bangladesh would not have been created without India's military intervention and rapid regional recognition was important for the new states of the former Yugoslavia and Czechoslovakia. Given that the sovereignty of a 'nation-state' implies acceptance into the international system of states that has grown up since the 19th century, a key aspect of winning such support from powerful international sponsors is to assert the legitimacy of a territory's claim to nationhood (Aspinall 2001:2–3).

In this endeavour, however, GAM has not been conspicuously successful. This has, in part, been because it has generally found itself arguing against the prevailing climate of opinion in the centres of international power and influence. During the early years of GAM's existence in the 1970s and 1980s, when it had little presence on the ground in Aceh, Hasan di Tiro took up the rhetoric of anti-imperialism and Third World nationalism. This line of argument found little support (outside marginal activist groups) because it ran counter to the Cold War mentality of most Western powers. The then newly-established Suharto regime was seen as a beacon of stability, or at least anti-leftist order, in a region threatened by communism, as well as a secure place for new investment in seemingly scarce oil resources. As Fretilin found to its cost in 1975, striking the poses of Third World radicalism played into the hands of the generals in Jakarta (Aspinall 2001:9–10). The military benefit of training GAM activists in Libya was far outweighed by the political cost of being seen as an instrument of Colonel Gaddafi.

In later years, GAM has focused more on appealing to universalist norms such as the right to self-determination and has argued its case within the discourse of human rights (Aspinall 2002c:5–20). Underpinning all its international efforts has been the continuing project of creating a historical tradition of ethnic and religious identity and continuity. In the immediate post-Suharto era, casting the Aceh issue as a question of human rights had some effect, especially in the context of domestic Indonesian politics. International human rights groups such as Amnesty International and Human Rights Watch have an extended history of observing the conflict. But a major problem for Acehnese nationalists is that arguments about questions such as self-determination are as much legalistic as they are philosophical or normative. Thus, it may well be logical that the right to vote on self-determination for the East Timorese should also be extended to the Acehnese, but the reality is that the ambiguities that existed about the status of the former Portuguese territory are not present in relation to the former territories of the Netherlands East Indies. Unlike East Timor, the UN has never questioned the legality of Indonesian rule in Aceh and no sovereign state has ever suggested that Aceh is not rightfully a part of Indonesia.

Since the attacks of 11 September 2001 and the US declaration of its 'War on Terror', GAM has once again found itself in an unconducive global environment. The suggestion that the movement for autonomy or independence in Aceh is fundamentally driven by Islamist ideas or is even dominated by Islamic extremists had the potential to close many doors to GAM in Western capitals. Looking through the distorting lens of ideas about Islamic extremism and webs of global terror, the US (and Australia) have implicitly accepted the version of Acehnese history which emphasises a putative particularism of Acehnese culture and religious identity. The irony, as argued above, is that both TNI and GAM have contributed to such perceptions. In response to continuing conflict in Aceh, the governments of countries such as the US and Australia have limited themselves to expressions of understanding about TNI actions (although the US has made subtle overtures to the Indonesian government about finding a peace settlement). There has even been some sympathy, notably in non-official, pro-Jakarta quarters, that human rights abuses are mainly the fault of GAM. Such a position has been regarded in Washington and Canberra as an easy price to pay for Indonesian co-operation with anti-terrorism operations by Western security agencies and Indonesia's passive acquiescence to the West's particular ideological construction of the problem of terrorism.[14]

In reality, GAM has no history of association with foreign, Islamic fundamentalist movements[15] and there is no evidence of links with Southeast Asian Islamic terrorist networks such as Jema'ah Islamiyah, let alone Al Qaeda. There are, however, reports that GAM has rebuffed efforts by JI to build links with it (Jones 2003). An earlier connection with Libya was abandoned and, in any case, was opportunistic rather than ideological on GAM's part.[16] There is also no sign that support for Jakarta's war against GAM is any less popular amongst Muslims than other religious groups.

Finally, GAM has made little headway in winning international recognition because no regional country has shown that it has any interest in, or perceived advantage from, an independent Aceh, or that the crisis in the province has reached such as stage as to warrant their intervention (although Japan, which has a substantial investment in the Arun LNG plant, did host the failed May 2003 talks, and has since offered to do so again). The importance of foreign assistance for successful secessionist movements has already been noted, but such movements rarely achieve their objectives with only generalised international sympathy. Major developments usually only occur when important bordering or nearby states become directly involved, or there is another strategic interest. The examples of East Timor and Bangladesh, each of which has geographic and strategic importance, are such cases. Moreover, from a military point of view, guerrilla movements are not often triumphant unless they have neighbouring territories from which to operate or find sanctuary: the Viet Cong not only had North Vietnam for support, but they could also operate in Laos and Cambodia. By contrast, GAM's territory is bordered by ocean and thereafter the states of ASEAN, all of which vigorously eschew interference in each other's internal affairs, especially those of the senior member, Indonesia. Many ASEAN governments themselves face some kind of separatist movement, which further strengthens support for the state rather than the separatist movement. Although reports indicate that GAM obtains most of its arms from or through Thailand and Malaysia, there is no suggestion that this process has any official support.

Megawati's government: new elections and the future of reform

When President Megawati Sukarnoputri signed the decree of 19 May 2003 declaring martial law in Aceh, many commentators saw the move as part of her efforts to build popular support in the lead-up to Indonesia's national elections in April 2004. Most indications were that there was little popular sympathy for Acehnese separatism and that support for operations by the security forces was strong, particularly among the (sometimes intimidated) media, despite awareness of the TNI's appalling human rights record. Megawati was almost certainly prepared to reverse her previous stand and allow a return to the old 'security approach', because it might boost her image as a strong leader and defender of national unity in the lead-up to the elections, and to ensure continuing TNI support for her presidency.

But Megawati's unleashing of the military was symptomatic of problems within her administration that were deeper than mere political opportunism. The efforts to find a peaceful solution in Aceh failed to get beyond the initial stage of a ceasefire because they did not tackle the wider issues of how to address the grievances of the Acehnese or to re-integrate the province into the mainstream of national political life. Beyond an immediate end to insecurity and fear of extortion, intimidation or death at the hands of TNI, GAM or militias, the people of Aceh want recognition of past abuses, notably by the TNI, and a serious attempt to bring justice to the perpetrators (which seems unlikely for the TNI, given their stated objections). There has also been widespread suffering from loss of employment and economic opportunity, the displacement of thousands of people from their homes, the collapse of government services and shortages of basic items like food, clothing and medicine, all of which has been brought about by over a decade of conflict. This situation was, of course, radically exacerbated by the massive destruction caused to Aceh by the 2004 tsunami. Finally, there is the long-standing feeling that the unique history and culture of Aceh has been suppressed by successive regimes in Jakarta and that the resources of the province have been exploited for the exclusive benefit of non-Acehnese. Meaningful (as distinct from token) autonomy is widely seen as the only way for Aceh to exist within the framework of the Republic of Indonesia.

Neither the Wahid nor the Megawati administrations appear to have had the capacity to develop longer-term policy strategies or the persistence to see existing efforts to completion. The most promising initiative, the law on Special Autonomy for Aceh, had little effect on the reality of life in Aceh because, as mentioned above, it did not supplant the old Jakarta-centric power elites and provided few avenues through which non-GAM forces could build a political alternative based on acceptance of autonomy within Indonesia. Most national leaders apparently thought that the mere passing of the law would satisfy all reasonable demands. In the face of constant military opposition and GAM's insistence on raising the question of independence, the government caved into the force that has the most to gain by continued conflict—the army—and reverted to the strategy that has demonstrably failed since the 1980s.

This rather gloomy assessment reflects the fact that progress in many urgent areas of governmental reform has been disappointingly slow since the end of the Suharto regime. The Megawati government was unwilling to confront vested interests, including a corrupt and dysfunctional legal and judicial system and a civil service that is driven by patronage and corruption, to the detriment of the delivery of basic services like education, health and infrastructure. In the case of Aceh, this weakness in policy formation and implementation meant that a version of regional autonomy, while perhaps well motivated in principle, failed in practice because the apparatus of state could not actually deliver the promised benefits. Because of a failure to bring about a complete, or even significant, withdrawal of the military from civilian politics, the government was susceptible to pressure from the TNI and was afraid to confront the issue of past TNI abuses in Aceh. With attempted negotiations not producing immediate results (or with the results being undermined), the military was again being permitted to dominate policy on the problem of Aceh.

In addition to human rights and humanitarian concerns, Jakarta's handling of the matter revealed ongoing weaknesses within the Megawati administration. Even as the country moved towards its second democratic election, the processes of decision-making in the Indonesian state and economy had not changed significantly since the end of the New Order. The circle of political competition had widened a little since 1998, but the main players were basically the same as those who fought for the spoils under the watchful eye of Suharto. Suharto is gone and there is no longer an ultimate overseer of who gets what: new channels of patrimonialism have opened up in the national parliament and in the regional governments, but the practices of corruption, collusion and nepotism still provide the motive force for the exercise of power and the accumulation of wealth.

The bolstering of the military's political position that was implicit in allowing it to return to its previous role and to impose martial law in Aceh was a serious blow against reform and symptomatic of the Megawati administration's incapacity to overcome the vested interests that profited from the status quo. This was not only dangerous for Indonesia's future as a stable democracy, but it also threatened its economic prospects by deterring domestic and international investment. The conflict in Aceh was a part of the crisis of the Indonesian state and its ill-handling by the Indonesian Government exacerbated the crisis still further.

With the election of Susilo Bambang Yudhoyono as president in September 2004, there was some hope that there could be movement towards a resolution of the Aceh conflict. Certainly, Yudhoyono had noted this was among his key goals as president. However, in the period between September and the end of December 2004, there was, in effect, no progress on this front. There was, however, in November 2004 a quiet overture from the leadership of GAM to re-open a dialogue, and by mid-December it seemed that the new government might be preparing to respond. However, the tsunami that destroyed much of the populated areas of Aceh, including Banda Aceh, on 26 December 2004, changed the material and political dynamic of the province.

Not only did over 100,000 Acehnese die in the catastrophe, around a half a million were left homeless and much of the province and its infrastructure was destroyed. In response, the international community poured hundreds of millions of dollars into Aceh, along with more than 2,000 foreign aid workers, engineers and others from the militaries of the US, Australia and a number of other countries. This had the effect of forcing open the previously closed province and, with the TNI not only assisting in a limited fashion, but interfering in the aid delivery process through stockpiling, forcing payment of bribes by aid organisations, selling otherwise free aid supplies and so on. As well, the TNI shipped thousands of fresh troops into the province and escalated its campaign against GAM, closing off some areas to aid relief. In response, the UN, USA and many other members of the international community called on the warring parties to end their conflict. Given that GAM had declared a unilateral ceasefire from 27 December, this tended to fall to the TNI. The TNI responded by rejecting such calls and demanding that foreign militaries leave within three months.

Prospects

The collapse of the CoHA and the return of open armed conflict in Aceh could, in the first instance, be seen as a product of failures of judgement on both sides. On the government side, despite the singular efforts of then Security Affairs Co-ordinating Minister, Susilo Bambang Yudhoyono, the Cabinet as a whole failed to consider the wider issues involved in a peace plan, especially the timing and delicate handling that would need to be invested. GAM overplayed its hand by expecting that a ceasefire would bring favourable international attention to its cause, by blatantly using the ceasefire to bolster its political and military strength and by a mixture of intransigence and prevarication in negotiations, at least until the very end, by which time it was too late. TNI had already set the government on its preferred course of action. The process was made doubly difficult, of course, because the Indonesian military openly opposed the plans of the civilian government, lobbied for an end to the negotiations within the highest levels of government, undermined the security of international observers and provoked confrontations on the ground within Aceh. Last minute concessions by the GAM leadership came after the TNI, and hence the government, had already decided on reverting to military action.

Although TNI won a political victory within the Indonesian state and regained responsibility for defeating separatism in Aceh, the experience of the 12 months of martial law, and the reversion to a state of emergency thereafter, showed that there was little chance that the military would be any more successful than it had been in the past. GAM was forced into a military retreat, and there was a claim, based on unsubstantiated TNI statements, that GAM was suffering significant casualties.[17] But its leadership has remained intact and, like all guerrilla movements, it is successful as long as it is not completely eliminated. GAM is relying on the assumption that the conflict will cause civilian deaths, that the Acehnese population will blame TNI for these deaths and the tension and disruption to normal life brought by the military campaign. And TNI appears to be vindicating this assumption with vigour. The cycle of violence in Aceh since 1989 has progressively turned the people of Aceh against the central government and the current situation can only intensify this.

The only realistic scenario under which the current military offensive might succeed is if it were combined with a strategy of undermining the political position of GAM through a restoration of government services within the province and allowing the people of Aceh to develop alternatives to GAM. A two-track strategy of this kind would require TNI to keep its forces under tight discipline and to facilitate humanitarian relief. It would only work if there were elections for a new provincial administration in the near future and the law on Special Autonomy was redrafted with strong Acehnese involvement. In addition, the amendment of electoral laws to allow for the participation of regionally-based parties is critical for creating the possibility for political organisations (both those whose constituency might support GAM and those who do not) to participate in democratic politics without being tied to one of the existing major parties, all of whom are seen as being controlled from and by Jakarta.

There was no indication that either TNI or the central government saw the military retreat of GAM as an opportunity to create political alternatives to secessionism. A mentality of regarding assertions of regional identity as a threat to national unity tended to cast suspicion on any independent Acehnese organisation and on the people of the province as a whole. Special Autonomy as defined by Jakarta was unlikely to win credibility within Aceh and Jakarta was unwilling to trust Aceh to develop its own formula for autonomy within the Republic of Indonesia. In any case, the corruption and administrative incapacity of the Indonesian state apparatus, at both the national and provincial level, weakened any effort to re-establish effective government. The relapse into the 'security approach' appeared to be born of a sense of exasperation and resignation amongst the civilian politicians. The fact that it appeared to be popular with the Indonesian electorate, or at least via a media that was wary of offending the TNI, made it doubly tempting. But the reality was that attempts to enforce a military solution would probably bring nothing but an extended cycle of violence.

The political economy of the New Order in Aceh locked the province into a conflict with the centre, and the chances of finding ways out of the deadlock were blocked by interpretations of the past emphasising a lack of capacity to change an intrinsic identity, rather than as historically contingent phenomena that could be changed as they were in the past, through political negotiation and accommodation. The two sides, (essentially GAM and TNI) were stuck in a deadlock, while civilian government had allowed itself to become little more than a passive observer. This deadlock could only ultimately play into the hands of GAM, who viewed (probably correctly) that every TNI action is unlikely to defeat them militarily, but would drive more Acehnese into the independence camp.

The idea that continuing conflict would internationalise the issue (and break the deadlock to the benefit of pro-independence forces) was based on unlikely assumptions. In particular, comparing Aceh with East Timor ignored the historical and legal differences between the two cases (despite GAM claims to the contrary). Moreover, it failed to come to terms with the reality that the critical factor in allowing movement on the East Timor situation was the eccentric personage of BJ Habibie and his quixotic attempts to notch up a major policy achievement before the 1999 election. Any other incumbent of the post-Suharto presidency would almost certainly not have allowed the East Timor 'popular consultation' of August 1999. The relationship between TNI and the Megawati government—and the successor government of Susilo Bambang Yudhoyono—was such that the government would never flout TNI's wishes and call a referendum, whatever pressure there might be from powers in the region or further afield.

The result of this deadlock was twofold: continuing suffering for the people of Aceh and a dislocation of security policy in Jakarta. The armed forces have continued to get what they want in terms of resources and powers and Indonesia continues to be destabilised. The boost given to TNI can only be seen as a boost to the elements resisting political change in Indonesia. The 'nationalism' induced by the Aceh conflict diverted attention from the need to reform the TNI and to reduce its role in politics. It also diverted attention from other issues of democratic reform and provided justification for the inherently authoritarian tendencies of the Megawati administration and the closed circles of the Indonesian political class in general. The Yudhoyono government, which came to power with the explicit support of a large section of the TNI, appeared to be similarly trapped, despite Yudhoyono's personal reformist tendencies and aspirations. The Megawati presidency saw a series of assaults on civil rights in Indonesia, with the jailing of anti-Megawati demonstrators, continuing physical and legal attacks on the effective freedom of the press and the jailing and deportation of foreign activists and critical observers.

How long this situation could prevail was a critical, but open, question. The TNI's failure to solve the Aceh crisis continued to be swamped by 'nationalist' sentiment and rhetoric about defence of unity and integrity of the state. Amongst the political class, this state of affairs could probably have been prolonged indefinitely. But the crucial question was, how long would it be accepted by the Indonesian electorate or, indeed, by a compromised and cautious but still reformist president? Examples internationally do not give a lot of cause for hope: the Indian and Pakistani electorates appear to continue to accept the ongoing disaster in Kashmir and the Russian government's abuses and human losses in Chechnya do not seem to cause its administration irretrievable electoral damage. The immediate prospects are that the military and political stalemate, with its accompanying violence, political polarisation and dire humanitarian effects, will continue for the foreseeable future. In the absence of initiatives from policy-makers in Jakarta, there can be little optimism about relief of the continuing agony of Aceh.

The one chance, perhaps, was that with the massive rebuilding effort underway in Aceh as this was written, and the presence of the international community there with the attendant focus of the world's media, there was a small chance that the two sides could be brought together to talk again. There was clear willingness within GAM to do this and some willingness within the government (although its position appeared to reflect a range of agendas and perspectives). The main impediment to such talks and hence a potential resolution, however, appeared to be the TNI.

Endnotes

1 The formal name for GAM is the Aceh-Sumatra National Liberation Front (ASNLF).
2 Estimates of the military strength of GAM vary from 2,000 to more than 5,000.
3 Dirk van Hogendorp in 1800 (Vickers 1996:2).
4 One of the ironies of current constructions of present-day militant anti-government groups is that although Islamist extremist groups, such as Jema' ah Islamiyah, that stand in the tradition of Dar'ul Islam, are mainly composed of Javanese, they are not generally seen as representing some kind of Java-based tradition. GAM leaders, on the other hand, who often repudiate the heritage of Dar'ul Islam, or view it as a peculiarly local manifestation of separatist aspiration, are cast as the inheritors of Acehnese tradition.
5 The patrimonial networks of the New Order and the various elements of the Indonesian business class were first definitively analysed from a political economy perspective by Robison (1986). Harold Crouch (1978; 1979) presented a political scientist's picture, and Elson (2001) provides an important addition from a historian's point of view.
6 Wahid's first post-New Order visit to Aceh in May 1999 was a failure. He was jostled by student demonstrators and when he was heckled at a public meeting, he refused to speak and left the meeting (Barton 2002:270–71).
7 The total population of Aceh is about 4.3 million.
8 Editor's note: Acehnese opponents to this law claim it represents an alien interpretation of *syariah* and is therefore an imposition.
9 Former Thai foreign minister, Surin Pitsuwan, retired US General, Anthony Zinni, and former Yugoslav foreign minister and ambassador to Indonesia, Budimir Loncar.
10 The author would like to express appreciation to Dr Aspinall and Dr Crouch for allowing access to this draft paper.
11 According to Lowry (1996:167), some have argued that TNI 'actually chose to let the revolt [beginning in 1989] to unfold, perhaps to demonstrate to the Indonesian public and the regime the dangers of Islamic extremism and thereby reinforce the armed forces' role in protecting the state'.
12 The protection accorded the GAM leadership by Sweden has been a *cause celebre* in the Indonesian media, with government and parliamentary figures attacking the Swedish government and even calling for a withdrawal of diplomatic relations. The Swedish government's response is that the GAM members have not committed any crime under Swedish law and have the same rights as all Swedish residents or citizens.
13 Editor's note: It has not been established whether these 'splinter factions' are GAM, Acehnese bandits claiming to be GAM or, as has been shown in many cases, members of the security forces posing as GAM. The leadership of GAM

in the field says that it recognises the authority of the Swedish leadership group, and there are regular communications between them. In part at least, the propagation of the idea of splinter groups or factions within GAM has been a part of the TNI's strategy of attempting to foment discord within GAM and a sense of its illegitimacy among external observers.

14 Following the start of the military offensive in May 2003, the Australian Minister for Foreign Affairs, Alexander Downer, and the Minister for Defence, Robert Hill, expressed hopes for a return to negotiations, but emphasised that the matter was an internal Indonesian affair (*SMH* 2003a:9; *Canberra Times* 2003:2; *Age* 2003a:13). Downer also singled out for condemnation the 'violence perpetrated by the separatist movement' (*SMH* 2003a:9). While attending an ASEAN meeting in Cambodia, Downer defended the Indonesian military against foreign criticism, attacked 'terrible acts of violence' by GAM and praised Indonesia for allowing journalists and human rights groups into the province (*SMH* 2003b:11; *Age* 2003b:13). In fact, the Indonesian government introduced strict controls over the entry of journalists and human rights observers into the province. The government also emulated the US in Iraq by controlling media coverage by 'embedding' journalists amongst operational military forces. Following a TNI attack on a German tourist couple, resulting in the death of one and the injury of the other, all tourists were banned from entering Aceh.

15 Editor's note: In 2001, GAM explicitly rejected the presence of Laskar Jihad in Aceh, and similarly rejected overtures by Jema'ah Islamiyah in 2003. Following the introduction of the Islamic Defenders Front and Laskar Mujahidin members into Aceh in the wake of the 2004 tsunami, GAM said they were not welcome, challenged their Islamic credentials and called on them to leave. It is worth noting that both organisations were brought to Aceh with the assistance of the TNI.

16 The regime in Libya could not be described as Islamist and it has provided training to a wide range of nationalist and separatist groups, including the Irish Republican Army.

17 Editor's note: GAM claimed that the vast majority of casualties during this period were civilians, which tended to be confirmed by independent reports. The TNI similarly downplayed reports of its own casualties. However, based on their pre-existing numbers and reserve capacity, there was no doubt that GAM suffered proportionately more than the TNI during this period.

Chapter 8

Greed: the silent force of conflict in Aceh

Lesley McCulloch[1]

Aceh is the scene of Indonesia's worst internal conflict and poses the biggest challenge to the territorial integrity of the state. To assume that the conflict in Aceh has triggered the collapse of the local economic and political system would be quite wrong. The war in Aceh is not—as the Indonesian government would have us believe—due to the uncontrolled presence of the pro-independence Aceh Sumatra National Liberation Front (ASNLF—or Gerakan Aceh Merdeka—GAM). Nor can the increasingly brutal attacks on civilians be attributed simply to 'rogue elements' of the military: there has been no breakdown in the military chain of command in Aceh. In fact, a system of profit, power and protection that benefits certain groups has emerged, and it is this that largely explains the violent conflict. For example, the Indonesian Government, the Aceh political elite and the military all stand to gain from the continuation of the conflict, even as other sections of the community become increasingly impoverished.

Within the historic, nationalistic and economic themes that are usually thought to explain the causes of the conflict, three recurring factors are commonly used. The first is that the Acehnese are angry at the corrupt and predatory practices of non-Acehnese in the province, who they accuse of plundering their resources while giving very little in return. The second is the widespread anger at the repression and human rights abuses suffered at the hands of those acting on behalf of the Jakarta-based government. And finally, an argument most commonly confined to those involved in the hierarchy of GAM, is that Aceh was never legally part of Indonesia and that there is therefore a legal basis for independence. These 'understandings' of the conflict have some validity. But this is all rather simplistic and misses one critical element. It is argued here that there exists a more sinister set of motives that fuel—at least in part—the conflict in Aceh.

This chapter will focus on economic factors to explanation of the recent war in Aceh and its pervasiveness over almost three decades, suggesting that the conflict in Aceh is, to a degree, due to the opportunism of one of the warring parties—the security forces. Elements within this party are thus able to pursue their own alternative agenda of enrichment, rather than security and conflict resolution. The thrust of the argument is that greed is the silent force of the conflict in Aceh.

The current situation of martial law, imposed on 19 May 2003, introduces a caveat to this 'greed' hypothesis, but does not discredit it. The military's economic activities at the institutional and individual levels have been adversely affected by the increase in intensity of the conflict and by the changes in operational procedures under martial law. This is causing a split between those who do not benefit directly or who are more professionally minded and want to see martial law maintained—for the 'good of the nation'—and those whose profiteering has been adversely affected, and who are now lobbying for the situation to be downgraded to a civil emergency. The first group argue on the basis of unity of the state and national security, while the latter group have identified several reasons for downscaling: lack of funds for a large scale military campaign to continue; a realisation that the separatist movement cannot be successfully eliminated using a traditional security approach, and disquiet in the international community at the harsh approach taken by Megawati's administration to the problem.

While not diminishing the importance of the above reasons for the eventual inevitable downgrading of the military operation, a second understanding that relates to the issue of 'greed' is the desire of the military and the police to reclaim the 'profit space' that has been lost to them during martial law. The effective 'profit space' in a conflict is quite narrow, and is dependent on a fine balance of relatively low intensity conflict, a significant but controllable level of militarisation and a level of autonomy with which the local military is able to effect its command and control. The current, heightened military operation has squeezed that space, adversely affecting the profiteering of the military and the police.

An understanding of the pursuit of profit by the security forces in Aceh will add to conventional analysis of the dynamics of the conflict, the currently stalled peace process and the predicted changing nature of the military operation.

Indonesia's economic development

Throughout Indonesia, the population has experienced uneven development. Many outlying areas—Aceh is but one—have not enjoyed the same level of economic and social benefits as other areas of Indonesia.[2] When one considers that many of those areas have vast natural resources, it is not difficult to understand why many have come to believe they are almost totally disengaged from the local economy. In Aceh, there has been disenchantment with the Republic for many years. The province received little attention until the mid-1970s, when the boom in liquefied natural gas (LNG) and the presence of PT Arun attracted the rich, powerful and corrupt to Aceh.

The province has a wealth of natural resources, manufacturing and agricultural capacity. Oil resources have dwindled in significance in recent years, but gas, particularly LNG, remains highly profitable. In addition, there are fertiliser and cement plants; the forests harbour valuable wood and the coastal waters are rich fisheries. The province is very fertile, and commercial crops such as palm oil, rubber, coconuts and coffee grow with ease. Much attention—at the national and international level—has focused on the production of natural gas in the north of the province around Lhokseumawe and the impact of the conflict on production. Aceh produces a third of the country's liquefied natural gas exports. But the conflict has disrupted production on several occasions. The temporary closure from March to July 2001 caused remarkably little anxiety among the majority of Acehnese. This intransigence can be attributed to the fact that most feel they receive little or no benefit from the presence of the LNG facilities. But for the Indonesian Government, who lost about US$100 million per month during the closure, and of course for the company, such a volatile security situation must be addressed as a priority.[3] The conflict is not conducive to the smooth running of international business interests and as such is of grave concern to the domestic political and business elite. Under the control of a Jakarta-based government, it was inevitable that the majority of Acehnese would see few, if any, of the benefits of their rich natural resource base. The close relationship the Suharto regime had with foreign capital affected the way the resources were exploited and the distribution of the benefit. The central government's policy toward Aceh is very obviously influenced by ExxonMobil and the American government that has consistently lobbied Jakarta to prioritise protection of these foreign interests.

In recent years, foreign governments have been more aggressive in their representation of domestic business interests overseas, especially when oil, gas and other natural resources are concerned. The US is also concerned with maritime trade routes. Aceh's proximity to the all-important Straits of Malacca is another reason why not only the American Government, but also many others, are so eager to see an end to the conflict there. In a 1992 presidential election campaign speech, Bill Clinton said that the economic wellbeing of the US 'must become a central defining element of our national security policy' (Clinton 1992). He also said that he would elevate economics into the realms of American foreign policy, which is exactly what he did on taking presidential office in 1993. This was not so much a new policy, but rather signalled an increasing commitment to existing approaches.

ExxonMobil's production in Aceh does not contribute to the oil and gas needs of the US directly. But the profits from that operation are significant, and it falls within the remit of foreign policy and strategic objectives. To this end, the US has condoned the increasing level of militarisation around the plant, putting continuing productivity above the security of those who live nearby.

The presence of ExxonMobil has done little to lift the local people out of poverty. This lack of socio-economic development is of apparent concern to local politicians who now recognise that the disproportionate scale of poverty in Aceh and the influence the conflict has on this—and vice versa—can no longer be ignored. Even before martial law was declared, Vice-Governor Azwar Abubakar lamented

> Seventy percent of villages in Aceh are poor. This is a real problem for us. These people are disenchanted with our efforts and are more inclined to support the rebel movement. We are trying our best to use aid from Jakarta to give people the feeling of hope for the future. For example, we are building drainage systems for the agricultural sector. This has two advantages. First it increase agricultural production, and the second we can employ many people to build the drains and pay them a wage.[4]

What has caused the escalating tensions in Aceh that has contributed to so much suffering and poverty? It is not a simple conflict-poverty correlation. Geoffrey Robinson (2001:214) has suggested that:

> the New Order regime itself was largely responsible for the serious and protracted violence in Aceh...the demise of the New Order state, and its replacement by a less authoritarian, less militaristic, less centralized variant, could bring a swift end to the unsettled conditions that have plagued Aceh in recent years'

Unfortunately this rather optimistic note has not been borne out by subsequent events. The violence has only intensified, and the military has been able to consolidate its control.

Rather than any of these preconditions for peace eventuating with the fall of Suharto, the trend has been one of an escalating conflict. By the time Suharto fell from power in 1998 the conflict had already taken on a momentum of its own. The main stakeholders were now the political, military and business elite whose agenda was quite different from the movement for democracy that was gaining momentum. The hopes expressed by Robinson and shared by many (including some Acehnese) have been dashed by the three Presidents since Suharto. Despite the rhetoric of diplomacy to solve the problem, Megawati has allowed the pursuit of a security approach. Even during the most recent failed peace initiative, the Cessation of Hostilities Agreement

(CoHA), the number of reported violations of the agreement was higher by TNI and police than GAM (JSC 2003). And Megawati has allowed the military to go much further than previous presidents: she declared a state of martial law in Aceh on 19 May 2003. This has resulted in the most brutal of crackdowns on the civilian population.

Root causes of the conflict

There have been several stages in the debate about the root causes of the conflict in Aceh. The first is the discourse on economic injustice and political self-determination predominant in 1976–79 and again in 1989–90 (perhaps even later). The second phase really began in 1991. Attention turned to the actions of the military as information became available about their actions over the previous years. And by 1998, the media had more freedom and began to tell the world the truth about what had happened in Aceh, and as a result, there were several fact-finding missions to the region in mid-1998. General Wiranto (then commander of the armed forces) visited Aceh in August 1998 and shocked the Republic by apologising for human rights violations during the period when Aceh was designated a *daerah operasi militer* (militarised zone—DOM). He declared the DOM status would be lifted. The criticism about past violations soon spread and the calls for more investigations into human rights abuses gained momentum. It is interesting to note that every President since Suharto has apologised for the atrocities committed in Aceh.

This chapter proposes a third phase of investigation into a significant contributor to the real causes of the conflict in Aceh: the economic interests of the military and the police. Although such interests are not a new phenomenon, the cause and consequence relationship has not been properly explored.

Economic motives

In Aceh, people feel aggrieved that the profits from their resources have been 'plundered' by the policies of the Government in Jakarta. In November 2000, Syarifudin Tippe, the then senior military commander in Aceh, conceded that of the financial gain to Jakarta from Aceh's natural resources, less than 5% was actually returned to the province (*Pustaka Cidesindo* 2000:48).

In the early 1970s, a large liquefied natural gas field (LNG) was discovered in Aceh. Operations to extract the resource a few years later were followed very quickly by the onset of the conflict. Anger over existing economic disparities 'became more pronounced when oil companies discovered major pockets of natural gas in the district of North Aceh…With construction of pipelines taking place in 1976, local dissent saw a commensurate rise' (Conboy 2003:261). In 1976 Hasan di Tiro, the GAM leader now in self-imposed exile in Sweden, declared Aceh 'independent'. Hasan said:

> We had no choice but to declare our independence and defend our country—against the Indonesian government and elite. It was obvious they [the Indonesians], would deny the Acehnese not only their political right to a nation state, but also the wealth and resources that would come from the American presence [Exxon] in Aceh. We knew they would not share the profits with us—the poor Acehnese. We had to stop the neo-colonialism, it was very dangerous for us.[5]

Official recognition that less than a fair share of the benefits of Aceh's resources remains in the province, and that this might be one of the major factors fuelling the push for independence resulted in the province receiving 'special autonomy' in January 2002.[6] The legislation stipulated that for a period of eight years, 70% of revenue from Aceh's oil and gas would be returned to the province, thereafter the share would drop to 50%.

The policy has already failed as a confidence-building measure, and has not silenced the call for independence by a majority of Acehnese. Many have rejected the new law, saying it is unwelcome and has been 'imposed' by Jakarta. There is disquiet about the diminishing rate of return over time from oil and gas and unease about some other aspects of the law.[7] There is widespread belief that the new autonomy law has created opportunity for the minority to increase their economic and political power, but reduced opportunity for the majority. There is popular suspicion that Governor Abdullah Puteh and other political, military and business elites will be the main beneficiaries. The 'imposition' of this autonomy law has only served to unite the Acehnese even more against the 'common enemy', Jakarta.

Beyond these two issues, the increased level of militarisation due to the presence of ExxonMobil and the grievance over the share of benefits from resources that remains in the province, there has been little systematic attention given to the economically motivated actions and processes involved in generating and sustaining the conflict in Aceh. To view these economic factors only in terms of profits being denied by Jakarta is somewhat simplistic. Other economic activities have given the war a distinctive dynamic.

It is generally assumed that the primary motive of the military in Aceh is to defeat the 'enemy'—the independence movement—in order to achieve peace and stability and to maintain the unity of the state. At the same time, after the 1999 events in East Timor, the military is still working to regain the credibility and trust of most Indonesians. It is also broadly accepted that the conflict has produced the collapse of the local economic and political system; that we are witnessing mindless and senseless violence; the uncontrollable proliferation of militia and the breakdown of the military chain of command. One system has been replaced by another, which favours the interests of the government in Jakarta, the Aceh political and business elite, and the military—while impoverishing other sectors of the community. So, the conflict is facilitating economic opportunities for a minority while destroying them for the majority. The professionally driven motives of the security forces have been replaced by economic ambition to profit from Aceh's resources. To facilitate such profiteering and enrichment the military and the police now have a vested interest in maintaining a level of conflict that justifies their presence.

The discussion about the conflict in Aceh—the plundering of resources and the widespread call for justice against those who have been accused of extrajudicial killings, torture, rape and other abuses of human rights—is usually understood within the context of the motivator grievance. But a second factor, the greed of the few—the political, business and military elite—should not be ignored.

Towards a new understanding of the conflict in Aceh

Recognition of the presence of economic motives and commercial agendas in conflict situations is not new. A growing body of literature is concerned with linking the economic gain of one party or another to civil war. Most of the literature on so-called 'war economies' however, tends to focus on the prevalence of natural resources in conflict (see Collier & Hoeffler 1998; Elbadawi & Sambanis 2000; Berdal & Malone 2000; Duffield 1994). This literature moreover, touches only superficially on the economic interests of the state-sponsored security apparatus. Its primary focus is instead on the opposition groups that operate in such areas.

In a World Bank project, Collier and Hoeffler (2001) suggest civil wars can be explained in terms of greed and grievance. They argue that the grievance motivators that often dominate the discourse on causes of civil wars: inequality, political rights, ethnic polarisation and religious fractionalisation are 'relatively insignificant'. They argue that an econometric analysis based on the levels of opportunity available to groups to rebel adds more to explanations of violent conflict than the more narrow grievance focused analysis. According to Collier and Hoeffler, greed and grievance predict civil war, the ability to finance rebellion being one of the main quantitative indicators that help explain this type of conflict. With this in mind, they assert that resource-rich states experience a higher incidence of civil war, and that 'a particularly powerful risk factor [for civil war] is dependence upon primary commodity exports' (Collier & Hoeffler 2001:2).

The rationale of such commonly perceived wisdom is that natural resources—more readily than manufacturing output—provide the financing rebel groups need to challenge the state. Furthermore, since predation and extortion is indeed more accessible to rebel groups in relation to natural resources, rebellions are 'feasible and perhaps even attractive' (Collier & Hoeffler 2001:16). Gossman argues in a similar vein that rebels profit from looting these natural resources, thus suggesting that the prevalence of such greed motivated conflict is all too common (Gossman 1999:267–83). The problem with this model is that while acknowledging the role of the military in the collection of predatory tax and extortion, the focus tends to be on the revenue raising activities of the so-called 'rebels,' placing the emphasis on the rebel groups as the instigators and protagonists of the violent conflict.[8] Collier (2000), in his own work that distinguishes between greed or grievance motivated civil wars, also falls into this trap of assuming it is predominantly rebel groups who 'aspire to wealth by capturing resources extra-legally'. He acknowledges however, the methodological problems involved in making such a general assessment. As Collier (2000:93) concedes, acquiring concrete data on this issue is extremely problematic, because: 'rebel organizations that are sufficiently successful to get noticed are unlikely to be so naïve as to admit to greed as a motive'. Moreover, in terms of garnering external support, Collier (2000:92) argues that 'narratives of grievance play much better with the international community than narratives of greed'.

Of the four main factors that constitute narratives of grievance, Collier suggests income inequality is one of the most dominant.[9] But he then goes on to dismiss understanding civil wars in terms of grievance as 'unimportant and perverse', arguing that economic agendas are of primary importance (Collier & Hoeffler 1998:4). He concludes that rebellions based on grievance are doomed because 'the basic theories of social science would predict that they are unlikely to occur' (Collier & Hoeffler 1998:7). Yet the inequitable distribution of resources is an economically motivated grievance.

In his analysis of the relationship between resources and conflict in Aceh, Ross tends to agree with the Collier-Hoeffler model that an identifiable set of pre-requisites exist that make a state more prone to civil war (Ross 2002). He also places emphasis on the ability of the rebel group to fund a challenge to the state. According to Ross, this may come from several sources, for example, 'lootable' primary commodities, the country's overseas community, or states sympathetic to their cause or antagonistic toward their government.[10] In addition, Ross suggests that by applying the Collier-Hoeffler model to a micro level of analysis of Aceh, rather than a country, he is able to offer a 'more fine-grained analysis' of the conflict. In his attempt to fully understand the conflict in Aceh, Ross offers advice on a discussion of the 'entrepreneurship' of the founder of the ASNLF—Hasan di Tiro. Ross suggests that it is more than just the presence of natural resources that has led to the onset of war there. He acknowledges the role of the unequal distribution of benefits from these resources, and adds that the presence of a larger and more aggressive military has exacerbated tensions. Ross further argues that the issue of funding 'cannot explain GAM's successful re-emergence and the new civil war, since 1991' (Ross 2002:4). He fails to explore this further and his conclusions tend to emphasise the conventional: that the economic motives of the conflict can be understood predominantly within the confines of this rather narrow framework—availability and denial of natural resources.

This chapter concedes that revenue and profit lost is indeed a source of grievance for the Acehnese, and Ross is quite correct in identifying the increased level of militarisation as another salient factor to the level of violence. But the emphasis of the argument presented here is that the economic interests of the military and the police should be specifically identified as one of the primary motivators of the conflict. These 'professionals' appear free to openly participate in exploitative economic practices. This has led to the almost wholesale destruction of the economic and social fabric of Acehnese society; and it is only within the context of this larger picture that an accurate profile of the conflict can be drawn.[11]

In the case of Aceh, the historical and recent causes and consequences of the conflict are intertwined and should be viewed as part of a continuum. Thus the work of Collier and Hoeffler and the project at the World Bank in general (the focus of which is on the catalysts of these conflicts) remain relevant. There is a direct correlation between the events of 1976—the founding of GAM, the declaration of Aceh's independence—and the beginning of operations to exploit the oil and gas resources. Similarly, this extraction operation and payments for security—official and unofficial—by ExxonMobil to the military, has led to increasing levels of militarisation in the vicinity which has in turn given the local miliary increased ability to engage in and benefit from criminal opportunism.

The dominant paradigm on economies and war has tended to focus on the nation state as the unit of analysis. Very little micro (sub-state) level analysis has been conducted. But it is often in areas such as Aceh where the most intense relationship between war and economy can be found.[12] There can be no doubt that the conflict in Aceh has caused the gross violations of human rights, widespread poverty, food insecurity, a significant number of IDPs and a lack of access to education and health care.[13] It has also caused unemployment and underemployment. And in many areas of the province, because farmers were too afraid to tend their fields, many were experiencing a shortage of food.

This chapter argues that in the case of Aceh, it is the state security apparatus that has had an impact on the longevity and intensity of the conflict, seeking to maintain the war and also arguing for the deployment of additional troops. It is not only the abundance of natural resources available in the province that provides opportunity for economic enrichment—the involvement in the economy of these actors is more all-inclusive than this implies. The security forces have become an integral part of the functioning economy and society, in part, explained by the legacy of *dwifungsi* in the Republic, but also because of some very special circumstances that exist in Aceh.[14]

While the majority of Acehnese are ensnared in a vicious cycle of underdevelopment and poverty, a virtuous cycle of socio-economic gain has developed for a minority—the political, military, police and business elite. The military's civilian paymasters hold neither political nor economic authority over the armed forces. Politically, the central government must rely on the support of this very powerful sector of the state. And economically, the central budget is unable to allocate sufficient funds to increase military salaries or provide the operational costs to the level required by the military and the police. Military Chief General Endriartono Sutarto has said that the government remains unable to provide for the armed forces and so the businesses will continue (*Kompas* 2002). This is nothing more than a political excuse for allowing the military as an institution, and its members, to pursue profit. The military hierarchy use this as a rationale of convenience. In Aceh, personal enrichment has become a significant pillar of the conflict; remove such opportunism and the nature and intensity of the conflict would change.

It is a common misconception that these 'for profit' activities are born of necessity due to a lack of funding, and that the level of profiteering might be a new, post-1997 economic crisis, phenomenon. This is a falsehood. The level of profiteering has not changed over the decades, but the nature has. The difference is that there is now more involvement in the informal and illegal economies. This is due not to any reaction to any change in financial circumstances, but to restrictions on the involvement of serving military and police personnel in business, and the beginning of a process of auditing and attempts at increased transparency and accountability by the Indonesian

Government. In some measure this is a response to pressure from the international community, including the IMF. The involvement of the IMF in the Indonesian economy because of the economic collapse has allowed the institution leverage it previously did not have, but this is where the relationship between the economic crisis, and the military and the police business complex, ends.

Those who attempt to understand the economic factors driving the conflict in Aceh tend to focus on the lack of benefit to the province from LNG revenue.[15] It is widely accepted that the controversy surrounding the presence of ExxonMobil's interests in northern Aceh is based on a perception that Aceh sees little benefit from this natural resource. And indeed, many of the villages in the area surrounding Lhokseumawe (the location of the plant) are among the poorest in Aceh. Too afraid to farm the fields because of the level of violence in the area, and with their infrastructure destroyed in 'sweeping' operations by the locally based military, the civilians suffer social and economic impoverishment as a direct result of the economic activities of the security personnel in their area. Furthermore, most of the employees at ExxonMobil, PT Arun and related facilities are non-Acehnese. Most of the social and economic advantage is indeed, accrued elsewhere—in Jakarta or even further afield. And more recently, the Acehnese political elite also stand accused of 'diverting' profits.

The Collier-Hoeffler model does not deny that those other than rebels can benefit from the abundance of natural resources. Members of the military may be soldiers by day but 'rebels' by night, suggesting that soldiers may (by night) participate in similar extortion and other economic activities that are assumed to be the exclusive domain of the recognised rebel group. But in Aceh, the situation is quite different. The level of professionalism in the military and the police operating in Aceh is, on the whole, extremely low. These soldiers are rebels day and night, preferring to spend more time pursuing personal enrichment than professional duties. Such predation and rent-seeking has come at substantial expense to the Acehnese people and the economy. The true motivations for war are often deliberately 'silenced' by these influential beneficiaries.

Military 'business'

The role of the military as an economic actor has been an acceptable part of Indonesian life for decades, 'sought after' by the military, and viewed as necessary and legitimate by a majority of the population (McCulloch 2001). This chapter employs a broad definition of 'military business', including not only the profit making enterprises in which the military as an organisation is involved, but any activity that brings economic or material benefit to either individual members or to the organisation.

The military initially became involved in business as a response to the inability of the government to adequately provide for their welfare and running costs. The territorial command structure helped to establish and protect these interests. One of the Indonesian military's most reform-minded officers, Major General Agus Wirahadikusumah, is quoted as saying 'We all know that the military is acting as a parasite. Who backs and supports the discotheques, brothels and narcotics rings if not the military or the police? Let's be honest about it...' (Bourchier & Hadiz 2003:307). In today's Indonesia, the official defence budget accounts for only one-third of what is actually spent by the military (McCulloch 2001). Since the fall of Suharto, military financing has become one of the key components of the reform rhetoric. But, it seems that the government cannot afford to make up the short-fall between funds required and the amount available. And so the military business complex will be left largely on the periphery of the reform agenda for the foreseeable future.

The military's vast national business complex is found at all levels (depth) and in most sectors (breadth) of the economy. It is a system comprising a complex network of *yayasan* (charitable foundations), companies and co-operatives; and operates in the formal and informal economy, often including illegal activities. Indeed, the value of the military's business activities is greater in the informal than the formal economy (McCulloch 2001).

The military has come to rely on the off-budget funds that these business activities provide. At the national level the military's economic interests include natural resource extraction, manufacturing, construction, finance and the service sector.

The profits from these economic activities are used in several ways:

For the 'communal good' of the military

Business activities make a significant contribution to welfare, operational capabilities and maintenance of the military and the police.

As 'slush funds'

These are held by individual officers, who keep scant, if any, record of income and outgoings. This is the case even when the profits come from the official businesses to these informal funds.

As 'off-salary' income

Many mid- to high ranking officers have come to rely on these additional 'salaries' which are commonly used to purchase large houses, cars and overseas medical care. These officers also buy the loyalty of subordinates, who have also become reliant on this income.

Even the official businesses and co-operatives operate in the informal economy. The ad hoc activities of these officially structured commercial ventures and profits generated are used not only to boost the bank accounts of certain individuals, but also to 'top up' the welfare benefits, firepower and operating capacity of the military and the police. Significant sections of the services are involved at this level. But it is more commonly maverick groups and rogue individuals within the military who are the main actors. The number of personnel involved is not insignificant. Although some may be 'reluctant entrepreneurs', most participate.

Military 'business' in Aceh

For years the economic activities of the military and the police in Aceh has certainly been aided—never impeded—by the conflict. Traditionally, a small amount of the profit has been used for local 'slush funds' for the military or the police as organisations, but the profits have predominantly been used as off-salary incomes for individuals, rather than as a local 'slush fund'. Under the current situation of martial law, the nature, level and profitability of these 'enterprises' has changed. Before discussing the nature of these changes, let us focus on the military's economic and material interests and how they have underpinned the conflict in Aceh.

The military's economic interests in Aceh can be found mostly in the informal economy. Indeed, many of the activities are illegal. Such profiteering is criminal opportunism.

For many years it has been a 'common secret' that in Aceh some elements of the military have been involved in illegal logging, the drugs economy (though less so now than in the past) and providing additional 'protection' for oil palm plantations, oil, gas and other companies. There have also been rumours that the military and/or the police are part of the supply chain of arms and other equipment to the ASNLF. While such activities are extremely difficult to quantify as no balance sheets exist, factual evidence is available in some, though not all, cases. The anecdotal evidence is, however, very compelling.[16] Military and police personnel often enjoy substantial material gain while on a tour of duty in Aceh. There is a standing military joke that when sent to Aceh on a tour of duty, one will return home either very rich or dead.

The 'military in business' operates in the province by monopolising local production, extraction, transport and processing of some natural resources; price controlling; appropriating land for themselves and on behalf of other parties; and many other commercial activities. It is virtually impossible to do business in Aceh without dealing with the military.[17]

The Acehnese generally feel their natural resources have been 'plundered'—not only by the policies of the Indonesian Government and by the local political and business elite—but also by the locally-based military and police. Such perceptions of injustice have contributed to rising levels of resentment that has fuelled the calls for independence, which in turn has led to an increase in the level of violent conflict. The military and the police themselves are seen as responsible for denying local people their 'rightful' access to such resources. Moreover, they are seen to act on behalf of other actors—be they state or private—who also seek to deny these 'rights'.

The level and type of involvement in this *criminal opportunism*, by the military and the police is dependent on several variables: location; local commanders; availability of 'lootable' commodities; level of professionalism in a particular unit, and local civil–military relations. In Aceh, the following are the main (although not the only) economic interests:

Drugs

The involvement in the drugs economy is less so now than in the past. It is, of course, an illegal trade in itself. The security forces 'encourage' locals to harvest the crop for a predominantly military market. The price paid is significantly below market value—the majority of profit accruing to armed forces personnel while the farmers live in poverty and fear.[18] This has been an increasing cause of conflict. Aceh Merdeka, reputedly involved in the drugs trade in the past, has now firmly stated that:

> we [Aceh Merdeka] will do everything in our power to enforce the law in respect to the drugs trade. We are not involved in this evil trade. This issue has brought us into further direct conflict with the security forces that continue to participate in this valuable trade.[19]

In late 1999 in Banda Aceh, 23 soldiers were accused of involvement in the Tengku Bantaqiah massacre.[20] The killing of Tengku Bantaqiah and 50 or more of his followers in July that year was witnessed by two villagers who report that a combined military force under the command of Korem 011

Lilawangsa carried out the attack.[21] The three police officers assigned to escort 12 of the prisoners to Jakarta were apprehended by air force personnel for smuggling 430 kilograms of marijuana on board the military aircraft used to transport the prisoners. And in early 2001, a police helicopter pilot was arrested by air force personnel for marijuana trafficking. He flew 40 kilograms from Aceh and admitted that the marijuana belonged to Aceh Besar Police Chief, Lieutenant Colonel Ali Hussein.

In January 2002, local police received information that a certain military truck belonging to TNI was transporting drugs. The truck was stopped by police, checked and indeed found to be full of marijuana. There was a skirmish as the TNI attempted to prevent the police from impounding their valuable cargo. One policeman and two members of the military were injured in this incident. Such incidents are not unusual, and contribute to increasing levels of tension between TNI and the police. A journalist from the Aceh daily newspaper *Sermabi* said 'there are many incidents such as these, but we are afraid to report the details'.[22]

Again, in late November 2002, a haul of 675 kilograms of marijuana was brought into the Polda station in Banda Aceh. A senior officer said 'it [the marijuana] came from Pulau Aceh where the military supervises its cultivation. We got information that truck was carrying drugs, and also that the local military commander in Pulau Aceh paid the truck driver and his four companions'.[23]

Arms

Another of Aceh's 'common secrets' is that the military has been part of the supply line of weapons to the independence movement, and that transactions take place on two levels: the first is that individual military personnel sell their weapons to the Aceh Merdeka and report them as 'seized in battle'. But perhaps more worrying is that certain key military personnel have provided a supply line for specific weapons. A spokesperson for the movement, who of course preferred to remain anonymous, said: 'Yes, it is true, we do receive weapons from the military—ammunition too. It is a very reliable source. But recently the cost of these weapons has increased, so we may be looking for alternative avenues' (*Tempo* 2000a).

In July 2000, the Baktiya local police seized a truck from just in front of the local police station that was carrying 15,000 bullets and two automatic rifles. The bullets were clearly marked 'manufactured by PT Pindad', the army's own defence manufacturer (*Tempo* 2000a). The local police suspected that military in Jakarta had sent the weapons and ammunition by prior order from GAM, a theory confirmed by a local resident:

The army has been sending guns through here for GAM for some time now, ammunition too. I know for sure because even a member of my own family is involved. He told me that sometimes they pay the police to turn the other way, and to allow the weapons to pass. You believe me? It's crazy, but true.[24]

Logging

The military's involvement in illegal logging is extensive. Companies— many of them foreign-owned—pay the military and the police to 'look the other way' as they log out of their permitted area. The security authorities also commonly provide false documentation for export. Ad hoc logging by locals find armed forces personnel an insatiable market. The illegally felled timber is then often passed onto unlicensed sawmills for processing.

The European Union-funded Leuser Development Project, based in Medan since the mid-1990s, was puzzled when the rate of logging within the protected area increased.[25] The project eventually realised that the police and the military—the very people they were relying on to prevent the illegal logging— were in fact the loggers. A senior member of staff admitted:

> Our regular monitoring is becoming increasingly depressing. The forest cover is decreasing in the more easily accessible areas, and this is where much of the wildlife is. We know that the military and the police are involved as they have threatened several of our [Indonesian] staff.[26]

There are often reports of 'incidents' between the military and the police. In South Aceh, the two services have an agreement to use different routes to transport their illegally felled logs. During floods there are often problems as one group attempts to transport via the other's route. Such inter-service rivalry has led to an increase in violent conflict.

On the island of Simeulue, to Aceh's west, the wholesale destruction of forests is due in large part to the collusion of the local government, the police and to a lesser degree, the military. There is strong evidence to suggest that the local police and military provide 'protection' to the companies, are paid to ignore the illegal logging and are also involved in facilitating shipping.[27]

In response to concerns about flooding and other environmental damage, the Bupati issued an order on 5 June 2001 that all logging should cease until further permission was granted. But Thai company PT Panto Teungku Abadi continued to log. Only when the local people blocked the roads into the forest, and threatened to turn against the local police, did the law enforcement agency attempt to enforce the law.[28] Related to the logging, there has been an illegal trade in wildlife—birds and small mammals have been taken from the forests for sale elsewhere in Indonesia.

Protection

The military has been involved in 'protecting'—for a 'fee'—companies such as ExxonMobil, PT Arun, oil palm, coffee and rubber plantations, and many more. In the early relationship between Exxon and the Indonesian Government, provision was made for the military to protect the company's operations. It was never made clear the source of the perceived threat, only that the company would be operating in a volatile security environment. Exxon was not alone in 'contracting' the services of the Indonesian military for security. In what is now West Papua, Freeport had signed a Contract of Work in 1967 with the government, which locked them into what has essentially become a 'protection racket' by TNI.

During confidential discussions with a source previously involved in the 'negotiations' between ExxonMobil and the authorities, I was told that not only does the company pay the military officially for its security services, but the company also began very early on to pay 'small sums of money "here and there" to local military commanders for their co-operation'.[29] Investigations by Kontras suggest that the company paid the 1,300 (as at October 2001) armed forces guarding the facilities at Lhoksukon a daily allowance of around Rp 40,000 (Kontras 2001).[30] The report also suggests that ExxonMobil paid a substantial monthly allowance to the local military command, and provided transportation facilities, offices, posts, barracks, radios, telephones, dormitories and other equipment.[31] The same company source cited earlier also revealed that:

> The problem was never with Jakarta as such, not with the military hierarchy there. The biggest problem has always been with the local military. Basically, once we started to pay we were backed into a corner. The demands always came in for more money. It is true the Indonesian military is under-paid and under-equipped, and the housing they are provided is terrible. But is it the company's place to subsidise the Indonesian military? And anyway, my sense is that at least some of the money paid by the company never made it to local funds but was kept by some of the individuals negotiating.

The company now has what can be termed a 'mutually beneficial relationship' with the military. There is, of course, a genuine desire by the security forces to protect Exxon's operations, and attacks against the company's installations and infrastructure have been minimal. For its part, the local GAM commanders have always stated quite emphatically that:

> we never attack ExxonMobil's buildings or operations, why would we do that? We do of course attack the military, and if they are near the ExxonMobil facilities then that might be seen as an attack on the company when in fact it is not.[32]

The weight of benefit lies with the military in its relationship with the company. The local military command (Aceh wide) has come to rely on the financial and logistic 'support' of the company. There is no doubt that benefits are accrued to the military's local operational and running costs: cash, food, the use of buildings and equipment and other 'services' are among the 'incentives' to maintain a presence there. And the commanding officers themselves benefit from the regular payments made to them to maintain their local co-operation and to secure operations.

On occasion, when there has been a direct attack on the company's facilities, the military themselves have often been accused of being responsible. This is why the company is now trapped in a similar 'protection racket' relationship to that of Freeport West Papua. The money made from petty economic activities in addition to cash payments by the commanders ensures the lower ranking officers are also satisfied. The problems with lack of professionalism and poor discipline of the troops guarding the oil and gas operations although publicly acknowledged, have never been addressed by local commanders in Medan or TNI HQ in Jakarta (*Tempo* 2002).

In addition to 'protecting' Exxon, the military is commonly used by companies to seize land for plantations and then prevent the locals from reclaiming their land. Many are killed or injured while trying to protect their property. The Medan office of human rights NGO the Legal Aid Foundation, *Yayasan Lembaga Batuan Hukum Indonesia* (LBH) reports that land disputes (in particular, involving the military), is the fastest rising case-load.

Fishing

Local fishermen are forced to sell their catch—or at least part of it—to the military or the police at a price below market value. These armed entrepreneurs then normally sell to agents at a vastly inflated price. And at sea, the Indonesian Navy often board vessels for 'inspection'. A story not uncommon in Aceh is told by a fisherman from Lampulo, Banda Aceh:

> The navy signalled they wanted to board our boat for inspection, so we had no choice but to allow them to. They seized all our fish and siphoned off our fuel. They had been tailing us all day, so they knew we had good fish on board. We tried to get to land, but the fuel ran out before then and we drifted for five hours. Another fishing boat from our village [Lampulo] saw our boat in trouble and helped us ashore.[33]

In addition, many fishermen say they must pay the local police or military a regular amount for 'protecting' their boats. In Lampulo the amount 'is between

Rp 50,000—Rp 100,00 every two weeks. But in Idi Rayeuk [East Aceh], it was as much as Rp 1 million'.[34]

Coffee

The situation is similar to fishing and logging. Coffee farmers have been forced to sell their coffee to the military at almost half the market rate. And, in some areas of Central Aceh, the military backed militia have driven the locals off the plantations altogether. These plantations now have a dual use—as militia training camps, and as a source of revenue for military and militia, who have taken over the coffee production. In the villages of Pondok Gajah and Sidodadi, there was an attempt to resist the militia and the military's pursuit of profit. But the price paid by the local people was high, and:

> many of the men were taken away and shot when they tried to negotiate the price of the coffee. We were told Rp 2,000 a kilo was the maximum they would pay. But on the market, we could get Rp 5,000. They killed our men, and then they burned our houses.[35]

The impact on levels of human rights abuses from all this economic activity is substantial. Those who dare to resist are killed, tortured or disappear, and their houses, boats or shops are burned. They generally suffer personal and economic ruin. Throughout Aceh, the destruction of people's homes and livelihoods by the military and its militia is highly visible. There are many cases of destruction by the military (often in conjunction with the militia) of almost entire villages.

Since this chapter defines 'business' very broadly, many other activities are included. For example, activities such as the illegal tolls and levies paid by those who travel by road. This is commonplace all over Aceh. The main trading route from Medan to Banda Aceh (a journey of about 12 hours by bus) is particularly profitable for the military and the police. At the 38 military and police checkpoints (as at February 2002) on that road, buses and many other vehicles pay a total of around Rp 250,000–300,000 in illegal tolls per trip.[36] Trucks pay even more to pass. The higher the value of the load, the more they have to pay. In general, the total is between Rp 700,000 and 1 million per trip.

In most areas the military and the police help themselves to food and other items in restaurants and coffee shops. The owners are too afraid to protest. In Matang near Bireuen, an area well-known for its coffee shops, the owners are poor, angry, but powerless. Every evening at around 7pm, the local police visit and expect three packets of cigarettes. If the shops don't have the cigarettes, cash is accepted. One coffee typically costs Rp 1,000 (the 'donation' to police welfare is around Rp 20,000). In interviews with several owners, the story was similar:

> The first 20 cups of coffee sold each day are for nothing. Of course we dare not say anything, they would only take five packets instead of three. This is the way in Aceh. With each protest, the price will increase.[37]

And in the shops and markets whatever they need is available gratis. Just as coffee, fish and other commodities are sold by the military at 'above market' rates, so too is petrol. For example, in Takengnon (Central Aceh), the locals are often too afraid to buy petrol elsewhere. A local journalist said 'this petrol is brought from Bireuen. When the military has a supply to sell, we would not dare to buy elsewhere. The trade in many commodities is similar in Central Aceh: the military controls much of the local economy'.[38]

To protest against human rights abuses by the armed forces, the ASNLF called for a three day strike, 16–18 January 2002. Most businesses closed for the three days. In Langsa (East Aceh) store owners and market traders who refused demands by the local police and military to open for business during the strike—as most did—had to pay a 'fine'. Traders interviewed said they knew this would happen, but would rather obey the strike and pay the requested Rp 50,000.[39]

Most building, road (and other) contractors will confide that the military and/or police routinely expect to receive between 8 and 10% of the total value of the contract. The contractor simply makes allowance for this in the tender—thus having a detrimental impact on local government budgets. In addition, vehicles are routinely seized and owners are asked to pay a 'fee' for their release.

Arbitrary and unofficial arrests have become more common in some areas. A 'fee' is charged for the release of the 'accused'. The 'fee' can be anything from between Rp 1 million for a becak driver, to an almost limitless amount for a businessman.[40] Data collected from 149 civilians arrested in the period December 2001 to January 2002 in the Bireuen district shows that family and friends of 29 of those arrested paid for their release. The total amount was more than Rp 67 million.[41] The 'distortion' of the local economy by all these 'business' interests is incalculable.

During martial law, the 'petty' economic interests such as those described here have flourished. There are many examples of security forces profiting from the changed situation. From West Aceh, for example, there have been many reports of military checkpoints demanding Rp 25,000 per vehicle—an extortionate amount of money in Aceh— whether for a motorbike, car, truck or bus. Those who resist have been beaten.[42]

In Lokop, in a remote, mountainous area of East Aceh, the local administration complained that of Rp 17 million allocated for emergency funds, seven million was taken by the military. There are six local military posts. Each was given Rp 2 million to help with operational costs (Acehkita 2003). The farmers of Lokop are also being forced to sell their produce at less than the market value to support the spirit of the nation's struggle against GAM (Acehkita 2003).

The introduction of the new red and white KTP (residency cards) in Aceh has given the military and the police a new avenue for profit. The scheme was a response to allegations that in some areas GAM had taken KTPs from residents. The martial law authorities have been tasked with issuing the new cards in Aceh. The rationale was to separate the civilians from members of GAM, on the assumption that GAM members would not apply for a new KTP, anyone found to be without one would be arrested and charged. The cards are supposed to be free, but in reality cost between Rp50,000 to Rp 300,000—in some cases even more. While such petty businesses have benefited, the larger economic concerns of the military have fared less well.

The protection businesses, especially at ExxonMobil, continue to flourish under martial law but the drugs economy, fishing, logging and the trade in wildlife has become problematic. The local people who were 'employed' to produce the marijuana and cut trees, facilitate the logging and catch the birds and other wildlife previously trafficked, are too afraid to leave the villages. The fishermen are no longer going to sea: afraid of putting themselves at risk of piracy which has increased in recent months, or looting of their catch usually by the Indonesian navy or other sectors of the armed forces. In addition, the deployment of troops from other areas, and the desire by the military hierarchy in Jakarta that at least some semblance of order and control of its armed forces be promoted to the domestic and international audience has meant that the scope for unwieldy military business has been adversely affected by the conflict. The supply of weapons to GAM from the military at both levels—the more structured ordering process, and the more ad hoc acquisition—has also suffered.

Megawati's presidency

When President Megawati Sukarnoputri came to power in July 2001, many had high hopes that her government would have the political will and the capacity to bring a peaceful end to the bloodshed in Aceh. Megawati has however, declared the unity of the Republic as one of her top priorities. To this end she has been persuaded by the military that a security approach is the only way to deal with secessionist movements on the periphery. In Aceh, this has led to an increase in the level of violence during Megawati's presidency. Megawati's first year in office, 2001, was particularly brutal, with around 2,000 people—80% of them civilians—dying as a result of the violent conflict.[43] More recently there has been a rapid and dramatic increase in the number of victims: in the first four months of martial law—19 May to 19 September 2003—the chief of armed forces, Major General Endriartono Sutarto, said that 897 people had died in the conflict, and he conceded 304 were unarmed civilians. Data from Komnas-HAM and the local LBH office indicate the real figure may well be double and the percentage of civilians is probably much higher. In an open letter issued by SIRA on 21 September 2003, a total of 2,636 conflict-related deaths were been recorded. Moreover, the special autonomy law that was to 'quieten' the voices of dissent has instead fanned the flames, and the 'additional revenue that Aceh was to receive from the autonomy legislation is being ploughed directly back into military operations' (Jones 2003).

The presence of the giant oil producer ExxonMobil in Aceh and its related LNG facilities has influenced government security policy toward the province. In early 2001, during the presidency of Abdurrahman Wahid, ExxonMobil feared that production might be disrupted due to increasing security concerns. The immediate response of the government in Jakarta was to consider the deployment of additional armed forces. When the company did eventually suspend operations, the predicted military response was indeed forthcoming. Wahid then issued Presidential Decree IV facilitating a security solution to the problem. The long-term ramifications of the passing of that decree were not part of Wahid's intentions. Nevertheless, it was the beginning of a mobilisation of increasing troop numbers to Aceh which did not decrease during the CoHA and that escalated just prior to and just after the end of the CoHA. The declaration of martial law and the subsequent state of emergency gave the generals *carte blanche* to operate under their own initiative. However, not known for their propensity for strategic thinking or planning, the military commanders failed to predict the detrimental impact on their economic activities.

In September 2004, Megawati was unceremoniously dumped from the presidency in Indonesia's first direct presidential elections. In her place, the former Politics and Security Co-ordinating Minister, Susilo Bambang Yudhoyono, was elected. Yudhoyono came to power saying that he would clean up corruption and resolve the Aceh conflict. His singular attempt to address the Aceh problem was to call on Acehnese separatists to lay down their arms and accept an amnesty to return to civil society. The offer was, in effect, for GAM to surrender and was studiously ignored. However, in

November 2004, GAM altered its position and began to re-engage the Indonesian Government in secret dialogue. By December 2004, it appeared that Yudhoyono was responding, with off-the-record reports that he had begun to assemble a team of negotiators. At least part of the secrecy surrounding this move was to ensure that it could, if at all possible, proceed without the interference of the TNI. The TNI had made it clear that it did not support a negotiated settlement and had, in practice, worked to undermine such a process ever since it effectively undermined the CoHA.

The end of CoHA and the declaration of martial law not only increased military pressure on GAM, it also disrupted TNI business activities in Aceh. Funding for the TNI's post CoHA campaign had come from a central government allocation. However, like all such operations, it was also extensively funded by non-official sources, including businesses, criminal activities and the diversion of funds from other government departments. The human rights campaigner Munir was said by sources close to him that he was about to expose the TNI's sources of funding from other government departments and, allegedly, pay-offs to very senior political figures, when he suddenly died on a flight to Amsterdam a few days before the September 2004 presidential elections. An autopsy showed that he had been poisoned with arsenic. However, while the TNI had apparently derived funding from other government departments, it was struggling to fund its increased campaign in Aceh.

On 26 December 2004, a massive tsunami hit Aceh, killing more than 100,000 people and destroying most of the infrastructure and many of the buildings in the province. The international aid effort that was mounted to redress the immediate disaster and to help rebuild the province, which ran into the billions of dollars, was nothing if not a magnet to the TNI. As a consequence, the TNI began to stockpile food aid, which in many cases it sold, to demand bribes from aid agencies in order to allow the road shipment of goods and to herd the almost half a million homeless Acehnese into refugee camps where it controlled the flow of aid. All of this represented a windfall for the TNI. It also pushed to have foreign militaries removed from Aceh and to end, as soon as possible, the presence of international aid agencies. As when schools had been burned after the declaration of martial law in May 2003, the TNI stood to benefit from its own companies tendering, with little or no competition, for aid and reconstruction work at inflated prices.

Conclusion

The historical (1970s) motivation for, and the degree and nature of the violent conflict in Aceh can only be fully understood when the criminal opportunism and the more general profiteering of the armed forces is utilised as a priority context for analysis. The military's role in the economy has become uncontrollable. The lack of a sufficient budget from the central government does not explain, nor does it justify, the type of economic activity seen in Aceh or the business practices employed there. In addition, such profiteering largely explains the lack of professionalism that has led to the scale of death and destruction witnessed in the province, and the rorting of massive aid inflows in the post-tsunami period.

The focus of the dominant discourse—on human rights abuses, the contribution of the LNG to the country's economy and the 'greed' of the Free Aceh Organisation—is merely a diversion. These factors, either individually or together, fail to explain the real motivation of the conflict: the profiteering of the military and the police.

The Collier-Hoeffler model offers an interesting foundation for further investigation. In concluding that most civil wars are greed motivated, but that grievance must also be given some credence as a powerful motivator, their study does pose some salient questions that can be applied more generally to conflict analysis. This chapter has argued that in the case of Aceh however, a more powerful motivator has, and continues to be the greed of the few: the military and the police. The Collier-Hoeffler model does not accommodate this factor.

Since the powerful minority are beneficiaries of the conflict, they may feel less inclined toward finding a peaceful solution. If conflict facilitates their inflated income; peace will only serve to decrease it. In Aceh, the level of violent conflict which sustains the military's profit space is limited and volatile. While it is true that 'peace will depend upon those groups which gain from peace being more influential than those which gain from continued war' (Collier 1999:10), it is also the case that the intensity of the war must not be allowed to escalate exponentially. And in Aceh, those who stand to gain economically—from 'relative peace' and 'relative war'—hold not only the political persuasion, but also the 'firepower'.

In an article on military professionalism in Indonesia, Kristiadi (2001:93–110) argues that an increase in military salaries would lead to higher levels of professionalism. Thus, by extension, implying a cessation to these illegal economic activities. But in reality, even a five-fold increase in military salaries would not compensate serving personnel for the 'off-salary' income resulting from the criminal opportunism in places such as Aceh. To suggest otherwise ignores the desire for increased profitability, by whatever means, that characterises Indonesia's elite politics. Increased government contributions to the TNI merely increase its profit margin; they do not decrease its criminality.

The high level of militarisation, predatory economics and lack of civil accountability in Aceh are a lethal combination. But it is the enrichment of the armed forces specifically, that is the main motivator of the suffering and disempowerment of the unarmed majority: greed is the cause of the nature and intensity of the conflict, while grievance is merely its consequence.

Endnotes

1. Post-2003 text in this article was contributed by the editor.
2. For example West Papua, Kalimantan and Riau are just a few of the provinces that have been disproportionately impoverished.
3. ExxonMobil is the second largest producer of LNG in the Republic. Indonesia's exports of LNG are dependent on its production.
4. Personal interview, Banda Aceh, January 2002.
5. Interview with Hasan di Tiro, April 2003, Sweden.
6. The law that granted special autonomy to Aceh is Law No 18, 2001.
7. For example, the law gives more power to the local governor and regents over Aceh's public sector budget. Many Acehnese do not trust these local political elite, many of whom have recently come under scrutiny for embezzling. It also makes provision for the legal system of the province to be based on the Islamic Syariah. The Syariah Court was inaugurated in Aceh on 4 March 2003. This has drawn widespread criticism from many in Aceh who claim the 'imposition' of Syariah was nothing more than a political move by Jakarta to attempt to portray Aceh as radically Islamic and thereby alienate the international community.
8. This is not an uncommon position to adopt. Keen also de-prioritises the benefits accrued by the military's final set of short-term economic benefits that may arise from conflict are those institutionalised benefits accruing to the military (Berdal & Mallone 2000:31).
9. The others being 'raw ethnic or religious hatred', 'lack of political rights' and 'government economic incompetence'.
10. Other conditions that make it easier for armed rebellion to take place, according to the 'model' are high rates of poverty, recent violent conflict in the country (province), a homogeneous ethnic and religious community and a mountainous and difficult terrain (Collier 2000:93). Collier measures the economic opportunities in civil war using three variables: availability of primary commodities, percentage of society made up of young men and education. This chapter, however, concentrates only on the first.
11. The author acknowledges that the Aceh Merdeka Movement might not also benefit financially from the conflict environment. But the most significant plundering and profiteering can be attributed to the entrepreneurial military and police, and is viewed by the majority of Acehnese as more problematic than any revenue-raising enterprises undertaken by the independence movement (although the latter is often viewed as highly problematic by outsiders). A local politician who requested anonymity said:

> Everyone knows that 'the movement' is involved in extortion and robbery. Otherwise how would they survive? What is often overlooked is that many Acehnese give money of their own volition. Further, there is a very high tolerance among the Acehnese people to the revenue raising tactics of GAM—especially more recently when they appeared

to be more considerate'. The 'business' activities of Aceh Merdeka is not the focus of this paper. Such economic activity has been facilitated by, but is not the cause of the continuation of the conflict.

12   There are several places of conflict in Indonesia where economic motives can easily be identified. For example, in Kalimantan, West Papua, Maluku, Riau and in many other areas where there is, or has been, low intensity conflict.

13   OCHA Consolidation Report No 148 reported that almost 11,000 people were displaced in just eight districts on 1 October 2003. Some estimates have put the total number of IDPs in Aceh at 50,000.

14   On the dual function of the military see, for example, MacFarling (1996).

15   Kell (1995) suggests that the rise of the independence movement in the mid 1970s is directly related to the growth of the beginning of exploitation of the oil and gas reserves near Lhokseumawe in North Aceh (see Sjamsuddin 1984).

16   The nature of this study means that most sources of information must remain anonymous. Many of those interviewed on this issue were initially reluctant to speak, fearing for their lives. This of course, leaves the study open to criticism regarding the quality of sources. Even academic work must recognise that one cannot always produce concrete evidence to support an argument. My loyalties lie with those who either asked to remain anonymous or those whose interests I think are better served by remaining so. I have the utmost admiration for those who, despite their fear, agreed to speak with me.

17   Interview with the manager of a plantation company, East Aceh, January 2001.

18   A farmer involved in this trade said 'Of course I am aware it is illegal to grow and harvest this crop. But I am afraid to stop as the military would shoot me and kill our animals, so what would my family do then?' Confidential interview, December 2001.

19   Interview with Teungku Isnander, spokesperson for the ASNLF Central Bureau of Information, Banda Aceh, December 2001.

20   In April and May 2000, one civilian and 23 soldiers were found guilty of the killing of the Muslim cleric Tengku Bantaqiah and over 50 of his followers in West Aceh in July 1999. They were sentenced to between eight-and-a-half and ten years' imprisonment.

21   Tragedi Beutong Ateuh, Laporan Data Koalisi HAM Aceh, 23 July 1999. The report details that members of the combined unit were Pasikan Yonif 131 and 133, and one platoon from Battalion 328 Kostrad.

22   Interview, Banda Aceh, May 2002.

23   Interview, Polda station, Banda Aceh, 23 November 2002.

24   Interview with resident of Baktiya, January 2001.

25   The project was intended to fund conservation of the Gunung Leuser National Park in North Sumatra and Aceh.

26   Confidential interview, Medan, November 2000.

27 Many interviews with locals uncovered strong anecdotal evidence that PT Panto Teungku Abadi was paying significant sums of money to the local police while neglecting to pay the local villagers for road access.
28 Witnessed by the author.
29 A former employee of ExxonMobil who was, for a time, directly responsible for the negotiations and 'payments' made to the local military. A precondition of his agreeing to be interviewed was that his identity remain undisclosed. The interview took place in the US, April 2002.
30 The number of soldiers guarding these facilities increased to around 5,000 by February 2002.
31 The Kontras report alleges that ExxonMobil pay a sum of Rp 5 billion per month. This is denied by the company, and since Kontras has no 'hard evidence', it remains only an allegation.
32 Interview with Tengku Jamaica, spokesperson of GAM command Unit Pase, North Aceh, 17 January 2002.
33 Interview with local fisherman, November 2001. This man was so afraid of telling his story that he travelled to another district of Aceh to be interviewed. There are many similar stories from others who must also remain anonymous.
34 Interview with fisherman, Banda Aceh, November 2000.
35 Interview with former resident of Pondok Gajah., December 2002. The interview took place in North Aceh, as several Pondok Gajah residents had fled from Pondok Gajah, fearing the militia and military would return.
36 In November 2000, the number of blocks on the same stretch of road was 12.
37 Interview, Bireuen, January 2002.
38 Confidential interview, Takengnon, January 2002.
39 Interview on 19 January 2002, Langsa. Of 18 market traders and store owners asked, 12 admitted having to pay a 'fine'.
40 The highest amount I have heard of being paid is Rp 40 million. A building contractor refused to pay the 8% requested, and was 'kidnapped' during the night from his home.
41 Data collected by the author.
42 See website www.acheh-eye.org for reports of incidents during martial law.
43 Data from LBH

Chapter 9
Security forces in Ambon: from the national to the local

Muhammad Najib Azca

Introduction

The conflict that plagued Ambon from late 1999 was largely settled by 2002, despite occasional outbreaks of violence. But it continues to stand as an example of where state institutions did not quell the conflict, at least initially, but contributed to it. In this respect, one of the critical factors that prolonged the conflict in Ambon was the partisan role played by the security forces.[1] Rather than preventing and stopping conflict, as is their normative role, the security forces often neglected, supported, instigated or otherwise became involved in the conflict. As a result, the conflict was protracted.

This chapter will examine the profile and the dynamics of the security forces in five spheres: tension between the security forces and society; internal tension in the army; tension between the army and the police; tension between the government and the military; and internal police tension. Each sphere will be analysed at the local and national levels respectively, to portray the possible parallels and the interplay between them. The focus is primarily on the post-Suharto era, though some features of Suharto's New Order will also be discussed, since these clarify the context and the origins of the problems. I will argue that the security forces during Indonesia's transition period provided fertile soil for their partisanship in the conflict. A tentative conclusion is drawn about the landscape of the security forces in the conflict in Ambon and the nature of their partisanship in communal–religious unrest.

Theoretical view

To analyse the dynamics of the role of the security apparatus in Ambon, the conflict is placed in its socio-political context: the transition era from authoritarian rule to democracy. Such a transition is usually characterised by the lack of government ability to deal with the many problems that arise due to a kind of vacuum of authority. The risk of an outbreak of communal conflict increases in the early phases of democratisation, according to Snyder (2000:310): 'Nationalist and ethnic conflicts are more likely during the initial stages of democratizations than in transition to full consolidations of democracy'.

Each transition is commonly characterised by uncertainty as its main feature, as argued by O'Donnell and Schmitter (1986:6):

> Transitions are delimited, on the one hand, by the launching of the process of dissolution of an authoritarian regime and, on the other hand, by the installation of some form of democracy, the return to some form of authoritarian rule, or the emergence of a revolutionary alternative.

Thus, the transition period can be defined as the passage from authoritarian rule to another form of, as yet uncertain, government. There is no single track of transition experience among those countries, which have accomplished democratic transitions. However, based on the experiences of several countries, Ethier (1990:5-6) outlines several types of democratic transition. The first type is driven by external factors. The second comes about as a consequence of violent revolt on the part of certain internal socio-political forces, while the third type of transition—evolutionary or continuing transition—is initiated from within a political regime. Referring to recent studies, Ethier concludes that recent democratic transitions in Southern Europe, Latin America and Southeast Asia fall into the third category.

Whatever category of transition process occurs common problems emerge in developing and consolidating democratic political systems. Huntington (1991:209-10) distinguishes two kinds of problem. First, there are transition problems, originating directly from the phenomenon of regime change from authoritarianism to democracy—creating and establishing new constitutional and electoral systems and removing pro-authoritarian officials and replacing them with democratic ones. Second, there are contextual problems, originating from the character of the society, its economy, culture and history, whatever the form of government. Huntington argues that the authoritarian rulers were not able to solve these problems and, possibly, neither will the democratic rulers. Communal conflict, regional antagonism, poverty and socio-economic inequality fall into this category.

In Indonesia, the transition followed Ethier's third type. Democratic transition initiated from within the authoritarian regime has some particular characteristics. According to Alfred Stepan (1986:72), in this a kind of transition, the main actors within the ruling authoritarian coalition will endeavor to maintain their long-term interests in the new political context by resisting political reform and hence avoiding marginalisation. This resistance, Stepan argues, may take a variety of forms. Firstly, the power holders may attempt to check the liberalisation policies if the costs of tolerance are greater than the costs of repression. Secondly, they may seek to reconstruct in the successor democratic regime the formal and informal rules that secured some of their main interests in the previous regime. Thirdly, the security apparatus of the authoritarian regime may endeavor to keep their privileges entirely.

Another likely characteristic of the transition period, according to O'Donnell and Schmitter (1986:24), is resistance from hard-line supporters of the old regime who are anxious that political reforms will eliminate and even annihilate their privileges and prerogatives. The hard-line supporters will most likely struggle at all costs to restore the triumph of the old regime. One of the critical elements among these hard-line supporters is commonly the military, which was usually a dominant force of the old regime. Therefore, in some cases, communal conflicts which take place in countries during democratic transition are likely to be associated with a particular group of the military, which was marginalised by political reforms.

This chapter will approach the conflict in Ambon through the neo-patrimonial[2] perspective as used by David Brown to analyse the Aceh case. Rather than use a corporatist perspective to analyse Indonesia, Brown (1994:112) prefers to apply a neo-patrimonial perspective to explore what has happened in that country. According to him, the most prevalent feature of the Indonesian state has been elite factionalism and the personal use of governmental power. He argues that the neo-patrimonial state provides a patronage umbrella under which communalism can be mobilised by cohesive elites in the service of national integration (Brown 1994:121). But the promise is a fragile and tentative one, as the tension within neo-patrimonial regimes will endanger political stability and unity. Furthermore, he suggests that the inherent fragilities of the neo-patrimonial state stimulate the development and politicisation of ethnic communalism, either in the form of integrative communal, patronage networks, as the mobilisation of ethnicity for purposes of electoral opposition, or as ethno-regional rebellion.

As has been happening in Aceh, national politics has played a critical role in the conflict in Ambon. As a result of the neo-patrimonial networks that developed during Suharto era, the linkage between national and local factors, as well as its actors, was prominent. Therefore, this chapter will discuss linkages, parallels and the interplay between national politics and the local dynamics of the security forces that led to their partisanship in Ambon.

Van Klinken's (2001:2) to a certain degree expresses a similar view by highlighting patronage networks, particularly at the provincial level. He also underscored the instability of these networks during the transition period, which significantly influenced the nature of the conflict in Maluku.

The approach here highlights different features of the role of the security forces during the conflict in Ambon, which are different to those given by Aditjondro (2001a; 2001b), Tomagola (2000) and Hefner (2001). While Aditjondro, Tomagola and Hefner focus primarily on national factors and actors as the key variables causing the prolonged conflict in Ambon, the situation is much more complex than they presented in the 'grand narrative' of a military-provoked religious communal conflict.

Aditjondro (2001a:119; 2001b:164) contends that the persistence of inter-religious killings in Ambon is the outcome of systemic behaviour of the TNI (Tentara Nasional Indonesia, the Indonesian National Military), designed to advance TNI interests. In his paper, local military and civilian actors were perceived merely as extensions and instruments of national actors without having tensions and causing dynamics of their own. Tomagola (2000) claims that the prolonged religious conflicts in Ambon were provoked and orchestrated by some army generals in Jakarta for the sake of their economic and political interests. Hefner (2001) argues that the prolonged conflict in Ambon was the outcome of the political resistance of 'old' political elites, following President Suharto's resignation in May 1998.

Without necessarily rejecting such an interpretation, it is hard to provide strong evidence for it. This chapter therefore goes in a different direction by arguing that the interplay of national and local factors led to the partisanship of the security forces in the conflict. I will not present a 'grand narrative' or a single 'big scenario' or 'conspiracy'. Rather, I will show that it was a complex of parallel actions and an interplay of local and national factors that contributed to the protracted clashes in Ambon.

National setting of the conflict in Ambon

The Ambon riot first erupted on 19 January 1999—eight months after the fall of Suharto on 21 May 1998. Just prior to President Suharto being toppled, there were two major outbreaks of riots in Jakarta (13–14 May) and Surakarta (20–21 May). In the following days during the early post-Suharto era, a series of communal conflicts erupted throughout the archipelago. Two clashes occurred prior to the 19 January riot in Ambon, namely, on 22 November 1998 in Ketapang Jakarta and on 30 November 1998 in Kupang, East Nusa Tenggara. Some people draw a possible direct connection between these two conflicts and the 19 January riot in Ambon. The Ketapang violence had caused the deaths of some Christian Ambonese thugs, whose colleagues returned to Ambon just before the riot erupted. The Kupang conflict was incited by the speech of a retired, Christian army officer who was alleged to have deliberately provoked the conflict (Ecip 1999:15–38).

Indonesia's transition period was marked by the emergence of communal riots throughout the country. Tadjoeddin (2002:34–5) contends that the outbreak of communal violence was an important feature of this transition period. The scale of violence and the number of incidents and deaths increased significantly over time. While in 1997 there were 12 incidents and 127 deaths, the number increased significantly to 75 incidents and 1,300 deaths in 1998. In 1999, the number of incidents rose slightly to 139 and the number of deaths to 1,442 and then continued in 2000 with a further increase in the number of incidents (170) but a decrease in the number of deaths (1,150). However, the number of deaths presented by Tadjoeddin is more likely an under-estimate if, for example, we include the documented deaths in Maluku, where more than 3,000 were killed in the first two years of the conflict.[3] Similar outbreaks of mass violence can be seen as an indication of the chronic crisis facing Indonesia as a whole. According to International Crisis Group (2000a), the lack of resources, capacity to govern and national cohesion in addressing the national crisis was evident in Maluku as well as in the rest of the country.

The landscape of the security forces

The fall of Suharto on 21 May 1998 marked a new stage in Indonesian history: the end of the New Order regime. What would happen to the TNI, which was the backbone of the New Order regime?

Major General Agus Wirahadikusuma (1999) wrote:

> ...Suharto's resignation has been interpreted as the end of ABRI's 'invulnerability'. Since then, hardly a day goes by without ABRI being slandered and cursed. It used to be that no one dared to touch the military, but now ABRI's very existence is under attack. ABRI is not only blamed for causing the people of Aceh, Lampung, Tanjung Priok, Irian Jaya and East Timor to lose their family members, but also for its involvement in the disappearance of student and political activists, and because it was unable to prevent the loss of hundreds of lives during the conflict in May 1998. Moreover, it is [now] being demanded that ABRI retreat from politics (Kammen 1999).[4]

Thus, the panorama of military-society relations after the toppling of Suharto was quite tense. Following the extensive exposure by mass media of the massive human rights violations and power abuse by TNI in the New Order era—in Aceh, West Papua and East Timor—as well as the kidnapping of pro-democratic activists, the poor image of the TNI reached its nadir. The abrupt breakdown of its public profile, according to ICG (2000b:3), led to a significant decline in the military state of mind and brought TNI to a defensive position never before experienced. Then, the abolition of 'Dwifungsi ABRI' (dual-function of the military) became a major demand of the pro-democratic movement (Said 2002:169) Furthermore, a research team from the Indonesian Science Institute (Lembaga Ilmu Pengetahuan Indonesia—LIPI), even argued that Dwifungsi ABRI was 'the source of the national disaster' (Sumber Bencana Nasional) (Bhakti et al 2001:59).

Responding to the public demand for the eradication of Dwifungsi ABRI, the TNI Headquarters then declared on 5 October 1998 a set of political reforms within TNI called 'Paradigma Baru' (the New Paradigm) of the TNI.[5] This new paradigm, according to *Indonesia* (2001:141), redefined the role of the military in politics in terms of power sharing with civilian forces, impartiality in elections and between political parties, and separation of the police from the military. Not long after its launch, it was criticised by Wirahadikusuma (1999c:7) who stated that TNI needs more than just 'redefinition, re-actualization, and reposition'; rather, it required a whole change of its perspective and concept of 'perang rakyat semesta' (entire people's war). Furthermore, according to Bhakti et al (2001:285-7), the internal reforms made by TNI were just half-hearted (*reformasi setengah hati*) since they were only a response to public blame and criticism and therefore aimed to persuade people to accept TNI's non-military roles.

The inauguration of the new political stance by TNI therefore did not automatically repair its legitimacy and regain public trust. In the wake of its declaration for the new paradigm, the so-called 'Semanggi' incident occurred on 13 November 1998, when army and police troops shot students protesting against the holding of a special session of MPR, which led to nine students being killed and hundreds being injured. Therefore, as argued by Crouch (1999:137), this incident negated the security forces' efforts to repair their public image and brought them back to rock bottom.

The situation was so poor that even police and military posts became the target of mass attack, particularly in the capital and in many big cities. According to Defence Minister Juwono Sudarsono, in the middle of 12 July 2000, 150 police and army posts were attacked by masses in one month.[6] The media reported that some army and police members took off their uniforms outside their offices and only dared to wear them around their military complex. The morale of soldiers had deteriorated in part because of commissions to investigate human rights abuses in Aceh and East Timor, and some middle- and low-ranking officers and soldiers were brought to court, although nobody of high rank was in fact penalised (*Indonesia* 2001:135).

Even though the profile of the security forces in the post-Suharto era has significantly declined, they, particularly the army, still control huge residual resources through which it is possible to exercise political influence. According to the International Crisis Group (ICG 2000b:ii–iii), there are at least three resources belonging to TNI that contribute to its political influence: firstly, its territorial structure throughout the nation; secondly, its strong representation in the state and military intelligence services; and thirdly, its access to funds through business enterprises and other tools. Furthermore, there are some indications of military officers' involvement in some activities that seem planned to erode the government's authority, such as antagonism to government policy in Aceh, Maluku, West Timor and West Papua.

Thus, the image of the security forces at an early stage of the post-Suharto era was one of demoralisation. Contrary to their superior and lordly performance under the New Order era, these forces behaved with a lack of confidence and a host of anxieties about public scrutiny. However, they still held enormous, residual, political resources to influence the political sphere. In sum, the complicated mixture of their weak legitimacy and their huge residual political resources in the setting of uncertainty during the early stage of democratic transition led to their poor performance in dealing with the many social conflicts that erupted during the post-Suharto era.

Tension between the security forces and civil society in Ambon before the 19 January violence reached a peak in the Batu Gantung incident on 18 November 1998.[7] The large student demonstration in which about 5,000 students participated focused on the demand to abolish Dwifungsi ABRI and the responsibility of the Armed Forces Commander, General Wiranto, for the military shooting at the Semanggi incident in Jakarta. This ended in a clash between students and soldiers in front of the headquarters of the Pattimura Army Resort Command, or Korem, and resulted in 63 students, one lecturer, 24 soldiers and three spectators being injured (Aditjondro 2001a:103; Kastor 2000:197–204; Kusuma 2000:93; Rio Pelu 2002).[8]

Following this incident, the Maluku Governor called a meeting between the Korem Pattimura Commander, Colonel R Hikayat, and religious and community leaders. At this meeting, Hikayat was blamed and criticised by some leaders, especially those representing the Christian community. Furthermore, he and his deputy, Lieutenant Colonel Gatot Sumarwoto,[9] both Javanese, were asked to resign and leave Ambon (Kastor 2000:197–207; Kusuma 2000:94–5). After this clash, relations between the security forces and Ambonese society deteriorated significantly. Many soldiers were scared to wear their uniforms in public. (Kusuma 2000:94).

However, poor relations between security forces, particularly the army, and society, particularly the Christian community, had begun years before. The strain arising from the plan to rebuild the mosque in the Batumerah army barracks was one of the causes. There was a dispute between the Maluku Protestant Church (Gereja Protestant Maluku—GPM) and the Pattimura Korem regarding ownership of the land to be used to rebuild the mosque. The dispute had begun when the Korem Commander was Colonel Amir Syarifuddin (1994–96) and continued under Colonel Hikayat (1997–99) (Kusuma 2000:82–9).

Hikayat's first test arose from political contestation regarding the election of the Maluku Governor in 1997. The rivalry was mainly between Freddy Latumahina, a Christian Ambonese, Ruswan Latuconsina and Saleh Latuconsina, who were both Muslim Ambonese. Latumahina was supported mainly by Golkar, consisting mostly of Christians in Ambon, while Saleh Latuconsina was supported mainly by the national leadership of Golkar and the bureaucracy, who were mostly Muslims. Under the guidance of the Commander of ABRI, General Feisal Tanjung, Hikayat supported Saleh Latuconsina, who was then elected Governor. This case, according to an informant who was a key figure in the Korem, caused Hikayat's relationship with the Christian Ambonese political elite to deteriorate (interview in Jakarta 24 November 2002).

Another primary cause was actually the leadership style of Hikayat.[10] According to a middle-ranking officer in Ambon, compared to previous Korem Commander, Colonel Sudibyo, whose background was in territorial management, Hikayat's approach toward people was relatively poor. His style of leadership was somewhat stern and inflexible, typical of the operational soldier. An illustration was given by an officer who worked in the information section, that Hikayat's relationship with journalists was poor. In Sudibyo's era financial support was provided by the Korem for journalists but this was cancelled by Hikayat. As a result his relationship with journalists in Ambon was not harmonious. The fact that the press in Ambon was predominantly Christian while Hikayat is a devout Muslim was another barrier[11] (interview in Ambon, 6 October 2002).

Internal army tension

The emerging tension within the army in the late Suharto era, according to Kammen and Sidarth (1999:12), was visible in 1988. Conflict between President Suharto and many senior officers was indicated by the sudden dismissal of General Beny Murdani as Commander of the Armed Forces, just before the March session of the MPR. The military leadership was alienated when the 1988 MPR session elected the titular military general Sudharmono to be Suharto's Vice President. This situation deteriorated further with the Dili incident on 12 November 1991, the rivalry for the leadership of Golkar and the election of the Vice President in 1993.

Angry and potentially threatened because of the military's defiance, Suharto then switched his political strategy to embrace Islamic groups by supporting the foundation of the Association of Indonesian Muslim Intellectual (Ikatan Cendekiawan Muslim se Indonesia—ICMI) in December 1990. Hefner (2000:159) suggests that Suharto's ICMI initiative punished the ABRI leadership for its actions, but was also an effort to balance the president's loss of support among the military with a new base among Muslims.

Subsequently, Suharto encouraged factionalism among the military, particularly the army (Hefner 2000:151; Kingsbury 2001b:98–9). In 1994, President Suharto replaced several of the most prominent critics of ICMI in the military command with figures sympathetic to what Hefner called 'regimist Islam'. He identified four officers—Feisal Tanjung, Hartono, Syarwan Hamid and Prabowo — who represented the ascendant 'Islamic' wing of the armed forces.[12] Inter-factional tension was growing especially between the so-called 'green' (regimist Islam) wing and the 'red and white' (secular nationalist) wing.[13]

On 6 June 1997, Suharto exacerbated the tension between the two groups by appointing the middle-of-the-road General Wiranto as army Chief of Staff and, in 1998, as Commander of ABRI and Minister for Defence and Security. This, according to Crouch (1999:128–9), was part of a divide-and-rule strategy because at the same time Suharto was rapidly promoting his son-in-law, Prabowo Subianto, to key positions in the army. Prabowo was appointed to lead Kopassus (Special Forces) and then Kostrad (Army Strategic Reserve Command), key commands of elite troops. The factional tension within the army was then manifested in sharp rivalry between General Wiranto and General Prabowo.[14]

In this period there was a kind of 'dual command structure' within the army. As described by *Indonesia* (2001:136), some individual generals used their own financial resources to hire 'rogue elements' and 'deserters'[15] to initiate extensive violence, provocations and killings. Some sections of the press exposed the involvement of rogue elements and army deserters in many violent cases during this period (for instance, *DeTAK* 1998). Thus, the Ambon conflict began at a time when the army command was fragmented and divided.

Mirroring what was happening on the national stage, the division and fragmentation within the army command in Maluku, to a certain degree, was also apparent. One example was the case of 'unofficial permission' involving some intelligence personnel before the 19 January riot. Since there were some indications of a possible clash in Ambon before then, the Korem Commander, Colonel Hikayat, refused to give permission to some intelligence personnel to take leave. However, the Deputy Commander, Lieutenant Colonel Gatot Sumarwoto, gave permission 'unofficially' to some personnel, including Captain Makmuri, the Commander of the Intelligence Team, to take leave. Therefore, important intelligence personnel were absent when the riot erupted. According to an officer, Colonel Hikayat became very angry at an internal meeting in the Korem (interviews with officers in Ambon, September 2002 and in Jakarta, 24 November 2002).

Another case occurred at an early stage of the conflict. After the massive attack by Muslims from Hitu on some Christian villages following the riot in Ambon city, intelligence information was received that the mastermind was Habib Husein bin Tahir, a cleric from Java, who was visiting Hitu. Colonel Saragih, Assistant for Intelligence at the Trikora Kodam,[16] believed that this information was true and therefore he ordered the arrest of Habib Husein. However, a key figure of the Korem thought that the information was wrong. On the contrary, he believed that Habib Husein had tried to persuade people to cancel the attack though he did not succeed. This Korem senior officer decided to counter the command: he ordered an officer to save Habib. Habib had planned to leave Ambon by plane. Some officers ordered by Colonel Saragih waited for him at Pattimura airport, but, warned and assisted by the Korem officer, Habib decided to go by ship from Ambon port. Thus, the arrest order made by the intelligence officer of the Kodam was countered by an order made by a senior officer at the Korem[17] (Kusuma 2000:136; interview with officers in Ambon, September 2002 and Jakarta, 24 November 2002).

Questions have arisen about Colonel Hikayat's identity. According to a respected, civilian intelligence source close to BIN (Badan Intelijen Negara, or National Intelligence Agency),[18] Hikayat was a close ally of Lieutenant General Prabowo Subianto[19] (interview in Jakarta 6 August 2002) Therefore, according to him, the eruption of the Ambon riot was due to rivalry between Wiranto and Prabowo on the national stage. It was intended by Wiranto's group to discredit and discard Hikayat as Prabowo's man. However, this allegation was rejected by Major General Saurip Kadi, Hikayat's classmate at Akabri and an opponent of Prabowo's political group. According to him, Hikayat was less likely to be a Prabowo supporter. However, it is likely that Hikayat was perceived to be an ally of Prabowo by Wiranto's network (Saurip 2002).

A different story of religious tension within the army is told by Brigadier General (Retired) Rustam Kastor, former Commander of the Pattimura Korem, and an Ambonese Muslim, who has sided with Islamic troops throughout the conflict. According to Kastor, he was the target of a 'discriminative' policy when he was a colonel and was reported by his rival as 'anti Christian' to then Commander of the Armed Forces General Beni Murdani, a Javanese Catholic.[20] As a result, he was 'frozen' as a colonel for 11 years, until he was promoted to Brigadier General in 1991, just three years before he retired[21] (Kastor 2002).

Military–police tension

Soon after the collapse of Suharto, one of the critical issues for the security forces was the separation of the police from the military. The integration of the police as part of the military, implemented under President Sukarno, has been a major cause of power abuse and led to militarisation of the police (ICG 2001:4, 9). Thus, one of the major steps taken by the military in its New Paradigm launched in October 1998 was to separate the police from the military.[22] Since then, the domestic security function has been formally taken over by the police, whereas the military formally focuses on the external defence function. In reality, however, the military still plays a major, internal security role.

The formal institutional separation between the police force and the military was inaugurated by the Commander-in-Chief, General Wiranto, on 1 April 1999, when ABRI was formally renamed the TNI. The police force was placed under the authority of the Department of Defence and Security concurrently headed by Wiranto (*Indonesia* 2001:141). A further step was taken on 1 July 2000, when President Wahid revealed a presidential decision moving the police from the Department of Defence and situating it directly under the President, earlier than the planned change on 1 January 2001. According to ICG (2001:9), the forwarding of the time line of the separation of the police from under the Department of Defence was to get rid of vagueness about its status and to facilitate foreign aid for police training.

The separation of the police from the military took place relatively smoothly at the elite level; however, several problems arose regarding the new pattern of military–police relations.[23] The transition of internal security to the police caused resentment amongst the military because it was being deprived of authority in a domain that was full of economic and political resources. Clashes began to break out between the police and the military, some over competition for resources and some regarding law enforcement. As Roosa (2003:10–11) notes, the security forces in many cases paradoxically became a source of insecurity. A dramatic instance was the attack launched by the Kostrad's airborne unit (Linud 100) on the Police Resort Office at Binjai, Medan, on 29–30 September 2002, which led to seven policemen and three civilians dying and one being injured.

Even though the army has formally withdrawn from domestic security responsibilities, paradoxically the army deployment to turbulent areas in the post-Suharto era has increased significantly. Kammen (2003:6–7) indicates that from 1998 to 2001, the army deployment to conflict areas such as West Papua, Aceh, Maluku and Poso, has increased considerably from 24 to 57 non-territorial battalions. According to ICG (2002c:3–4), at least 18,000 army troops were sent to East Timor to anticipate the referendum promised by President Habibie, held on 30 August 1999. There were about 17 army battalions deployed in Maluku by the time the civil emergency was declared in June 2000, compared to two battalions of police troops.

Tension between the army and police in Ambon were common some months prior to the 19 January riot. One incident involved a group of soldiers searching for illegal weapons rumoured to have been smuggled into Ambon from the Netherlands and Belgium. The search was carried out from May until November 1998 in some locations around Lateri. According to an army officer who joined in the search (Kusuma 2000:89–91), two issues of dispute arose between the army and the police. The first was over the occupation of particular locations, since the two institutions did the same work. The second involved the snatching away by the army and police of a witness who was supposed to know where arms were being stored. The witness, a Butonese, then disappeared, so that neither institution found the weapons.

The next conflict happened just before the 'Batu Gantung incident' on 18 November 1998. According to Kusuma (2000:93–5), Polda Maluku did not deploy its troops around the Korem headquarters to handle the massive student protest. This was contrary to an agreement reached at a co-ordination meeting between Polda and Korem in order to anticipate the student demonstration as part of the so-called 'Lilin-Ketupat' Operation.[24] However, according to Colonel Karyono—then Head of Polda Maluku—a large number of police were deployed along the way from the Ambon Port to Korem headquarters to secure and prevent chaos in the city. According to him, because there were a lot of army troops around the Korem headquarters he decided to deploy police troops in other locations which were in a critical situation (interview in Jakarta, 16 April 2003). A former key Korem figure, however, argued that similar instances frequently occurred, indicating a lack of police professionalism (interview with an officer in Jakarta, 24 November 2002).

More tension arose in the case of the Dobo riot on 15 January 1999. There was a petty dispute between Polda and Korem regarding how to handle the riot. Assuming that the case was serious, Korem Commander Colonel Hikayat suggested sending army troops to Dobo as support for police troops whose major responsibility was internal security. However, the Head of Maluku Police, Colonel Karyono, rejected army assistance because he was confident that the Brimob troops could deal with it. According to a former key figure of the Korem, Colonel Hikayat finally decided to send a small group of intelligence personnel to Dobo without the approval of the Kapolda Colonel Karyono[25] (interview in Jakarta 24 November 2002).

The tension between the Pattimura Commander and the Head of Maluku Police has been commented upon by Kastor (2000:23). According to him, the tension was widely rumored among government elites as well as being evident in the way they dealt with the riots. Interestingly, he argues that the tension between them was the outcome of a conspiracy involving Christians and RMS supporters, rather than personal or institutional rivalries. By contrast, Suparlan et al (1999:17–8) contend that the causes were probably their different approaches—the police emphasised discretion, whereas the army underscored its hierarchical structure and disciplinary principles.

Military–Government tension

Soon after the fall of Suharto, Habibie and Wiranto were the most powerful people on the Indonesian political stage. Habibie took the presidency, while General Wiranto remained military commander. In the disarray following Suharto's fall, each needed and benefited from the other.

> Wiranto could not afford to risk dismissal by Habibie while Habibie needed Wiranto to ensure that no challenge emanated from ABRI. By the end of 1998, however, it seemed that Wiranto needed Habibie more than Habibie needed Wiranto…In short, Habibie could replace Wiranto but Wiranto could not replace Habibie. The subordination of the military to the civilian president, however, cannot be understood without taking into account the dramatic collapse in ABRI's reputation (Crouch 1999:135).

Covert tension between the government and the military arose regarding the referendum policy to deal with East Timor announced by President Habibie in January 1999. According to *Indonesia* (2001:143), Wiranto did not openly oppose the policy but worked silently to ensure that the East Timorese chose autonomy. Thus, from then until the referendum produced overwhelming victory for the pro-independence side, and on 31 August 1999, huge military efforts were mobilised in East Timor. The lack of attention to the Ambon riot appeared in Wiranto's statement in the aftermath of the general election in 1999, when he stated that Aceh, East Timor and the upcoming general session of the MPR were the three most critical issues for the military (*Indonesia* 2001:142)

In contrast to relatively calm government–military relations under President Habibie, the situation changed significantly under President Wahid. Even though General Wiranto and several senior military officers were appointed in the cabinet, tension immediately rose. Soon after his election, President Wahid began to erode General Wiranto's position by, for instance, replacing some of his allies such as: Chief of Police General Rusmanhadi with Lieutenant General Rusdiharjo; Chief of BAIS TNI Lieutenant General Tysno Sudarto with Air Vice-Marshal Ian Santosa Perdanakusuma; and military spokeperson Major General Sudradjat with Air Vice-Marshal Graito Usodo (*Indonesia* 2001:145). At the same time, he appointed Lieutenant General Arie Kumaat as the Chief of Civilian Intelligence replacing Lieutenant General Zaini Maulani, a close ally of former President Habibie (Mietzner 2001:334).

Further tension arose between President Wahid and General Wiranto with the reorganisation plan of the army's territorial structure proposed by Wiranto. Rather than support the plan, Wahid backed the idea of dismantling the army's territorial structure as launched by Major General Agus Wirahadikusumah before a parliamentary committee on 13 December 1999. The strain increased when President Wahid appointed Major General Agus Wirahadikusumah as Commander Kostrad in March 2000 replacing Major General Djaja Suparman, a close ally of Wiranto. The tension reached its peak when the National Human Rights Commission for East Timor named General Wiranto and some army and police officers to be investigated (SDSC 2002). President Wahid finally suspended General Wiranto as Co-ordinating Minister on 14 February 2000, soon after returning from a long overseas trip, and General Wiranto formally resigned from his position on 16 May (*Indonesia* 2001:145–7; Said 2001:338–47).

Another climax was reached in October 2000 when Wahid tried to promote Major General Wirahadikusumah[26] as army Commander in place of General Tyasno Sudarto. This manoeuvre, however, was resisted by many senior army officers. A statement signed by 45 generals called on the army Chief of Staff, General Tyasno Sudarto, to bring Major General Wirahadikusumah before a military court for his undisciplined behaviour. The culmination of military resistance to Wahid was its support for the first memorandum issued by parliament on February 1, 2002 against him, which eventually led to Wahid being toppled from the presidency[27] (Said 2001:334, 351–3).

More locally, tension between the Korem and the local government, particularly at the level of the Ambon Municipality, arose over the plan to relocate a mosque in the Batumerah Army Barracks. As described by Kusuma (2000:82–9), the case started when the Korem was led by Colonel Infantry Amir Syarifuddin, a Muslim Bugis. The dispute between the Korem and GPM was over the ownership of a piece of land to be used to relocate the mosque. Responding to a complaint made by GPM, the Head of the Ambon Municipality then Colonel Infantry Yohannes Sudiono, a Catholic Javanese, decided to suspend the relocation.

The dispute continued under the next Korem Commander Colonel (Artillery) Sudibyo, a Javanese Muslim. According to an officer in charge of religious affairs (as quoted by Kusuma 2000:85), in a meeting held by Colonel Sudibyo in Korem Headquarters, the Head of the Ambon Municipality, was asked to issue a building licence for the mosque in the army barracks. Colonel Yohannes Sudiono replied that the problem was at the level of the staff of the municipal office in charge of land affairs. Sudibyo said that most of the Christian staff in his office refused to deal with Muslim affairs, such as issuing licences for the mosque and for the Muslim cemetery.[28]

The problem persisted until the tenure of Colonel Hikayat (May 1997–February 1999). Another plan to rebuild the mosque at the OSM army barracks faced a similar problem in getting a building licence from the Municipal office (Kusuma 2000:88). The tension and suspicion between the Head of the Ambon Municipality and the army continued at the time the conflict broke out, particularly involving Kostrad 431 troops from Ujung Pandang.[29] The Head of the Ambon Municipality, Colonel Christ Tanasale, suspected he was the target of a group of Kostrad 431 troops who were looking for him in his house.[30] Nevertheless, according to a Captain Infantry Imam, Operational Section Officer of Kostrad 431 (Kusuma 2000:217–9), the troops were looking for him in his house in order to get assistance for a water problem in the army barracks nearby.

The relations between the provincial government and Kodam Pattimura seemed to be relatively calm prior to, and in the early stage of, conflict under Colonel Hikayat's leadership. This situation arose as a result of a political alliance between Colonel Hikayat and Governor Saleh Latuconsina during the election of the Governor in 1998. Nevertheless, the relations between the Governor and Pangdam Pattimura became relatively tense in the latter phase of the conflict, particularly under Brigadiers General Max Tamaela, I Made Yasa and Mustopo (as Pattimura Kodam Commander).

Internal police tension

In the popular imagination for many years during the New Order era, the Indonesian National Police (INP) were seen as ineffective, inefficient, brutal and corrupt (ICG 2001a:7). Portraying the chronic problems of INP, former Chief of INP Kunarto (2000) described it as understaffed, inadequately equipped, completely corrupt and without institutional memory of institutional independence, as the outcome of the degradation of its power by the New Order and the appropriation of its authority by the army. Thus, the police were weak in the early stages of the post-Suharto era.

However, in contrast to the army's internal tension, there were no significant issues regarding religious affairs that emerged within the police. The rivalries among police elites were based on such issues as the academy graduation class, different origins and operational divisions, and personal groupings. Rivalries based on academy class were also common within the army (Kammen & Sidarth 1999). The rivalries based on different origins and operational divisions among the police were particularly between Brimob, the elite paramilitary troop, and criminal investigation (Reserse) section. The last feature was based on economic and political motives and networks among police—particularly its elites—regarding the issue of replacement of the Head of National Police by President Abdurrahman Wahid.

The internal police tension emerged significantly when President Wahid attempted to replace Kapolri General Surojo Bimantoro by Lieutentant General Chairuddin Ismail, without approval by the parliament. The controversy was incited by President Wahid's decision to install Lieutenant General Chairuddin Ismail as the Deputy Head of National Police on 2 June 2000. The position had actually been liquidated by his own decision in Presidential Decision (Keputusan Presiden, Kepres) number 54 on Organisation and Police Procedure made in 2001. Chairuddin replaced Commander General Pandji Atmasudirja who had retired. President Wahid's step provoked further dispute since at the same time he forced the Head of National Police, General Bimantoro, to resign. However, Bimantoro refused to resign (Kompas, 3 June 2001).

Supported by most political parties, General Bimantoro continued to fight and reject his successor. The controversy spread among active and retired police personnel, and divided the national police institution into two main groups: those who favoured and those who opposed the installation of the new Kapolri. A group of retired generals, including some former Heads of National Police, supported Bimantoro's manoeuvres. Nevertheless, a group of officers declared their support for Chairuddin to be the Head of the National

Police and suggested that Bimantoro accept President Wahid's decision. As a result, as reported by leading newspaper *Kompas* (13 July 2001), there was 'The Commotion of the Head of National Police' ('Geger Kepala Polri').

The dispute over the leadership of the National Police had repercussions in Ambon over the replacement of Brigadier General Edi Darnadi as the Head of Polda Maluku. Darnadi was previously the Head of Police in the Bogor Residency and successfully removed the Laskar Jihad from its 'war exercise' in Bogor in April 2000. He was alleged to be a sympathiser of Lieutenant General Chairuddin and probably signed the police officer petition to support Chairuddin as the new Head of the National Police.

In contrast to the local army troops estimated to be more or less evenly divided between Muslim and Christian personnel, the local police were predominantly Christians (about 70%) (ICG 2002:4). Therefore from the beginning of the conflict, local police, particularly Brimob, were perceived by Muslims as biased.

Nevertheless, compared to the army, internal tension among police personnel was more overt. One of the most dramatic incidents was the break down of the Brimob headquarters and armory in Tantui on 21 June 2000. In Tantui there were also the houses of Polda Maluku elites including the house of the Head and the Deputy Head of Polda Maluku. The collapse of the Tantui headquarters was probably the result of an internal clash among police which led to the death of the Brimob Deputy Commander Major Edy Susanto who was murdered by his own Christian subordinates (Gani 2002:174–5). Following this murder the Muslim militias, included the notorious Laskar Jihad troops and backed by 'undercover forces' ('Pasukan Siluman'), launched a massive attack on Tantui and succeeded in capturing it. In this clash both sides, Muslim and Christian, gained a huge number of weapons[31] (ICG 2002c:5; Gani 2002:176).

In the aftermath of the destruction of the Tantui headquarters, the police institution reached its nadir, as no police installation remained united. The police institution in Ambon was more or less divided into two parts: the regional police headquarters (Polda) Maluku was dominated by Christian personnel while the municipal police (Polres) Ambon were controlled by Muslim personnel (Gani 2002:78–90). As a result, the maintenance of security and enforcement of law in Ambon had obviously broken down. As noted by ICG (2002:421), if the military detained a Muslim agitator, for instance, they feared that if he was transferred to the Polda he would be tortured or even killed, but if he was transferred to the Polres he would be released. The same dilemma arose when Christian agitators were detained.

Following the collapse of the Tantui headquarters, 15 police housing complexes on Ambon island were divided into two camps along religious lines. Seven complexes were inhabited by Muslim personnel and eight by Christian personnel. When I was in Ambon in October 2002, two new complexes in Tantui were inhabited by both Christian and Muslim personnel (interview in Polda Maluku on 11 October 2002).

Internal police tension was also occurring between local Ambon troops and outside police deployed in Ambon (Bawah Kendali Operasi, BKO). The tension was caused by several factors: first, the economic and facilities gap between local troops and the BKO; second, the taking over of authority and 'additional' financial sources by BKO troops; third, abuse of power and authority by the BKO.

The salary given to BKO troops was about 30% higher than the local troops[32] and their facilities were better. Many local police had to pay rent since their houses had been burnt or damaged, while most BKO troops commonly paid nothing for accommodation. Moreover, BKO troops usually stayed in their working area and did not need to spend money for transportation to work. Furthermore some local officers, like my informant, were asked for contributions to supplement the BKO troops' daily food rations (interview in Ambon October 2002).

The next factor leading to the deteriorating of the situation was the reduction and later elimination of local police authority, since most of the police were alleged to be partisan in the conflict. The reduction of local police authority meant that police officers lost opportunities to gain 'additional' financial sources from private security jobs during the conflict, such as building or company protection, which were taken over by BKO troops.

Finally, the BKO troops often abused their power and authority with regard to local people. My informant said that some BKO troops often 'rented' motorbikes without paying the full amount, for instance, only paying Rp 2,000 for a full day (the standard payment was about Rp 10,000–20,000). Another issue was improper behaviour with local girls, including sexual harassment and pregnancy (interview in Ambon October 2002).

The tension between local police troops and members of the BKO sometimes resulted in open clashes. A local police officer even said that some local Ambonese police snipers shot at BKO troops because of those problems (interview in Ambon October 2002).

Conclusion

There was a close connection between developments at national and local levels with regard to the role of the security forces, before and during the early stages of the conflict in Ambon. However, it is an oversimplification to conclude that these developments at a local level were just extensions of the dynamics on the national stage. Although the use of a neo-patrimonial perspective to observe the conflict in Ambon is able to demonstrate some prominent features of national and local networks, it does not mean that the local developments were merely reflections and extensions of the national phenomena. This chapter has shown that there were also local dynamics of their own in the realms of government-security forces and, more particularly, within the police.

Nationally and locally, tension between the security forces and society were in parallel: the strain became acute when the public image of the security forces deteriorated significantly, leading to demoralisation of the troops. The clear linking of the 'Semanggi incident' on 13 November 1998 in Jakarta to the 'Batu Gajah incident' on 18 November 1998 in Ambon, was a striking example of the close connections between the national scene and the local situation.

The deep, internal army tension, which had appeared at the national level in the late Suharto era and in the early stages of the Habibie presidency, seemed to be reflected to a certain degree in the local setting. Suspicions and distrust emerged within the army according to their different religious affiliations. The interplay of national and local factors was evident in communication between soldiers at these different levels during the massive religious clashes in Ambon. However, the linkage between national and local connections was not as clear as what happened in the realm of security–society tension.

The realm of army–police relations has also become tense. In the aftermath of the separation of the police from the military, the relationship between them has been uneasy at the national and local levels. However, national tension was mostly latent compared with the manifest tension at the local level. A lack of co-operation and co-ordination between them in Ambon has reduced the ability of the security apparatus to deal with social unrest.

A dynamic tension between the government and the security forces coloured the conflict. At the national level, tension between the President and the army had been changing along with its elites. Whereas the indecisiveness of security forces policy was the main feature in the Habibie era, it contributed significantly in opening a space for non-Ambonese actors (such as the Laskar Jihad in mid-2000) to play a bigger role in the conflict in the Wahid presidency. At the local level, the tension changed as the conflict developed and as elites within the security forces changed: before, and in the early stages of, the conflict, tension was more likely to occur at the municipal level rather than at the provincial level, but during the latter stages of the conflict tension also emerged at the provincial level.

Last, but not least, internal police tension undoubtedly contributed to the poor performance of the security forces. As a legacy of the army-dominated New Order regime, the police force had generally become a very weak institution. As a result, during the conflict in Ambon the police was quite powerless to deal with the situation and during a particular period, the force was in a state of complete breakdown. The tension among police at local level was remarkable and does not seem to be a reflection of a national phenomenon.

In sum, the landscape just before and at an early stage of the Ambon conflict shows the insecurity of the security forces. A survey of the situation in the security forces during that period reveals some major weaknesses. Their public image was poor, their privileges was threatened by the political reforms, their morale had declined, their internal solidity was fragile and their co-operation and co-ordination network was questionable. At the same time, the security forces (particularly the army) still held huge residual resources through which they could exercise political influence. Therefore, it is not surprising that they were unable to effectively deal with the massive social upheaval that occurred in Ambon, and as a result they were caught up in it, playing a partisan role.

Endnotes

1. The term 'security forces' incorporates police, army, navy and air force. According to regulation (Tap MPR No VII/MPR/2000) the major responsibility for domestic security is now in the hands of the police, though they are able to call for support from other forces when necessary. A legal study of the separation of the police from the military was conducted by a team of the Faculty of Law at the University of Gadjah Mada, led by Muhammad Fajrul Falaakh (2001). In the case of the Ambon conflict, army deployment outnumbered the police, while the navy (particularly marines) and the air force played minor roles (ICG 2002:3). This chapter will focus particularly on the police and the army.

2. A discussion about Indonesia's New Order as a neo patrimonial regime, a bureaucratic polity or a bureaucratic authoritarian regime was presented by Dwight King. It is based on Weber's notion of patrimonial rule, which was reinterpreted by Eisenstadt and Gunther Roth in the new context of 'detraditionalized, personalized patrimonialism' (King 1982:107).

3. I thank Dr Jaap Timmer for pointing out this matter. Tadjoeddin's work is based on only two national press sources, *Kompas* and *Antara*. This is most likely the main cause of its lack of accuracy.

4. For the original, Indonesian version, see Wirahadikusumah (1999a; 1999b).

5. The New Paradigm of TNI were, first, change in position and method to one where [ABRI] is not necessarily in the forefront; second, change from the concept of occupying to influencing; third, change in the method of influencing from direct to indirect ways; fourth, readiness to engage in political role sharing (joint decision-making in the case of important national and governmental issues) with other components of the nation. English version translated by Crouch (1999:138–9). The original source is Wiranto (1998:17–18). According Salim Said (2002:169) the New Paradigm launched first on 18 July 2003 by General Wiranto in Bandung. The declaration of 'New Paradigm' was the follow up of the seminar held by Sesko AD, 23–24 September 1998.

6. The statement was published by *Suara Pembaruan* on 13 July 2000 (Indonesia 2001:136).

7. The student demonstrations were interpreted by Rustam Kastor (2000:33), a retired Brigadier General and the former Commander of Korem Pattimura (1987–90), as part of a deliberate effort by Christians to undermine the TNI. Rio Pelu, a student of Unpatti and the Head of Islamic Student Association (HMI) Ambon Municipality in 1998, who actively participated in and organised those protests, gave a different account. According to him, the demonstrations were part of the national student movement demanded the abolition of Dwifungsi ABRI. An Unpatti student and HMI activist, Tahir Karepesina, was seriously injured in the 16 November protest (Rio Pelu 2002).

8. Kusuma's thesis is an interesting work since he is an army officer assigned to Ambon from 1997. He graduated from the department of history at UGM before joining in the army. He took leave from his duty in Ambon to undertake post-

graduate study at UGM from July 1999 to December 2000. In his thesis, Captain Kusuma used his own experiences and observations from his time in Ambon and also interviewed some colleagues. Though most of his informants are Muslim, in several cases he attempted to present both sides of the story.

9   The fact that Lieutenant Colonel Gatot Sumarwoto is Catholic supports the theory that there was tension between the security forces and society rather than a religious issue as perceived by Rustam Kastor.

10 Hikayat is an infantryman who graduated from Akabri in 1973 and was Assistant of Operations at Kodam Trikora (1996–97). During a military operation he to freed several hostages of the Papuan Freedom Movement in Mapenduma, Papua, July–August 1996. Previously he was a lecturer at Sesko AD (1996), Middle Officer Assistant (Paban Madya) at Army Headquarters (1992–96) and the Head of District Military Command (Kodim) Bangli, Bali (1990–92). Hikayat was then promoted to Commander Korem Pattimura (May 1997–February 1999). His term ended on 1 December 1998; however, as there was no person appointed as the new Commander, he was still in the position as the conflict erupted on 19 January 1999.

11 An anonymous former senior officer in Maluku explained that Hikayat supported Muslim groups in Maluku as they were, in Hikayat's view, underdeveloped compared with the Christian side (interview in Jakarta at 24 November 2002). This matter was perceived in very different way by Christian camp.

12 Salim Said (2001:144–6) gives a different account. According to him, the rise of General Feisal Tanjung and General Hartono to the peak of military command was the outcome of a long cultural and historical process to integrate Muslim people into the nation-state of the Republic of Indonesia, rather than the outcome of a power struggle in national politics. A brief note needs to be added about Salim Said. He was a scholar close to Centre for Policy and Development Studies (CPDS), a think tank founded by General Hartono and Lieutenant General Prabowo. For CPDS and the politics of the military in the late Suharto era, see Sulistyo (2001:296–300).

13 The so-called 'green' officers were those with an 'Islamic' political orientation and particularly those who supported the foundation of ICMI, whereas the so-called 'red and white' officers were those who had a 'Nationalist' political orientation and opposed ICMI. The latter group was usually assumed to sympathise with General Murdani. This distinction, however, was criticised by some observers (see Mietzner 1998).

14 The high tension and disarray within the army command was observed by the TGPF (Tim Gabungan Pencari Fakta, *the Joint Fact Finding Team*) for the May 1998 Riot in its report. See also Sulistyo (2001:299–300).

15 These 'rogue elements' and 'deserters' were also identified as off-line or non-official military, sometimes retired Kopassus members or those operating on clandestine projects.

16 At the time the 19 January riot erupted, the Pattimura Commander was under the Kodam Trikora, which its headquarters located in Jayapura, Irian Jaya. This

structural hierarchy changed when the Pattimura Korem was upgraded to be the Kodam on 15 May 1999.

17 The senior officer informant said that sources told the Kodam Commander Trikora, Major General Amir Sembiring, that the Korem Commander, Colonel Hikayat, was biased in dealing with the conflict in Ambon. The large number of Christians arrested compared to Muslims was reported as an indication of his bias. Therefore Christian leaders and officers asked for more balanced treatment. The order to arrest Habib Hitu, according to him, was a policy to accommodate this pressure but based on inaccurate information. Religious affiliation may have been significant since Major General Amir Sembiring and Colonel Saragih were Catholics, while the Korem senior officer was a Muslim (interview in Jakarta on 24 November 2002).

18 The authority of this civilian source was confirmed by another civilian member of BIN. At first, he said that he did not know him, but after he met with his senior intelligence officer he gave high respect to him as 'man who has very wide network'.

19 Hikayat was associated with Prabowo when he was Assistant of Operations at the Trikora Kodam (1996–97) during the successful military operation to free hostages taken by the Papuan Freedom Movement in Mapenduma, Irian Jaya, in July–August 1996. At that time, Major General Prabowo was Commander of Kopassus and involved in the operation. After this success, Hikayat was promoted to be the Commander of Pattimura Korem (1997–99).

20 The exact reason he was reported to General Benny Moerdani is not clear. In an interview he said that when he was Commander of the Pattimura Korem he got in to trouble with the Christian Golkar leader Zeth. Sahubura, who had, according to him, ambitions to be the Maluku Governor.

21 His promotion was probably supported by General Wismoyo Arismunandar, his classmate at Akabri, who graduated in 1963. When Rustam Kastor was Commander of the Pattimura Korem, Wismoyo was Commander of the Trikora Kodam. An Ambonese Muslim close to Kastor told the author that Kastor and Wismoyo have close personal relationship, and during the conflict in Ambon, Kastor frequently contacted and asked for assistance to Wismoyo (interview in Yogya in July 2002).

22 Under the military, the police also received military training. It can be called 'the sixty percent police' since about 40% of its educational curriculum was military. In this period, the police were handicapped in co-operation programs with overseas police because its position as part of military (Satjipto Rahardjo, quoted by Said 2001:287)

23 The tensions between army and the police, particularly Brimob, have their origins in the early stage of Independence. Brimob, was placed directly under the Prime Minister and equipped with weapons and equipments more sophisticated than the army. It then incited tensions and clashes between them (Suryohadiprojo 1996:298).

24 *Lilin* is an Indonesian word that means candle, and is seen as the symbol of Christmas, while *ketupat* is the name of traditional food especially produced during the Eid Fitri holidays. Thus, the so-called 'Lilin-Ketupat' operation was conducted by Indonesian police during Christmas and Eid Fitri.

25 Kapolda Colonel Karyono, who graduated from Akpol in 1970, is more senior than Colonel Hikayat. Police and army cadets share their first year (the formation period) at the armed forces academy (Akademi Angkatan Bersenjata Republik Indonoesia—Akabri) located in Magelang, Central Java. After that the army cadets stay in Magelang and the police cadets go to the police academy (Akademi Kepolisian—Akpol) at Semarang.

26 When General Wiranto was listed as one of those listed as responsible for the violence in East Timor by the Joint Committee for Fact Finding. Major General Wirahadikusumah, then the Commander of the Wirabuana Kodam, responded publicly to ask Wiranto to resign, which provoked anger among senior officers (Said 2001:343–5).

27 This incident was a repetition of what happened in 1995. At that time the Acting Army Commander, Colonel Zulkifli Lubis, refused to accept a decision made by Prime Minister Ali Sastroamidjojo to appoint Colonel Bambang Utoyo as the new Army Commander. It led to the fall of Ali Sastroamidjojo's cabinet (Said 2001:351–2).

28 Kusuma (2000:85) writes that the Head of the Ambon Municipality gave an illustration that even the Pancasila mosque located in Kebung Cengkeh, which was inaugurated by Minister of Religious Affairs, had not been issued a building licence. The Head of the Municipality also said that there were about 932 documents relating to Muslim affairs stacked on his desk.

29 An account widely rumoured among Christian people tells that these troops were deployed because of an appeal made by Hasyim Marasabessy, Suaidi's brother, who was the Head of Religious Affairs Department in Maluku, after his house in Karang Panjang was attacked by Christians (Kusuma 2000:132).

30 The Head of the Ambon Municipality told the story about a group of Kostrad 431 troops looking for him, allegedly to murder him, in a meeting with the Task Force Commander, ABRI's Special Team and governmental officials in Halong Navy Base, Ambon, at 2pm on 11 April 1999 (Kusuma 2000:217).

31 Major General Firman Gani (2002:80), the Head of Regional Police Maluku (June–October 2000), estimated that more than 1,000 weapons of different types were in the hands of combatants.

32 Because two thirds of all local police troops were on duty at the time, national police headquarters paid salaries for two thirds of the troops and distributed these funds to all of the troops on deployment. The result was that each police officer received two thirds of his or her salary (interview with police officer in Polda Maluku in October 2002).

Chapter 10

East Timor in transition: an Australian policy challenge

Clinton Fernandes

Australia supported Indonesia's occupation of East Timor for 24 years. In 1999, the Indonesian president, BJ Habibie, agreed to allow the people of East Timor a vote on whether they wanted independence or 'wide-ranging autonomy' within Indonesia. More than 78% of voters opted for independence. In response, violence and destruction by the Indonesian military and its militia proxies, which had been a feature of the lead-up to the ballot, broke with a wave of fury, leaving about 80% of all buildings and infrastructure destroyed, between 2,000 and 6,000 people dead[1] and a third of the population of 800,000 forced at gun point into neighbouring West Timor.

This event precipitated Australian intervention at the head of a multilateral military force under the auspices of the United Nations. Military links between Australia and Indonesia were summarily cancelled and there were occasions in the first few days of intervention when it seemed possible that Australia and Indonesia would go to war. Tensions in the East-West Timor border area remained high for months after, with numerous incursions and clashes between the two sides. Hostility in Indonesia towards Australia and its peacekeeping presence in East Timor has remained high, especially among so-called 'nationalists' and large sections of the military, more than four years after the event.

This chapter analyses the Australian government's policy towards East Timor, and consequently Indonesia, and how it was forced to change through three phases.

In the first phase, the government tried to preserve the status quo by insisting that East Timor was irreversibly a part of Indonesia. This ended when the Indonesian Government itself terminated the status quo by announcing plans for a ballot on autonomy or independence.

In the second phase, it provided diplomatic and material support for the Indonesian military's attempt to manipulate the outcome of the ballot. This ended in disaster when an outraged Australian public stampeded the government out of its entrenched position.

In the third and final phase, it scrambled to make Indonesia withdraw so that a peacekeeping force could be deployed.

Phase one: preserving the status quo

In the federal election of March 1996, the Liberal-National coalition won a decisive victory over the Australian Labor Party, and John Howard replaced Paul Keating as Prime Minister (Williams 1997). The Asian financial crisis was still more than a year away, and President Suharto seemed secure as Indonesia's president. The new government published a White Paper on Foreign Affairs and Trade, confirming that it would maintain its predecessor's policy towards Indonesia:

> In recent years government-to-government relations have developed very favourably and a substantial relationship is now in place across a wide range of technical, economic, cultural, defence and educational fields. The challenge is to sustain and widen it (DFAT 1997:61).

During the last full term of the Suharto regime (1993–98), there were signs of increasing unrest throughout the archipelago. Struggles for self-determination continued in East Timor, West Papua and Aceh, and there was the bloody spectacle of ethnic cleansing in West Kalimantan. Riots occurred in Java, where economic inequality and the Suharto family's kleptocratic rule angered many Indonesians. Amnesty International reported that in East Timor 'arbitrary detention and torture remain a part of everyday life' (Savill 1996:14).

For the Howard government it was business as usual. As the Suharto regime cracked down on pro-democracy demonstrators in July 1996, there were no official expressions of criticism or even disapproval. Foreign Minister Alexander Downer declared the military crackdown to be an 'internal affair' and hoped it would 'settle down quickly' (Hartcher 1996:14). Deputy Prime Minister Tim Fischer called Suharto 'perhaps the world's greatest figure in the latter half of the 20th century' (Lague 1996:15). When Jose Ramos-Horta and Bishop Carlos Belo were awarded the 1996 Nobel Peace Prize in recognition of the East Timorese cause, Australia—like Indonesia—did not send an ambassador to Oslo for the award ceremony. Ramos-Horta, a resident of Sydney, was unable to secure a meeting with Howard on his return to Australia (Da Silva 1997).

The Australian public, however, saw the matter very differently. On his return from Norway, Ramos-Horta addressed packed halls in Sydney, Melbourne, Canberra and Perth. Australian governments had been able to manage domestic opposition to Indonesia's occupation of East Timor by pointing to the 'fact' of Indonesian sovereignty. Crucially, Australian governments could rest secure in the knowledge that no parliamentary opposition would argue seriously for self-determination for the Timorese. This bi-partisanship was obvious to Indonesian observers like Teuku Rezasyah

(1996), who pointed out that 'Australian foreign policy changes from one regime to another are largely incremental, not radical', and that both major political parties are 'willing to cultivate a cordial relationship with Indonesia, regardless of the latter's position on East Timor. They remain steadfast in their attitude even though local backbenchers and the media are pushing for tougher Australian measures against Indonesia'.

The bi-partisan political consensus was fractured by the Australian Labor Party's spokesman on Foreign Affairs, Laurie Brereton. Indonesia, he argued, was beginning to go through a 'process of political transition in which President Suharto's New Order government will sooner or later give way to a successor regime, the precise nature of which is at present highly uncertain' (Brereton 1996). He noted that the emergence of an indigenous democracy movement in Indonesia was 'a critical development of potentially far-reaching significance', and that unless a role were 'found for this movement in the political process...further turmoil and conflict may follow'. Brereton took the lead in changing Labor's policy on East Timor, calling for 'a process of negotiation through which the people of East Timor can exercise their right of self-determination' (ALP 1998). The ALP adopted the new policy on self-determination in January 1998.

As intense pressure built on Suharto at this time, several political activists were abducted, tortured and killed (Aspinall 1999:41–58). During the first months of 1998, military crackdowns resulted in hundreds of people being injured. Protesting students at Jakarta's Trisakti University were shot by soldiers and more than 1,100 people were killed in Jakarta alone. Chinese women and children were made the target of a systematic campaign of murder and rape (Bourchier 1999:149–67). The Australian Government condemned none of these atrocities, and no moves were made to downgrade defence co-operation. Instead, it lobbied the International Monetary Fund to relax some of the conditions of the reform package to prevent social unrest threatening the regime (Johnstone 1998:2).

Suharto resigned in May 1998 and was replaced as president by BJ Habibie. The people of East Timor and their supporters overseas sensed the opportunity provided by the leadership change. Students at the University of East Timor organised free speech forums nearly every day during the first two weeks in June 1998 (Greenlees 1998b). They discussed the reform process and demanded the release of political prisoners. Protests in Dili were accompanied by protests in the Indonesian heartland of Java, where thousands of university students of East Timorese descent picketed the offices of the Indonesian Ministry of Foreign Affairs (*SCMP* 1998). The military leadership, already unsettled by these mass mobilisations, was further stunned by a helicopter crash near Dili that killed most of its high-ranking officers in the military command responsible for East Timor (AFP 1998a).

In his first television interview as president, Habibie had ruled out a referendum in East Timor (Greenlees 1998a). The increasing unrest in East Timor, the heightened international interest in post-Suharto Indonesia and Habibie's own need to establish his democratic credentials led him to offer what he called 'special status' a week later, 'under one condition that East Timor is recognised as an integrated part of the Republic of Indonesia' (Reuters 1998a). This offer was immediately rejected by the newly-formed East Timorese Student Solidarity Council, which demanded a UN-supervised referendum on independence (Roosa 1998).

The Australian government provided diplomatic cover for Indonesia's offer of autonomy by talking down the chances of a referendum. In a visit to Jakarta in July 1998, Alexander Downer dismissed calls for a referendum, saying that East Timor was 'obviously a very divided place. There is no point trying to solve the issue with a quick fix' (McDonald 1998:15). Later that month, Downer traveled to the Philippines for annual talks between the Association of South-East Asian Nations and its chief partners. He re-affirmed his government's rejection of calls for self-determination: 'I do not think that immediately moving into some sort of active self-determination in East Timor is a solution at all' (*Courier Mail* 1998:17).

The economic situation in Indonesia was plunging to new depths. In the second quarter of 1998, real GDP was 16.5% below that for the same period in 1997. The exchange rate was at Rp 11,000/US$1. This was more than four times lower than the previous year. Imported goods had become prohibitively expensive. As a consequence, total imports had fallen to almost half the pre-crisis level. Inflation was sky rocketing. The price of food was soaring and the purchasing power of the rupiah was plummeting. Wage earners had lost more than a third of their real incomes. Domestic unrest was threatening to get out of control. To compound all this, oil prices—a key source of government revenues—were stagnating at US$10–12 per barrel (McGillivray & Morrissey 1999:3–26). In the midst of all this, international activism about East Timor was a problem that President Habibie simply did not need. Buffeted from all sides, he moved to take some more steam out of the East Timor issue, announcing that 1,000 combat troops would be withdrawn from the territory, with more to come (Reuters 1998b). Alexander Downer praised the decision to withdraw troops, calling it 'a step in the right direction' (Stewart 1998:7).

A few months later, a Sydney-based activist, Andrew McNaughtan, smuggled a large number of Indonesian army personnel records out of East Timor. The records showed that Indonesia's claims of withdrawal and demilitarisation in East Timor were lies (AAP 1998). Downer tried to downplay the issue, saying he was 'attempting to verify the authenticity of the documents' (Daley 1998). However, the dramatic exposure of the personnel records and the extensive details contained therein made it clear that the Indonesian authorities were lying. Shortly after this episode, the Dili massacre was commemorated by thousands of East Timorese, who gathered at the Santa Cruz cemetery and demanded self-determination (AFP 1998b; Reuters 1998c). In December 1998, major demonstrations brought Dili to a halt, as pro-independence youth commemorated the anniversary of Indonesia's invasion with protests, roadblocks and scuffles with Indonesian police (Reuters 1998d).

Sensing that the independence of East Timor was once again a live issue, Australian Prime Minister John Howard moved to assist the Indonesian Government. He wrote to Habibie on 19 December 1998, suggesting that 'the East Timorese desire for an act of self-determination' could be addressed 'in a manner that avoids an early and final decision' (DFAT 2001). Howard approvingly cited the Matignon Accords,[2] which 'enabled a compromise political solution to be implemented while deferring a referendum on the final status...for many years'. Indonesia too, he suggested, could adopt the formula of 'a substantial period of autonomy' followed by 'an act of self-determination by the East Timorese at some future time' (DFAT 2001). The Indonesian military's political and economic weaknesses were temporary; at some time in the future, it would once again be strong enough to crush East Timorese demands. Self-determination would have to be delayed until such time. Howard's letter, therefore, was designed to diffuse the issue and postpone self-determination indefinitely. The Deputy Secretary of DFAT explained a year later that 'a very important part of our thinking at the time that the Prime Minister dispatched his letter was that Indonesia had only one last chance to keep East Timor as part of Indonesia' (Dauth 1999).

An electronic copy of the letter was transmitted by cable to Australia's Ambassador in Jakarta. The original would arrive later, via diplomatic bag. The ambassador presented the cable to President Habibie, who rejected it angrily. It appears that he was annoyed by the colonial analogy with New Caledonia (Greenlees & Garran 2002:87–101). However, he and his closest advisers had a technocratic, not a nationalist, understanding of the problem that confronted them. They recognised that, given the extent of international and domestic opposition, the Indonesian state would be further endangered if a part of it were not excised. Furthermore, they had played no part in the decision to invade East Timor, yet were bearing the diplomatic burden it had caused. When the original arrived via diplomatic bag, Habibie scribbled his thoughts on it and sent copies to five ministers: 'if the question of East Timor becomes a burden to the struggle and image of the Indonesian people and if, after 22 years, the East Timorese people cannot feel united with the Indonesian people...it would be reasonable and wise if...East Timor can be honourably separated from the unitary nation of the Republic of Indonesia...' (Greenlees & Garran 2002:87–101).

Habibie discussed the idea of a rapid process of separation via a referendum with members of his cabinet and his close advisers. Extensive discussions occurred at the 25 January meeting of cabinet's Political and Security Committee, and two days later at a meeting of the full cabinet. Most cabinet members were of the view that Indonesia would win the referendum. Much later, Foreign Minister Ali Alatas would recall that most members of cabinet 'were then very convinced we would win the referendum. Everything was painted with optimism' (Tempo 2000b).

The new policy was announced by Foreign Minister Ali Alatas and Information Minister Yunus Yosfiah on 27°January 1999. Thus ended the Indonesian and Australian governments' policy of preserving the status quo. The Habibie government was forced into its policy change by a rapidly deteriorating situation and constant pressure from below. It was compelled to cut away a problem that had become too difficult to handle. Furthermore, influential sections of Indonesian opinion believed that a ballot would result in a win for the autonomy proposal.[3] The Asian financial crisis and the subsequent collapse of the Indonesian economy caused uncertainty and confusion at the elite level.

Phase two: providing political cover for the Indonesian military

In order to ensure that the ballot delivered a result in favour of autonomy, the Indonesian military (Tentara Nasional Indonesia—TNI) began to intensify operations under the guise of proxy forces, known as 'militias'. The military had to pretend that it was not the main source of repression and violence but a force for peace between East Timor's 'warring factions'. The problem was the all too visible evidence that it was recruiting, arming, training and organising the militias.

It took a foreign ally to provide diplomatic cover in the international arena. Such an ally would run the propaganda line that East Timorese society was not united on the question of independence but divided between rival factions, which were so hostile to each other that only the presence of the military was preventing a civil war. It would argue that the militias were somehow distinct from the military. Ideally, a foreign ally would work to reduce international intervention in order to guarantee a victory for the autonomy proposal. Under the Howard Government, Australia played this role. An examination of the government's actions leads to the unpleasant but unavoidable conclusion that it complemented the strategy of plausible denial, and functioned to reduce the prospect of international intervention.

The lead-up to the ballot was marked by a contest between the government's diplomacy on the one hand and, on the other, a vigorous and re-energised solidarity movement that campaigned in Australia and overseas, a parliamentary opposition that kept the Howard government on the back foot, and a constant series of leaks of classified material that severely embarrassed the government.

The Alas massacre of November 1998 is today acknowledged to have been the beginning of the militia terror campaign after the fall of Suharto. Approximately 50 people were said to have been killed and houses and property destroyed as a reprisal for an attack by resistance fighters (Martinkus 2001:83–7). When reports of the massacre became public, DFAT claimed that only nine people had been killed, and that three of them were Indonesian soldiers. This claim was based on a visit by the Australian Army Attaché[4] and was presented by Alexander Downer as a significant inquiry that resolved questions of human rights abuses (Martinkus 2001:111–15). It later became clear that the DFAT assessment was doing no more than providing public relations cover for the Indonesian military; rather than an inquiry, the visit by the Australian Army Attaché turned out to have been only a routine tour to introduce his successor to various military contacts in the area (*West Australian* 1999). The Army Attaché had visited Alas for only a few hours, and was accompanied at all times by Indonesian military personnel, whose presence served to intimidate any potential witnesses. Under no circumstances could the DFAT assessment be regarded as a genuine attempt at uncovering the truth. To present the visit as a human rights investigation, as Downer did, was in effect to take the pressure off the Indonesian military.

On 5 December 1998, the news wires carried reports that Indonesia's military chief in Dili, Colonel Tono Suratman, intended to arm civilians to fight pro-independence rebels. Suratman said that he would equip volunteers with guns 'in order to protect villages that are prone to rebel attacks' (AP 5 December 1998). On the heels of this report, the East Timor International Support Centre warned that this plan was not intended to protect villages but to terrorise them:

> A 'people's defence force' is just a cruel excuse to create another paramilitary group in East Timor. This defence force will be used by ABRI to do their dirty work, and being out of uniform they are unaccountable for the abuses they might commit (ETISC 1998).

In a Current Intelligence Brief dated 6 January 1999, Australia's Defence Intelligence Organisation (DIO) reported the first killings by pro-integrationist militias, noting that they were proxies for ABRI:

> ABRI's decision to arm local militias has drawn its first blood. As long as ABRI continues to contract-out some of its security responsibilities, more clashes are likely...ABRI recognises that using force against pro-referendum groups will continue to attract international criticism. So using force against the referendum movement looks likely to continue to be subcontracted (Ball 2002:246).

However, none of the intelligence leaks had begun at that stage. The government's public statements were well and truly in line with the Indonesian military's disinformation campaign, secure in the belief that it could conceal its knowledge of the matter from an increasingly concerned public. Downer, for instance, said that he could not confirm reports that the Indonesian military were arming militias in East Timor: 'The Indonesian military are denying this...It's obviously very hard for us to verify one way or another' (Downer 1999a).

In light of Colonel Suratman's statement, pleas by the East Timor International Support Centre and warnings contained in DIO's Current Intelligence Brief, Downer's statements—whatever his intention—had the effect of providing diplomatic cover to the Indonesian military's activities. Following meetings with the Indonesian Government, Downer was asked whether he raised the militia issue. He replied:

> Yes, with Ali Alatas [Indonesia's Foreign Minister] I did...And he explained to me that they weren't giving arms out to pro-integrationists. But what they were doing was what they were doing in all the provinces...and that is that they do have some civilian people who help in a policing function (Downer 1999b).

No leaks had occurred at that stage, and the government's statements were at their most loquacious. Its utterances fit comfortably with the Indonesian Government's own rhetoric, and followed clear themes. First, the facts are in dispute. Second, the Indonesians have given assurances. Third, 'rogue elements' might be responsible. All themes are on display in the following statement by Downer:

> If it's happening at all and there is concern that it could be happening, if it's happening at all, it certainly isn't official Indonesian Government policy, it

certainly isn't something that's been condoned by General Wiranto, the head of the armed forces. But there may be some rogue elements within the armed forces who are providing arms of one kind or another to pro-integrationists who have been, you know, fighting for the cause of Indonesia...The Indonesian Government when we've raised it with them, including when I raised it with Ali Alatas the other day, have said that it certainly wasn't happening, that they weren't arming paramilitaries, there was some arming of the informal police support group who are civilians in East Timor but that applies in all of the provinces of Indonesia. There is nothing different or unusual about that, so I mean, I do accept the Indonesian Government's word for it, that it's not official Indonesian policy, but on the other hand it may be that some soldiers informally are doing this (Downer 1999c).

Despite numerous reports—private and public—to the contrary, Downer continued to assert that the Indonesian military was not engaged in a proxy war:

[W]e accept that is not the official policy of ABRI or the Indonesian government, [but] there is a risk that some rogue elements within ABRI may be or may have been providing arms to the so-called paramilitaries in East Timor (Downer 1999e).

Six days after this statement, the Liquiça massacre occurred. The circumstances of this massacre were unambiguous: on 6 April 1999, a number of militia went to Liquiça village accompanied by army and police. They surrounded a church where villagers were sheltering, dragged two priests out of the church compound and took them to the local military district headquarters. Once the priests were removed, Indonesian troops began to throw tear gas into the church. When the refugees ran out, blinded and trying to save themselves, the militia rushed towards them. Women and children were attacked with fists, sticks, rifle butts, stones, arrows and machetes. More than fifty people died and seven were injured during this attack. Afterwards, the militia forced the local people to hoist the Indonesian national flag (Robinson 2002:256–7; Christalis 2002:129–35).

The Howard Government moved into damage control mode. Commenting on the massacre, Downer followed the established themes:

Well, look, they [the military] were present, I understand, at the incident but there again, there's a debate about what part they played...[O]ur report is that you're getting very conflicting accounts, wildly different accounts of what actually happened, but what you can be sure of is that some people did die, some people were injured and it was a very violent and unfortunate incident and we hope that such an incident doesn't occur again (Downer 1999f).

He later refused to release the report prepared by Australian diplomats into the massacre (Newman 1999).

Eleven days after the Liquiça massacre, militia groups in Dili attacked the houses of prominent independent supporters and the local newspaper office. At that very moment, the Irish foreign minister, David Andrews, was in Dili on a scheduled visit (TAPOL 1999). Andrews was accompanied by Tom Hyland of the East Timor Ireland Solidarity Campaign, which had been instrumental in building support for East Timor at the European Union. Andrews ended his visit immediately and returned to Jakarta, where he raised the alarm about the mass murders. Hyland tapped into the solidarity movement, rapidly escalating the international pressure on Indonesia. As a result, Alexander Downer made a public call for the Indonesian military to disarm the militias. Howard telephoned Habibie to express his concerns, and the two agreed to meet in Bali to discuss the situation (DFAT 2001:78). After this meeting, where President Habibie was accompanied by senior Indonesian military personnel, the Howard Government resumed its program of providing diplomatic cover. Downer was effusive in his praise of the Indonesian authorities, saying that there wasn't 'any doubt that the Indonesians through this process are committed to the laying down of arms…we have no reason at all to doubt their goodwill' (Downer 1999g).

Containing international pressure

The governments of Indonesia and Australia were trying to prevent or minimise international involvement. The full weight of Australian diplomacy was brought to bear in pursuit of this goal. On 22 February 1999, the Secretary of DFAT, Ashton Calvert, met US Assistant Secretary of State Stanley Roth in Washington. Roth was of the view that a full-scale peacekeeping operation in East Timor was essential. Calvert, stating the Australian Government's position, made it clear that Australia wouldn't support peacekeepers, and continued to run the 'factions' line:

> One of the central themes to achieving a resolution was to convince the Timorese that they had to sort themselves out, and to dispel the idea that the UN was going to solve all their problems while they indulged in vendetta and bloodletting (Lyons 1999:25–9).

Had the government been committed to an international peacekeeping presence, it would have leapt at the opportunity, not rejected it. For Howard, though, the objective was to minimise international involvement and give Indonesia a free hand in East Timor. It pursued this objective consistently. The transcript of the Calvert-Roth meeting was leaked to the media some months later (Daley 1999). Had the transcript of the Calvert–Roth meeting not leaked, the Australian public would not have found out about the government's secret rejection of Roth's proposal until 2029, when the archives open up under the thirty year rule. By contrast, the real-time leak resulted in a swift escalation of political pressure.

On 5 May 1999, an agreement was signed at the United Nations headquarters in New York. The 5 May Agreement, as it came to be known, provided for an autonomy proposal to be put to the East Timorese people. If they accepted this proposal, the East Timor issue would be considered solved once and for all. If they rejected it, authority would be transferred to the UN, allowing East Timor to begin its passage to independence. Indonesia would have complete responsibility for maintaining security (Marker 2003:144–60). Two days later, the Australian Defence Force began planning for logistic support to the ballot. This was known as *Operation Concord* (ANAO 2002:28–9). In parallel with this operation, planning was also begun for *Operation Faber*, which involved military observers who would serve with the United Nations Assistance Mission in East Timor (UNAMET) (ANAO 2002:29).

However, Defence planners began work on another plan as well. Known as *Operation Spitfire*, its aim was to evacuate foreign observers (ANAO 2002:29). Now that Indonesia had gained control over 'security', it would be in a position to destroy pro-independence supporters regardless of the result of the ballot. The Indonesians were of the view that they would win the ballot. However, just in case they did not, they would need to move rapidly to reverse the result. Under these circumstances, foreign observers would impede any Indonesian action. They would have to be removed from the territory, just as they had been when Indonesia first invaded in 1975. *Operation Spitfire* would fit in with the Indonesian military strategy: the evacuation of all foreign observers would mean that the Indonesians could act without witnesses. Planning for *Operation Spitfire* began on 11 May 1999. It was designed to evacuate personnel, not keep the peace (Wilson 2003:6–11).

Back in Australia, Downer kept deflecting calls for a stronger international presence, saying:

> We hope that there won't be a need for a peacekeeping force because if you need a peacekeeping force, you need a peace to keep and peace first has to be negotiated and we hope that when the peace is negotiated it will be a peaceful peace that won't require a peacekeeping force (Downer 1999d).

Downer sought to make his meaning clearer. The situation in East Timor didn't warrant the presence of peacekeepers. And peacekeepers should not be put in harm's way; rather, the 'factions' should negotiate 'a peaceful peace that won't require a peacekeeping force':

> [W]e're not passionately of a desire to send Australian troops into danger and it would only be a complete fool who would want to do that. They have

lives, we don't want them to risk their lives or for them to lose their lives. We have a responsibility to them (Downer 1999d).

There was a curious illogic at the heart of the Australian Government's position. On the one hand, it was arguing that the violence was of a level that would cause peacekeepers to risk their lives ('they have lives, we don't want them to risk their lives or for them to lose their lives'). On the other hand, the violence was not that serious, because a small unarmed presence would suffice ('administrative assistance, observers, some technical assistance, perhaps some people to assist with policing functions and we hope it won't be more than that' [Downer 1999d]). So East Timor was safe enough for the matter to be resolved peacefully, yet dangerous enough to cause the deaths of peacekeepers. If the Foreign Minister was of the view that troops should not be placed in harm's way, the obvious question arose: what exactly are troops for?

This conundrum could be resolved by only one explanation—the Government would say and do anything to prevent an international peacekeeping presence. John Howard visited the US in July. He praised the Indonesian Government instead of stressing the urgency of the situation with US President Bill Clinton:

> We discussed Indonesia and Timor at very great length over lunch. I said that Indonesia deserved from the world perhaps a little more credit and a little more praise and understanding for the transition that was occurring in that country towards a more democratic system of government... (Howard 1999)

This public statement of support, without criticism of the violence or concern about the military–militia links, sent a clear signal to the Indonesian authorities. The government's diplomacy continued in this fashion in the lead-up to the ballot.

On the day of the ballot, 30 August 1999, the TNI's control over the militia was demonstrated by the near-total absence of intimidation (Robinson 2002:260–1). There was a huge turnout of voters, and the results were announced on Saturday 4 September 1999. Despite the climate of fear, the one-sided pre-ballot election campaign, the presence of dubious voters from West Timor and the fact that many voters did not believe their votes were secret, 78.5% of registered voters opted for independence from Indonesia[5] (Martin 2001:94).

State-sponsored terrorism

The Indonesian authorities moved rapidly to reverse the ballot result by creating new demographic facts on the ground (McDonald 2002). They evacuated foreign observers to Australia and drove East Timorese across the border to West Timor (Robinson 2002; Martinkus 1999). The dramatic scenes of human suffering served to blind many observers to what was really going on. The Indonesian military needed to remove all foreigners from East Timor so that it could execute its plan without the impediment of outside attention (Robinson 2002:263). Therefore, for all its sensationalism and violent imagery, the execution of the terror campaign was carefully controlled. The military campaign would work sequentially as follows:

Use the militia proxies to contain and remove foreign observers.

With foreigners unable to report, use the militia to attack the local population and use transport and logistics assets to move them across the border.

Provoke a desperate retaliation from the vastly outnumbered armed resistance (the Armed Forces for the National Liberation of East Timor, or FALINTIL), thereby drawing it into a conventional war.

Announce that TNI was forced to intervene between the 'factions', and then, freed from restraints, attack and destroy FALINTIL in conventional warfare.

Create new facts on the ground, ensuring that the results of the ballot were irreversibly overturned.

To complement the Indonesian strategy, the Howard Government continued to make public statements that took the pressure off Indonesia. Foreign Minister Downer, for instance, argued that President Habibie, Foreign Minister Alatas, General Wiranto and others were 'all trying to do the right thing'. Other commanders were also 'trying to do the right thing' (Downer 1999h). The problem, once again, lay with a few 'wild elements within the Indonesian military' (Downer 1999h) acting on their own.

Step 1: Contain and remove foreign observers.

Foreigners were treated very differently to native East Timorese (Robinson 2002:263–5). They were intimidated and corralled into confined areas where they could not provide eyewitness reports to the outside world, but they were largely unharmed (Martinkus 1999). There was good reason for this: the Indonesians remembered all too clearly the diplomatic difficulties they encountered in Australia and elsewhere following the killings of six Western journalists in 1975. By comparison, the deaths of tens of thousands of East Timorese in the aftermath of the 1975 invasion, and the deaths of hundreds of thousands of Indonesians in 1965–66, did not cause quite so many difficulties with Western governments. The Australian evacuation plan fitted in with the Indonesian strategy. Between 6 and 14 September, 2,478 foreign observers, journalists and international and local staff were evacuated by RAAF and RNZAF C130 Hercules transport aircraft to Darwin (Wilson 2003:6–11).

Ian Martin, the head of UNAMET, ordered the evacuation of UN staff, journalists and observers from the besieged compound on 8 September (Martin 2001:98–9). This evacuation would have resulted in the rape or murder of the 1,500 refugees sheltering there. Outraged, the international staff collectively refused to be evacuated until all the refugees had first been taken to safety (Martinkus 2002b:24–5; Christalis 2002:236–48). As a consequence, the refugees were airlifted to Darwin. It was only when this evacuation was guaranteed that the international staff left the compound.

Step 2: With foreigners unable to report, use the militia to attack the local population and use transport and logistics assets to move them across the border.

East Timorese, in contrast to foreign observers, were attacked and forced out of their homes. They were rounded up and taken via land and sea transport to West Timor and elsewhere (Martinkus 1999). According to the United Nations and a subsequent investigation by Indonesia's National Human Rights Commission, approximately 70% of the buildings in East Timor had been destroyed. Vital infrastructure was crippled, leaving Dili and major towns without running water, electricity or telephones (KPP-HAM 2002:15–59). Approximately 250,000 people are thought to have been driven across the border. Thousands of frightened East Timorese ran for the hills or into the UN compound, which was surrounded and isolated (Martinkus 1999; Christalis 2002:213–48). They were the targets of an organised campaign, planned and directed by senior Indonesian generals, whose aim was to reverse the ballot and create new demographic facts on the ground (McDonald 2002).

Step 3: Provoke FALINTIL[6] into fighting a conventional war.

This terror campaign would have the added benefit of provoking FALINTIL into a desperate retaliation, thereby drawing it into something approaching conventional warfare, where the TNI clearly had the advantage. A FALINTIL reaction would allow the Indonesians to claim that it had to intervene between the 'factions'. The pressure on FALINTIL was indeed severe. In Uai Mori on the northern coast, Taur Matan Ruak (Operational Commander, FALINTIL) was receiving reports of the devastation and finding it almost impossible to remain in cantonment. Speaking by satellite telephone to Xanana Gusmao on 7 September, the day of Gusmao's release from house arrest, Matan Ruak conveyed his feelings to Gusmao. Gusmao implored him to stay in the cantonments and after further frantic messages, Matan Ruak agreed (Greenlees & Garran 2002:231).

Step 4: Announce that TNI was forced to intervene between the 'factions', and then, freed from restraints, attack and destroy FALINTIL in conventional warfare.

The Indonesian strategy failed at this point. While it imposed martial law under the pretext of 'intervening between the factions', and continued to claim that the ballot had been rigged (Martin 2001:97), it was unable to go any further, and was compelled to retreat from East Timor once and for all. Under the terms of martial law, soldiers could openly 'stop anyone and search them for weapons, arrest anyone suspected of creating disturbances for 20 days without a warrant, and shoot on sight anyone who breaks the curfew' (Sudrajat 1999). The effect of this was to turn East Timor into a free-fire zone, meaning that TNI could attack and destroy FALINTIL in conventional warfare. Indonesia talked up the violence and the dangers, knowing that Western governments were reluctant to accept casualties. Ali Alatas spoke of the 'failure of this kind of mission when there is no peace yet to be kept' and warned that 'any nations willing to send peacekeepers to the province would have to shoot their way in' (AFP 1999).

The immediate US reaction to the ethnic cleansing campaign was that it was not contemplating military intervention. At the regular Pentagon briefing on 7 September 1999, Defense spokesman Kenneth Bacon talked about 'regrettable and unfortunate problems in East Timor' (Ellis 1999). National Security Adviser Sandy Berger also signalled the Indonesians that, although they had to wind up operations quickly, the US would not intervene:

My daughter has a very messy apartment up in college, maybe I shouldn't intervene to have that cleaned up. I don't think anybody ever articulated a doctrine which said that we ought to intervene wherever there's a humanitarian problem (Berger 1999).

The assessment of the TNI leadership appeared to be that it could stave off international pressure long enough to create new facts on the ground. It could afford to ignore UN officials like Mary Robinson, the High Commissioner for Human Rights, who called for the convening of a 'special session of the UN Commission on Human Rights' (Lubetkin 1999). In addition, the president of the UN Security Council, Arnold Peter van Walsum, stated that the Council would not authorise the deployment of foreign forces without the express consent of the Indonesian Government: 'I can assure you the Security Council will not give the green light if there is no permission on the part of the Indonesian government' (Aita 1999).

The Australian government continued to make public statements that took the pressure off Indonesia. Calls for troops to be sent in were deflected by a standard response: Australia can't invade Indonesia. Australia's Defence Minister said:

> We're not going to go in there and invade Indonesia. That would be, you know, tantamount to creating a very substantial war, and that would I think result in a lot of unnecessary loss of life for both nations...Let's invade the world's fourth most populous country' is probably not a very brilliant idea (Downer 1999i).

Of course, hardly anyone was calling for an invasion of Indonesia. In addition to the obvious fact that Western powers had just conducted a real invasion (of Yugoslavia's province of Kosovo), East Timor was never a part of Indonesia. What was being demanded was an end to evacuations of foreign observers and more diplomatic pressure on Indonesia. Instead, the Australian government was still claiming that the Indonesian authorities were 'all trying to do the right thing' (Downer 1999h). It seemed as if the Indonesian military's actions would go unchallenged. But another, more powerful force was awakening.

The Australian public was outraged at what it saw and demanded an immediate deployment of troops. Kerry Myers, letters editor at the *Sydney Morning Herald*, noted that the public response 'was quite overwhelming':

> Readers were shocked, angered, saddened, appalled by the terrible, terrible story...Letters attacked the government, specifically the Prime Minister and the Foreign Minister, for what the writers saw as hand-wringing inaction...And as the week wore on there was the chilling realisation that there was to be no rescue for the East Timorese (Myers 1999).

The union movement swung into action, dramatically increasing pressure on the government. In Sydney, the first serious protest action occurred on Monday 6 September, when activists in the international solidarity movement and several hundred trade unionists protested outside the Sydney office of Garuda Airlines. They demanded the withdrawal of Indonesian troops and the insertion of a peacekeeping force. That week, there were more and more protests, increasing in size and anger. Approximately 4,000 building workers walked off the job. They were joined by workers from a number of other unions. Garbage workers—with the full support of Randwick Council—refused to pick up garbage from the Indonesian Consulate. Printing workers refused to handle paper products made in Indonesia. The Australian Nurses Federation declared its support for all the ongoing actions and announced that it had placed several of its members on stand-by to go to East Timor, if required. Education unions called for two minutes silence to be observed in all public schools. The Maritime Union of Australia (MUA) prevented the loading of cargo on all Indonesia-bound ships. The *Bunga Teratia III* was delayed in Port Botany until its owner agreed not to transport 16 cargo containers bound for Indonesia. In Newcastle, the *Cape Horn* was prevented from loading produce bound for Indonesia. In Brisbane, the *Chekiang* was not allowed to leave until 30 containers headed for Indonesia were unloaded. In Melbourne, AU$22 million worth of products were left stranded. In Adelaide, the MUA took 20 containers to a warehouse and refused to release them until East Timor was free. The International Transport Workers Federation called on its 500 affiliates around the world to follow the MUA's example and 'organise appropriate protest action against Indonesian commercial interests including air and sea traffic coming from or bound for Indonesian ports and airports' (Labor Council 1999).

At a special ACTU meeting, unions were urged to place bans on all Indonesian Government and commercial interests in Australia. In Melbourne, rank-and-file anger had taken the union leadership by surprise. Leigh Hubbard, secretary of the Victorian Trades Hall Council, said that 'a lot of these members are ahead of the leadership on this one' (Labor Council 1999). At Melbourne airport, passengers travelling to Indonesia were prevented from boarding a Garuda Airlines flight due to depart at 11am (Cleary 1999). Their path had been blocked by construction workers at the airport terminal, who gave them leaflets which apologised for the blockade, but explained why it was taking place. Subsequently, the CFMEU's Victorian leadership signalled its intention to take similar action against other Garuda flights until the violence in East Timor ended. It also informed Qantas that it would oppose any attempt to take on displaced Garuda passengers (Labor Council 1999).

The Australian Services Union declared that it was also imposing bans on Garuda Airlines. The Transport Workers Union banned the loading of all Indonesian bound freight at Melbourne airport. This occurred despite threats from employers. For instance, Qantas staff in Melbourne were warned that they could be prosecuted under the Workplace Relations Act and the Trade Practices Act if they refused to handle or delayed the handling of Garuda freight. Staff responded by intensifying their actions.

Defiance was spreading throughout the union movement. The Communications, Electrical and Plumbing Union, which also represents postal workers, imposed national bans on all mail, telecommunication services and fault repairs to the Indonesian Consulate and to Indonesian businesses. The

Australian Workers Union stepped up the pressure, telling BP, Caltex and Shell not to order Indonesian oil because its members would refuse to process it. This was significant because of the union's strategic location—one-third of Australia's crude oil imports came from Indonesia. The Textile, Clothing and Footwear Union of Australia agreed to support any campaign to stop the violence. It called for all state and federal instrumentalities, including the Sydney Organising Committee for the Olympic Games and the Sydney Paralympic Organising Committee and all companies manufacturing in Indonesia, to suspend production contracts immediately. The major rally on Saturday 11 September was held at the Archibald Fountain at Hyde Park. Attended by approximately 15,000 people, it soon turned into a march through Sydney's central business district. This rally had an unusual feature—members of the public were coming out of the shops to join the procession. The 15,000 marchers were drawing more and more people carrying shopping bags.[7]

Policymakers were alarmed that the Australian public was starting to ask why the US response was so feeble, and contrasting it with the promptness that always characterised Australian military deployments in support of US objectives; public support for the US alliance might begin to decline. There was already considerable bitterness and dismay at American reluctance to respond to Australia's requests. The Australian Government was failing in its policy of allowing the Indonesian military to shape the outcome of the ballot.

Phase three: scrambling to act

Stampeded out of its position by the public, the government finally did what it could have done months earlier—ensured that the US exert pressure on Indonesia to allow peacekeepers in. The problem was that for the whole of 1999, the government had lobbied to keep peacekeepers out. It now worked frantically to allow international forces to enter East Timor in order to prevent a political crisis in Australia. Contrary to Howard and Downer's earlier claims, repeated even today when asked why peacekeepers weren't sent in before the ballot, four days of diplomatic pressure is all it took for Indonesia to agree to foreign troops.

The earlier US stance was based on its calculation that it 'must put its relationship with Indonesia, a mineral-rich nation of more than 200 million people, ahead of its concern over the political fate of East Timor, a tiny impoverished territory of 800,000 people that is seeking independence' (Becker & Shenon 1999). However, once it realised that the alliance was in jeopardy, the Clinton administration acted swiftly. As a senior official said, 'We don't have a dog running in the East Timor race, but we have a very big dog running down there called Australia and we have to support it' (Hartcher 1999:8).

The US ensured that its message to the Indonesian military was delivered in person—Admiral Dennis Blair, Commander-in-Chief of the US forces in the Pacific, met General Wiranto in Jakarta on 8 September 1999. He informed him of the US's decision to suspend its military ties with Indonesia (Wolfson 1999). The Clinton cabinet openly demonstrated its determination to impose order in East Timor. Defence Secretary William Cohen warned that 'the international community has a number of levers we can pull on. There are serious economic consequences to be sure' (Cohen 1999). State Department spokesman James Rubin also reminded his audience that 'Indonesia's relations with the international community, including the United States, are at risk' (Rubin 1999). The Chairman of the Joint Chiefs of Staff, General Hugh Shelton, telephoned Wiranto several times during the week after the announcement of the referendum result. President Clinton warned that 'if Indonesia does not end the violence, it must invite—*it must invite*—the international community to assist in restoring security' (Clinton 1999a, emphasis in original). He also accused the TNI of direct involvement: 'It is clear the Indonesian military is aiding and abetting the militia violence...This is simply unacceptable' (Clinton 1999b).

The coincidental timing of the APEC meeting in Auckland was crucial. It allowed the Australian to lobby the leaders and other key players in the member states of APEC (Grattan 1999b:1). The TNI could read the writing on the wall. In a visit to Dili on Saturday 11 September, while the APEC meeting was occurring in Auckland, General Wiranto conceded that he could not 'rule out the possibility of accelerating the arrival of the peace-keeping force' (Dodd & Hartcher 1999). In an emergency debate in the UN Security Council on 12 September 1999, US envoy Richard Holbrooke finally 'warned Indonesia that it faced "the point of no return in international relations" if it did not accept an international peacekeeping force' (Dodd & Hartcher 1999).

Indonesia's resistance ended within hours. On 12 September 1999, Habibie emerged from a special Cabinet meeting, stood alongside Wiranto and announced that his government had decided to allow a UN force into East Timor (Grattan 1999a:9). Wiranto's presence beside Habibie sent a clear signal that the TNI had agreed to support the decision.

In addition to lobbying the Americans frantically, the Australian Government had been scrambling to organise the deployment of troops. This force, known as INTERFET (International Force East Timor) 'was not presented with the stresses and demands of sustained combat' (ANAO 2002:52). According to the military logistician, Lieutenant-Colonel Susan Smith, the 'risks attendant on this concept of operation would have been magnified if the East Timorese militia had mounted any serious opposition to INTERFET. As it turned out...the logistic system was not tested by a tempo of operations that called for high levels of ammunition usage or other combat supplies' (Smith 2001). As the Chief of the Australian Defence Force concluded, the force 'was not presented with the stresses and demands of sustained combat' (ANAO 2002:52). These and other conclusions confirm the assessment of an academic specialist on Indonesia that the militia were 'a gutless gang of thugs who rarely had any idea of what it was they were actually doing...should a proper, disciplined and genuinely neutral police or military force enter the territory, the violence would disappear almost immediately' (Kingsbury 2000a:185).

The government's constant obfuscation of this basic fact served to take the pressure off the Indonesian military; its statements had the effect of providing diplomatic cover to the architects of the state-sponsored terror campaign. Ultimately, its policy of solidarity with the Indonesian military was foiled when an outraged public forced it to send troops into East Timor.

Endnotes

1. Official UN estimates of the death toll, based on bodies recovered, was around 1,600. However, a large number of bodies were strongly believed to have been dumped at sea or otherwise not recovered. Unofficial estimates put the death toll at three to four times the official rate.
2. Only weeks before, Alexander Downer had celebrated the 10th anniversary of the Matignon Accords, which had been signed between the Government of France and constituencies in New Caledonia. These accords effectively deferred a decision on New Caledonia's final status for more than a decade.
3. As has subsequently been shown in Aceh and West Papua, such 'autonomy' is functionally meaningless and was assumed to be so by most East Timorese at the time.
4. And the International Committee of the Red Cross, who visited Alas in the presence of the Indonesian military.
5. For the record, 344,580 rejected the 'special autonomy' proposal and 94,388 accepted it.
6. Falintil was the acronym for the National Liberation Force of East Timor, the army established by the first Fretilin government in 1975, which subsequently became the anti-Indonesian guerrilla force.
7. The author was an eyewitness to these and other protest actions (see Fernandes 2004).

Chapter 11

East Timor border security

Damien Kingsbury

When the first UN 'Peace Keeping Force' (PKF) entered East Timor in late September 1999, their first move after securing Dili and the coast road was to form a pincer movement to prevent the realisation of the public threat by militia leaders Joao Tavares and Eurico Guterres to partition the two western-most districts of Bononaro and Cova Lima. The movement, then, was to prevent the continuing loss of civilian life and destruction of property (although the latter was largely complete by this stage), the kidnapping of more civilians to West Timor and the removal of critical documents. The PKF also needed to establish that, if pressed, it would not avoid conflict. The main confrontation occurred a couple of kilometres west of the village of Hatolia along the hill overlooking the Lois River valley, where dozens of militia were shot by PKF troops after refusing to surrender (Anon A 2002), along what is now colloquially known as 'Militia Ridge'. Like much of what happened in East Timor after the introduction of the PKF, this was not publicly reported nor widely known.

By 2005, the widespread belief outside East Timor was that all was fairly quiet along the East Timor–Indonesia border. However, as with the shootings of dozens of militia near Hatolia in late September 1999, much was not officially reported. This was largely an attempt to preserve the appearance of increasingly cordial relations between Indonesia and East Timor, and between Indonesia and Australia, and to calm respective 'nationalist' or justice-inspired emotions that had the potential to destabilise the tripartite relationship. After 2002, the main public concerns with the Indonesia–East Timor border region revolved around the issues of cross-border trade, and smuggling. The main private concerns focused on continuing militia activity and the role played by the Indonesian military, the Tentara Nasional Indonesia (TNI). This chapter considers these issues, in particular, as an illustration of the confluence of economic considerations with other agendas pursued by the TNI.

Background

After three months of cross-border forays, in December 1975 Indonesia officially invaded East Timor, annexing the territory the following year (Pour 1993:383–403). This annexation was not recognised the United Nations, and was deemed illegal under international law. It has been widely estimated that during the period of Indonesia's occupation, at least 150,000 of the territory's population of around 698,000 were killed or died from related causes (Kiernan 2003; ACFOA 1991:3). In order to establish itself in East Timor, the TNI appropriated local businesses and homes, began (or continued) direct trading relations with Singapore, and assumed control of the local economy.

Following the resignation of Suharto as Indonesia's president, at the beginning of 1999 his successor, BJ Habibie, announced that East Timor would be allowed to vote on whether it wished to remain a part of Indonesia, or to separate. On 30 August 1999, following months of growing violence and destruction by TNI proxy militias, 78.5% of registered voters chose to leave Indonesia, precipitating the murder of, officially, more than 1,500 people and unofficially at least double and perhaps as many as four times that number (Anon B 2000; Anon C 2002; Emmerson1999:357). About 250,000 East Timorese either fled or were herded across the border into West Timor. In response to widespread domestic criticism, the Australian Government organised a coalition of interested countries to contribute to a UN-sanctioned International Forces in East Timor, which quickly became the peace-keeping force of the UN Transitional Administration in East Timor (UNTAET) and later, UN Mission in Support of East Timor (UNMISET). Peace-keeping forces flushed militia units from Dili and along the northern coast, circling back in the above-mentioned 'pincer movement', trapping many militia members in the Hatolia area. For several weeks after the PKF arranged itself along the East Timor–West Timor border, there were aslo 'militia' forays into East Timor, few of which were publicly acknowledged. It was clear from the equipment found on some 'militia' that they were almost certainly regular TNI personnel and assumed to be serving or former members of Kopassus. After the loss of two PKF lives in such border contact, three UN personnel were murdered by a militia mob in Atambua, not far from the East Timor border. While most of those East Timorese who had been forced to flee to West Timor returned over the following two years, around 28,000 or so chose to stay in West Timor, some fearing instability in East Timor, but most having links to or sympathy for the integrationist movement. It was these people who formed the backbone of local trade across the border.

The brief period of cessation and the resumption of militia activity was reliant upon the status of the militia's 'centre of gravity' (defined as 'that characteristic from which a military force derives its freedom of action'), which was the direct support and involvement of the TNI. The cessation of militia activity was not therefore ended by military force as such, but by pressure from the United States on the TNI to cease the militia operation. Perhaps the clearest sign of this expression of US intent was the landing in December 1999 of the fully armed US Marines 11th Expeditionary Unit (Special

Operations Capable) in East Timor, with the public role of delivering relief supplies. This was later supported by further aid projects delivered by US Marines. However, once the façade of normality was established, was largely preserved in the public eye and the US Marines left in December 2002, despite the common perception that all remained stable, the TNI took advantage of again being free to act (Anon X 2003).

The reform agenda

The conventional view of Indonesian politics and the TNI in the period following May 1998 was that the state was undergoing a process of democratic transition and that the military was itself undergoing a process of reform (Singh 2001). Elaborations of this view held that, after 40 years of authoritarian, military-backed government, Indonesia was following the Latin American example of shedding military intervention in civil affairs through military 'professionalisation' (Stepan 1976), corresponding with what Huntington (1991) referred to as the 'Third Wave'. Surrounded by the rhetoric of *reformasi* (reformation) and the TNI's *paradim baru* (new paradigm), it was indeed possible to believe that fundamental change was afoot. However, entrenched aspects of Indonesia's political and economic history, ethnic composition and physical geography all composed a different context to that of Latin America (and even Thailand—see Crone 1991), while the TNI itself was compromised by its reliance on private and often illegal business, hence contributing to a different outcome than the successful moves away from military domination in Latin America. Even in Latin America, the success of bringing the military under civilian control was sometimes limited (Farcau 1996:ch5). As Philip (1985:356) succinctly put it: 'The military does not behave in any simple or one-dimensional way which can be deduced *a priori*...contemporary observers have been strikingly wrong in their expectations of military behaviour'. One might have said the same for observers who suggested that the TNI would, after 1998, be relatively weakened or successfully reform.

It has been suggested by numerous observers that Indonesia's process of *reformasi* halted around the time President Abdurrahman Wahid was deposed from office in a constitutional coup in July 2001, to be replaced by his more conservative vice-president, Megawati Sukarnoputri. There is little doubt that the senior echelons of the TNI were opposed to Wahid's continuing presidential tenure and helped undermine his presidency. After his presidency ended, the TNI assumed greater political authority and autonomy, in cabinet, in constitutional affairs and in security matters. The TNI's own process of 'professionalisation' removed it from presidential control, but at the same time also removed it from presidential accountability. The factionalism that damaged the TNI's capacity to act cohesively in the later years of Suharto's New Order government was largely resolved by early 2000, with the key 'Red and White' and 'Green' factions coalescing through their common opposition to allowing East Timor to achieve independence, and later efforts by President Wahid to promote reformist-minded generals. While distinctions within the TNI remained, they were largely personality-based and not fundamental to its operation.

Similarly, the period of factionalism, especially from around 1993 until 1999–2000, allowed the TNI to leave unchallenged the view that its operational lines of command were ineffective and that 'rogue elements' or *oknum* (military gangsters) operated outside of the formal structure. This was a blind to conventional TNI lines of control for covert policies, such as the organisation of East Timor's militias. Especially given the TNI's high degree of coherence around opposition to East Timor's independence and its use of East Timor to justify a regional presence, it is therefore not surprising that after the TNI mended its internal differences elsewhere, this previously agreed policy position remained intact.

TNI business

There is a view of Indonesian politics that has it that the TNI's primary consideration is not protection of the people, the imposition of 'stability or even the unity of the state. This view claims that the TNI's primary interest is its own enrichment (McCulloch 2000). To this end, the TNI's territorial function and its engagement in Indonesia's troubled provinces are primarily aimed at securing and enhancing the TNI's business interests, both legal and illegal. A competing view of the TNI's involvement in business has simply been as a means to an end—that it would be unable to survive without engaging in extensive business activities, that this has been the TNI's practice since the days of the Revolution (1945–49) and that this practice is, if not formally endorsed, not actively discouraged by the government. The state recognises that it cannot afford to sustain the TNI in its current form, providing as little as one quarter of the TNI's total income (Widjojo 2002; Evans 2001; ICG 2001b).

Of the TNI's total income, the 'black' income was thought by various analysts to be in the order of double its legal off-line income. That is, assuming an on-line budget of approximately US$ one billion, legal business activities would bring income up to around US$ two billion dollars, while illegal income would add approximately that much again, to a total of US$ four billion or more. Of this, diverted funds were used to top up salaries, which were and continue to be fixed at unsustainably low levels, and for other discretionary purposes (ICG 2001b:13; McCulloch 2000:10, 12–14) Illustrating the extent of these activities and the problems in controlling them, in early 2001 the East Kalimantan police chief said that it was difficult to control petrol and diesel smuggling because he thought that only the Department of Religion was not involved. *(Gatra* 2001:89) Petrol and diesel fuel smuggling has since become a significant issue in Indonesia–East Timor border relations.

Use of off-line income

The TNI's off-line or informal income is used for a range of purposes, although because most income is hidden, via the network of largely unaccountable 'charitable foundations' *(yayasan)*, the exact level of income and its usage are not precisely known. As with its manpower allocation, the TNI's business activities are spread across the archipelago, although they tend to be concentrated in and around Jakarta and in the wealthier, commodity producing provinces.

The off-line income derived by branches of the TNI was used in three primary ways. The first was to buy capital goods and equipment for the TNI and its personnel, including the so-called 'welfare' function. The second was for reinvestment into the businesses. The third was by way of cash payments primarily to senior officers, although to TNI members of all ranks where they have access to differing levels of business activity or through patronage networks. Salaries for junior TNI personnel do not adequately cover their living costs, especially for those with families, so there is a 'top-up' function for their income through direct cash payments or, more usually, free or subsidised goods, education, health benefits and housing. Officers receive a slightly better income, but as a consequence of ingrained notions and requirements of patronage, they are expected to display significantly higher levels of wealth as well as to disburse such wealth, and this is well beyond their formal income. So, they too receive cash payments from various sources, usually through military *yayasan* (from which profit is skimmed), from their own private businesses (which have TNI and other private business directed towards them and which can place undue pressure on existing competition) and from percentage pay-offs from businesses under their 'protection'.

The territorial structure is the prime institutional linkage through which wealth is created and distributed within the TNI. Members of the TNI who can manipulate their position, which basically means ranks of non-commissioned officers and above, undertake 'favours' for more senior officers, and are in turn 'looked after'. Such 'services rendered' can include quite conventional or mundane day-to-day military duties, as well as special favours.

In this sense, there is little distinction between official and non-official military duties, especially in the Army. Being 'looked after' frequently means having education provided for a soldier's children, but can also mean cash payment or granting opportunities through which easy money can be earned, such as establishing legal or black businesses, paying commissions on or directing purchases to such business or encouraging non-military businesses in dealing with such military linked businesses. Rutherford (2001:193) also claimed (with considerable evidence) that:

> Military officers have a stake in the designation of certain areas as 'unstable'. Former commanders often live out their retirement in East Timor or Irian Jaya so they can reap the harvest of profitable business deals made in the areas under their command.

Being 'looked after' does not necessarily correspond to the performance of particular favours, but is a type of irregular retainer that may increase in response to particularly notable acts.

In what amounts to a patron–client relationship, junior officers may owe allegiance directly to officers several rungs up or outside their own direct command structure. This can then create confusion about where orders actually originate, as opposed to where they are supposed to originate. By way of illustration, a captain who might formally have line responsibility to a district colonel might acknowledge actual allegiance to an officer in a completely different command line. Such patron-client relations may initially be established when junior and senior officers work in the same command and then separate, but retain their mutual obligation. Or, it may somewhat less frequently originate through association with officers already established in such a separated patron–client relationship, such as a captain who owes allegiance to a brigadier-general in a separate line of command might bring in a colleague for a particular purpose, who would then also join that particular patron-client network (though usually at a lower level). Such relationships are, according to a confidential intelligence assessment, 'totally endemic' to the TNI.

As a consequence of the pervasiveness of patron-client relations outside line commands, it can be difficult to know who to deal with in terms of issuing orders. That is, an officer who has formal line command in one area may actually work for another, and may ignore or be unable to follow conventional line command orders. This in part explained why, although President Habibie had issued clear orders for the TNI and police to provide a secure environment for the ballot on independence in East Timor in 1999, the variously issued orders were subverted through the chain of command. What can at best be described as the official ambiguity of commitment to the referendum process by the TNI and police made this subversion that much easier. It also explains why, although one element of the TNI (Kostrad) can claim (perhaps not entirely convincingly) to oppose illegal, cross-border activity, such activity can continue with the support of other military elements.

Income for these purposes is derived from three revenue streams. The first is businesses owned and operated by branches of the TNI, usually through (still tax exempt but now theoretically auditable) *yayasan* (charitable foundation) and co-operatives, including businesses in natural resources and agribusiness, finance, real estate, manufacturing and construction. The second is through 'grey' areas such as the leasing out (or imposition) of military services and surcharges imposed on purchases, along with mixing private and military business interests. The third and most lucrative source of income is through the black market, in particular, smuggling of oil or oil products, and illegal mining and logging.

History of TNI business in East Timor

By the early 1990s, the TNI or individuals close to them, such as President Suharto and his family, controlled virtually the entire economy of East Timor. This was one of the interconnected reasons why East Timor was so hard for the TNI to give up, and why it wishes to re-establish economic links, legal or illegal. By way of illustration, Suharto's son, the now disgraced Tommy, owned shares in Mobil Oil through the Perth-based Genindo Western Petroleum, which explored for oil off East Timor's south coast, as well as owning local sugarcane plantations. He and his brother, Bambang Trihadmodjo, owned most of PT Elnusa, which drilled for oil on and off shore in East Timor, as well as operating a tanker fleet and air charter service to East Timor. Suharto crony, now jailed, Bob Hasan owned timber plantations, Suharto's daughter Tutut owned the bottled water company Aquamor as well as coffee production, export and marble mining companies, and Suharto's grandson Ari Sigit owned other bottled water ventures, textile manufacturing and, with militia group Garda Paksi (Youth Guard for Upholding Integration) organiser Gil Alves, also collected the alcohol sticker tax. Two key planners and executors of the East Timor invasion, General Benny Murdani and Colonel Dading Kalbuadi, owned the Batara Indra Group, which in turn ran hotels, cinemas, sandalwood plantations and construction and infrastructure projects. Suharto's youngest daughter, Titiek, was in business with Colonel Tono Suratman, who was deeply implicated in the death and destruction around the 1999 ballot, in Kima Surya Lestari Mutiara. Titiek's husband, Prabowo Subianto, spent several years as an army officer in East Timor, mostly with the TNI's special forces, Kopassus. The Governor of East Timor, Abilio Soares, owned the Anak Limbau Group, while Basilio de Araujo, who headed the pro-integration Forum Perdamai,

Demokrasi dan Keadilan, ran the Provincial Investment Board (Kingsbury 2003:193 fig 5.1). This wealth 'was built over three decades from a skein of companies, monopolies and control over vast sectors of economic activity in Indonesia. The Suharto family on its own or through corporate entities controls some 3.6 million hectares of real estate in Indonesia, an area larger than Belgium. That includes nearly 40% of the entire province of East Timor' (Aditjondro 1997; 1999; Colmey and Liebhold 1999).

Legal cross-border trade

Not surprisingly, a large proportion of cross-border trade between East Timor and Indonesia is quite legal, so far as public recognition of the practice, including the payment of taxes, is concerned. Apart from markets and shipping through the port at Dili, all such cross-border trade arrives through the Technical Co-ordination Line (TCL) posts of Motaain on the Indonesian side and Batu Gade, Bobonaro district, on the East Timor side of the north coast of the island. The TCL was the functional border until a more formal arrangement was negotiated. Such trade from Indonesia includes fuel (petrol, diesel and kerosene), manufactured goods, processed foods and, to a much lesser extent, motor vehicles. Trade from East Timor primarily includes coffee beans and sandalwood.

There were two markets established within the TCL, which operated on a 'day pass' (stamp on the wrist) system. One, which attracted a few hundred people per day, was based at Batu Gade-Motaain, while the other, attracting a few thousand people per day, was at Turiskain, on the Loes River between Balibo and Maliana in the Bobonaro district. These markets operated on alternate days—Monday, Wednesday and Friday at Motaain, and Tuesday, Thursday and Saturday at Turiskain. The establishment of the markets at these previously major refugee crossing points was primarily the idea of the then Bobonaro District Administrator, Joao Vicente, and was intended to regulate cross-border trade by providing a legitimate and agreed site for trade between people on both sides of the border, to reduce a demand for goods that encouraged smuggling.

There had also been four market sites in Cova Lima district—on low-lying land near the southern coast at Selele; to the north in lower mountains near Fatu Maen; at a relatively remote and inaccessible point in the mountains at Fato Lulic; and near the border with the Bobonaro district, deep in the mountains at Lebos. It should be noted that access to the last three points, for local people, was almost exclusively by foot or pony, which limited tradeable goods to a maximum of around 60 kilograms per pony. The roads in this part of East Timor were generally poor, in the most part not sealed or deeply broken up and most commonly just pot-holed and rutted dirt or rock, in places extremely steep, and often little more than narrow tracks running along precipices at altitudes of up to 1,500 metres. The almost complete impenetrability of this part of East Timor to wheeled transport, apart from more competent (and expensive) four wheel drive vehicles, meant that local people had very limited access to the outside world, and it was usually easier for them to reach points across the border in West Timor than to come to towns, usually farther away, in East Timor.

While Bobonaro district had implemented a day pass system, such a system had not been implemented in Cova Lima, which meant that any trade across the border, even for limited purposes, had to be conducted under a conventional visa. Apart from the three day delay in Dili for obtaining an Indonesian visa (assuming people could get to Dili, which from Cova Lima was often uncertain due to the extremely poor condition of the roads), such a visa cost US$35, and was generally good for only one visit. East Timorese visas were available at the border, but cost US$25. In a region where most people were lucky to earn an average of US$1 per day, the visa system was geographically and financially prohibitive, and consequently encouraged illegal border crossings and smuggling. Following a series of problems (noted below) and a consequent low level of legal use of the border markets in Cova Lima, they were closed in early 2003. This only further encouraged illegal border crossings and smuggling. Meanwhile, local people who had family on both sides of the border, or in some cases even farmed land across the border, continued to cross illegally to avoid the prohibitive visa costs, and when doing so, often undertook a small amount of trade while they were there, thereby avoiding the compulsory 5% tax on the value of goods officially crossing the border. This tax applied to general dutiable goods, but was less than the excise attached to soft drinks (US50c per litre), alcohol (US$1.50 per litre) and tobacco (US$15 per kilogram), electronic goods and motorcycles (10%), or perfume and cars (15%) (UNTAET 2000).

While the border market system appeared to help regulate local cross-border trade, it was not entirely free from problems, especially from the Indonesian side. Militia members openly operated stalls at the markets (at Turiskain at the front of the market in the best selling spot) and imposed a 'tax' or surcharge on Indonesian stall holders. It is worth noting that the militia who were active in 2003 and into 2004 were drawn from the same cadre base as the 13 militias that comprised the anti-independence movement of 1999, but were formed into a single organisation, the Pasukan Pejuang Integrasi (Integration Struggle Troops—PPI, also referred to as Perjuangan Pro

Inegrasi—Struggle for Integration). The PPI, originally formed as the overarching militia organisation in July–August 1999, ahead of the East Timor ballot on independence, was formally headed by Joao Tavares, although second in command, Eurico Guterres, assumed operational control in 2001. At Motaain and Tursikain, Indonesian police charged all entrants to the market a 'fee' of US10 cents (Rp1,000) per person, while at the markets in Cova Lima they imposed a 'fee' of US25 cents (Rp2,000) per person. This led to resentment when market goers were asked to pay tax on the goods they had bought, their response being that they had already 'paid tax' (UNMO 2003a).[1]

The border markets were closed by the TNI in October 2003 following the killing on 25 September of an Indonesian citizen of East Timorese origin, Vegas Biliato, near Turiskain by BPU members. After a significant increase in smuggling, two markets, at Baru Gade and Turiskain, were re-opened in January 2004.

The TNI, trade and smuggling

Not surprisingly, given its limited revenue base, the militia also imposed a 'tax' upon West Timorese market stallholders and, beyond this, were deeply involved in smuggling. In part, the imposition of a 'tax' and smuggling directly funded their own activities. However, given the militias' client relationship with the TNI, a proportion of the money raised by the militia was forwarded to their patrons, who were local TNI officers. The TNI also provided goods directly or through front companies for sale in the markets and for smuggling across the border.

The TNI and Polri also profited from border trade by controlling the money exchange in the region, doing so at near enough to extortionate rates. The rates for (illegally) exchanging US dollars at the border was Rp8,000, which was close enough to the market value at that time. However, the exchange rate Rp10,000 to the US dollar, making a neat 20% profit on all financial transactions. Not only was this exchange rate mechanism highly favourable to making large, quick profits, it was aslo quite public. At the Motaain border police post, uniformed Polri were openly buying and selling money across the police post counter. This engagement in illegal money changing was not unusual for Polri in West Timor, which had an established history of extensive engagement in illegal businesses, such as gambling and prostitution, particularly in Kupang. Indeed, Polri and the TNI had a history of armed conflict over their attempts to control or monopolise illegal businesses in Kupang, paralleling such sporadic armed conflict in other parts of the country. Polri formally separated from what was the Armed Forces of the Republic of Indonesia

(Angkatan Bersenjata Republik Indonesia—ABRI) on 1 April 1999. However, Polri remained subservient to the TNI (as ABRI was renamed after the split) and was still under TNI operational command in conflict areas (as West Timor was classified to be) (Davies 2001:11; Kingsbury 2003:134–6). In the West Timor border district, however, there was little tension between Polri and the TNI, as most TNI members were from Kostrad and on a high rate of rotation, unlike the Territorial army who were permanently based in West Timor, although generally away from the immediate border area due to their lack of military competence.

In the Cova Lima district, and to some extent in Bobonaro district, smuggling was complicated by the various agendas of the militias and their TNI masters. Despite the official position of the Indonesian Government— that it recognises the independence of East Timor and wishes to work with it in a constructive manner—many amongst Indonesia's political elite, certainly within the TNI and not least among the militia, retain irredentist aspirations for East Timor. Such irredentist claims have found support from no less a figure than Indonesia's then Defence Minister, Juwono Sudarsono, who reiterated the militia allegation that UNAMET 'cheated' in the conduct of East Timor's 1999 ballot and that the East Timorese military resistance organisation, Falintil, engaged in armed activities (Tedjasukmana 2000). Similar claims have been made by a number of other political figures in Indonesia in an attempt to de-ligitimise the outcome of the ballot, which in turn attempts to re-legitimise irredentist claims. As field co-ordinator of (and participant in) a large NGO observer group to that ballot, the author confirms that UNAMET conducted an almost entirely unblemished electoral process, while the TNI-supported militias killed, raped, burned homes and intimidated in the pre-ballot period. That is, there were massive irregularities in the ballot process conducted by the TNI-backed militias. Similarly, with Falintil in voluntary cantonment (which the author witnessed), there was no military activity by that force during the campaign period (and only one significant incident prior to the campaign period, in retaliation for the TNI murder of two youths in the Bobonaro district who refused to join the local militia).

To this end, the frequent psychological warfare operations ('psyops') being conducted by militia and TNI across the border were intended to and had the effect of ensuring that many people in the East Timor border region felt highly insecure (Vicente 2003; da Carmo 2003; Adriano 2003). An example of such psyops was the repeated statement that: 'We plan to bring the Red and White (Indonesian flag) back to East Timor'. This was broadcast on West Timor radio, found on documents circulated across the border and stated by militia members in interaction with East Timorese, usually while engaging in illegal trade. Such psyops were probably at their most intense in the East Timorese enclave of Oecussi, on the north coast of West Timor, but also quite pronounced in Cova Lima and somewhat less noticeable in Bobonaro (probably due to the higher profile of the PKF in this area). However, while Bobonaro was spared some of the psyops, on 4 January 2003 between 20 and 30 armed militia members wearing TNI uniforms (without insignia) and carrying automatic weapons, murdered seven former resistance leaders in the villages of Tiarlelo and Laubuno near the town of Atsabe, southwest of Dili (with some attackers being captured by villagers). This was followed by an attack by a smaller group of armed men on a bus on 24 February and another group attacking a peace-keeping patrol on 27 February. There were also numerous though unofficial reports of similar incidents in the Bobonaro and Cova Lima districts (UNMO 2003b; BPU 2003). While 'psyops' were an important part of the incursions, it was also likely that militia incursions into East Timor were to gather intelligence on the presence of PKF and Forcas de Defesa Timor L'este (East Timor Defence Force—FDTL) troops—a detachment of the latter being based on Cova Lima, near the town of Zumalai, well away from the border.

A significant reason that militia infiltration and smuggling could not be controlled was that the RDTL Border Patrol Unit (BPU)was too small—around 200 people at the end of 2003. This was further complicated by the BPU's relatively brief training, their lack of basic equipment including guns, water canteens, food and permanent shelter (which at Batu Gade was constructed, unofficially, by the Australian peace-keeping battalion). The BPU had, according to the local BPU instructor, 'no capacity for pro-active interdiction', which was critical to securing the border (Shappf 2003). However, with the introduction of the BPUs, it was intended that the PKF in border areas would be scaled back and take a less 'robust' profile (this term being used to describe the Australian peace-keeping presence by a senior US UNMO in November 2000), meaning that infiltration was increasing rather than decreasing, as confirmed by 20 separate arrests in early 2004 (ETAN 2004). As a consequence of cross-border infiltration, however, at the end of May 2003 the UN decided to slow the rate of PKF withdrawal from the border region, extending the commission of the two battalions and international police near the border until May 2005, at which time the UN presence in East Timor was to come to an end.

In that the militia increased its infiltration activity and engaged in psyops, this seemed to run counter to its engagement in cross-border trade and smuggling. At one level, these activities do appear to be irreconcilable. Relations with partner smugglers and border traders were generally positive, and where there remained an element of intimidation, it was to indicate the power differential between the two groups, which recalls elements of traditional relationships across different social groups. A number of incursions by militia were made by smuggling parties (this was established when the parties were arrested and the militia members' identities were confirmed) and indeed, such smuggling parties might have been largely comprised of militia, although a number of new members were not formally identified with the '1999 generation'. In that business engagement clashed with political opposition, the need to raise money was of primary importance to the militias, and given the seller's market nature of arrangements, did not strongly conflict with the respective positions in a 'power relationship'. In this respect, what appeared on the surface to be competing agendas for the militia and their TNI bosses actually worked.

Apart from the difficulty in accessing the main towns of East Timor, the costs of crossing the border and taxes, according to two Suai *lia nain* (traditional guardians and mediators of rules and custom), it was in many cases simply 'easier' for many local people to engage in illegal cross-border trade than to trade legally (Ospina & Hohe 2001:38; da Carmo 2003; Adriano 2003). The lower cost of goods from West Timor and greater accessibility combined to make smuggling an attractive proposition. However, they did recognise that the infiltration of militia members complicated the situation, and indeed, noted that most of the local community wanted the border to remain closed to limit militia infiltration. Adriano and da Carmo identified the militia members as belonging to Laksaur Merah Putih[2] (LMP), which was responsible for the murder of at least 300 people, whose names are listed on a memorial to 'Black September' in Suai, and probably many more throughout Cova Lima in September 1999. They further said that the members of LMP were from West Timor and were 'native Indonesians' (meaning not East Timorese). Adriano and da Carmo also said that, amongst the smugglers, were men they identified as members of the TNI, although these men wore civilian clothing. They also said that the TNI controlled the exchange of dollars and rupiah.

In terms of goods being smuggled across the border into Cova Lima, da Carmo and Adriano said this included motor vehicles (especially motorcycles), cigarettes, fuel (petrol, diesel and kerosene), electrical and electronic goods, salt, sugar, rice and clothes. The motorcycles smuggled across the border were new or, more commonly, used vehicles, many of which did not come with any papers, indicating they had been stolen. The motorcycles with papers may have been purchased or extorted from their owners. Regarding the prevalence of smuggling in this district, the author actually witnessed a smuggler on the border near Lebos, where the track runs very close to West Timor. This smuggler's dozen or so plastic containers strapped to his pony's back indicated that he was about to pick up a supply of fuel. Upon sighting the author's vehicle, the smuggler dashed down the side of a steep slope to avoid what he seemed to think might be apprehension. The point at which the smuggler was crossing was directly opposite a post of TNI Kostrad Battalion 721.

A UN official stationed in Cova Lima also confirmed that there was a lucrative border trade in smuggled alcohol, saying the appeal was that it was cheaper than buying the same alcohol in East Timor. This indicated that no tax was being paid on alcohol in Indonesia and hence, having come via TNI and militias, was through import/export businesses directly connected with the TNI. Apart from vehicles, da Carmo and Adriano described most smuggled goods as comprising basic needs. Traded or smuggled goods from East to West Timor included coffee, sandalwood, candles, peanuts and oil nuts. The parish priest at Suai, Reverend Manuel Simao Barreto, added that timber, corrugated iron and other building materials were also smuggled from West to East Timor. He said the actual site of the sale of smuggled goods that he was aware of was always just inside the West Timor border.

Reverend Barreto also noted Cova Lima's vulnerability to militia/smuggler infiltration, primarily due to the physical isolation of the district from the rest of East Timor, poor roads, and its proximity to crossing points into West Timor (Barreto 2003). There was only one road accessible between Suai and the capital, Dili, via Ainaro, and it was in very poor condition; in many places it would be considered a four wheel drive track and was normally closed during the wet season (November to May). The three other 'roads' to Cova Lima were generally not traversable by conventional vehicle and in some cases only by foot or pony. Reverend Barreto noted that emergency relief supplies distributed by the church were airlifted into Suai, although there was also a weekly UN ferry service from Dili.

Reverend Barreto said that smugglers used what had previously been conventional trade routes between East and West Timor, and that this was largely driven by necessity for the East Timorese. In particular, he noted that food insecurity often forced people from Cova Lima to buy goods from West Timor, and that LMP members dominated the cross-border smuggling, many of whom were on a list he had of 48 militia who had been clearly identified as having committed major crimes, such as murder and rape, on or about 6 September 1999. Reverend Barreto said that the list of 48 did not include less serious crimes, such as the burning of homes, whom he had pardoned, and it was not possible to pardon the perpetrators of the more serious crimes. This interview took place next to the small cairns marking the sites where Father Hilario Maderia, Father Tarcisius Dewanto and Father Francisco Soares were murdered. 'There is still a very significant militia threat,' he said. As with militia who had been arrested in the Bobonaro district, Reverend Barreto said that villagers who had reported to him sightings of militia said the militia wore Indonesian military uniforms without badges, and carried automatic weapons. This was consistent with descriptions of militia members arrested by the Thai battalion stationed in Cova Lima (BPU 2003) and the Australian battalion in Bobonaro (UNMO 2003b).

Suai had been destroyed in 1999, and by 2004 the town had still not returned to normal. Around half the houses in Suai and surrounding districts remained burnt shells. Reverend Barreto said that many people had not returned to Suai because of continuing fear of militia raids, because they were sympathetic to militias, because they were being forced to stay in West Timor, or because they were dead. He said there were approximately 5,000–7,000 people from Cova Lima still in West Timor who were not connected with the militia. Militia members in this area continued to extort 'protection' payments from refugees in West Timor, especially if they wanted to return to East Timor. As a consequence of militia incursions, psyops and smuggling, Reverend Barreto said that: 'Security is most important, and it will become urgent when UNMISET leaves the country'.

Smuggling across the border in the Bobonaro district was generally similar to that in the Cova Lima district, although there were no reports of motorcycles being smuggled. In particular, the TNI was said to be directly involved in the smuggling of sugar and rice from Belu *kabupaten* to the Bobonaro district (Anon A 2002). Beyond such food staples, the smuggling of fuel was also extensive, if primarily on a small or local scale, and undertaken and controlled by TNI non-commissioned officers. The attraction in smuggling fuel was that in Indonesia it cost about a fifth of the retail price in East Timor, and even less when purchased wholesale. By way of illustration, kerosene was officially Rp600, or US6 cents per litre (depending on the exchange rate), although up to Rp1,100 in Atambua, diesel Rp1,150 per litre and premium petrol Rp1,550 per litre. In East Timor, by comparison, it was around US50 cents a litre for diesel and premium petrol (Rp4,000–5,000 depending on exchange rates) and around US60 cents (Rp5,000–6,000) for kerosene (Anon A 2002). So rampant was the smuggling across the border that at one stage there was actually a fuel shortage in the Belu district in West Timor, which abuts East Timor (ETAN 2002).

The supply of fuel from West Timor has been a recurring theme in East Timor. In one ironic arrangement in the early phase of the PKF, in 2000, according to senior UNTAET staff, the New Zealand Battalion then stationed in Cova Lima was supplied with petrol from West Timor through the TNI (Kingsbury 2000b). This petrol, and subsequently most of the legal fuel to East Timor, was supplied by the Indonesian state-owned oil company Pertamina (at US34 cents a litre wholesale, or nearly triple the retail price in West Timor), through its licensed distributor PT Jagad Adilaut in Bima and Kupang. The West Timor branch of PT Jagad Adilaut was run by Purwo Subekti, while PT Jagad Adilaut was headquartered in Jakarta. The Pertamina depot in Dili also housed Indonesia's diplomatic mission until early 2003, and according to a UN security report was the site of intelligence activities (Dodd 2001), which meant involvement of TNI's Military Strategic Intelligence Organisation (Baden ABRI Intelijen Strategis—BAIS), which was represented throughout the TNI's territorial structure and had close links with the TNI's Special Forces (Kopassus). Further cementing this connection, in September 2003, a senior officer from Indonesia's National Intelligence Agency (Baden Intelijen Nasional—BIN), Ahmad Bey Sofwan, was appointed ambassador to East Timor. BIN and BAIS retained very close working relations. Former Defence Minister Juwono Sudarsono noted that Pertamina 'play[ed] a role as a funding channel to the TNI' (Fabiola 2003). Regardless of the TNI's direct link to PT Jagad Adilaut, it could in any case purchase fuel from this distributor at the wholesale price and transport it in TNI fuel tankers, selling it at well above Indonesia's internally capped retail price.

TNI organisational structure in West Timor

The TNI organisational structure in West Timor allowed perhaps the clearest insight into the focus and purpose of the TNI in that part of Indonesia. Most notable was the promotion of Lieutenant-Colonel Djoko Subandrio, as head of *kecamatan*-level District Military Command (Komando Distrik Militer— Kodim) 1605 Belu to colonel, and head of the Strategic Command Centre based at Atambua. In particular, although this move was announced as the creation of a Strategic Command Centre (and at one stage touted as a possible new Kodam[3]), it was formally identified to UNMO officers by the TNI as a 'satgas' (*satuan tugas*), which is a generic term for 'function unit', though more commonly understood as 'duty unit'. The term 'satgas' is used to identify any special purpose unit, ranging from intelligence to special operations to militia control. It is unusual within the TNI for a Kodim head to receive a second 'tour of duty' at a particular post and to be promoted at the same time. It is also unusual for the TNI to create a Strategic Command Centre, this being outside the TNI's conventional command structure, especially while at the same time maintaining the original Kodim, in this case Kodim 1605 at Atambua, under Lieutenant-Colonel Anip. Similarly, it is most unusual to have a colonel appointed to a geographic position so closely located to another colonel (in this case, Muswarno Musanip) at the *kabupaten*-level, battalion strength Military Resort [Garrison] Command (Komando Resort Militer—Korem) 162 at Kupang, in the western part of West Timor. It is worth noting that the TNI's Military Liaison Officer, Lieutenant Fauzi Nurdin, who was part of Army Strategic Reserve (Komando Strategik Angkatan Daerah—Kostrad) Battalion 321 stationed along the border in the Belu *kabupaten*, said that if the author had particular inquiries about the TNI in West Timor, he should be initially directed to Colonel Muswarno Musanip at Korem 162 in Kupang, and thence to Major-General Agus Suyitno at brigade strength Military Command Area (Komando Daerah Militer—Kodam) X Udayana at Denpasar, Bali (which is ordinarily headed by a brigadier-general). This completely bypassed the most senior local officer, Colonel Djoko, which was in accordance with conventional organisational lines of command but which, thereby, located this geographically senior officer outside of the nominal command structure. This in turn indicated Colonel Djoko's 'special' or non-conventional military status and role. He had succeeded Lieutenant-Colonel Sigit Yuwono as TNI head at Atambua, where the latter had been executive chairman of the committee overseeing the 1999 influx of refugees to West Timor (Ketua Pelaksana Urusan Pengungsi Timtim) and as such, was one of the key organisers of the forcing of East Timorese into West Timor. Then Lieutenant-Colonel Djoko was the regional commander appointed to head Kodim 1605 when, on 6 September 2000, PPI militia based in and around Atambua attacked the Atambua office of the UN High Commissioner for Refugees (UNHCR), murdering three UNHCR employees. Lieutenant-Colonel Djoko said that he would crack down on the militias as a consequence of the attack, which saw the UN withdraw from West Timor. However, at a weapons handover by the militia on 26 September, militia members seized back their weapons from Polri, who did not attempt to stop them. Given the pre-existing (and very well documented) links between the TNI, and to a lesser extent Polri and the militias, it is highly likely that Lieutenant-Colonel Djoko had direct administrative control over the militias at that time, and indeed that this was a primary focus of his original appointment, having succeeded Lieutenant-Colonel Sigit in this role. One credible TNI observer said that it 'can probably be assumed that he was involved in training and arming the militias for forays into East Timor (Anon D 2003). The establishment of a *satgas* at Atambua and the continued public presence of militia members there and nearby, indicated that Colonel Djoko's new position was primarily to run the militias and their activities within West Timor and across the border into East Timor. As late as May 2002, the military commander at Kupang, Colonel Muswarno, said there were as many as 20,000 militia still in West Timor (*Jakarta Post* 2002), although this figure almost certainly included families and sympathisers (active PPI militia members were limited to perhaps 3,000, according to various unofficial estimates). One militia member, clearly dressed in TNI boots, camouflage pants and TNI-type sweatshirt (black with yellow writing on the back) calmly walked past the UNMO liaison post at Motaain while the author was there. Given his stature and bearing, this person would have not been distinguishable from an ordinary (if tall and muscular) Kostrad soldier but for his hair, which fell well past his shoulders. It is possible, of course, that this man was in fact TNI. However, if that was the case, it should be noted that the only group in the TNI that allows long hair is Detasemen Sandi Yuhda (Denha) of the Special Forces (Kopassus). Denha is the covert 'dirty tricks' unit of Kopassus, and specialises in covert activities, including intelligence gathering, assassination and the training of militias. Alternatively, he could have been a *milsus*, or *militer khussus* (special military), who are usually former Kopassus personnel who have resigned but come back as freelance agents for particular projects. *Milsus* were known to be operating in East Timor in 1999. If they were retained to oversee the operational aspects of the militia in West Timor, they would operate through the *satgas* under the command of Colonel Djoko.

Other militia members I encountered in Atambua were less physically impressive, being shorter, more unkempt and, in one case at least, less disciplined (although in making it clear he knew my name he was employing the type of psyops common in East Timor in 1999). This unkempt militiaman was almost certainly connected to a Polri sergeant-major, Adonis Apollo, to whom I was introduced at the Motaain UNMO post and who was later identified as being a former militia organiser in Maliana in East Timor in 1999 (UNMO 2003b).

In terms of TNI deployment in the first half of 2003, Kodim 1605 at Atambua comprised TNI Territorial (non-specialist) troops and militia members; Kostrad Battalion 321, of around 700 men, was located along the border in Belu *kabupaten*, opposite the Bobonari district, physically separate from but within the same command formation as the Territorial troops; Kostrad Battalion 721 (also around 700 men) was located along the border in Boas *kabupaten* opposite Cova Lima, similarly organised to Territorials; and a 'detachment' of Kostrad Battalion 407 was located at the border around the enclave of Oecussi on the north coast of West Timor, again linked to the Territorials. There are formally two detachments to a battalion, although a detachment can in practice be up to 500 men of a 700–800 man battalion, or any group at less than full battalion strength (due to other deployments or staffing issues). Along with Battalion 407, and absorbed into the Territorial structure, were members of the since disbanded Battalion 745, which was comprised largely of East Timorese and was based in the Los Palos district at the eastern end of East Timor. This was confirmed by a member of Battalion 745 who made himself known to me at Kefamenanu, near Oecussi. Battalion 745 had a reputation for considerable brutality in any case, and in its withdrawal from Los Palos in late September 1999 murdered the people it came across on the road back, including a European journalist in the suburb of Becora in Dili, as well as burning everything not already destroyed. The author had earlier encountered members of Battalion 744 at the Motaain border post, mixed with Kostrad troops stationed there at the time (January 2000).

According to Lieutenant Fauzi, the TNI intended to draw down on its forces along the border from mid-2003, corresponding to a similar draw-down by the PKF (the operational function of which was renewed until May 2005). The existing Kostrad battalions in West Timor were deployed to Aceh to assist in the imposition of martial law from May 2003. The replacement was intended to reduce the three Kostrad battalions to three detachments, not including Territorial troops. The difference in numbers, Lieutenant Fauzi said, was made up by police and would be under police command. While on the surface this looked like a 'civilianising' of the border, the effect could have been to reinforce an even more militarised version of the status quo. Indonesia's National Police (Polri) often function as a part of the army (Davies 2001:24), especially the Mobile Brigade and Polri's 'counter-terrorist' unit, Gegana, which was mobilised in military operations in Aceh. More critically, in operational terms, nominally 'police' 'BKO' units (*bawa kendali operasi*—under operational control) comprise highly trained soldiers from Kostrad and Kopassus who are seconded to Polri and are formally identified as police, even though they are trained and equipped as soldiers and perform a purely military function (also mobilised in Aceh). The structure was in place for such BKO units to be operational in West Timor, and given demonstrably close links between PPI militia and Polri at the border, it would be possible to segue into such an arrangement without disrupting strategic or tactical considerations.

Notably, too, the Polri relationship with the militia was close and active after Indonesia's occupation of East Timor, and will remain active, it seems, and into the foreseeable future. Polri's active engagement in illegal trade, including money changing, and its history of running illegal businesses in West Timor, mean that the functional positioning of Polri as a state agent parallels that of the TNI in relation to a range of border-related issues, notably where the more permanent Territorial troops did not have a presence.

This potential military imbalance and the pressure being applied across the border by way of psyops, was widely expected in East Timor to play a role in negotiations between the government of Indonesia and the government of East Timor over the formalisation of the demarcation of the border between the two states and the conditions of passage across it (including access to the enclave of Oecussi). Although there was no formal reason why such negotiations had not already begun, the Indonesian Government had continued to defer them to an unspecified future time, thought to be after the UN had formally ended its presence in East Timor, or at least after the PKF had been formally removed. If this was the case, Indonesia would be well placed to step up pressure, through means it would be able to formally deny, to achieve an outcome on border issues it regarded as most suiting its various requirements. Indeed, if one was to take the irredentist claim seriously as a medium to longer term proposition, negotiations over the border could open the way to a wider claim, including such matters as territorial waters, claims to off-shore mineral (oil and gas) rights and the repatriation of remaining, pro-integrationist militia members. Based on destabilisation activities (political opportunism, public disturbances) and calls for reintegration with Indonesia by the Jakarta-backed (and deceptively named) Committee for the Popular Defence of the Democratic Republic of East Timor (CPD-RDTL) (Kingsbury 2002:164), the repatriation of remaining pro-integration forces would act as a further means of destabilising East Timor's already uncertain political environment. In this there was a view that irredentist claims could be achieved without formal military incursion, through holding a future ballot on voluntary re-incorporation into Indonesia. With widespread post-independence aspirations within East Timor not being met (in many cases because they exceed even that which was available under Indonesia), some East Timorese look back on the period of Indonesian occupation with an almost child-like sense of nostalgia. Given the political naivety of many East Timorese (though this quality is far from exclusive to East Timorese), there is considerable scope for gathering political support for simplistic solutions to complex problems, which is the CPD-RDTL's stock in trade (and historically, the prime vehicle of populist/fascist movements).

Conclusion

The activities of the TNI and the PPI militia serve a number of inter-related and mutually reinforcing functions, consistent with the profile of the TNI as the former occupier of East Timor and in terms of the complex of agendas that inform its territorial presence throughout Indonesia and that of its specialist divisions. The first of these inter-related functions is legal and illegal business activities that help fund the TNI, and in this case the otherwise poorly financed PPI militia. This accords not just with the contemporary localised practice of the TNI, which as an actor and as a patron benefits from it, but this also legal and illegal business practices throughout the archipelago and in particular where the TNI has a long-established high level presence, such as Aceh and West Papua. Securing an income requires a high level of local political control to ensure that local constituents do not object vocally to such practices. In the case of West Timor, this is achieved by PPI militia control of refugee camps and high levels of intimidation in the wider region. Thus once secured, the PPI militia and its TNI patrons can engage in their (nominal) core function, which is 'defence', in this case understood as intelligence gathering and psychological and destabilisation operations aimed at the 'enemy'. This in turn strengthens the PPI militia/TNI position that has informed and continues to inform issues of border relations, in particular the timing and scope for negotiations over the shape and terms around the as yet to be formalised border between East Timor and Indonesia. In the final sense, all of this establishes a pro-active position from which to 'facilitate' the possible re-integration of East Timor into Indonesia, through unsubtle 'encouragement'. This in turn rationalises the core function of the TNI and addresses the sense of legitimacy that the TNI and even the PPI militia feel about themselves. Such 'legitimacy', however, disguises a range of self-serving interests, not least, in full circle, is that of economic benefit. However, this locally reconstructed sense of 'legitimacy' strengthens the TNI's claim to participation in political processes around what it regards as core issues of the state, and in which it has demonstrated that it intends to take a long-term leading role which, in turn, rationalises the TNI's high profile in Indonesian political society and helps protect its self-serving economic interests.

Endnotes

1. This was confirmed by Joao Vicente (2003), who had closely monitored the situation at the markets.
2. This name was 'Laksaur', not the common Indonesian term for militia, 'laskar'.
3. In July 2004, the Indonesian navy announced that it would build a new naval base at Saumlaki on Tanimbat Island, east of East Timor and just north of the international sea border with Australia, as a means of countering the development of a military force in East Timor.

Bibliography

AAP (Australian Associated Press) 1998, *Indonesia admits 18,000 troops may be in East Timor*, 30 October

Abat, FU 1993, *The day we nearly lost Mindanao: The CEMCOM story*, FCA, Inc, Manila.

Abdullah, T 2003, 'Teungku Daud Beureueh: the rebellious freedom fighter', *Tempo*, Special Edition, 25 August.

Abinales, PN 1998, '"Muslim" political brokers and the Philippines nation–state' in Trocki, CA (ed), *Gangsters, democracy and the state in Southeast Asia*, Cornell University Southeast Asia Program, Ithaca.

—— 2000, *Making Mindanao: Cotabato and Davao in the formation of the Philippine nation–state,* Ateneo de Manila Press, Quezon City.

Abuza, Z 2002, 'Terrorism in Southeast Asia and international linkages', presentation sponsored by the USINDO Open Forum and Johns Hopkins School of Advanced International Studies, Washington, 4 December.

Acehkita 2003, 'Bau "VOC" di Lokop?', Acehkita.com, 12 September.

ACFOA (Australian Council for Overseas Aid) 1991, *East Timor: keeping the flame of freedom alive*, Development Dossier No 29, Fitzroy.

Aditjondro, G 1997, 'Suharto and his family: the looting of East Timor', *Green Left Weekly* 3 September.

—— 1999, 'Timor: business interests are behind Indonesia's fight to hold on to East Timor', *Sydney Morning Herald* 8 May.

—— 2001a, 'Guns, pamphlets and handie-talkies. How the military exploited local ethno-religious tensions in Maluku to preserve their political and economic privileges' in Wessel, I and G Wimhofer (eds), *Violence in Indonesia*, Abera Verlag Markus Voss, Hamburg.

—— 2001b, 'Di Balik Asap Mesiu, Air Mata dan Anyir Darah di Maluku' in Salampessy, Z and T Hussain (eds), *Ketika Semerbak Cengkih Tergusur Asap Mesiu, Tragedi Kemanusiaan Maluku di Balik Konspirasi Militer, Kapitalis Birokrat, dan Kepentingan Elit Politik*, Tapak Ambon, Jakarta.

Adriano, F 2003, interview at Suai, 6 May.

AFP (*Agence France Presse*) 1995, 'Ramos signs military modernization law', Agence France Presse, 23 February.

—— 1996, 'US refuses to include Spratlys in defence treaty with Manila', Agence France Presse, 10 December.

—— 1998a, 'Eleven, including general, killed in East Timor helicopter crash', 4 June.

―――― 1998b, 'East Timorese hold solemn celebration of 1991 Dili massacre', 12 November.

―――― 1999, 'Indonesia demands time before world judges East Timor martial law', 9 September.

―――― 2003, 'Ba'asyir says Hambali's arrest to boost President Bush's Popularity', *Jakarta Post* 20 August.

Age 2003a, 21 May.

Age 2003b, 20 June.

Agencies/*Jakarta Post* 2003, 'Westerners trained in al-Qaeda camp in Indonesia, claims official', 18 January, reproduced in *Ummahnews.com* 17 October.

Aglionby, J 2002, 'Jakarta dispatch epidemic of ignorance', *Guardian*, 12 September.

Aita J 1999, *UN mission will urge Indonesia to accept foreign peacekeepers on Timor*, USIS Washington File, US Information Agency, 7 September.

ALP (Australian Labor Party) 1998, *National conference resolution*, Sydney.

Ambon Information Website, www.websitesrcg.com/ambon/Transmig.htm

ANAO (Australian National Audit Office) 2002, *Management of Australian Defence Force deployments to East Timor*, Audit Report No. 38, Canberra.

Anderson, B 1983, *Imagined communities: reflections on the origins and spread of nationalism*, Verso, London.

―――― 1990, *Language and power: exploring political cultures in Indonesia*, Cornell University Press, Ithaca.

―――― 1991, *Imagined communities*, 2nd revised edition, Verso, London and New York.

Anon A 2002, interview with senior military officer directly involved in this campaign at the time.

Anon B 2000, interview with United Nations civilian investigating officers, Dili November.

Anon C 2002, interview with an Australian military intelligence officer.

Anon D 2003, correspondence from TNI observer, 14 May.

Anon X 2003, private communication from confidential source.

Ansari S 1998, 'The Islamic world in the era of Western domination' in Robinson F (ed), *Cambridge Illustrated History of the Islamic World*, Cambridge University Press, Cambridge.

AP (Associated Press) 1998, *Indonesian military to arm civilians*, 5 December.

Apdal, MS and C Thayer 2003, *Security, political terrorism and militant Islam in Southeast Asia*, ISEAS, Singapore.

Asmarani, D 2002 'Militant Muslim bodies admit receiving cash from Osama's terror network, but insist there were no strings attached', *Straits Times*.

Aspinall E 1999, 'The Indonesian student uprising of 1998', in Budiman A, B Hatley and D Kingsbury, *Reformasi: crisis and change in Indonesia*, Monash Asia Institute, Clayton.

—— 2001, 'Sovereignty, the successor state and universal human rights', paper to *Political fault-lines in Southeast Asia: movements for ethnic autonomy* conference, Southeast Asia Research Centre, City University of Hong Kong 15–16 October.

—— 2002a, 'Modernity, history and ethnicity', *Review of Indonesian and Malaysian Affairs* 36(1).

—— 2002b, 'Modernity, history and ethnicity: Indonesian and Acehnese nationalism in conflict', in Kingsbury, D and H Aveling (eds) *Autonomy and disintegration in Indonesia* Routledge Curzon, London.

—— 2002c 'Sovereignty, the successor state and universal human rights: history and the international structuring of Acehnese nationalism', *Indonesia* 73, April.

Aspinall, E and H Crouch 2003, 'The peace process in Aceh', paper presented to the East–West Center, 30 April.

Associated Press 2002, 'War on terror', INFID's Short News Overview No 103: 9–14 August.

Ba'asyir, AB 2000, 'Sistem Kaderisasi Mujahidin Dalam Mewujudkan Masyarakat Islam', address to *Kongres Mujahidin I Indonesia*, 5–7 August, Yogyakarta., www.geocities.com/kongresmujahidin/.

Babbage, R 2002, 'The new terrorism – implications for Asia Pacific governance', paper presented to Australian Security in the 21st Century Seminar Series, Menzies Research Centre, Parliament House, Canberra, 11 December.

Ball D 2002, 'Silent witness: Australian Intelligence and East Timor' in McDonald H, D Ball, J Dunn, G van Klinken, D Bourchier, D Kammen and R Tanter (eds), *Masters of terror: Indonesia's military and violence in East Timor in 1999*, Strategic and Defence Studies Centre, Canberra.

Baraja, AQ 2000, 'Kebangkitan dan Keruntuhan Khilafah', address to *Kongres Mujahidin I Indonesia*, 5–7 August, Yogyakarta, www.geocities.com/kongresmujahidin/.

Barber, B 1995, 'Beijing eyes South China Seas with sub purchase', *Washington Times* 7 March.

Barnabasfund.org 2003, 'Laskar Jihas alive and well in Papua', 5 March, www.barnabasfund.org/News/Archive/Indonesia/Indonesia-20030305.htm, accessed 17 June 2005.

Barreto, Rev Manuel Simao 2003, interview at Suai cathedral, 6 May.

Barton, G 1991, 'The international context of the emergence of Islamic neo-modernism in Indonesia' in Ricklefs, MC (ed), *Islam in the Indonesian social context*, CSEAS Monash University, Clayton.

—— 1994, 'The impact of Islamic neo-modernism on Indonesian Islamic thought: The emergence of a new pluralism' in Bourchier, D and J Legge (eds), *Indonesian democracy: 1950s and 1990s*, Monash Asia Institute, Clayton.

—— 1995, 'Neo-modernism: a vital synthesis of traditionalism and modernism in Indonesian Islam', *Studia Islamika* 2(3).

—— 1996, 'The liberal, progressive roots of Abdurrahman Wahid's thought' in Barton, G and G Fealy (eds), *Nahdlatul Ulama, traditional Islam and modernity in Indonesia*, Monash Asia Institute, Clayton.

—— 1997a, 'Indonesia's Nurcholish Madjid and Abdurrahman Wahid as intellectual *ulama*: the meeting of Islamic traditionalism and modernism in neo-modernist thought', *Islam and Christian–Muslim relations* 8(3).

—— 1997b, 'The origins of Islamic liberalism in Indonesia and its contribution to democratisation', in Schmiegelow, M (ed), *Democracy in Asia*, St Martins Press, New York.

—— 2001a, 'Islam and politics in the New Indonesia' in Issacson, JF and C Rubenstein (eds) *Islam in Asia: changing political realities*, Transaction Press, New Brunswick.

—— 2001b, 'The prospects for Islam' in Lloyd, G and S Smith (eds), *Indonesia today: challenges of history*, Institute of Southeast Asian Studies, Singapore.

—— 2002a, *Abdurrahman Wahid, Muslim democrat, Indonesian president: a view from the inside*, UNSW Press and University of Hawai'i Press, Sydney and Honolulu.

—— 2002b, 'Islam, politics and regime change in Wahid's Indonesia' in Weiss, JM (ed), *Tigers' roar: Asia's recovery and its impact*, ME Sharpe, Armonk.

—— 2003, 'Indonesia at the crossroads: Islam, Islamism and the fraught transition to democracy', paper to the *Islam and the West: the impact of September 11* conference, Monash University and University of Western Australia, Melbourne, 15–16 August.

Bartu, P 2000, 'The militia, the military and the people', in Kingsbury, D (ed), *Guns and ballot boxes: East Timor's vote for independence* Monash Asia Institute, Clayton.

Becker E and P Shenon 1999, 'With other goals in Indonesia, US moves gently on East Timor', *New York Times*, 9 September.

Beckett, J 1993, 'Political families and family politics among the Muslim Maguindanaon of Cotabato' in McCoy, AW (ed), *An anarchy of families: state and family in the Philippines*, University of Wisconsin Center for Southeast Asian Studies, Madison.

Berdal, M and D Malone (eds) 2000, *Greed and grievance: economic agendas in civil wars*, IDRC/Reinner, Boulder.

Berger S 1999, Press Briefing by National Security Advisor and National Economic Advisor, Briefing Room, White House, 8 September.

Bergin, P 2001, *Holy War, Inc: inside the secret world of Osama Bin Laden*, Touchstone Books, New York.

Bertrand, J 2000, 'Peace and conflict in the southern Philippines: why the 1996 peace agreement is fragile', *Pacific Affairs* 73(1).

Bhakti, IN, H Cahyono, MH Basyar, M Nurhasim, R Sihbudi and S Yanuarti 2001, *Militer dan politik kekerasan orde baru*. Mizan, Bandung.

Binder, L 1988, *Islamic liberalism: a critique of development ideologies*, University of Chicago Press, Chicago.

Blanche, B 1996, 'The Spratly's task force', *Jane's Intelligence Review* 8(4), 1 April.

Boland, BJ 1971, *The struggle of Islam in modern Indonesia*, Martinus Nijhoff, The Hague.

Bonner, R 2003, 'Officials fear new attacks by militants in Southeast Asia', *New York Times*, 22 November.

Booth, K 1977, *Navies and foreign policy*, Croom Helm, London.

Bourchier, D 1999, 'Skeletons, vigilantes and the Armed Forces' fall from grace' in Budiman A, B Hatley and D Kingsbury 1999, *Reformasi: crisis and change in Indonesia*, Monash Asia Institute, Clayton.

Bouchier, D and V Hadiz (eds) 2003, *Indonesian politics and society*, Routledge, New York.

BPU 2003, discussion with RDTL Border Patrol Unit police officer at Selele, Cova Lima district, 4 May.

Brereton L 1996, 'Australia and Indonesia: A Labor perspective', Speech to the 2nd Indonesian Students' Conference, University House, Australian National University, 21 August.

Brown, D 1994 *The state and ethnic politics in Southeast Asia*, Routledge, London and New York.

Brownfeld, A 2002, 'Al-Qaeda goes south east', *Jane's Defence Weekly* 14 October.

Bull, H 1977, *The anarchical society: a study of order in world politics*, Columbia University Press, New York.

Burke, J 2003, *Al-Qaeda: casting a shadow of terror*, IB Tauris, London.

Canberra Times 2003, 21 May.

Carpenter, W and D Weincek 1999, 'Chinese defence build-up on track', *Global Defence Review*, www.global-defence.com/asia/asia1.htm.

Carranza, P 1995, public lecture on Philippines' Naval Policy for the 1990s, Malaysian Institute of International Affairs, Kuala Lumpur, 12 April.

Chalk, P 2002, 'Al Qaeda and its links to terrorist groups in Asia' in Tan, A and K Ramakrishna (eds), *The new terrorism: anatomy, trends and counter-strategies*, Eastern Universities Press, Singapore.

Chang, F 1996, 'Beyond the unipolar moment: Beijing's reach in the South China Sea', *Orbis* 40(3).

Chauvel, R 2002, *The land of Papua and the Indonesian State: essays on West Papua* vols 1 and 2, Working Papers on Southeast Asia, Monash Asia Institute, Clayton.

Christalis I 2002, *Bitter dawn*, Zed Books, London.

Chulov, M and P Walters 2003, 'JI deeply divided on use of violence', *Australian*, 14 August.

Cleary P 1999, 'Australia reviews Defence ties, scraps joint exercise', *Australian Financial Review*, 11 September.

Cline, L 2000, 'The Islamic insurgency in the Philippines', *Small Wars and Insurgencies* 11(3).

Clinton, W 1992, 'A new covenant for American security', *Harvard International Review*, Summer.

—— 1999a, Statement on East Timor, 9 September, www.clinton6.nara.gov/1999/09/1999-09-09-statement-by-the-president-on-east-timor.html, accessed 18 October 2002.

—— 1999b, 'Statement on East Timor', *Voice of America*, 9 September.

Cloughley, B 1995, 'ASEAN at arms: a defence profile', *International Defence Review* 28(12).

Coedes, G 1968, *The Indianized states of Southeast Asia*, East–West Center Press, Honolulu.

Cohen W 1999, 'Remarks on East Timor', *Voice of America*, 8 September.

Collier, C 2002, 'Spoiling for a fight: dangerous days in the Southern Philippines', paper presented to Asian Studies Association conference, Hobart, 2 July.

Collier, P 2000, 'Doing well out of war: an economic perspective' in Berdal, M and D Malone (eds), *Greed and grievance: economic agendas in civil wars*, IDRC/Reinner, Boulder.

Collier P and A Hoeffler 1998, *On economic causes of civil war*, Oxford Economic Paper 50.

—— 2001, *Greed and grievance in civil war*, World Bank Development Research Group, Washington.

Colmey, J and D Liebhold 1999, 'Suharto, Inc', *Time* 24 May.

Conboy, K 2003, *Kopassus: inside Indonesia's Special Forces*, Equinox, Jakarta.

Connor, W 1993, *Ethnonationalism: the quest for understanding*, Princeton University Press, Princeton.

Conversi, D (ed) 2002, *Ethnonationalism in the contemporary world: Walker Connor and the study of nationalism* Routledge, London and New York.

Corbin, J 2002, *The base: Al-Qaeda and the changing face of global terror*, Pocket Books, New York.

Courier Mail 1998, 'Warning against quick-fix for E Timor', 29 July.

CR (Conciliation Resources) 1999, 'Accord: an international review of peace initiatives', www.c-r.org/accord/acc_min/, accessed 6 April.

Crone, D 1991, 'Military regimes in Indonesia and Thailand' in Kennedy, C and D Louscher, (eds), *Civil–military interaction in Asia and Africa*, EJ Brill, Leiden, New York.

Crouch, H 1978, *The army and politics in Indonesia*, Cornell University Press, Ithaca.

—— 1979, 'Patrimonialism and military rule in Indonesia', *World Politics*, 31(4).

—— 1996, *Government and society in Malaysia* Allen and Unwin, St Leonards.

—— 1999, 'Wiranto and Habibie: military–civilian relations since May 1998' in Budiman, A, B Hatley and D Kingsbury (eds) *Reformasi: crisis and change in Indonesia* Monash Asia Institute, Clayton.

da Carmo, A 2003, interview at Suai, 6 May.

Da Silva W 1997, 'The politics of the prize', *Australian Financial Review Magazine*, 27 March.

Daley P 1998, 'Fear over troops switch on Timor', *Age*, 31 October.

—— 1999, 'US marines set for Dili', *Age*, 10 August.

Dauth J 1999, *Hansard*, Senate Committee on Foreign Affairs, Defence and Trade, 9 December.

Davies, M 1999, 'Indonesia/East Timor: TNI generals in Dili plan "Scorched Earth" operation to precede withdrawal from East Timor' (unclassified) unpublished paper, 3 September.

Davis, A 1998, 'Islamic guerrillas threaten the fragile peace on Mindanao', *Jane's Intelligence Review*, May.

—— 2003, 'Resilient Abu Sayyaf resists military pressure', *Jane's Intelligence Review*, 1 September, internet edition.

Davis, M 2002, 'Laskar Jihad and the political position of conservative Islam in Indonesia', *Contemporary Southeast Asia* 24(1).

Dawood, D and Sjafrizal 1989, 'Aceh: the LNG boom and enclave development' in Hill, H (ed), *Unity and diversity: regional development in Indonesia since 1970*, Oxford University Press, Oxford.

Denny, D 2003, Washington File staff writer, transcript of interview with Ambassador Cofer Black, 'Counterterrorism indicators "all very positive," Cofer Black says', 11 September.

DeTAK 1998, 'Pengakuan Desertir Kopassus: Target Kelompok Cikarang Gagalkan Kongres PDI', 3–9 November, [*The Kopassus deserter's confession: the Cikarang's group target is the PDI Congress*].

DFAT (Department of Foreign Affairs and Trade) 1997, *In the national interest*, Canberra.

—— 2001, *East Timor in transition: an Australian policy challenge*, Brown and Wilton, Canberra.

Ding, A 2003, 'The PRC's military modernization and a security mechanism for the Asia-Pacific' 31(8).

Dodd, M 2001, 'UN fears sabotage of East Timor elections', *Sydney Morning Herald* 17 March.

Dodd T and P Hartcher 1999, 'Humiliation for Jakarta', *Australian Financial Review*, 13 September.

Downer A 1999a, interview, ABC Radio, 5 February.

—— 1999b, press conference, 25 February.

—— 1999c, interview on *Sunday* program, Nine Network, 7 March.

—— 1999d, press conference, Australian Parliament House, Canberra, 14 March.

—— 1999e, speech to the National Press Club, Canberra, 31 March.

—— 1999f, interviewed by Glen Milne, *Face to Face*, Channel Seven, 11 April.

—— 1999g, ABC Radio, 27 April.

—— 1999h, interview on *Meet the Press*, Channel Ten, 5 September.

—— 1999i, press conference, Hyatt Hotel, Auckland, 10 September.

Downing, J 1996, 'China's maritime strategy - part 2: the future', *Jane's Intelligence Review* 8(4).

Duffield, M 1994, 'The political economy of internal war: asset transfer, complex emergencies and international aid' in McRae, J and A Zwi (eds), *War and hunger: rethinking international responses*, Zed, London.

Dunn, J 1983, *A people betrayed*, Jacaranda, Sydney.

Ecip, SS 1999, *Menyulut Ambon, Kronologi Mermbatnya Berbagai Kerusuhan Lintas Wilayah di Indonesia*, Mizan, Bandung.

Elbadawi, I and N Sambanis 2000, *How much war will we see? estimating the incidence of civil war in 161 countries*, World Bank, Washington.

Ellis S 1999, 'US expects Indonesia to protect people of East Timor', USIS Washington File, US Information Agency, 7 September.

Elson, R 2001, *Suharto: a political biography*, Cambridge University Press, Cambridge.

Emmerson, D 1999, 'Voting and violence: Indonesia and East Timor in 1999' in Emmerson, D (ed), *Indonesia beyond Suharto: polity, economy, society, transition*, ME Sharpe, New York.

Environment Australia 1997, *Australia's ocean policy, international agreements*, Background Paper 2, October.

ETAN (East Timor Action Network) 2002. *West Timor Press Summaries*, New York, 24 January.

—— 2004, *Illegal border crossers cause rift between TL and TNI*, 28 April.

Ethier, D 1990, 'Processes of transition and democratic consolidation: theoretical indicators' in Ethier, D (ed) *Democratic transition and consolidation in Southern Europe, Latin America and Southeast Asia*, Macmillan Press, London.

ETISC (East Timor International Support Centre) 1998, press release, Sydney, 7 December.

Evans, G 2001, 'Indonesia's military culture has to be reformed', *International Herald Tribune*, 24 July.

Evans, KR 2003, *The history of political parties and general elections in Indonesia*, Arise Consultancies, Jakarta.

Fabiola Desy Unidjaja 2003, 'TNI nothing more than mercenaries: analysts', *Jakarta Post* 17 March.

Fakhry, M 1983, *A history of Islamic philosophy*, Columbia University Press, New York.

Falaakh, MF et al 2001, *Implikasi Reposisi TNI-Polri di Bidang Hukum*, Fakultas Hukum Universitas Gadjah Mada, Yogyakarta.

Farcau, B 1996, *The transition to democracy in Latin America*, Praeger, Westport and London.

Fargo, Admiral TB 2003, US Navy Commander, US Pacific Command, statement on US Pacific Command Posture, before the House International Relations Committee, Subcommittee on Asia and the Pacific, 23 June.

Fealy, G 1994, 'Rowing in a typhoon: Nahdlatul Ulama and the decline of constitutional democracy' in Bourchier, D and J Legge (eds), *Indonesian democracy: 1950s and 1990s*, Monash Asia Institute, Clayton.

—— 1996, 'The 1994 NU Congress and aftermath: Abdurrahman Wahid, Suksesi and the battle for control of NU' in Barton, G and G Fealy (eds), *Nahdlatul Ulama, traditional Islam and modernity in Indonesia*, Monash Asia Institute, Clayton.

—— 2001, 'Islamic politics: a rising or declining force?' in Kingsbury, D and A Budiman (eds), *Indonesia: the uncertain transition*, Crawford House Publishing, Hindmarsh.

—— 2002, 'Is Indonesia a terrorist base? The gulf between rhetoric and evidence is wide', *Inside Indonesia*, July–September.

Fernandes C 2004, *Reluctant saviour*, Scribe, Melbourne.

Finin, GA 1991, 'Regional consciousness and administrative grids: understanding the role of planning in the Philippines' Gran Cordillera Central', PhD dissertation, Cornell University.

Frake, C 1998, 'Abu Sayyaf: displays of violence and the proliferation of contested identities among Philippine Muslims', *American Anthropologist* 100(1).

Fuentes, WJ 1998, 'Negotiating an agenda for peace and self-rule in Moroland', *Mindanao Focus* 4.

Fulghum, D 1995 'New Chinese fighter nears prototyping', *Aviation week and Space Technology* 142(11).

Gallager, M 1994, 'China's illusory threat to the South China Sea', *International Security* 19(1).

Gani, F 2002, *Perjalanan Panjang Anak Bangsa Menuju Perdamaian*, Lembaga Humaniora, Jakarta.

Garnadi, H 1999, Memo M53/TM p4-OKTT/7/99 (General Assessment if Option 1 fails), Office of the Minister of State for Co-ordinating Politics and Security, Republic of Indonesia, Dili Command Pos, 3 July.

Garver, J 1992, 'China's push through the South China Sea: the interaction of bureaucratic and national interests', *China Quarterly* December.

Gatra 2001, 'Penyulundupan: manikmati kencing solar', 10 February.

Geertz, C 1960, *The religion of Java*, Free Press, New York:.

Gellner E, 1983, *Nations and nationalism*, Cornell University Press, Ithaca and London.

George, TJS 1980, *Revolt in Mindanao: the rise of Islam in Philippine politics*, Oxford University Press, Kuala Lumpur.

Ghosh, N 1994, 'Philippine military keen to modernise', *Straits Times*, 31 August.

Gomez, HM Jr 2000, *The Moro Rebellion and the search for peace: a study on Christian–Muslim relations in the Philippines*, Silsilah Publications, Zamboanga.

Gonzales, FL 1999, 'Sultans of a violent land' in Gaerlan, K and M Stankovich (eds), *Rebels, warlords and Ulama: a reader on Muslim separatism and the war in southern Philippines*, Institute for Popular Democracy, Quezon City.

Gossman, H 1999, *Kleptocracy and revolution*, Oxford Economic Papers.

Gowing, P 1979, *Muslim Filipinos: heritage and horizon*, New Day, Quezon City.

Grattan M 1999a, 'PM's pressure for UN military mission vindicated', *Age*, 13 September.

—— 1999b, 'How PM's triumph comes at a cost', *Age*, 14 September.

Greenlees D 1998a, 'Habibie rules out Timor referendum', *Australian*, 4 June.

—— 1998b, 'East Timor students soak up freedom', *Australian*, 13 June.

Greenlees D and R Garran 2002, *Deliverance*, Allen and Unwin, St Leonards.

Gunaratna, R 2001, 'The evolution and tactics of the Abu Sayyaf group', *Jane's Intelligence Review*, July.

—— 2002, *Inside Al Qaeda: global network of terror*, Columbia University Press, New York.

—— (ed) 2003, *Terrorism in the Asia-Pacific: threat and response*, Eastern Universities Press, Singapore.

Gutierrez, E 1999, 'The reimagination of the Bangsamoro: 30 years hence' in Gaerlan, K and M Stankovich (eds), *Rebels, warlords and Ulama: a reader* on *Muslim separatism and the war in southern Philippines*, Institute for Popular Democracy, Quezon City.

Gutierrez, E and M Danguilan Vitug 1999, 'ARMM after the peace agreement: an assessment of local government capability in the autonomous region of Muslim Mindanao' in Gaerlan, K and M Stankovich (eds), *Rebels, warlords and Ulama: a reader on Muslim separatism and the war in southern Philippines*, Institute for Popular Democracy, Quezon City.

Harris, G 1956 *North Borneo, Brunei, Sarawak*, Human Relations Area Files, New Haven.

Hartcher P 1996, 'Howard's discomfort over Jakarta', *Australian Financial Review*, 29 July.

—— 1999, 'The ABC of winning US support', *Australian Financial Review*, 13 September.

Hassan, K 1993, 'KL's choice of Russian and US fighters sparks debate', *Straits Times*, 14 July 1993.

Hefner, RW 1997a, 'Introduction' in Hefner, RW and P Horvatich (eds), *Islam in an era of nation states: politics and religious revival in Muslim Southeast Asia*, University of Hawaii Press, Honolulu.

—— 1997b, 'Islamization and democratization in Indonesia', in Hefner, RW and P Horvatich (eds), *Islam in an era of nation states: politics and religious revival in Muslim Southeast Asia*, University of Hawaii Press, Honolulu.

—— 2000, *Civil Islam, Muslims and democratization in Indonesia*, Princeton University Press, Princeton.

—— 2001, Muslim–Christian violence in Maluku: the role of national politics, www.uscirf.gov.hearings/13feb01/hefnerPT.php3.

—— 2002, 'Islam and Asian security' in Ellings RJ and AL Friedberg (eds), *Strategic Asia 2002–03: Asian aftershocks*, National Bureau of Asian Research, Seattle.

—— 2003, 'Political Islam in Southeast Asia: assessing the trends', keynote address to the *Political Islam in Southeast Asia* conference, Southeast Asia Studies Program, Johns Hopkins University, Washington, 25 March.

Heginbotham, E 2002, 'The fall and rise of navies in East Asia: military organizations, domestic politics, and grand strategy', *International Security* 27(2).

Heinzig, D 1976, *Disputed islands in the South China Sea: Paracels — Spratlys — Pratas — Macclesfield Bank*, Otto Harrassowitz, Wiesbaden.

Hill, Senator R 2003, Minister for Defence, 'Regional terrorism, global security and the defence of Australia', speech given to the RUSI Triennial International Seminar, Canberra, 9 October.

Hirschkorn, P, R Gunaratna, E Blanche and S Leader 2001, 'Blowback: the origins of Al Qaeda', *Jane's Intelligence Review* 13(8).

Hobsbawm, E and TO Ranger (eds) 1983, *The invention of tradition*, Cambridge University Press, Cambridge.

Hoffman, B 1998, *Inside terrorism*, Columbia University Press, New York.

Holley, D 1988, 'China, Hanoi count losses in isles clash', *Los Angeles Times*, 17 March.

Howard, J 1999, doorstop interview at the White House, Washington, 12 July.

HRW (Human Rights Watch) 2001, 'Indonesia: the war in Aceh', August.

—— 2004, *Malaysia: Security Act detainees launch hunger strike* New York, 2 March.

Huang, R 2002. 'In the spotlight: LJ', Center for Defense Information, Washington, 8 March.

Huntington, S 1991, *The third wave: democratization in the late 20th century*, University of Oklahoma Press, Norman.

—— 1997, *The clash of civilizations and the remaking of world order*, Touchstone, New York.

—— 1999, *The third wave: democratization in the late 20th century*, University of Oklahoma Press, Norman and London.

Hutchcroft, P 1998, *Booty capitalism*, Cornell University Press, Ithaca and London.

Hutchinson, J and A Smith (eds) 1996, *Ethnicity*, Oxford University Press, Oxford.

ICG (International Crisis Group) 2001a, *Indonesia: national police reform*, Available: www.crisisweb.org/projects/asia/indonesia/reports/A400054_05092001.pdf, accessed 19 April 2001.

—— 2001b, *Indonesia: next steps in military reform*, ICG Asia Report No 24, 11 October, Jakarta/Brussels.

—— 2001c, *Indonesia: violence and radical Muslims*, 10 October.

—— 2002a, *Al-Qaeda in Southeast Asia: The case of the 'Ngruki Network' in Indonesia*, Jakarta and Brussels, 8 August.

—— 2002b, *Indonesia backgrounder: how the Jemaah Islamiyah terrorist network operates*, ICG Asia Report no. 43, Jakarta and Brussels, 11 December.

—— 2002c, *Indonesia: the search for peace in Maluku*, www.crisisweb.org/projects/asia/indonesia/reports/A400054_05092002.pdf, accessed 19 April 2002.

—— 2003a, *Aceh: a fragile peace*, 27 February 2003.

—— 2003b, *Aceh: why the military option still won't work*, 9 May 2003, www.crisisweb.org/home/index.cfm?id=1258&l=1. accessed 23 July.

—— 2003c, *Jemaah Islamiyah in South East Asia: damaged but still dangerous*, ICG Asia Report no. 63, Jakarta and Brussels, 26 August.

IDP (International Displaced Persons) 2002, *Philippines: GRP-CPP/NPA/NDF peace process (September 2002)*, Global IDP Database, Washington.

IDR (*International Defence Review*) 1994, 'China boosts presence in South China Sea', 1 May.

IISS (International Institute for Strategic Studies) 2002, *The Military balance 2002–2003*, Oxford University Press, Oxford.

Indonesia 2001, 'Current data on the Indonesian military elite January 1, 1999–January 31, 2001' 71.

IRIP News Service 2001, 'Laskar jihad', *Inside Indonesia*, July–September.

Jakarta Post 2002, 'No way to Oecussi through West Timor', *TheJakartaPost.com* 31 May.

Jalong, T 2002, 'A new wave of Penan blockades', Sahabat Alam Malaysia press release, 23 April.

JDW (*Jane's Defence Weekly*) 2002, 'Singapore reveals project delta frigate', http://jdw.janes.com/, posted 22 November.

JNI (*Jane's Navy International*) 2002, 'Malaysia acquires Scorpene submarines', http://jni.janes.com/ posted 13 June 2002.

Johnstone C 1998, 'Howard supports Suharto move to resign', *Courier Mail*, 20 May.

Jones, S 2003, *Aceh: how not to win hearts and minds,* International Crisis Group, 23 July.

Joon Num Mak 1994, 'Armed, but ready? ASEAN conventional warfare capabilities', *Harvard International Review* 16(2).

—— 2002, 'War? What war?' in Wilson, D (ed) *Maritime war in the 21st century*, Papers in Australian Maritime Affairs, No 8, Royal Australian Navy Sea Power Centre, Defence Publishing Service, Canberra.

JSC (Joint Security Committee) 2003, internal memorandum, February.

Jun Zhan 1994, 'China goes to the blue waters: the navy, seapower mentality and the South China Sea', *Journal of Strategic Studies* 17(3).

Kammen, D 1999, 'Akhir "Kedigdayaan" ABRI?' [The end of the Indonesian military's "invulnerability"?], paper presented at the 12th INFID Conference in Bali, 14–17 September, www.infid.or.id/oldconf/1999/Douglas.htm.

—— 2003, 'Security disorders', *Inside Indonesia*, January–March.

Kammen, D and S Chandra 1999, *A tour of duty: changing patterns of military politics in Indonesia in the 1990s*, Cornell Modern Indonesian Project, Ithaca.

Kastor, R 2000, *Fakta, Data dan Analisa, Konspirasi politik RMS dan Kristen menghancurkan umat Islam di Ambon-Maluku*, Wihdah Press, Yogyakarta.

—— 2002, author interview, Jakarta, 1 August.

Keen, D 1998, *The economic functions of violence in civil wars*, Oxford University Press: International Institute for Strategic Studies, Adelphi Paper 320.

Kell, T 1995, *The roots of Acehnese rebellion, 1989–1992*, Cornell Modern Indonesia Project, Ithaca.

Khilafa Online 2004, www.khilafah.e-syariah.net/, accessed 11 August 2004.

Kiefer, TM 1981 'The Tausug Polity and the Sultanate of Sulu: a segmentary state in the southern philippines', in Madale, NT (ed), *The Muslim Filipinos: a book of readings*, Phoenix Press, Quezon City.

—— 1986, *The Tausug: violence and law in a Philippine Moslem society*, Waveland Press, Prospect Heights.

Kiernan, B 2003, 'The demography of genocide in Southeast Asia: the death tolls in Cambodia, 1975–79 and East Timor, 1975–80', *Critical Asian Studies* 35(4).

King, DY 1982, 'Indonesia's New Order as a bureaucratic polity, a neopatrimonial regime or a bureaucratic authoritarian regime: what differences does it make?' in Kahin, A and B Anderson (eds), *Interpreting Indonesian politics: thirteen contributions to the debate*, Cornell Modern Indonesia Project, Ithaca.

King, DY and MR Rasjid 1988, 'The Golkar landslide in the 1987 Indonesian elections: the case of Aceh', *Asian Survey* 28(9).

Kingsbury, D (ed) 2000a, *Guns and ballot boxes: East Timor's vote for independence* Monash Asia Institute, Clayton.

—— 2000b, 'The new Timor: a Xanana republic', *Jakarta Post*, 16 December.

—— 2001a, *Southeast Asia: a political profile*, Oxford University Press, South Melbourne.

—— 2001b, 'The TNI in transition' in Kingsbury D and A Budiman (eds) *Indonesia, the uncertain transition*, Crawford House Publishing, Hindmarsh.

—— 2003, *Power politics and the Indonesian military*, Routledge Curzon, London and New York.

—— 2004, 'Political development' in Kingsbury, D, J Reminyi, J McKay and J Hunt, *Development: a new approach* Palgrave, London.

Kivlan, Z 2004, *Konflik dan integrasi TNI-AD*, Institute for Policy Studies, Jakarta.

Klintworth, G 1994/95, 'Greater China and regional security', *Australian Journal of International Affairs* 48/49.

Kompas 2002, 'Dilema bisnes militer', 2 October.

—— 2003, 25 February, cited in Aspinall, E and H Crouch, 'The peace process in Aceh', paper presented to the East–West Center, 30 April 2003.

Kontras 2001, 'The number of military guarding these facilities has increased to around 5,000 by February 2002', report, November.

KPP-HAM 2002, 'Full report of the Investigative Commission into Human Rights Violations in East Timor' in McDonald H, D Ball, J Dunn, G van Klinken, D Bourchier, D Kammen and R Tanter 2002, *Masters of terror: Indonesia's military and violence in East Timor in 1999*, Strategic and Defence Studies Centre, Canberra.

Krader, L 1976, *Dialectic of civil society*, Prometheus Books, New York.

Kristiadi 2001, 'Indonesia: redefining military professionalism' in Alagappa, M (ed), *Military professionalism in Asia*, East–West Center, Manoa.

Kusuma 2000, 'Berhenti Berkelahi Tidak Berhenti Bermusuhan, Analisis Konflik Etnik dan Agama di Ambon', MA thesis, Department of Sociology, University of Gadjah Mada, Yogyakarta.

Labor Council 1999, 'Details of Protest Actions', *Workers online* - official organ of the Labor Council of NSW.

Lague D 1996, 'The looming crisis with Jakarta', *Sydney Morning Herald*, 3 August.

Laksamana.Net 2002a, *Ambon: battlefield for Jakarta players*, 1 May.

—— 2002b, 'Gufron arrest may lead to Suharto's dark forces', 10 December.

Lambert, M (ed) 1993, *Jane's all the worlds aircraft 1993–94*, Jane's Information Group, Surrey.

Lansdale, E 1976, 'Practical jokes', in *US Department of the Army Psychological Operations*, DA Pamphlet, US Department of the Army, 525-7-1, April.

Laski, H 1934, *The state in theory and practice*, George Allen and Unwin, London.

Liddle, W. 2003. 'Indonesia's army remains a closed corporate group', *Jakarta Post*, 3 May 2003.

Lindsey, T (ed) 2000, *Indonesia: the commercial court and law reform in Indonesia*, Desert Pea Press, Sydneya.

Lok, J 1992, 'Spratly Islands rivalries bring regional navies into focus', *Jane's Defence Weekly* 18(8).

Lowry, R 1996, *The armed forces of Indonesia*, Allen and Unwin, St Leonards.

—— 1998–99, 'Indonesian Armed Forces' [Tentara Nasional Indonesia-TNI], Research Paper no. 23, Australian Parliamentary Library 1998–99.

Lubetkin W 1999, 'Robinson calls for Human Rights Commission Emergency Session on East Timor', USIS Washington File, US Information Agency, 7 September.

Lyons J 1999, 'The secret Timor dossier', *Bulletin*, 12 October.

MacFarling, I 1996, *The dual function of the Indonesian Armed Forces*, Australia Defence Studies Centre, Canberra.

Madale, N T 1992, 'The organic law for the autonomous region in Muslim Mindanao: contrasting views', in Turner, M, RJ May and LR Turner (eds), *Mindanao: land of unfulfilled promise*, New Day, Quezon City.

Majul, CA 1973, *Muslims in the Philippines*, University of the Philippines Press, Quezon City.

Mangold, T and G Goldberg 1999, *Plague wars: the terrifying reality of biological warfare,*: St. Martin's Press, New York.

Manila Times 2003, 10 March.

Manyin, M, R Cronin and L Niksch 2002, 'Terrorism in Southeast Asia', report for Congress, Washington, Congressional Research Service, Library of Congress, 13 December.

Marker J 2003, *East Timor: a memoir of the negotiations for independence*, McFarland and Company, London.

Marohomsalic, NA 2001, *Aristocrats of the Malay race: a history of the Bangsa Moro in the Philippines*, VJ Graphics Arts, Quezon City.

Martin I 2001, *Self-determination in East Timor: The UN, the ballot and international intervention*, Lynne Rienner, London.

Martinkus J 1999, 'The thin blue line', *Bulletin* 117(6192), 21 September.

—— 2001, *A dirty little war*, Random House, Milsons Point.

—— 2002a, 'An unwelcome mat in Papua', *Bulletin*, 30 October.

—— 2002b, Review of 'Deliverance', *Australian Book Review* 244.

—— 2003, 'Jihad in Papua', *Bulletin*.

McClintock, M 1992, *Instruments of statecraft: US guerrilla warfare, counterinsurgency, and counterterrorism, 1940–1990*, Pantheon Books, New York.

McCulloch, L 2000, *Trifungsi: the role of the Indonesian military as economic actors*, Bonn International Centre for Conversion, Bonn.

—— 2001, *The role of the Indonesian military in business*, Bonn International Centre for Conversion, Bonn.

McDonald H 1998, 'Ominous currents in the Timor Sea', *Sydney Morning Herald*, 17 July.

—— 2002, 'Australia's bloody East Timor secret' and 'Silence over a crime against humanity', *Sydney Morning Herald*, 14 March.

McDonald H, D Ball, J Dunn, G van Klinken, D Bourchier, D Kammen and R Tanter 2002, *Masters of terror: Indonesia's military and violence in East Timor in 1999*, Strategic and Defence Studies Centre, Canberra.

McGillivray, M and O Morrissey 1999, 'Economic and financial meltdown in Indonesia: prospects for sustained and equitable economic and social recovery', in Budiman A, B Hatley B and D Kingsbury 1999, *Reformasi: crisis and change in Indonesia*, Monash Asia Institute, Clayton.

McKenna, Thomas 1992, 'Martial law, Moro nationalism and traditional leadership in Cotabato', *Pilipinas* 18.

—— 1997, 'Appreciating Islam in the Philippines: authority, experience and identity in Cotabato' in Hefner, RW and P Horvatich (eds), *Islam in an era of nation–states: politics and religious renewal in Muslim Southeast Asia*, University of Hawaii Press, Honolulu.

—— 1998, *Muslim rulers and rebels: everyday politics and armed separatism in the southern Philippines*, University of California Press, Berkeley.

McLeod, R 2000, 'Soeharto's Indonesia: a better class of corruption', *Agenda*, 7(2).

McVey, R 1997, 'Nationalism, revolution and organization in Indonesian communism' in Lev, D and R McVey (eds), *Making Indonesia* Cornell University Southeast Asia Program, Ithaca.

—— 1990, 'Teaching modernity: the PKI as an educational institution', *Indonesia* 50.

Melchor, A 1973, 'Introduction' in Majul, C, *Muslims in the Philippines*, University of the Philippines Press, Quezon City.

Menaul, S 1982, 'The Falklands campaign: a war of yesterday?', *Strategic Review* 10(4).

Mietzner, M 1998, 'Godly men in green', *Inside Indonesia*, January–March.

—— M 2001, 'The first 100 days of the Abdurrahman presidency: an evaluation' in Kingsbury D and A Budiman (eds), *Indonesia, the uncertain transition*, Crawford House Publishing, Hindmarsh.

Milivojevi, M 1989, 'The Spratly and Paracel Islands conflict', *Survival* 31(1).

Milne, R and D Mauzy 1999, *Malaysian politics under Mahatir*, Routledge, London and New York.

Misuari, N 2003, author interview, Fort Santo Domingo, Santa Rosa, Laguna, 31 March.

Morris, C 1998, *An essay on the modern state*, Cambridge University Press, Cambridge.

Morris, E 1985, 'Aceh: social revolution and the Islamic vision' in Kahin, A (ed), *Regional dynamics of the Indonesian revolution*, University of Hawaii Press, Honolulu.

Mueller, J 2000, 'The banality of "ethnic war"', *International Security* 25(1).

Murphy, D 2002, 'Indonesian cleric fights for a Muslim State', *The Christian Science Monitor*, 2 May.

—— 2003a. 'How Al Qaeda lit the Bali fuse: part one', *Christian Science Monitor* 17 June.

—— 2003b. 'How Al Qaeda lit the Bali fuse: part two', *Christian Science Monitor* 18 June.

Muslim, MA 1999, Sustaining the constituency for Moro autonomy' in *Accord: an international review of peace initiatives*, www.c-r.org/accord/acc_min/, accessed April.

Myers K 1999, 'Postscript', *Sydney Morning Herald*, 13 September.

Nakamura, M 1983, *The crescent arises over the banyan tree: a study of the Muhammadiyah movement in a Central Javanese town*, Gadjah Mada University Press, Yogyakarta.

Nazaruddin Sjamsuddin 1985, *The republican revolt: a study of the Acehnese Rebellion*, Institute of Southeast Asian Studies, Singapore

Nemets, A and T Torda 2002a, 'Most recent trends in the development of the Chinese aviation industry and their strategic implications', 2 May, www.newsmax.com.

—— 2002b, 'PLA Navy: from 'green water' to 'blue water' – part II, 30 July, www,.newsmax.com.

Newman J 1999, response to question on notice, *Senate Hansard*, Australian Parliament House, Canberra, 22 March.

Noble, LG 1976, 'The Moro National Liberation Front in the Philippines', *Pacific Affairs* 49(3).

—— 1987, 'The Muslim insurgency' in Schirmer, DB and S Rosskamm Shalom (eds), *The Philippines reader: a history of colonialism, neocolonialism, dictatorship and resistance*, South End Press, Boston.

Novichkov, N 2002, 'China expected to buy a third batch of SU-30MKK', *Jane's Defence Weekly*, 10 September.

NST (*New Straits Times*) 1992, 'China plans to be regional naval power', Kuala Lumpur, 7 April.

O'Donnell, G and C Schmitter 1986, 'Tentative conclusions about uncertain democracies, part IV' in O'Donnell, G, C Schmitter and L Whitehead (eds), *Transition from authoritarian rule: prospects for democracy*, Johns Hopkins University Press, Baltimore.

O'Rourke, K 2002, *Reformasi: the struggle for power in post-Soeharto Indonesia*, Allen & Unwin, St Leonards.

Ospina, S and T Hohe 2001, Traditional Power Structures and Community Empowerment and Local Governance Project, final report, CEP/PMU, ETTAUNTAET and World Bank, Dili, 6 June.

Philip, G 1985, *The military in South American politics*, Croom Helm, London.

Polanyi, K 1957, *The great transformation*, Beacon Press, Boston.

Pour, J 1993, *Benny Moerdani: profil prajurit negarawan*, Yayasan Kejuangan Panglima Besar Surdiman, Jakarta.

Pratt, P (ed) 2000, *Jane's exclusive economic zones, 2000–2001*, Jane's Information Group.

Pustaka Cidesindo 2000, 'Aceh di Persimpangan Jalan', Jakarta, November.

Rabasa, AM 2003, *Political Islam in Southeast Asia: moderates, radicals and terrorists*, Oxford University Press, London.

Rahman, F 1979, 'Islam: challenges and opportunities' in Welch, AT and P Cachia, *Islam: past influence and present challenge*, Edinburgh University Press, Edinburgh.

—— 1982, *Islam and modernity/transformation of an intellectual tradition*, University of Chicago Press, Chicago.

Ramage, Douglas E 1995, *Politics in Indonesia: democracy, Islam and the ideology of tolerance*, Routledge, London.

Raman, B 2004, 'Thailand and International Islamic Front', South Asia Analysis Group Paper No. 890, 1 September.

Ravenholt, A 1962, *The Philippines: a young republic on the move*, D Van Norstrand Company Inc, Princeton.

Reeve, S 1999, *The new jackals: Ramzi Yousef, Osama bin Laden and the future of terrorism*, Northeastern University Press, Boston.

Reid, A 1979, *The blood of the people: revolution and the end of traditional rule in northern Sumatra*, Oxford University Press, Kuala Lumpur.

—— 1988, *Southeast Asia in the age of commerce, 1450–1680: the lands below the winds*, Yale University Press, New Haven.

Rengah Sarawak 2002, www.rengah.c2o.org/news/.

Ressa, M 2002, 'Al Qaeda links to Indonesian violence', CNN, 13 August.

—— 2003, *Seeds of terror: an eyewitness account of Al-Qaeda's newest center of operations in Southeast Asia*, Free Press, New York.

Reuters 1998a, Habibie interview with the BBC, 10 June.

—— 1998b, *Some Indonesian troops to leave East Timor*, 24 July.

—— 1998c, *East Timor remembers dead with anti-Jakarta sentiment*, 12 November.

—— 1998d, *East Timorese protestors mark invasion anniversary*, 8 December.

Rezasyah T 1996, 'Uncovering Australian foreign policy making: the prevalence of a dominant bureaucracy', *Indonesian Quarterly*, XXIV(4).

Rio Pelu 2002, author interview in Yogyakarta, 27 October.

RLR (Reuter Library Report) 1992, 'Manila expects US help if attacked in Spratlys', 13 April.

Roberts, G 1971, *A dictionary of political analysis*, Longman, London.

Robinson F 1998, 'Knowledge, its transmission and the making of Muslim societies', in Robinson F (ed), *Cambridge Illustrated History of the Islamic World*, Cambridge University Press, Cambridge.

Robinson, G 1998, 'Rawan is as Rawan does: the origins of disorder in New Order Aceh', *Indonesia* 66, October.

—— 2001, 'Rawan is as Rawan does' in Anderson, B (ed), *Violence and the state in Suharto's Indonesia*, Southeast Asia Project, Cornell University, Ithaca.

—— 2002, 'The fruitless search for a smoking gun', in Colombijn F and J Lindblad (eds) 2002, *Roots of violence in Indonesia*, ISEAS, Singapore.

Robinson, N 1999, *Islam: A concise introduction*, RoutledgeCurzon, London.

Robison, R 1986, *Indonesia: the rise of capital*, Allen & Unwin, St Leonards.

Rodell, PA 2002, 'The Philippines: *Gloria in Excelsis*' in *Southeast Asian affairs 2002*, Institute of Southeast Asian Studies, Singapore.

Rodil, BR 1994, *The minoritization of the indigenous communities of Mindanao and the Sulu Archipelago*, Alternate Forum for Research in Mindanao, Davao City.

Roosa J 1998, *Suharto's fall: a new era in East Timor*, Estafeta, East Timor Action Network.

—— 2003, 'Brawling, bombing, and backing', *Inside Indonesia* January–March.

Ross, M 2002, 'Resources and rebellion in Indonesia', paper prepared for the Yale–World Bank project on *The Economics of Political Violence*, March.

RS (Republic of Singapore) 2003, *The Jemaah Islamiyah arrests and the threat of terrorism*, White Paper, Ministry of Home Affairs, 7 January.

Rubin J 1999, daily press briefing, US Department of State, 8 September.

Rutherford, D 2001, 'Waiting for the end in Biak' in Anderson, B (ed), *Violence and the state in Suharto's Indonesia*, Cornell University Press, Ithaca.

RWS (Reuters World Service) 1995, 'Indonesia satisfied by China's Natuna explanation', 21 July.

Saad, Hasballah 2003, 'Generations of Acehnese born amid war', *Jakarta Post*, 13 May.

Said, S 2001, Militer Indonesia dan politik, dulu, kini dan kelak, Pustaka Sinar Harapan, Jakarta.

—— 2002, Tumbuh dan Tumbangnya Dwifungsi, Perkembangan Pemikiran Politik Militer 1958–2000, Aksara Karunia, Jakarta.

Salamat, Sheikh H 1998, 'Perhaps the Moro struggle for freedom and self-determination is the longest and bloodiest in the entire history of mankind', *Nida'ul Islam*, 23(5).

Saleeby, N 1963, *The history of Sulu*, Filipiniana, Manila.

Saurip Kadi, Major General 2002, interview, Jakarta, 21 November.

Savill R 1996, 'Award of Nobel Peace Prize fails to lift East Timor gloom' *Daily Telegraph*, UK, 11 December.

Scaff, AH 1955, *The Philippine answer to communism*, Stanford University Press, Stanford.

SDSC (Strategic and Defence Studies Centre) 2002, *Masters of terror: Indonesia's military and violence in East Timor in 1999*, Australian National University, Canberra.

Shambaugh, D 1994, 'Growing strong: China's challenge to Asian security', *Survival* 36(2).

Shappf, P 2003, interview with BPU instructor at Border Patrol Unit compound, Batu Gade, 7 May.

Sherwood, R 1999, 'Implications for naval roles' in MacKinnon D and R Sherwood (eds), *Policing Australia's offshore zones: problems and prospects*, Centre for Maritime Policy, University of Wollongong.

—— 2000, 'Oceans governance and its impact on maritime strategy' in Wilson, D and R Sherwood (eds), *Oceans governance and maritime strategy*, Allen & Unwin, St Leonards.

Shiying, P 1993, 'The Nansha Islands: A Chinese point of view', *Window* 2(36).

Sinaga, S 1995, 'Natunas "belong to Indonesia"', *Straits Times*, 22 July.

Singh, B 2001, *Civil–military relations in democratising Indonesia: the potentials and limits to change*, Strategic defence Studies Centre, Australian National University, Canberra.

Sipress, A and E Nakashima 2003, 'Obscure cleric who dreamed of regional Islamic rule', *Sydney Morning Herald*, 3 September.

SIPRI (Stockholm International Peace Research Institute)1994, *SIPRI yearbook 1994*, Oxford University Press, Oxford.

—— 2002, *SIPRI yearbook: world armaments and disarmament*, Almquist and Wiksell, Stockholm.

Sjamsuddin, N 1984, 'Issues and politics of regionalism in Indonesia: evaluating the Acehnese experience' in Lim Joo-Jack and S Van (eds), *Armed separatism in Southeast Asia*, 1984 ISEAS, Singapore.

—— 1985, *The republican revolt: a study of the Acehnese Rebellion*, Institute of Southeast Asian Studies, Singapore.

SMH (*Sydney Morning Herald*) 2003a, 21 May.

—— 2003b, 19 June.

Smith, A 1986, *The ethnic origins of nations*, Oxford University Press, Oxford.

—— 1991, *National identity*, University of Nevada Press, Reno.

Smith S 2001, '*a handmaiden's tale: an alternative view of logistic lessons learned from INTERFET*', Australian Defence Studies Centre.

Snyder, C 1982, 'Building multilateral cooperative security' in Samuels, MS (ed), *Contest for the South China Sea*, Methuen, New York.

—— 1989. 'The Falklands Islands War of 1982: A legal, diplomatic and strategic evaluation', MA dissertation, Brock University.

Snyder, J 2000, From voting to violence, democratization and nationalist conflict, WW Norton & Company, New York and London:.

SCMP (*South China Morning Post*) 1998, '10,000 students rally in Dili as defiance grows', 19 June.

Stepan, A 1976, 'The new professionalism of internal warfare and military role expansion' in Lowenthal, A (ed), *Armies and politics in Latin America*, Jolmes and Meier, New York and London.

—— 1986, 'Paths towards democratization: theoretical and comparative considerations, part III' in O'Donnell, G, C Schmitter and L Whitehead (eds), *Transition from authoritarian rule: prospects for democracy*, Johns Hopkins University Press, Baltimore.

Stern, J 2003, 'The Protean Enemy', *Foreign Affairs* 82(4).

Stevenson, J 2003, 'The two terrorisms', opinion-editorial, *New York Times*, 2 December 2.

Stewart I 1998, 'Downer hails Timor troop withdrawal', *Australian*, 28 July.

Stewart, J C 1972, The Cotabato conflict: impressions of an outsider', *Solidarity* April.

Storey, I and Jou Ji 2002, 'Chinese aspirations to acquire aircraft-carrier capability stalled', *Jane's Intelligence Review* 14(2).

Suara Pembaruan 2002a, 10 October.

—— 2002b, 11 October.

Sudrajat E 1999, Statement by TNI chief spokesman, *Voice of America*, 7 September.

Sulistyo, H 2001, 'Greens in the rainbow, ethnoreligious issues and the Indonesian armed forces' in Hefner, RW (ed), *The politics of multiculturalism, pluralism and citizenship in Malaysia, Singapore, and Indonesia*, University of Hawai'i Press, Honolulu.

Suparlan, P et al 1999, 'Laporan hasil penelitian, Kerusuhan Ambon dan rekomendai penanganannya', University of Indonesia and Perguruan Tinggi Ilmu Kepolisian, unpublished report.

Suryohadiprodjo, S 1996, *Kepemimpinan ABRI, Dalam Sejarah dan Perjuangannya*, Penerbit Intermasa, Jakarta.

Tadjoeddin, MZ 2002, *Anatomy of social violence in the context of transition: the case of Indonesia 1990–2001*, United Nations Support Facility for Indonesian Recovery, Jakarta.

Tan, A 2000, *Armed rebellion in the ASEAN States: persistence & implications*, Strategic and Defence Studies Centre, Australian National University, Canberra.

—— 2002, 'Terrorism in Singapore: threat and implications', *Contemporary Security Policy* 23(3).

Tapol 1999, *Bulletin Number 152*, Indonesia Human Rights Campaign, London.

—— 2003, *The Bali blast and beyond*, Bulletin Online 169–70 January–February.

Tarling, N (ed) 1999, *The Cambridge history of Southeast Asia, volume two: from c.1500 to c.1800*, Cambridge University Press, Cambridge.

Taylor, J and K Munson 1995, 'Gallery of Far East/Pacific airpower: fighters', *Air Force Magazine*, November.

Tedjasukmana, J 2000, 'Wiranto had it coming', *Time*, 28 February.

Tempo 2000a, 'Lagi, polisi temukan senjata dan ribuan peluru', 25 July.

Tempo 2000b, Santa Cruz incident a turning point in our diplomacy, 18–24 September.

Tempo 2002, 'TNI terlibat bisnis di Aceh', 25 November.

Tomagola, TA 2002, author interview, Jakarta, 14 November.

Trijono, Lambang 2001, *Keluar dari kemelut Maluku*, Pustaka Pelajar, Yogyakarta.

Tsamenyi, M and M Herriman 1996, 'Introduction' in Tsamenyi, M and M Herriman (eds), *Rights and responsibilities in the maritime environment: national and international dilemmas*, Centre for Maritime Policy University of Wollongong.

Tyler, P 1995, 'Chine revamps forces with eye to sea claims', *New York Times*, 2 January.

—— 1996, 'Chinese get top Russian jets as military leaders win round', *Globe and Mail*, Toronto, 8 February.

UNMO 2003a, interview, not for direct attribution, with senior UN Military Observer Group officer in Bobonaro district, May.

UNMO 2003b, Series of separate interviews, not for direct attribution, with UN Military Observer Group officer in Bobonaro district, May.

UNTAET 2000, UNTAET/Reg/2000/12 *On a Provisional Tax and Customs Regime for East Timor*, 8 March 2000.

USA 2002a, 'East Asia overview', *Patterns of global terrorism*, Department of State, April.

—— 2002b, *Patterns of global terrorism – 2002*, Appendix B, Office of the Coordinator for Counterterrorism, Department of State.

Van Bruinessen, M 1996, 'Traditions for the future: the reconstruction of traditionalist discourse within NU' in Barton, G and G Fealy (eds), *Nahdlatul Ulama, traditional Islam and modernity in Indonesia*, Monash Asia Institute, Clayton.

—— 2002a, 'Genealogies of Islamic radicalism in post-Suharto Indonesia', *South East Asia Research* 10(2).

—— 2002b, *The violent fringe of Indonesia's radical Islam*, International Institute for the Study of Islam in the Modern World, Leiden.

—— 2002c, 'Wahhabi influences in Indonesia, real and imagined', paper presented to Journee d'Etudes du CEIFR et MSH sur la Wahhabisme, ecole des Hautes Etudes en Sciences Sociales/Maison des Sciences de l'Homme, Paris, 10 June.

Van Klinken, G 1999, 'What caused the Ambon violence?', *Inside Indonesia Digest* 60, October–December.

—— 2001, 'The Maluku wars: bringing society back in', *Indonesia*, 71.

Van Zorge 2003, 'Trade your M–16 for 16M[illion]', *Van Zorge Report on Indonesia* V(8), 6 June.

Vicente, J 2003, interview at Maliana, 3 May.

Vickers, A 1996, *Bali: a paradise created*, Periplus, Hong Kong.

Vitug, MD 2002, 'The big shift', *Newsbreak*, 29 April 29.

Walters, G 1992, *Gulf lesson one – the value of air power: doctrinal lessons for Australia*, Air Power Studies Centre, RAAF Base Fairbairn, Canberra.

Weber, M 1978, *Economy and society: an outline of interpretive sociology*, Roth, G and C Wittich (eds), University of California Press, Berkeley

Weekly, K 1996, 'From vanguard to rearguard: the theoretical roots of the crisis of the Communist Party of the Philippines' in Abinales, P (ed), *The revolution falters: the left in Philippine politics after 1986*, Southeast Asia Publications, Cornell University, Ithaca.

Wen-Chung Liao 1995, *China's blue waters strategy in the 21st century: from the first islands chain toward the second islands chain*, Chinese Council of Advanced Policy Studies, Taipei, September.

West Australian 1999, 8 January.

Widjojo, A 2002, 'Indonesia's changing security structure and its implications for US policy', address to United States–Indonesia Society, Washington DC, 21 February.

Williams, C 2003, 'Keeping tabs on the war against terrorism', *Canberra Times*, 14 May.

Williams P 1997, *The victory*, Allen and Unwin, St Leonards.

Wilson D 2003, *Warden to Tanager: RAAF operations in East Timor*, Banner Books, Queensland.

Wirahadikusumah, Major General A 1999a, 'Hubungan Sipil-Militer: Visi, Misi dan Aksi', seminar paper, Department of Political Science, Faculty of Social and Political Studies, University of Indonesia, 24–25 May.

—— 1999b, 'Hubungan Sipil-Militer: Visi, Misi dan Aksi' in Wirahadikusumah, A et al, *Indonesia Baru dan Tantangan TNI, Pemikiran Masa Depan*, Pustaka Sinar Harapan, Jakarta.

—— 1999c, 'Reformasi TNI' in Wirahadikusumah, A et al (eds), *Indonesia baru dan tantangan TNI*, Pustaka Sinar Harapan, Jakarta.

Wiranto 1998, *ABRI Abad XXI, Redefinisi, Reposisi, dan Reaktualisasi peran ABRI dalam kehidupan bangsa*, Armed Forces Headquarters, Jakarta.

Wolfson P 1999, statement by Under-Secretary of State to the US Congress, *Voice of America*, 9 September.

Wolters, OW 1999, *History, culture and religion in Souheast Asian perspectives*, Southeast Asia Program Publications, Cornell University, Ithaca.

Wong CW and C Lourdes 2003, 'Nik Aziz's son named in report', *Star* Kuala Lumpur, 2 January.

Wortzel, L 1994, 'China pursues traditional great-power status', *Orbis* 38(2).

Wurfel, D 1988, *Filipino politics*, Cornell University Press, Ithaca and London.

Yates, D 2002, 'Feature: Muslim liberal takes on militants in Indonesia', *Reuters*, 8 September.

Yeong, M 1992, 'China's new assertiveness', *Business Times*, Singapore, 27 August.

You Ji 1995, 'A test case for China's defence and foreign policies', *Contemporary Southeast Asia* 16(4).